CW00548610

Multilingual Environments
in the Great War

Also available from Bloomsbury

Making Sense of People and Place in Linguistic Landscapes, edited by Amiena Peck, Christopher Stroud and Quentin Williams
Multilingual Memories, edited by Robert Blackwood and John Macalister
Multilingualism in the Public Space, edited by Robert Blackwood and Deirdre Dunlevy
The Language of War Monuments, by David Machin
Words and the First World War, by Julian Walker

Multilingual Environments in the Great War

Edited by
Julian Walker and Christophe Declercq

BLOOMSBURY ACADEMIC
LONDON • NEW YORK • OXFORD • NEW DELHI • SYDNEY

BLOOMSBURY ACADEMIC
Bloomsbury Publishing Plc
50 Bedford Square, London, WC1B 3DP, UK
1385 Broadway, New York, NY 10018, USA
29 Earlsfort Terrace, Dublin 2, Ireland

BLOOMSBURY, BLOOMSBURY ACADEMIC and the Diana logo are trademarks of
Bloomsbury Publishing Plc

First published in Great Britain 2021

Cover design: Rebecca Heselton
Cover image © Julian Walker

A catalogue record for this book is available from the British Library.

Library of Congress Cataloging-in-Publication Data
Names: Walker, Julian, 1954- editor. | Declercq, Christophe, 1971- editor.
Title: Multilingual environments in the Great War / edited by Julian Walker
and Christophe Declercq.
Description: London; New York: Bloomsbury Academic, 2021. | Includes
bibliographical references and index. |
Identifiers: LCCN 2020050808 (print) | LCCN 2020050809 (ebook) | ISBN 9781350141346
(hardback) | ISBN 9781350141353 (ebook) | ISBN 9781350141360 (epub)
Subjects: LCSH: World War, 1914-1918–Language. | Languages in contact. | Language
and languages–Political aspects. | War and society. | Sociolinguistics.
Classification: LCC P130.5 .M85 2021 (print) | LCC P130.5 (ebook) | DDC 940.3/1–dc23
LC record available at https://lccn.loc.gov/2020050808
LC ebook record available at https://lccn.loc.gov/2020050809

ISBN: HB: 978-1-3501-4134-6
ePDF: 978-1-3501-4135-3
eBook: 978-1-3501-4136-0

Typeset by Deanta Global Publishing Services, Chennai, India

To find out more about our authors and books visit www.bloomsbury.com and
sign up for our newsletters.

Contents

Illustrations

Figures

Tables

Contributors

Javier Alcalde holds a PhD in Social and Political Sciences from the European University Institute, Florence. He teaches at Universitat Oberta de Catalunya and Universitat Autònoma de Barcelona. His latest publications are 'Comparative language policy', in F. Grin et al. (ed.) *The Routledge Handbook of Language Policy and Planning*; 'A special relationship: the Esperanto movement and pacifism in Zamenhof's time' in V. Beckmann and L.R. Feierstein (Ed.) *Language as Hope. L. L. Zamenhof and the Dream of a Cosmopolitan Wor(l)d*, Hentrich & Hentrich; 'Pacifism' and 'Esperanto' in D.A. Snow et al. (ed.) *The Blackwell Encyclopedia of Social and Political Movements*; 'Esperanto' in M. Musto and B. Amini (ed.), *Routledge Handbook of Marx's Capital: A Global History of Translation*.

Stefano Bannò is a PhD student in Cognitive Science at the University of Trento and Fondazione Bruno Kessler with a project on automatic scoring of spoken language proficiency. He is also a musician and a teacher of Italian and History in a high school of his home town. His research interests span from dialectology and sociolinguistics to phonetics and natural language processing.

Hillary Briffa holds a doctorate in War Studies from King's College London, asking whether small states can have a Grand Strategy. She is a teaching fellow at the Royal College of Defence Studies (Belgravia) and the Joint Services Command and Staff College (Swindon), both part of the Defence Academy of the United Kingdom. She also teaches at Birkbeck University of London, Queen Mary University of London and King's College London. In 2015, she was appointed an Associate Fellow of the Royal Commonwealth Society, and in 2016 became a recipient of the US State Department's inaugural Emerging Young Leaders award. Her First World War interest was sparked by research initially carried out at the University of Malta in 2013 and is ongoing as independent archival research. Extracts feature as the chapter 'Malta in the First World War' in Palgrave-Macmillan's 2016 edited volume *Languages and the First World War: Communicating in a Transnational War* (eds Walker and Declercq).

Jamie Calladine is a postgraduate researcher specializing in cultural and sporting histories of First World War internment and the early development of German football. His research into Ruhleben originated from his relation to Steve Bloomer, the former Derby County and England footballer who was interned in the camp. Jamie works within the heritage sector following the completion of a Master of Arts in Museum Studies in 2019. He is the founder and trustee of Rams Heritage Trust, a charitable trust dedicated to the heritage of Derby County FC. His current projects include an upcoming book on the instrumental role of British migrant workers – including those interned at Ruhleben – in the early growth of football and sports in Germany.

Mark Connelly is Professor of Modern British History at the University of Kent. His main research and teaching interest is the First World War. He is particularly interested in the commemoration of the Great War, and is currently working on a book about battlefield tourism in the 1920s and 1930s. He also works closely with the Commonwealth War Graves Commission, and also convenes a lecture series in collaboration with the In Flanders Fields Museum, Ieper. His most recent publication is *Great Battles: Ypres* (with Stefan Goebel).

Christophe Declercq is a senior lecturer at CenTraS, University College London, and a lecturer at KU Leuven, Brussels Campus. Christophe has been working on Belgian refugees in Britain 1914–19 for well over a decade. On the subject, he has taken part in several commemoration projects – academic as well as popular outreach – in both Britain and Belgium and worked with the BBC and VRT (Belgian television) on multiple occasions. Through his PhD subject, he has ventured into the domain of cross-cultural communication at times of conflict, either in a historic setting (including two books on languages and the First World War, co-edited with Julian Walker, Palgrave-Macmillan 2016) or in a contemporary setting. His most recent publication is *Intercultural Crisis Communication: Translating, Interpreting and Languages in Local Crises* (Bloomsbury 2019, with Federico Federici). He is a board member of LIND (Language Industry, DGT) and CTTT (Centre for Language, Technology and Application, KU Leuven).

Véronique Duché is A.R. Chisholm Professor of French at the University of Melbourne. Her interdisciplinary research focuses on the history of the French language, literature and culture. She has published extensively on French literature, in particular fictional works published between 1525 and 1557, and edited several sixteenth-century novels. She has recently directed the first volume of the *Histoire des Traductions en Langue Française. xve et xvie siècles (1470-1610)* (Paris, Verdier, 2015). Another strand of interest is the language of Australian soldiers during the First World War.

Iaroslav Golubinov is a historian from Samara, Russia. He has worked in Samara University, but since 2019 he has held the position of senior researcher at the Institute of History and Archeology, Ural Branch of the Russian Academy of Sciences. He was an author for the '1914-1918-online – International Encyclopedia of the First World War', the journals *Le Mouvement Social*, *Scando-Slavica* and others. Dr Golubinov's articles in journals and book chapters were devoted to the problems of the economic, social and cultural life of Europe and Russia during the Great War as well as issues of its commemoration currently. He prepared the chapter for this volume as part of the project 19-18-00221 funded by the Russian Science Foundation.

Jonathon Green is the world's leading lexicographer of Anglophone slang. His dictionary – updated every three months – can be found online at https://greensdictofslang .com. He has also created a number of Timelines of Slang, accessible here: http:// thetimelinesofslang.tumblr.com/. His latest book, *Sounds and Furies* (Little, Brown Book Group ltd.), an attempt to chart of the relationship of women to slang as recorded from the Wife of Bath to Mumsnet and beyond, appeared in 2019.

Marguerite Helmers is Professor Emerita at the University of Wisconsin Oshkosh. Her research focuses on cultural history and visual communication from the First World War era. Recent publications include the book *Harry Clarke's War: Illustrations for Ireland's Memorial Records, 1914-1918* and the edited collection *Harry Clarke and Artistic Visions of the New Irish State*. Helmers is a past research fellow at the Center for Twentieth Century Studies (UW Milwaukee), the Institute for Research in the Humanities (UW Madison) and the Humanities Institute at University College Dublin.

Jiří Hutečka is an associate professor at the Institute of History, University of Hradec Králové, Czech Republic, specializing in the cultural and social history of modern warfare. In his current research, he focuses on military and gender history of the First World War, and has published a number of scholarly articles on experiences of Czech-speaking soldiers of the Austro-Hungarian army during the war and its immediate aftermath. His most recent book *Men under Fire: Motivation, Morale and Masculinity among Czech soldiers of the Great War, 1914-1918* (early version published in Czech in 2016) was published in early 2020 by Berghahn Books.

Chris Kempshall is a historian focusing on allied relations in the First World War as well as popular representations of warfare. He has taught on war and European history at the Universities of Sussex, Kent and Goldsmiths College, London. He is a senior research fellow at the Centre for Army Leadership, Royal Military Academy Sandhurst. He is the author of *The First World War in Computer Games* (Palgrave, 2015) and *British, French and American Relations on the Western Front, 1914–1918* (Palgrave, 2018). He is also writing *History and Politics in the Star Wars Universe* due to be published by Routledge in 2021.

Mart Kuldkepp is Associate Professor of Scandinavian History and Politics at University College London (UCL). He completed his PhD dissertation about Estonia's 'Nordic' identity in the First World War at University of Tartu, Estonia in 2014, and joined UCL in 2015. His research mainly concerns Baltic and Nordic political history in the first decades of the twentieth century. He has published on the plans to draw Sweden into the First World War on the side of Germany, German propaganda targeting Estonian civilians and prisoners of war, the fate of deserters from the Imperial Russian Army who managed to escape to neutral Sweden, anti-German attitudes in Estonia after the 1918 German occupation and so on.

Amanda Laugesen is a historian and lexicographer, and is currently director of the Australian National Dictionary Centre at the Australian National University. As well as being chief editor of the *Australian National Dictionary: Australian Words and Their Origins*, she is the author of a number of books and articles, with a focus on the history of Australian English, the history of the book and publishing, and the cultural and social history of war. Her most recent book, *Rooted: An Australian History of Bad Language*, is forthcoming in 2020 with NewSouth Publishing.

Gwendal Piégais is a PhD student in contemporary history at the Université de Brest and the Université de Strasbourg. Since 2017, he has been writing a doctoral thesis about the Russian Expeditionary Force in France and in Macedonia during the Great War. His first research led him to the military history of and to the history of intelligence services during the First World War, before turning to the military history of France and Russia. He published 'Le déserteur, source de renseignements du Secret Service' in the *Cahiers d'études du renseignement*, and 'Le corps expéditionnaire russe en Macédoine, 1916-1920. Combats et mutineries sur un front périphérique'. His focus now is on the history of the Macedonian Front and on the history of Imperial Russia.

Jane Potter is Reader in Arts at the Oxford International Centre for Publishing Studies, Oxford Brookes University, where she teaches on the undergraduate and master's programmes in Media, Journalism and Publishing and supervises PhDs. Her publications include *Boys in Khaki, Girls in Print: Women's Literary Responses to the Great War, 1914-1918* (Oxford University Press, 2005), *Three Poets of the First World War: Ivor Gurney, Isaac Rosenberg and Wilfred Owen* (Penguin Classics, 2011) edited with Jon Stallworthy, *Wilfred Owen: An Illustrated Life* (Bodleian Library Publishing, 2014) and, with Carol Acton, *Working in a World of Hurt: Trauma and Resilience in the Narratives of Medical Personnel in War Zones* (Manchester University Press, 2015).

Julia Ribeiro S. C. Thomaz is a PhD student in French Literature at the Université Paris Nanterre and in History at the École des Hautes Études en Sciences Sociales. She works on constructing a corpus of French poetry of the First World War and on using it as a historical source about the experience of combat. She is a collaborator of the *Poésie Grande Guerre* project, dedicated to building an online relational database of French poets of the Great War. She is a founding member of the *Une Plus Grande Guerre* network for early-career scholars. She holds a master's degree in History from the EHESS and an undergraduate degree in Social Sciences from the Universidade de São Paulo (Brazil).

Cristina Ilea Rogojină is a PhD student in Humanities, Ovidius University of Constanta, with a research on proper names in Romanian folktales, in a linguistic and anthropological approach. With a BA in Romanian Language and Literature – English Language and Literature and an MA in Romanian Studies, she is Assistant Professor in the Department of Romanian, Classical and Balkan Philology at the above-named university. She is also member of various research centres, participating in National and International Conferences.

Connie Ruzich is a professor of English at Robert Morris University; she holds a PhD from the University of Pennsylvania. She is the editor of *International Poetry of the First World War: An Anthology of Lost Voices*, published by Bloomsbury (2020) and the author of 'Distanced, Disembodied, Detached: Women's Poetry of the First World War', appearing in *An International Rediscovery of World War One: Distant Fronts*, published by Routledge (2020). Ruzich was a 2014–15 Fulbright Scholar at the University of Exeter; her essays on the First World War history and poetry have appeared on numerous online sites. Her blog, *Behind Their Lines*, discusses lesser-known poetry of the Great War.

Anne Samson is an independent historian specializing in the First World War in sub-Saharan Africa. She runs the Great War in Africa Association (https://gweaa.com) and has published and presented widely on the topic especially on East, Central and Southern Africa. She has three books to date, two on the war in Africa and more recently a biography on Lord Kitchener inspired by his not wanting to involve Africa in the conflict (*Kitchener: The man not the myth*, Helion, 2020). For a full list of her publications and talks, visit www.thesamsonsedhistorian.worpress.com. Her interest in the use of language in the East Africa campaign derives from her work on the diversity of troops and how they managed to form a coherent functioning force.

Fabian Van Samang studied Modern History (1994–8) and International Relations and Conflict Prevention (1998–9) at the Catholic University of Leuven (Belgium). In his doctoral dissertation (2008), he argued how a specific National Socialist discourse shaped the decision-making process that led to the destruction of the European Jews. For this study he received the 'Prix de la Fondation Auschwitz – à la mémoire de Richard Suffit' (2009). He has written substantially on the history of war and genocide, on ghettoization policy and NS-language. He currently works as editorial secretary for the academic journal of the Auschwitz Foundation, *Getuigen. Tussen geschiedenis en herinnering*, and as editor-in-chief for *Tijdschrift voor Mensenrechten* (Journal of Human Rights).

Julian Walker is the co-director of the Languages and the First World War project, and he lectures at The University of the Arts London. Coming from a background in sociolinguistics, education and fine art, he has written a number of books on the history of the English language and social history. He is the co-author of *Trench Talk* (2012), the author of *Words and the First World War* (Bloomsbury, 2017) and has recently completed *Tommy French* (Sword and Pen, 2021), a study of the British soldiers' encounter with the French language. He is currently researching popular magazines from the period of the war.

Steve Witt has been the director of the Center for Global Studies (CGS) at the University of Illinois since 2015. Witt's faculty appointment is as associate professor in the library, and he has been head of the International and Area Studies Library since 2011. In the library, he is currently the subject specialist for Japanese Studies and Global Studies. Witt is also editor of *IFLA Journal*, the flagship journal of the International Federation of Library Associations and Institutions. Witt's research focuses on the trajectory and impacts of international developments in library and information science, placing global trends in librarianship and knowledge production in the context of wider social and technological developments. He is currently working on a long-term project that aims to complete a global history on the public information campaigns of the Carnegie Endowment for International Peace (CEIP) to 'internationalize' the minds of the world population through library collections, book distribution and academic networking. He spent a sabbatical in the spring and summer of 2019 at Hitotsubashi University in Tokyo, Japan, as a visiting research professor to develop this project further.

Preface

Christophe Declercq and Julian Walker

Multilingual conflict

The First World War was the first global conflict; its impact was felt worldwide. The war was destructive beyond imagination. The breadth of knowledge of the destruction at the time exceeded previous awareness of loss of life in both numbers and geographical spread. The conflict also brought about fundamental changes to international politics, warfare, technology, medicine and the balance of power between social classes and genders. Developments affected social structures and attitudes, and social and cultural shifts were framed in language that had to accommodate new realities, horizontally across the many nation states involved in the conflict, vertically within each of the national societies or its constituent parts. Borders were redefined or deliberately drawn without respect for historic or ethnic boundaries and suffering. After several partitions in the late eighteenth century, Poland had struggled for survival for over a century until it was re-established in 1923. Spheres of influence in the Middle East were shaped by the Sykes-Picot Agreement, by deceit and mistrust over the Balfour Declaration, by a botched independent Kurdistan and by the unresolved Armenian genocide. The language of the politics involved and its reception in printed media all related to insular spaces and the territory of the nation state, regardless of the validity of its borders. However, the concept of the national homeland, perceived as a geographically securable entity, included the idea of a supreme home language (Shell 2001: 2). The fault lines during the war – trenches at the front, support lines, support and supply at home – established a kaleidoscope of interconnections at various levels: political, military, group and individual, all of which yielded more complex linguistic spaces. Ignoring both static and mobile populations and workers who used multiple languages for distinct purposes, abstract linguistic boundaries were reinforced by and connected to pseudo-scientific anthropometric boundaries, such as Dominian's claim for an east-west line in Belgium dividing Walloon-speakers from Flemish speakers, which also 'marks the separation of the tall, blond, long-skulled Flemings from the short, dark, round-skull Alpine Walloons' (Dominian 1917: 21).

Following the publication of *Trench Talk* (2012) – a study of British wartime slang and new terminology – the Languages and the First World War project (LFWW) developed from meetings between a military historian, a sociolinguist and a translation scholar. In developing connections and comparative models of the changes affecting language in a period of sustained international conflict, the project brought a new way of looking at societies in that conflict, and a model for looking at society in conflict in a century that was to a large extent shaped by the Great War. The project undoubtedly benefited from the increased academic and general focus brought by the centenary, and added to the depth and breadth of thinking about the ways that the twentieth century was shaped by the national, familial and personal stories of the war. However, although as a case study of history the war carries a wealth of material for study, it is unlikely that people will relate to the war again on such a scale. One result of this is that the views and opinions of the war that have been produced by the end of the centenary period are likely to be those that will remain as predominant and orthodox in popular mythology for future generations. We hope that this third book will consolidate the position of language study in the overall structure of thought about the lived experience of the conflict, and that its extension to exploring the position occupied by comparative sociolinguistics within conflict and conflict resolution studies will be a lasting contribution.

Language in multilingual environments: Multilinguism

In looking at the concept of multilinguism, the period and the experience of the First World War brings to light many concepts that now appear startling. Multilinguism, a dense concept with rich application, can be thought of as the use of languages, often language fragments, in a given social grouping, in which the distinctive use of specific languages may indicate such phenomena as social status difference, or a religious application. Multilinguism also describes what happens when groups of distinct language speakers meet and have to create a lingua franca. In both approaches to multilinguism, locality itself no longer alone drives the local language(s), but designated geographical areas become linguistic spheres in which languages corelate mutually and act through third codes. This becomes most apparent at times of crisis or conflict.

In the First World War, crises were typically localized tentacles within the overall conflict, local particles of the war where newly created social structures emerged as a consequence of military action. The conflict affected the existing linguistic intricacies of any sample of land that carried language issues within it. In the area bounded by Antwerp, Dunkirk, Arras and Charleroi for instance, existing Flemish-Walloon tensions in Belgium – a linguistically driven political difference, but also a social one as French was the language of social advancement – and very localized forms of Flemish formed an attractive opportunity for the Germans, who occupied nearly all of Belgium, to attempt to bolster Flemish identity within Belgium, including establishing a first Dutch-speaking university in Ghent in 1916, which had been solely Francophone until then. The establishment caused a rift among Flemish nationalists, many of whom did not support collaborating with the German forces. Once beyond Flemish-Walloon antagonism, Belgians existed in imposed vacuum, created deliberately or out of ignorance.

Although the term 'Boche' – originating from the Franco-Prussian war – was initially used to refer to German soldiers, it became a vehicle for French citizens to refer to any German, but also to Belgians and even people from Luxemburg. French citizens from the northernmost part of France – Nord-Pas-de-Calais, part of which is still known as *Frans-Vlaanderen*, 'Flanders in France' – were labelled as 'Boches du Nord'. Because over 300,000 Belgians fled into France during the early stages of the war and about two million French people fled their occupied northern territories, the term 'Boches du Nord' was also applied to all those refugees and internally displaced French people, groups that were regarded as foreign as they moved to different areas. 'Boches du Nord' was attached to a fluid entity of German soldiers, Germans, Belgians, Luxemburgers, Belgian refugees and French refugees. This mutation of the word 'translated the extent of the cultural mobilization affecting both civilians and combatants' (Roynette 2016: 27). Here multilinguism transcended the locality of the language and travelled along the lines set out by conflict and crisis. This also created tensions among the French themselves, as citizens from the most northern French regions considered themselves patriots for having stalled the German advance, but they were labelled as foreigners nonetheless by French people from Paris and more southern parts (Cobb 1983; Lyons 2008). Moreover, the application of that single term 'Boche' proved a meaningful device as it was reiterated at the start of the Second World War.

If 'Boches du Nord' had grown in use through the deliberate choices of language users, then the relation with the British in terms of the multilinguism in the said area – a true microcosm – could not be more contrasting. This was highlighted by the traditional monolinguism in the main wealth-producing areas of the British Isles, which supplied the majority of the British troops. But monolinguism also came to the fore because the introduction of troops from the British Empire and its lines of contact brought in a large number of languages, many of them associated with status positions in an imperial hierarchy. This gave rise to the potential for encounters between languages such as Flemish and Chinese in Flanders to bypass the dominant European languages in the area, and the revitalizing of lost connections in meetings between French-speaking locals and French-speaking Canadian troops. Notably, a phrasebook giving Urdu phonetic transcriptions of French phrases for Indian Army troops bypassed English altogether.

According to the War Graves Commission, the Indian Army grew from some 150,000 soldiers at the start of the First World War to nearly 1.4 million by the end of the conflict. Approximately 74,000 Indians lost their lives in the war years and the immediate post-war period (CWGC 2020). The majority of those Indian soldiers served overseas (their perspective), 138,000 of whom were deployed in the Ypres Salient alone (Statistics 1922: 777). India at the time had not yet undergone a partition and forces had been drawn from all parts of the subcontinent. Although more than half the Indian forces were of Punjabi origin (Das 2018: 213), other ethnic groups were represented as well. Sikhs, Jats, Garhwalis, Pathans, Rajputs, Dogras, Gurkhas, Bengalis, Mahars, Kachins, Punjabi Muslims and Anglo-Indians all contributed to the war effort but also represent a multi-ethnic case in point that along the Western Front alone the world had come together in terms of language variety.

Personal experiences of multilinguism

Home fronts too became environments of multilinguism, with prison camps, the movements of troops, both real and imagined, and cultural events which celebrated alliances, such as the Japanese theatre productions in London in the autumn of 1914, the French *Grand Guignol* season in 1915 and the multilingual revues throughout the war: 'The Ambassadors Theatre, with its brilliant Anglo-Franco-Belgian company, has now added the charming Japanese actress, Mme Hanako, to the Thespian representatives of the nations to which we are allied' (*The Bystander*, 11 November 1914).

Specific and less memorialized environments, such as prison camps and the mixed nationality regiments of the French Army, functioned as linguistic crucibles, and are represented in this volume. Two memoirs show how broad the spread was of languages to be found in these situations – the American poet E.E. Cummings' memoir, *The Enormous Room* (1922), and M. Macdonald's *Under the French Flag* (1920) – and both tell anecdotes showing how wide a range of languages might be found crammed into a small space. Cummings served with the Norton-Harjes Ambulance Corps in France. His openly anti-war sentiments – he had been a conscientious objector who eventually signed up – came to a boiling point when he refused to condemn the Germans. In September 1917, he was arrested by the French authorities and imprisoned for several months. Cummings records an extraordinarily multilingual environment, where he is 'the focus of a group of indistinct recumbents who were talking about me to one another in many incomprehensible tongues . . . where ten invisible recumbents [in the dormitory] yelled . . . in six languages' (Cummings 1922: 60), and where he is assailed 'from all directions, by at least thirty voices in eleven languages (I counted as I lay Dutch, Belgian, Spanish, Turkish, Arabian, Polish, Russian, Swedish, German, French and English) at distances varying from seventy feet to a few inches' (Cummings 1922: 57). In *The Enormous Room*, language use is not one of clear and outspoken multilingualism, but more one that aims to overcome 'the discrepancy between language and experience' as well as the 'corrosive effects of this discrepancy on the human psyche' through the use of a code that does not come from the native tongue, nor from a language that Cummings masters let alone understands. They serve as 'new relationships between language and experience' (Gaull 1967: 646).

> 'Vous ne voulez pas de café?'
> The threatening question recited in a hoarse voice woke me like a shot. Sprawled half on and half off my paillasse, I looked suddenly up into a juvenile pimply face with a red tassel bobbing in its eyes. A boy in a Belgian uniform was stooping over me. In one hand a huge pail a third full of liquid slime. I said fiercely: 'Au contraire, je veux bien.' And collapsed on the mattress.
> 'Pas de quart, vous?' the face fired at me.
> 'Comprends pas,' I replied, wondering what on earth the words meant.
> (Cummings 1922: 58)

Wartime experiences created new relationships with language and between languages – but typically in a partial or fragmented manner, creating loss of facility and therefore grasp of reality. E.E. Cummings was not the only author to endure a sense of linguistic loss and a sense that conventional language had lost touch with reality if it was by non-conventional language use that reality was overcome (see also Linehan and Linehan 1979). For M. Macdonald as well, new relationships had to be developed without properly being taught another language, but the necessity was urged by the situation: 'the old school-yard [functioning as the camp yard] was transformed at mealtimes into a modern tower of Babel' (Macdonald 1917: 14). There Macdonald came into contact with Russians, Poles, Spaniards, German-speaking Alsatians, Italians, Romanians and Americans all serving in the 30th company of the 289th Regiment, and incidentally came into contact with Senegalese troops and German prisoners.

As exemplified by Cummings and Macdonald's experiences, personal memoirs of the war describing a range of environments indicate how multilinguism was less an exception than something which came to be seen as normal.

> To be a corporal in the Ninth Infantry, it is said, a man must be able to speak eight languages, one for each soldier in his squad. The same could be said with almost equal truth of our regiment. I don't know whether it is this mixture of many nationalities that gives my family its flavour; be that as it may, Company A has more color, more character, more individuality to the square inch than I had dreamed any such group could possess. (Morse 1920: 10)

> We have a strange mixture of French nationalities down here, so that we get all kinds of French accents and all kinds of patois. Some of the men don't even understand each other the Basques especially seem quite out of it, as they speak an entirely different language, and apparently one which even Frenchmen, living in the country round, find the greatest difficulty in learning, unless they have been brought up to it from childhood. (Cator 1915: 47)

Popular perceptions of multilinguism, the use of pidgin and Esperanto

The melting pots of the prison and the training camp functioned not only as places where foreign languages could be heard and learned to various degrees, but places where the relatively new constructed languages, Esperanto and Volapük, might come into their own. Esperanto was widely used in communication between home and prisoner-of-war, whilst the documented use of Volapük challenges the idea of globally dominant languages – French, English or German – or even the dominant status of Esperanto within constructed languages. The view of the multilingual environment at this time must be extended to include the perception of languages which were in their origins and nature both multilingual and stood beyond the national aspects of languages. Calvet points out that the growth of constructed languages moved with the slide to a Europe-wide war in the early twentieth century 'as if these projects were attempts to avert the catastrophe appearing on the political horizon' (Calvet 1998: 197). Esperanto evolved to meet the needs of its speakers, with the creation of a parallel form Ido, which appears alongside Esperanto in a set of translations of a propaganda document in 1915 (Calvet 1998: 197), whilst Volapük, the first constructed language to achieve wide usage, experienced success and failure in a short timescale. Calvet notes that 'ten years after its appearance, 25 journals were being printed in the language,

283 societies had been established, and there were textbooks in 25 languages. An academy was founded, which was not slow to discuss reforms. The intransigence of the inventor caused all of these to fail and provoked a schism then a crumbling away from 1889.' (Calvet 1998: 197). It is quite surprising then to see it in use at all during the war.

But apart from their actual use, constructed languages had a mythological status at the time, Esperanto coming, like 'pidgin', to be used to describe the ad hoc construction of lingua franca terms and exchanges, with varying degrees of success seen in terms of their relation to standard forms and their actual value in the field. In this way, a complex set of relations emerges in the contact between bi- or multilingualism in the individual, learning foreign languages, and successful, that is, pragmatic communication, a reductio ad absurdum of Macdonald's and later Ogden's idea of the 'basic' form of a language (in Macdonald's case 500 words (Macdonald 1917: 100), in Ogden's case 850 words (Ogden 1930), but in the case of the average British Expeditionary Force (BEF) private in France, probably less than 20 words). This application of Esperanto for something quite other than the actual language was not limited to English. In October 1917, the excitable journal *La Vie Parisienne* (n.p.) described the mingling of English and French in advertising as 'Desesperanto'. Whilst there was perhaps mock-shock in the reporting of a product labelled 'Paris-Londres, Writing pad, containing 100 feuilles Cream Laid superfin', the journal asked, 'We ask for the meaning of this strange language, and the tribe it is aimed at. Is it English, is it French? Is it an object destined for sale on the British Front?' Continuing its assessment of this kind of language as more appropriate for Africa than Europe, the article continued: 'For the love of God, speak French, merchants! You can't always avoid having a Swiss or Spanish accent; but try to speak French. Or at least, learn English.' The article concluded with a racist implication that this kind of language was suitable only for black people.

For some years, the actuality of pidgin, a term applied to a range of languages constructed primarily for trade purposes, had been subverted by imperial characterizations of colonized peoples as unable to speak standard English. Pidgin languages arise 'very suddenly in contact situations, where they are used by speakers with different language backgrounds to fulfil certain basic communicative functions (e.g. trade)' (Romaine 1988: 2); in these linguistic meetings, there is a 'prestige language of the dominant group in a situation of language contact' (Romaine 1988: 3) which supplies the vocabulary, much of the grammar of the 'native languages of the subordinate groups' being retained.

The imperial narrative preferred to see pidgins used within the British Empire less as examples of sociolinguistic change and development, than as proofs of social hierarchy. Pidgins thus were seen as displaying the superiority of one speaker over another, and inherently bolstered the fiction that one language, and thus culture, was better than another. Thus, when the language of basic communication between British soldiers and French traders was described as 'pidgin-French', there was little doubt who was being seen as the more civilized. On 25 August 1916, the *Sheffield Independent* carried an article about the encounter between English and French, its title, '"Pidgeon" French – A New Esperanto Breaking Out In Flanders', carrying both a sense of brotherhood and hierarchy. This can be compared with a report on the 1914 Christmas truce meetings being conducted in 'cockney French and pidgin English' (*The Daily Mirror*,

6 January 1915), in which a more equitable comparison is made. The 1916 article began by describing the tension that was arising because of the British trying to learn French, whilst the French were trying to learn English, producing a chaos that would only be resolved by the return of the armies to their homes, leaving France to revert to its own language. The article questioned, 'which of the two languages is going to give in?', the 1914 parity having by now become a struggle for domination.

In *In Kultured Kaptivity, life and death in Germany's prison camps and hospitals* (1918), Ivan Rossiter described the ad hoc lingua franca from the point of view of someone who appeared to know what a pidgin language was:

> A new 'language' has been born of this war, in the German prison camps, and is a medium of conversation between the different nationalities, being made up of German, Russian, French and English, resembling somewhat pidgin-English. It serves the purpose admirably, although it would be impossible for anyone but a prisoner in a German camp to understand it. (Rossiter 1918: 139)

Rossiter noted that after the war there would be a surprising number of former POWs who 'will be able to converse at least in French, and who will know something of German or Russian or both'. However, there is no mention here of the pidgin of the camp, and the inverted commas around 'language' indicate the interim status of what had developed, neither dialect nor language, something specific to the circumstance and likely to disappear at the cessation of hostilities. In popular perception 'Esperanto', despite its intrinsic anti-nationalism, and 'pidgin' both became excuses for evading the challenges of multilingualism and for retrenching the comfort of monolingualism.

War language in a crisis and its relevance now

As this book was being edited, the response to the global coronavirus epidemic was providing echoes of how states managed the crisis of 1914–18. Nation-based blaming, particularly the normalized attribution of the origin of Covid-19 to China, echoed the shaming of Germany for atrocities in Belgium in 1914 and the labelling of the influenza pandemic of 1918 as 'Spanish flu'. The merging of blame between a wet-food market and a research laboratory echoed the popular blaming of the start of the war on a mixture of Prussian militarism and pan-German imperial expansionism. This was even enforced upon Germany through the 'war guilt' clause of the 1919 Versailles Treaty (Britannica n.d.).

Early on in the British government's renewed response to the corona pandemic, the second daily press conference given by 10 Downing Street – on 17 March 2020 – put the country on a wartime footing through the use of wartime language: Prime Minister Boris Johnson decided to mirror French President Macron, who looked at battling the coronavirus as being at war. Johnson spoke of the virus as an enemy that could be deadly and that in order to win the fight, the enemy had to beaten: 'we must act like any wartime government' (BBC News 2020). The forecast of the death toll in Britain would make the coronavirus the worst crisis there since the 43,000 casualties of the Second

World War Blitz.[1] Until 16 March – when the first real measures were announced – the approach of the British government to the virus outbreak – at a time when the virus had already claimed many lives across Europe, and already fifty-five people in the United Kingdom – had been very low key, a go-it-alone and 'take it on the chin' attitude that was rife with Dunkirk and the Blitz spirit references.[2]

The Daily Telegraph (DT) compared the United Kingdom's new line of measures to increasingly self-isolate – proper lockdown sanctions – to the Second World War in a manner favourable to the government, and *The Daily Mail* (DM) even resuscitated Dame Vera Lynn (102 years old) to summon the Blitz spirit and pull together. Both populist newspapers referred to both world wars pretty much daily. A sample of those can be found in the following text:

'When it comes to the Coronavirus, Britain is right to keep calm and carry on (DT, 13 March)

In a move that will evoke some Blitz spirit, major businesses like Rolls-Royce and JCB have said they are ready to join the 'national effort' to help the NHS cope, amid calls for firms to switch to producing ventilators. (DT, 16 March)

I'm determined to Blitz spirit this virus. (DT, 16 March)

This week, the British public has been asked to channel its 'Blitz spirit', while many older people have said that if they can survive the war, they can survive this. (DT, 17 March)

Britain has gone to war with the Coronavirus. (DT, 20 March)

The psychology of rationing: will Britons battling coronavirus find a new Blitz spirit? (DT, 20 March)

'Selfless spirit' of war years can help Britain in coronavirus fight, says Dame Vera Lynn. (DT, 20 March)

It has become commonplace to compare the coronavirus to the Second World War, but our domestic economy continued to function even at the height of the Blitz. (DT, 28 March)

She [The Queen] also invoked Dame Vera Lynn as she promised tens of millions of watching Brits: 'We will meet again' (DM, 5 April)

War on coronavirus: Germans don't use WW2 rhetoric to describe the pandemic response because they associate it with loss – but Britain and the US are happy to invoke the 'Blitz spirit.' (DM, 20 April)

Dame Vera Lynn calls for VE Day style celebrations when Britain finally conquers coronavirus pandemic as she compares battle against killer infection to World War II. (DM, 29 April)

At last! The spirit of Beaverbrook is with us again . . . and in a stunning coincidence, the brains behind a wonder coronavirus test is the grandson of the press baron whose dynamism helped win the war. (DM, 20 April)

Others were much less impressed by the use of war references and were quite convinced of their inappropriateness: 'The "Blitz Spirit" Won't Protect Britain From the Coronavirus' (*The Atlantic*, online, 12 March), 'Why the cruel myth of the "blitz spirit" is no model for how to fight coronavirus' (*The Guardian online*, 19 March).

As ever, the British press was split over wartime language references: 'Thousands Of Europeans Have Left Britain This Week Because Of The Coronavirus – It is well and truly a Dunkirk in reverse' (*buzzfeed*, 21 March) stood in stark contrast to 'Coronavirus "Dunkirk spirit" praised as British labs re-purpose to carry out COVID-19 test' (*The Daily Express*, 2 April). Vera Lynn also resonated in a speech by Queen Elizabeth, who addressed the nation regarding the coronavirus crisis and whose core message was that the crisis could not last forever and that despite the fight ahead, 'we'll meet again'. The Queen also said that 'the situation reminded her of her first ever broadcast in 1940, when she and her late sister Margaret spoke from Windsor to children who had been evacuated from their homes to escape bombing raids by Nazi German aircraft' (*EurActiv* 2020). The connotation of the British spirit during the Second World War was evoked clearly. Inspired by the Queen's address to the nation, Vera Lynn and Katherine Jenkins recorded a new version of 'We'll Meet Again', the proceeds of which were entirely intended for the charity NHS Together.

However, in America, where the government's response to the corona outbreak was underperforming even more, the British government's response to the coronavirus had been labelled 'a disaster' (*Washington Post*, 16 March 2020). By mid-March, American politicians were still on a par with their French and British counterparts and resorted to military rhetoric in an attempt to comfort their fellow-Americans: 'We are going to defeat the invisible enemy' (President Donald Trump, 17 March press conference)[3], 'We're at war with a virus' (Democrat Joe Biden, NBC News 15 March). The use of these words was designed 'to give an appearance of solidity to pure wind' (Orwell 1946: 120): a virus is not an external challenge that can be defeated. Moreover, during the handover between the Obama and the Trump administration, officials of the former relayed to officials of the latter on how they had been working on a case study that modelled the worst influenza since 1918. Instead of taking the matter to heart, Trump hired John Bolton, who disbanded the National Security Council's global health security team, exactly one century after a previous pandemic, the decimation that was the Spanish flu (Weinstein 2020).[4] When President Trump changed tack mid-March – after weeks of downplaying the threat – he addressed the nation, and instead of a benign rallying call for self-support like the British queen's in her address, the American president announced from the Oval Office an 'aggressive and comprehensive effort to confront a foreign virus' (Trump 2020). If Trump was able to frame the virus as a foreign attack, then war language could displace blame (Levenson 2020). The president subsequently moved to his personal Twitter account and added that the American government would be supporting industries 'that are particularly affected by the Chinese Virus' (Trump 2020). However satisfying the military rhetoric might be for political purposes, the metaphors comparing the efforts to stop coronavirus to a military war fit in many ways. The war metaphors mobilize people – or so politicians using the phraseology believe – to 'do their bit', as the phrase was in 1914–18. People 'understand the sacrifices that have to occur during wartime and they understand the massive mobilization of resources needed in a war' (Levenson 2020).

Just as during the First and the Second World War, in coronavirus times the 'home front' was a global sphere broken down to isolating nations, fluid combatant entities – fighting the virus by staying low or by being involved in health care – and small bubbles of families sheltering; typically the socio-cultural association was at its most limited linguistically. On the home front, measures in place to try and contain the rapid spread of the highly contagious virus, and help limit the number of casualties, included hand-washing, social distancing, self-isolation, quarantine, cutting down public services, limited economic activity, restricted access to goods and more. However, the impact of the rhetoric and the continued announcement of measures on the one hand and ever-increasing numbers of infected people and deaths on the other was felt most by those who endured the consequences of those measures. And the people did act exactly along the lines of what public health experts had been warning about for years: by stockpiling supplies (Levenson 2020). If Matt Hancock, the British health secretary, called on the British to emulate their grandparents' behaviour during the Blitz, then the generations of spring 2020 immediately turned to a response that conflicted heavily with the much-used pride of resisting nightly pounding and loss of life (Bagehot 2020): the true British grit of the Dunkirk and Blitz spirit pulled together alright, but just like anywhere else in the world, by descending on shops in panic mode. This was not solely the British response to politicians' flag-waving but a common reaction shared across many, many countries. There is no escaping the cringeworthy repetition of war metaphors: 'selfish supermarket panic buyers betray Blitz spirit . . . testament to a wilful refusal to consider the welfare of others' (Vine 2020). Conveniently ignoring the wartime phenomena of looting, profiteering and black marketing, the self-directed story of the Blitz spirit, 'largely a confection, a propaganda ploy applied to keep up morale . . . sealed into the mythology of the war which, as the victors, the British wrote' (Dejevsky 2020), could even be rolled out to attack those who debased its role as presiding spirit. Just as rationing was the response to the government's perception of the social dangers of inequal access to food in 1917, so in 2020 supermarkets imposed rationing on shoppers, limiting the amount of selected products that could be bought and the number of members of a family who could shop at any one time. A culture of the social-distanced queue has developed in the United Kingdom, as it did in Russia of 1914–18 (see Golubinov, Part III, Chapter 11, in this volume), with extensive lines created by two metre gaps.

The patterns of behaviour extended beyond national propaganda and hoarding. Social media comments on the inappropriateness of using war metaphors in the management of the pandemic asked whether health-workers should be described as 'frontline workers' – who by miracle can be galvanized by the mere fundamental support of neighbourhood clapping – or those who contracted coronavirus should be described as 'fighting' the disease, should they 'win' or 'lose' their 'battle with the disease'. In purely health terms, such comments were seen as misleading, as an intubated patient in a coma was in no position to consciously fight the disease. Such easy terminology presented a simple story, of unprovoked attack and stalwart defence, papering over more complex interpretations.

Within a couple of weeks of the outbreak of the First World War commercial, marketing writers were using war terminology to help sell their products, ranging from the fairly drole 'Business as Usual, during European alterations' in *The Boot and Shoe Retailer*, 11 September 1914, to 'It's a long way to Tipperary but it doesn't seem a long way if you are wearing Wood-Milne rubber heels and tips' in *The Daily Sketch*, 10 December 1914. Some of these can be perhaps excused, as they were advertisements for products such as cigarettes, toffee and shaving soap, which were of direct use by soldiers. But there were advertisements that made puns on the Somme/some, as on 21 February 1917 *The Tatler* carried an advertisement for Gibbs' shaving soap with the headline: '"Somme" shave – It is really "some" soap, this Gibbs's.' Commercial companies sponsored food parcels and phrasebooks for soldiers, making sure that their names were associated with the product. Was this support or exploitation, or both?

As then so in 2020, television advertisements for major companies have run sequences indicating support for the NHS, with their company tags at the end. Again, the moral ground had blurred edges: health-workers need to relax, and surely many would benefit from the products of a major multinational communications company; many people were going hungry and undoubtedly benefited from the charitable distribution of food by a major supermarket chain; much extra revenue accrued from customers who were persuaded that in buying the products of these companies they were supporting the companies' support. Responsibility was spread among the population, but with a company logo attached. The end recipients of the revenue included health services, those who benefited from the charity, and the bank balances of the companies involved.

The exploration of the past for links and models for the present is as old as the concept of history itself; it is an activity which we are more accustomed seeing practised more in the environment of the anniversary of an historic event rather than at the time of international crisis. As the centenary of the First World War itself became history, there appeared a strong probability that the positions established in 2018, the responsibilities, the strategies, the stories, the viewpoints, would become the orthodoxies presented for the foreseeable future; the story would settle, be wrapped up and shelved to make way for the anniversary of the following war. The current period of global emergency has disrupted this, as we look more than we had expected at the influenza epidemic of 1918–19. Governmental rhetoric of Covid-19 has been much vocalized in terms of conflict, which in itself has facilitated the path towards international accusation; but examination of the role of language in situations of crisis may show us what we are doing, and what we are in danger of doing. It is a duty we owe to the present, to the past and to the future.

Notes

1   Figures on Blitz casualties from Gilbert 2017. By the time of submitting the texts for the volume, official figures of corona-related casualties were about to pass 40,000 (Clarke 2020), even though figures of excess deaths were almost 60,000 (Voce 2020).

2   Following the government's announcement of a limited social reprieve for Christmas 2020 a joke on social media proposed playing a football match against the virus, a clear reference to the 1914 Christmas truce on the Western Front.

3 A clip of the press conference is still available from *The New York Times* (https://tinyurl.com/yd9dvtdk), but might be offline soon. Not many US sources reference the sentence verbatim anymore.
4 By the time of writing, the number of people infected with corona worldwide stood at 6.3 million, whereas estimations for the Spanish influenza go as high as 500 million. Figures for the deaths in 1918–19 range between 20 and 50 million, whereas this was closing in on 400,000 for corona (figures by the Center for Disease Control and Prevention and the World Health Organisation, snapshot 3 June 2020).

References

First World War journals

La Vie Parisienne, Paris, 1863–1970.
The Boot and Shoe Retailer, 11 September 1914, 2.
The Bystander, 11 November 1914, 30.
The Daily Sketch, 10 December 1914, 13.
The Daily Mirror, 6 January 1915, 12.
The Tatler, 21 February 1917, 253.

Secondary literature

(Britannica) The Editors of Encyclopedia Britannica (no date), 'Treaty of Versailles', in *Encyclopedia Britannica online*. Available online: https://www.britannica.com/event/Treaty-of-Versailles-1919 (accessed 6 June 2020).
Calvet, J.-L. (1998), *Language Wars and Linguistic Politics*, Oxford: Oxford University Press.
Cator, D. (1915), *In a French Military Hospital*, London: Longmans, Green and Co.
Cobb, R. (1983), *French and Germans, Germans and French*, London: University of New England Press.
Cummings, E. (1922), *The Enormous Room,* New York: Boni and Liveright.
Das, S. (2018), *India, Empire and First World Culture: Writing, Images and Songs*, Cambridge: Cambridge University Press.
Dominian, L. (1917), *The Frontiers of Language and Nationality in Europe*, New York: The American Geographical Society of New York.
Gaull, M. (1967), 'Language and Identity: A Study of E. E. Cummings' "The Enormous Room"', *American Quarterly*, 19 (4): 645–62.
Linehan, T. and T. M. Linehan (1979), 'Style and Individuality in E.E. Cummings in The Enormous Room', *Style*, 13 (1): 45–59.
Lyons, M. (2008), *Reading Culture & Writing Practices in Nineteenth-Century France*, Toronto: University of Toronto Press.
Macdonald, M. (1917), *Under the French Flag*, London: Robert Scott.
Morse, K. D. (1920), *The Uncensored Letters of a Canteen Girl*, New York: Henry Holt.
Ogden, C. K. (1930), *Basic English*, London: Kegan Paul & Co.
Orwell, G. (1946), *Politics and the English Language*, London: Horizon.
Romaine, S. (1988), *Pidgin & Creole Languages*, Harlow: Longman
Rossiter, I. (1918), *In Kultured Kaptivity, Life and Death in Germany's Prison Camps and Hospitals*, Indianapolis: BobsMerrill.

Statistics of the Military Effort of the British Empire During the Great War, 1914–1920
(1922), London: His Majesty's Stationery Office.
Walker, J. and P. Doyle (2012), *Trench Talk: Words of the First World War*, Stroud: History
Press.

Online sources

Adedokun, N. (2020), 'Coronavirus "Dunkirk spirit" Praised as British Labs Re-purpose
to Carry Out COVID-19 test', *The Daily Express*. Available online, https://www.express.
co.uk/news/uk/1263881/coronavirus-uk-news-bbc-radio-4-today-covid-19-tests-paul-
nurse-francis-crick-institute (accessed 6 June 2020).
Bagehot (2020), 'Spirit of the Blitz', *The Economist online*. Available online: https://www
.economist.com/britain/2020/03/21/spirit-of-the-blitz (accessed 6 June 2020).
(BBC News) Coronavirus: 'We must Act Like Any Wartime Government' (2020), *BBC
News*. Available online: https://www.bbc.com/news/av/uk-51936760/coronavirus-we-
must-act-like-any-wartime-government (accessed 6 June 2020).
Clarke, S. and P. Gutierrez (2020), 'Coronavirus UK Map: The Latest Deaths and
Confirmed Cases Near You', *The Guardian online*. Available online: https://www.the
guardian.com/world/2020/jun/03/coronavirus-uk-map-the-latest-deaths-and-con
firmed-cases-near-you (accessed 6 June 2020).
(CWGC) Commonwealth War Graves Commission (2020), *India*. Available online https
://www.cwgc.org/history-and-archives/first-world-war/forces/indian-army (accessed
6 June 2020).
'Debating coronavirus: Sanders blasts, "Shut this president up," and Biden says, "This is
like a war"' (2020), *NBC News*. Available online: https://www.nbcnews.com/politics
/2020-election/debating-coronavirus-sanders-blasts-shut-president-biden-says-we-re-
n1159671 (accessed 6 June 2020).
Dejevsky, M. (2020), 'Coronavirus and the Myth of "Blitz spirit"', *The Spectator online*.
Available online: https://www.spectator.co.uk/article/coronavirus-and-the-myth-of-b
litz-spirit- (21 March 2020).
Gilbert, A. (2017), 'The Blitz', *Encyclopedia Britannica online*. Available online: https://ww
w.britannica.com/event/the-Blitz (accessed 6 June 2020).
Jenkins, H. (2020), 'The British government's Response to the Coronavirus has been a
Disaster', *The Washington Post*. Available online https://www.washingtonpost.com/outl
ook/2020/03/16/britain-coronavirus-disaster/ (accessed 6 June 2020).
Levenson, E. (2020), 'Officials Keep Calling the Coronavirus Pandemic a "war." Here's
Why', *CNN*. Available online: https://edition.cnn.com/2020/04/01/us/war-on-coron
avirus-attack/index.html (2 April 2020).
Lewis, H. (2020), 'The "Blitz Spirit" Won't Protect Britain From the Coronavirus', *The
Atlantic*. Available online: https://www.theatlantic.com/international/archive/2020/03/
britain-coronavirus-boris-johnson/607879/) (accessed 16 April 2020).
Lewis, R. (2017), 'Why the British Still Talk About the "Dunkirk Spirit"', *Time*? Available
online https://time.com/4860620/dunkirk-spirit-phrase-history-world-war-2/
(accessed 6 June 2020).
Nardelli, A. (2020), 'Thousands of Europeans Have Left Britain This Week Because of The
Coronavirus', *Buzzfeed*. Available online: https://www.buzzfeed.com/albertonardelli/
europeans-leaving-britain-coronavirus (accessed 6 April 2020).
O'Grady, S. (2020), 'Queen Elizabeth Channelled Blitz Spirit in Rare Address – but is this
Generation Up to the Task?', *The Independent*. Available online: https://www.independ

ent.co.uk/voices/queen-elizabeth-speech-coronavirus-uk-nhs-lockdown-boris-johnso n-a9448611.html (accessed 6 April 2020).

Overy, R. (2020), 'Why the Cruel Myth of the "blitz spirit" is no Model for How to Fight Coronavirus', *The Guardian*. Available online: https://www.theguardian.com/ commentisfree/2020/mar/19/myth-blitz-spirit-model-coronavirus) (accessed 6 June 2020).

Rawlinson, K. (2020), '"This enemy can be deadly": Boris Johnson Invokes Wartime Language', *The Guardian*. Available online: https://www.theguardian.com/world/2 020/mar/17/enemy-deadly-boris-johnson-invokes-wartime-language-coronavirus (accessed 17 March 2020).

Roynette, O. (2016), 'Problems and Challenges of a Historical Approach', in C. Declercq and J. Walker (eds), *Languages and the First World War: Representation and Memory*, 21–31, London: Palgrave-Macmillan.

Shell, M. (2001), 'Language Wars', *CR: The New Centennial Review* 1 (2): 1–17. Available online: https://www.jstor.org/stable/pdf/41949277.pdf?refreqid=excelsior%3Ac00 de1aa6c0f3c57ad192d0cf685169c (accessed 6 June 2020).

'The UK government's woeful response to the coronavirus outbreak' (2020), Comments section. *The Guardian*. Available online https://www.theguardian.com/uk-news/2020/ mar/19/the-uk-governments-woeful-response-to-the-coronavirus-outbreak (accessed 19 March 2020).

Trump, D. (2020), 'Trump: This Is The Most Comprehensive Effort To Confront A "Foreign Virus"', Oval Office broadcast 11 March. Available online: https://www.realcl earpolitics.com/video/2020/03/11/trump_this_is_the_most_comprehensive_effor t_to_confront_a_foreign_virus_in_modern_history.html (accessed 6 June 2020).

UK Urges Corona Tech Togetherness, Ahead of 'Digital Dunkirk' (2020), *Red Herring*. Available online https://www.redherring.com/europe/uk-urges-corona-tech-toget herness-ahead-of-digital-dunkirk/ (accessed 6 June 2020).

Vine, A. (2020), 'Coronavirus: Selfish Supermarket Panic Buyers Betray Blitz Spirit', *The Yorkshire Evening Post*. Available online, https://www.yorkshireeveningpost.co.uk/news /opinion/columnists/coronavirus-selfish-supermarket-panic-buyers-betray-blitz-spirit -andrew-vine-2506144 (accessed 6 June 2020).

Voce, A., S. Clarke, C. Barr, N. McIntyre and P. Duncan (2020), 'Coronavirus Excess Deaths: UK has One of Highest Levels in Europe', *The Guardian*. Available online: https ://www.theguardian.com/world/ng-interactive/2020/may/29/excess-deaths-uk-has-one -highest-levels-europe (accessed 6 June 2020).

Ward, A. (2020), 'Britain's WW2 Sweetheart Dame Vera Lynn, 102, Summons the Blitz Spirit in Rallying Cry to "pull together" and "weather the storm of coronavirus"', *The Daily Mail*. Available online: https://www.dailymail.co.uk/news/article-8125129/Dame -Vera-Lynn-102-summons-Blitz-spirit-amid-coronavirus-outbreak.html (accessed 6 June 2020).

Weinstein, A. (2020), 'The Casualties of the "War" on the Coronavirus', *The New Republic*. Available online: https://newrepublic.com/article/156949/casualties-war-coronavirus (accessed 6 June 2020).

'We'll meet again': Queen Elizabeth Invokes WW2 Spirit to Defeat Coronavirus (2020), EurActiv online, https://www.euractiv.com/section/politics/news/well-meet-again-qu een-elizabeth-invokes-ww2-spirit-to-defeat-coronavirus/ (6 April).

Abbreviations and acronyms

A/c	Aircraftsman
AEF	American Expeditionary Force(s)
AIF	Australian Imperial Force
ANZAC	Australian and New Zealand Army Corps
ASU	Arts and Sciences Union
AWOL	Absent without leave
BBG	Book of Belgium's Gratitude
BEF	British Expeditionary Force
CBI	Content Based Instruction
CEIP	Carnegie Endowment for International Peace
COB	Comité Officiel Belge
CUP	Committee of Union and Progress
DM	*The Daily Mail*
DT	*The Daily Telegraph*
ESBRN	Everyman Special Belgian Relief Number
FEI	Federazione esperantista italiana
FWW	First World War
GOB	Glory of Belgium
HMSO	*His/Her Majesty's Stationery Office*
ICRC	International Committee of the Red Cross
IKE	Itala Katedro de Esperanto
IMA	International Mind Alcoves
IWM	Imperial War Museum
k.u.k.	*kaiserlich und königlich*, Imperial and Royal
KAB	King Albert's Book
KAR	King's African Rifles
LTI	'Lingua Tertii Imperii: Notizbuch eines Philologen' (the Language of the Third Reich: A Philologist's Notebook)
MP	Military Police(man)

N&Q	Notes and Queries
NCO	Non-commissioned officer
NS	National Socialist
Oblt.	*Oberleutnant*, highest level of Lieutenant rank
OHL	*Oberste Heeresleitung*, Supreme Army Command
PGW	Poems of the Great War
PISA	Programme for International Student Assessment
PMGB	Princess Mary's Gift Book
POW	Prisoner of War
QWWF	Queen's 'Work for Women' Fund
RAF	Royal Air Force
RNC	Russian National Corpus
RSSILA	Returned Sailors and Soldiers League of Australia
RWU	Report on the work undertaken by the British Government in the reception and care of the Belgian refugees
THW	Times History of the War
TNA	The National Archives
UEA	Universala Esperanto-Asocio
USB	Swiss financial services company based in Zurich
WPB	War Propaganda Bureau
YMCA	Young Men's Christian Association

Part I

Multilingual environments

Introduction to Part I

Hillary Briffa

The very term 'First World War' highlights the expansive reach of the first total war waged between industrialized world powers whose empires spanned the globe. As the Allies postured offensively against the emerging peer competitors on the continent, a nationalist assassination in the Balkans led them, chain-ganged, into a conflict of unprecedented magnitude. The Central European Powers clashed with the entirety of the British Empire, India and the Dominions, the French Empire, Japan, the United States, and Russia in the early years of fire. Yet it was not just bullets and bayonets that crossed borders and occupied new spaces; soldiers and civilians carried their language and culture. Thus, the five chapters in this part explore the multilingual environments of the war, and the phonetic encounters that served purposes as wide ranging as riot suppression, or the trading of food stuffs with local chiefs.

As readers, we become foreign visitors ourselves, entering the German prisoner-of-war camps where one can almost hear the dialectal voices of the Italian prisoners in Bannò's meticulous study of the *Königlich-Preussische Phonographische Kommission*, singing in front of the gramophone and drafting passages that the recording linguists translated into standard language. Phonography pioneer Doegen's commission of German, Austrian and Swiss linguists, anthropologists and musicologists capitalized on the opportunity to study the exotic languages of their prisoners. The purpose of the commission was not limited to linguistic study, however; Bannò reveals how recordings were also leveraged for the war effort, in the teaching of foreign languages, and for propagandist ends, as Doegen strove to counteract allegations of prisoner maltreatment and to restore honour to Germany in the post-war period. As a rich educational repository, tourists to Berlin, far removed from the fronts, became aural explorers themselves as exhibitions of the sound collection fostered multilingual exchange. Thanks to Bannò's discovery and revival, the songs of the prisoners will continue to echo.

Like the caged Italian songbirds of Bannò's study, Javier Alcalde, too, takes us behind the bars that imprisoned conscientious objectors. Among this group, the auxiliary language of Esperanto was popular and Alcalde shines a light into these dark spaces of confinement, where the language flourished. An enterprising prisoner earned a salary by teaching the language to German officers. Esperanto magazines were published in prison camps. Even in captivity, there was creativity and cooperation. Tracing the roots of this internationalist language, the planned language of Esperanto was created by Zamenhof in 1887, intended to be used among people with different mother tongues. Two years prior to the conception of this international auxiliary language, the poet

Walt Whitman penned (in *Song of Myself*) the famous verse, '*I am large. I contain multitudes*'. These poignant words seem apt to describe Esperanto as presented in Alcalde's work. Its very nomenclature – meaning 'one who hopes' – demonstrates the expansive and profound purpose it was conceived to fulfil.

Rejecting presentism that relegates Esperanto to a marginal position, through Alcalde's study we come into contact with the Esperanto-speaking railroad workers passing through villages; doctors treating patients; humanitarian workers tending to the wounded and distributing clothing, medicine, and food; Boy Scouts; international scientists and jurists; and even the religious and the spiritual, all pursuing a neutral language of communication. Beyond the pragmatic ends, we learn not only of the war being fought in the trenches, but of the ideological war that was waged on behalf of ideals and the spirit of internationalism. The pacific vocation of the Esperanto movement was antithetic to the Great War, and Alcalde portrays not only the functional utility of the language, but its inherently globalist spirit. Its performative utterances advanced a social movement.

In opposition to the confined spaces of prisons, Anne Samson recounts the language learning taking place on the open decks of HM Forces ships, bound for East Africa. Samson homes in on the study of Kiswahili, as prioritized by the Colonial Office. Her lively work depicts the efforts of individuals, such as Lieutenant John Bruce Cairnie, struggling to learn the language and resolve misunderstandings with servants on board, whilst sailing across the Indian Ocean. Just as Cairnie's ship eventually reached port, so too does Samson transport the reader to East Africa – a theatre where the languages and dialects of some 177 ethnic or tribal groupings reveals the complex interplay between imperial and indigenous cultures and commands. She describes how local inhabitants proved invaluable to the war effort due to their knowledge of the terrain and language, understanding of the culture, and access to news. However, it was also important for those in leadership positions to learn the language: in practical terms, to deliver orders or interrogate potential prisoners; but so, too, for more intangible gains: building trust through mutual understanding.

Samson skilfully charts the day-to-day interactions in the camps. One labourer and herdsman of cattle describes how segregation was the norm in his experience, with only the leaders having contact with white soldiers; conversely, the 'whites' would be exclusively privy to information, may have had access to newspapers and were certainly delivering the orders. In so doing, Samson exposes the vertical and horizontal relationships prevailing during this period. As much as there are lessons to be learned regarding the practicality and functionality of language, and the complex sociopolitical dynamics playing out in the different regions, the chapters are also enriched by their immortalization of the journeys and lived experiences of a host of vivid characters. In addition to Cairnie, Samson notably introduces us to Van Deventer – an Afrikaans/Dutch-speaking South African who refused to speak English, following a particularly grim encounter with the British (to be discovered in her chapter). Gwendal Piégais, meanwhile, introduces us to the composer Paul Le Flem, whose ability to speak Russian elevated him from his initial war duties as a stretcher bearer to the interpreter of a special Russian regiment of the French army. His effort to improve the quality of life of former Russian soldiers working in France – including diet, living conditions and wages – demonstrates the centrality of interpreters' contributions, beyond translation. Just as linguistic skills enabled Paul Le Flem to climb the ranks, Piégais reveals how language skills enabled army recruits to become upwardly mobile in the stratified French society.

Piégais' chapter on French strategy provides, furthermore, for deeper understanding of the relationship between France and Central and Eastern Europe during the war. In particular, the analysis of the *Corps Expéditionnaire Russe en France* – the Russian Expeditionary force in France and Macedonia – imparts the struggles of the French and British army in their attempt to manage a multinational coalition, communicate with Ottoman prisoners and sustain peaceful relations with the occupied population in Northern Greece. With 40,000 Russian soldiers in the French army in 1916, Piégais pinpoints the challenges of interpreting and translating the Russian language during the war, emphasizing the difficulties and shortages in recruiting men with Russian linguistic skills. He is unequivocal about the importance of interpreters in this period, given that 'Languages were the bridge through which the allies could implement cooperation in the field, or even in unexpected theatres'.

Through Piégais' work, we therefore discover the multifaceted role of these linguists. Interpreters were interrogators, intelligence gatherers and inspectors of the behaviour in camps. They translated orders, documents and handbooks in a bid to homogenize the military practices of the multinational coalition. When Russian participation in the war ended with the Treaty of Brest-Litovsk in March 1918, the French had to contend with the 65,000 Russian POWs, freed from German camps and awaiting repatriation. Interpreters managed both the post and the prisoners; as tensions rose, Piégais reveals the essential dual role they played in both gauging troop morale in the field and preventing prisoner rioting in the camps.

Interpreter accounts therefore guided both the understanding of foreign language during this time and the expanding of our repository of historical knowledge through their study today. Indeed, Samson explains that 'Interpreters play an important role in our accessing accounts in languages not our own'. At the same time, Julian Walker introduces another medium intended to facilitate access to foreign languages during the war: phrasebooks published in France, Britain, Germany and the United States. Walker highlights the distinct purposes of these texts. Ranging from teaching books to travellers' phrasebooks, civilian engagement aids to military manuals, these served purposes as disparate as travellers' aides or interrogation scripts. The content spans the mundane (ordering tea), the militarized (asking after the passage of enemy troops or interrogating prisoners) and the outright mystifying (passionate encounters in Egyptian phrasebooks). Moreover, German copies in Allied hands were ridiculed for propagandist ends, fodder for caricaturized portrayals of the enemy.

The phrasebooks were not simply educational, however. The works had a prescriptive element, seeking to determine the course of action for various projected scenarios. Whether engaging with suspected spies, becoming separated from comrades, being fired upon or even seeking to deceive the enemy with false orders in their own language, the phrasebooks serve as a reflection of the types of situations soldiers were expected to encounter. The analysis of the phrasebooks is not limited to those involved in combat, however. Turning to civilians, away from the home front, and the displaced victims of the war, the study yields insight into the experience of locals seeking to accommodate Belgian refugees. Walker sensitively juxtaposes the proffered advice on food and household management (implicit of domestic coexistence) with the reality of the growing antipathy towards these arrivals and the anxiety they endured. Whilst phrasebooks were intended as tools for illumination, they were not always successful. Indeed, the comprehensive study scrutinizes the challenges of these attempts at linguistic exchange. Miscommunications in exchanging slang, faulty translations and the reinforcing of colonial and gender power dynamics in Egyptian-British relations all reveal the shortcomings of this very human process.

The stories within these chapters reveal the essentiality of language as 'the ultimate transmission belt' (to borrow Piégais' phrasing), a carrier of often fragmentary code. The reader follows in the footsteps of the soldiers, civilians, interpreters and advocates discovering new means of expression to reflect their new existence. When taken together, these five texts allow the reader to traverse multilingual environments where pragmatism and personalism coincide, ultimately the context of proper multilinguism; where characters share a fascination with the exotic or an appreciation for the musicality of language; but where language is also a source of conflict and a channel for rebellion. In these spaces, language is concurrently a functional tool, and an expression of the highest ideals. It is a source of connection and a source of contention.

1

Wilhelm Doegen and the *Königlich-Preussische Phonographische Kommission*

Translation, phonetics and phonography among the Italian prisoners in the German POW camps of the Great War

Stefano Bannò

During the summer of 2016, I learned through my supervisor Serenella Baggio (University of Trento) about the existence of *Berliner Lautarchiv*, an archive that keeps 4,503 phonographic records of folktales, poems, monologues and songs in more than 250 languages and dialects from all over the world, and, from 1 November of the same year, thanks to a scholarship of the Faculty of Letters and Philosophy of the University of Trento, I moved to the German capital to classify and analyse the Italian section of the archive. Among the impressive card index cabinets of the small room on the first floor of the *Institut für Musikwissenschaft und Medienwissenschaft* at Kupfergraben 5, I found sixty-four shellac discs containing 115 unpublished Italian dialectal recordings, produced in various German prisoner-of-war (POW) camps during the Great War on behalf of the *Königlich-Preußische Phonographische Kommission*, a commission established in October 1915 and made up of German, Austrian and Swiss linguists, anthropologists and musicologists who had seen war as a unique opportunity: the cultures and languages of near and especially distant and exotic peoples, often at risk of extinction, could be studied comparatively without undertaking hard and onerous expeditions around Europe and the colonial territories.

A few months before the outbreak of the war, on 27 February 1914, an ambitious teacher of English, Wilhelm Doegen, addressed a memorandum entitled *Vorschläge für die Errichtung eines Kgl. Preußischen Phonetischen Instituts* to the Prussian Ministry of Culture. In Doegen's plans, the institute with its sound recordings would give significant contributions to the study of cultural and 'spiritual' (*Kultur-und Geistesleben*) life of the peoples of the world and should not have been limited – despite the title of the memorandum – exclusively to the sphere of phonetics, but would have been useful also to anthropologists and musicologists. For this reason, Doegen had already thought of dividing the archive material into five sections in the planning stage: the first was dedicated to the languages of all the peoples of the world; the second to the German dialects; the third to the music and songs of all the peoples of the world; the fourth containing the voices of the most famous personalities of his time; the fifth and last section indicated as miscellaneous (Doegen 1925b: 9).

In October of the following year, the Prussian Ministry of Culture accepted Doegen's proposal and established the *Königlich-Preußische Phonographische Kommission* in collaboration with the *Seminar für Orientalische Sprachen* in Berlin (Evans 2006: 135). The commission also benefited from substantial financial contributions from the Kaiser's personal fund.[1] Doegen's academic credentials were not enough for him to be formally head of the commission, so Carl Stumpf, distinguished musicologist and founder of the *Berliner Phonogramm-Archiv*, was chosen as president (*Vorsitzender*) and director of the music department. However, de facto the central personality of the commission was Doegen, who was appointed administrative director (*Geschäftsführer*) and at the same time was tasked with dealing with the logistical organization of the recording sessions in the POW camps. Doegen's dream of recording 'die Stimmen, die Sprachen und die Musik aller Völker der Erde'[2] (Doegen 1925b: 9) could finally come true. The commission, composed of thirty-six scholars, was divided into nine sections: the music department led by Stumpf; the department of oriental languages, directed by the orientalist Eduard Sachau; the English-language department, coordinated by Alois Brandl, who was formerly Doegen's master; the department of comparative and Indo-European linguistics, chaired by the linguist Wilhelm Schulze; the Romance languages department, headed by the Swiss linguist Heinrich Morf until 1921, the year of his death, and later by the Alsatian Romanist Hermann Urtel; the department of Indian and Mongolian languages, led by the Indianist Heinrich Lüders; the department of anthropology, entrusted to Felix von Luschan; the African languages department, led by the Africanist Carl Meinhof; and finally, the phonetic recordings department, coordinated by Doegen himself. He was a very controversial figure and always presented himself as the true founder and factotum of the commission, but from the private correspondence of the scholars involved in the survey some sense of annoyance and distrust for the sometimes presumptuous and intrusive attitude of the *Geschäftsführer* emerges: Urtel did not have a high regard for his superior,[3] and von Luschan went so far as to plan an itinerary for his department in prison camps away from Doegen's entourage, specifically to avoid his presence (Scheer 2010: 307). As a result, since the survey activities of the musicologists and linguists of the commission were not supported by the presence of an anthropologist, they were not carried out according to the methods of anthropological research of that time: the Austrian counterpart of von Luschan, Rudolf Pöch, used to spend whole weeks in the camps for his surveys, whereas, on the contrary, Doegen and his team stayed in the camps only for the days that were strictly necessary to complete the recording sessions (Scheer 2010: 307). This aspect partly explains why the huge amount of written documentation that accompanies the sound recordings – at least for the section that I analysed during my research in Berlin – is mostly of linguistic interest.

Moreover, Doegen had to be proudly jealous not only of the phonographic (and linguistic) survey activities, but also of the collection of photographic material, about which he wrote: 'Meine Bildertafeln beruhen auf Photographien, die ich persönlich ganz selbständig und unabhängig von den lautlichen Aufnahmen in den Kriegsgefangenenlagern ohne Staatliche Mittel veranstaltet habe'[4] (Doegen 1925a: 6). In these circumstances, it is understandable that Urtel, in a letter dated 12 December 1916 and addressed to Friedrich Carl Andreas, recommended the utmost discretion with regard to some photographs attached to the letter and taken in Wünsdorf camp without the authorization of *Kommissar* 'Herr D.' – in all likelihood, just Doegen – who, if he had discovered such violation, would have made it a cause célèbre.[5] An official photographer of the *Kunstwissenschaftliches Institut of the University of Berlin* – named Mr Gerdes (Doegen 1925a: 6) – had followed the surveys of the phonographic commission and had taken photographs of the prisoners – probably the most 'exotic' ones – who had taken part in the recording sessions. Unfortunately, the majority of the photographs were not attached to the record and were lost after the war (Scheer 2010: 304).

It is worthwhile to go back to the Romance languages section, before delving into the contents of the Italian subsection. In addition to Morf and Urtel, it was composed of three distinguished Romanists namely Matthias Friedwagner, who worked on some Moldovan and Romanian recordings, Friedrich Schürr, who produced a dozen recordings of prisoners from Emilia-Romagna and Friuli, and Max Leopold Wagner, who produced only three Sardinian recordings. Although Morf was formally the head of the Romance linguistic department, he was rarely present in the survey activities in the POW camps[6] for health reasons.[7] In a letter dated 29 December 1915, the Swiss linguist wrote to Hugo Schuchardt about the golden opportunity offered by the enormous amount of linguistic material present in the prison camps and invited him to join him in Berlin for an inspection. He did not know a better Basque, Georgian and Berber specialist than Schuchardt.[8] In his reply, Schuchardt wrote to Morf about his student Urtel, an Alsatian Romanist specializing in Franco-Swiss dialects, who, in addition to possessing specific skills in Basque language, had already served as a censor of correspondence of French, British and Belgian soldiers in a prison camp near Hamburg[9] and later in Parchim *Lager*,[10] where he also began to study the Arabic language. On 1 February 1916, Urtel announced to his master that he had been called by Morf to Berlin to join the phonographic commission,[11] and a few months later the head of the Romance linguistic department sent a letter to Schuchardt to thank him for his valuable advice, because Urtel was working excellently.[12]

Considering that, by the end of the war, 1,651 recordings in 215 languages and dialects from all over the world were produced (Doegen 1925b: 12–13), Urtel's work in the prison camps, carried out between 1916 and 1918, was impressive: his name is featured in over 430 minutes mainly related to records of prisoners from the Basque and Romance language areas.

The long work carried out in more than seventy German POW camps earned Doegen the appointment to *Studiencommissar des Reichwehrministers in Gefangenensachen* in 1920 (Evans 2006: 181). With this assignment, the new German state entrusted him with the task of managing the propaganda activity produced in response to the attacks directed by the states of the Entente towards Germany in relation to the alleged mistreatment of prisoners during the war. Therefore, the activity of the phonographic commission in the prison camps was also used to try to restore honour to the German nation in the immediate post-war period (Doegen 1921b). In the same period, Doegen set to work to complete the ambitious goal he had been set at the time the commission was founded: 'die Schöpfung lebendiger Kulturkunden, die die Jahrtausende überdauern'[13] (Doegen 1925a: 6).

Already in 1917, thanks to rather substantial funding by Ludwig Darmstaedter (Doegen 1918: 7), Doegen had helped found the *Stimmensammlung zur Autographensammlung Darmstaedter der Königlichen Bibliothek*, a small phonographic archive containing the sound portraits of some political and academic personalities of that time. In November of the following year, he addressed the memorandum *Denskschrift über die Errichtung eines 'Deutschen Lautamtes in Berlin'* to the Ministry of Culture, with the dual purpose of exposing the results of the research activities of the phonographic commission and requesting the creation of an institution that could archive and preserve the records produced up till then and the ones that would be recorded through further surveys. Doegen also asked that the twenty-eight recordings of the Darmstaedter sound collection should be merged with the recordings produced during the war (Doegen 1918: 14). The ministry consented to the demands of the *Geschäftsführer* and, in 1919, entrusted him with the management of the entire collection of gramophonic recordings.[14] The phonographic commission disbanded and the recordings were separated: the musical recordings on Edison phonograph cylinders were destined for the *Berliner Phonogramm-Archiv*, whereas the recordings on shellac discs were given to the *Lautabteilung* of the *Preußische Staatsbibliothek*, officially founded on 1 April 1920 and placed under the direction of Doegen himself (Lange 2015: 4).

Within a few years, the news of the foundation of a sound museum in Berlin had a very wide echo all over the world, thanks to actual tours in which special projections and listening sessions of the photographic and phonographic material collected in the prison camps were shown[15]: in addition to German and European newspapers, several newspapers from overseas also described it as an incredibly forward-looking event.[16] However, in Doegen's plans, the archive could not merely be a simple recording collection. According to the German scholar, who was a specialist in glottodidactics, the record contained in the archive had to be employed for linguistic, phonetic and anthropological research (Doegen 1921a: 254) and would have undoubtedly been very useful to teach foreign languages both in school and as didactic tools for diplomats, academics and businessmen who maintained relations with colonial territories (Doegen 1918: 11).

Soldiers, translators, linguists, prisoners

In the years immediately preceding the foundation of the phonographic commission, Doegen had also dealt with the creation of educational tools for soldiers who would be sent to fight at the front. In 1915, he published a small quadrilingual dictionary entitled *Kriegsdolmetscher: Deutsch – Französisch – Italienisch – Englisch* (Amersdorffer and Doegen 1915). The work, divided into ten sections ('General', 'March!', 'Exploration and research', 'In the quarters', 'Food and drink', 'Security measures/Warnings', 'Requisitions, payment', 'Capture of prisoners', 'Relations with the injured' and 'Miscellany/Numbers/ Currencies') and laid out on four columns corresponding to the four languages, collects a series of words and short sentences inserted in typical war scenarios.[17] Words and sentences are accompanied by the respective phonetic transcription. Given the special purpose of the dictionary, in this case, Doegen decided not to employ a particular method of phonetic notation, but simply the German spelling rules in *Fraktur* and, in the introduction of the work, he only provided two simple rules:

> The tonic syllables have vowels in bold.
> The vowels preceding <h>, for example 'eh', 'oh', are long and closed (as in 'Lehm', 'hohl').

Doegen was a pioneer of phonography in glottodidactics, and, in 1910, he presented the new methodologies of gramophone recordings at the Universal Exposition in Brussels, where he was awarded the silver medal (Ziegler 2000: 118). One year before, he had published the first volume of a seemingly unfinished series of notebooks entitled *Doegens Unterrichtshefte*, of which the only volume apparently available to us is about the English language. The subtitle of the work, somewhat very significant, reads 'für die selbständige Erlernung fremder Sprachen mit Hilfe der Lautschrift und die Sprechmaschine' ('for self-taught learning of foreign languages with the help of phonetic transcription and gramophonic recordings'), and, in the heading, it is followed by a further warning: 'Die Erlernung der Fremdsprache ist auch ohne Sprechmaschine möglich' ('Learning a foreign language is also possible without the gramophone').

Great attention is paid to the usefulness of phonetic notation. Doegen had been a student of Henry Sweet, after he was sent to him by Alois Brandl (in turn, a student of Sweet himself), and had evidently taken advantage of one his most famous maxims: 'Phonetic notation helps the ear in many ways. The spoken word is fleeting, the written word is permanent' (Sweet 1899: 9). And, in the introduction of his *Unterrichtsheft*, Doegen claims that he borrowed Sweet's phonetic notation,[18] although, by carefully analysing the explanatory scheme of the phonetic notation contained in the work,[19] he seems to have found a compromise between the *Romic* alphabet, created by Sweet, the transcription method of the *Association Phonétique Internationale*, in turn inspired by *Romic*,[20] and some personal additions and re-elaborations.

In the early 1900s, the importance of the alphabet of the *Association Phonétique Internationale* had grown among the linguists in the Germanic linguistic area. The impact it had on Doegen was such that the German scholar adopted the alphabet as the standard phonetic notation system for all the phonetic transcriptions of the phonographic recordings produced by the *Königlich-Preußische Phonographische Kommission*, including the ones in Romance languages and dialects. This was quite unusual, since, generally in the Romance languages field (and not only them), the most common phonetic transcription system was based on *Romanists' Alphabet* (also called *Ascoli-Böhmer* alphabet).

Adapting to Doegen's guidelines was not always easy for the scholars involved in the surveys in the POW camps. If one looks at the phonetic transcriptions of the Italian recordings written by Urtel, one cannot help but notice several errors in the

use of the notation system imposed by the *Geschäftsführer* (Bannò 2016–2017: 209–
503). His training as a Roman philologist had naturally directed him to the use of the
Ascoli-Böhmer transcription system, which in his doctoral thesis he indicates as *die
gebräuchliche* ('the most used') (Urtel 1897: 6), a common notation in the Romance
linguistic field. We must also reiterate that Urtel showed a certain sense of intolerance
and annoyance towards Doegen, who had invited him to focus exclusively on the
phonetic transcription work of the prisoners' recordings to the detriment of his strong
interest in folk studies (Baggio 2018: 291–304). We can suppose, finally, that his
training as an 'all-round' Romanist had not provided him with the necessary skills to
master all the dialectal Italian varieties classified and recorded in the prison camps.

As has been said already, a small part of the recordings of the Italian section was
produced by Schürr, who, due to typographic reasons, had decided not to employ
the phonetic alphabet of the *Association Phonétique Internationale* and had chosen
to adopt his own transcription system based on *Romanists' Alphabet*.[21] In 1919, after
the phonographic commission had asked him to hand over the transcriptions of the
recordings made during his inquiries,[22] Schürr asked Doegen if a retranscription of
the interviews by means of the alphabet of the *Association Phonétique Internationale*
was necessary, however giving the impression that he was not very inclined towards
this idea, first of all, for reasons of graphic coherence with his previous publications
and, secondly, in order to avoid errors and inaccuracies.[23] Nevertheless, only for the
transcription of some Friulian recordings (PK1319, PK1320 and PK1323) he used the
phonetic notation system of the *Association Phonétique Internationale*, whereas, for
the remaining records that he produced (two from Emilia and one from Romagna), he
used his own transcription method. However, Schürr (1930: 319–26) later resumed the
Friulian recordings and rewrote the phonetic transcription using his own transcription
method (Bannò 2018–19). Instead, as for the Sardinian recordings produced by
Wagner, we only have available the attached *Personalbogen*, but the autograph texts of
the prisoners and the phonetic transcriptions are missing.

From a linguistic point of view, probably the most interesting aspect of the written
documentation that accompanies the sixty-four shellac discs of the Italian section
is the presence of dialectal texts. At the conference 'La Grande Guerre des gens
ordinaires', held at University of Montpellier, in which I participated as a guest speaker
in June 2018, Britta Lange (Humboldt Universität), whilst describing the dialectal
texts that accompany the French section of the archive, hypothesized that such texts
had not been produced by the prisoners, but more likely by translators who helped
the linguists-collectors during their surveys. It is true that Urtel occasionally used a
translator: during his visit to Chemnitz camp, Urtel was helped by a native speaker
from Douai;[24] moreover, as has been said already, Urtel himself had been employed as
a censor and translator in Parchim camp, where Carl Stumpf, head of the musicology
department of the phonographic commission, had involved him as a translator in the
recording sessions of French dialects;[25] from a letter sent by Morf to Urtel,[26] we even
get to know about some sort of 'tests' on interdialectal skills. After Morf gave Urtel
some instructions on how to administer the Parable of the Prodigal Son, one of the
most common elicitation systems in the collection, the Alsatian scholar informed his
superior that he had found 'a good Son', meaning that he produced a good recording

of the parable with a prisoner from Milan to whom he had shown Biondelli's Turin dialectal version; the prisoner exclaimed, 'it is a person from Turin who did this' (Baggio 2018: 291–304), and for this reason Urtel had chosen him as an informant and probably as a mediator. However, with regard to the Italian section, there is no doubt that the texts were written by the prisoners themselves. First of all, several sheets are signed by the respective authors and often there is a clear correspondence between their spellings and the personal data indicated in their *Personalbogen*. A significant example is the text of the Sardinian prisoner Giuseppe Loddo (PK1286): the clear and elegant calligraphy is well suited to his job: he was a *Schreiber* (accounting secretary?) in a pasta factory. Secondly, all the texts (more than fifty) have different spellings – with the exception, of course, of those cases in which a prisoner was required to write more than one text – and it is difficult to assume the presence of such a high number of translators in the camps. Furthermore, the massive presence of regionalisms, hypercorrections and other internal clues in the texts eliminates the hypothesis that they may have been written by the linguists-collectors or by the translators who were working with them. Only one single text was clearly written by Schürr: it is the dialectal text that accompanies the recordings of the Emilian prisoner Antonio Taruffi (PK1316, PK1317 and PK1318). Several clues support this hypothesis: the clear and flowing calligraphy, which is identical to other texts written by the linguist's hand; the widespread presence of the grapheme <k>; the high frequency of geminate consonants; the correct use of punctuations, including exclamation and question marks, that are usually ignored in the dialectal texts of other prisoners; the use of grave accent with tonic function even in positions other than the final syllable.

With the exception of this single text, therefore, an element of absolute novelty in the paper documentation of *Lautarchiv* is the precious chance of reading and analysing dialectal documents written by dialect speakers who were not linguists. The analysis of graphic 'errors' (spelling, use of diacritics, accents, capital letters and punctuation) reveals that the authors of the dialectal texts are popular-Italian speakers and have a medium-low education level. In the texts of the prisoners, forced to write in their respective dialects – not in standard Italian – we find, according to each case, influences of regional *scriptae*, influences exerted by the 'pressure' of the Italian spelling rules, elements that suggest at least some passive competence of literary Italian[27] and sometimes the possible graphic interferences of foreign languages.

But what were the steps followed before, during and after the recording sessions? In the miscellany *Unter fremden Völkern*, Urtel explains the criteria for choosing the informants and the elicitation techniques he used: the prisoners were chosen because of their origins and skills; their personal data were filed in very detailed *Personalbogen*, and they were asked to write – in their mother dialect – the passages that they would later sing or recite in front of the gramophone; the linguist in charge of the recording session analysed the text together with the prisoner who had drafted it, and he translated it into standard language (in our case study, Italian), to then carry out the phonetic transcription of the recording (Urtel 1925: 339). If we quickly review the *Personalbogen* of the prisoners of the Italian linguistic area, we immediately realize how meticulously the prisoners were selected: out of forty-one Italian soldiers interviewed, only one was semi-illiterate.[28] In cases like this, the informant was asked to sing a song and perform it in spoken form by heart or to speak freely, or, from time to time, the linguist stayed near the illiterate prisoner during the recording session and prompted him by reading the text sentence by sentence.[29] In short, apart from some rare cases, we are dealing with real translation activities, sometimes carried out by the prisoners in collaboration with the linguist in charge of the recording session.

In the variety of folksongs, folktales, poems and monologues, three elicitation systems which were commonly employed by dialectologists and geo-linguists active in the construction of linguistic atlases stand out: the Novella IX of Giornata I of *Decameron*, the Parable of the Prodigal Son and the *Normalsätze* elaborated by Schürr during his inquiries in Romagna and evidently borrowed from the *Normalsätze* by Georg Wenker, creator of the German linguistic atlas.[30] Fortunately, we have the three model-texts given to the interviewees: for the Parable of the Prodigal Son, Urtel used the version contained in the 1822 edition of Diodati's Bible,[31] of which we still have the printed text that he used in the camps in a leaflet; for Boccaccio's novella, he employed the 1857 edition of *Decameron* edited by Pietro Fanfani,[32] of which we also have a printed text; whereas, for the *Normalsätze*, Schürr employed a list of sixty sentences handwritten in Italian by himself.

On the occasion of the centenary of the Great War, the enhancement of the Berlin and Viennese recordings of Italian prisoners has required the collaboration of experts from different fields with the phonographic archives, with the primary objective of bringing these unique materials to light, after they were forgotten and ignored for too long.

A study of the Italian section of the Berlin archives, especially on a historical-archival and musicological level, has been carried out by Ignazio Macchiarella (University of Cagliari) and Emilio Tamburini (Humboldt Universität) and has been recently published together with a digital edition of all the Italian sound and written material (Macchiarella and Tamburini 2018).

I also actively participated in the work for the digital publication of the Italian dialectal recordings kept at the *Phonogrammarchiv* in Vienna, coordinated for the linguistic part by Serenella Baggio and for the technical and editorial part by Gerda Lechleitner and Christian Liebl (Lechleitner and Liebl 2019). A team of dialectologists from different regional areas has worked on twelve recordings (A. Arrigoni and M. Savini on Cozzo Lomellina; L. Coveri on Genoa; S. Calamai on Torri di Chiusdino and San Rocco on Turrite di Pescaglia; G. Manzari on Spinazzola; M. Maddalon and J. Trumper on San Marco Argentano; V. Matranga on Alcamo; R. Sottile on Sciacca and Pietraperzia; A. Dettori on Villaputzu; D. Mereu on Cagliari and N. Puddu on Arbus).

Some European countries at the forefront in the field of digital humanities, including Ireland and the United Kingdom, have taken steps to obtain and digitize the sound and written documentation of their interest some time ago.

An appeal I had the chance to make at the first conference on the project 'Voci della Grande Guerra' held at Accademia della Crusca in February 2017 consists of the proposal to acquire the materials of the Italian sections of *Lautarchiv* and the Italian recordings kept in other phonographic archives in Berlin, Vienna and Zurich (Bannò 2017: 275–8).

The rediscovery, now, of the dialectal voices of Italians, by far the first ones made available and replayable by the sound technology, is one of the most important effects of the centenary of the Great War.

Notes

1 The commission received the Kaiser's contributions in two parts: the first of 20,000 marks, the second of 30,000 marks (Doegen 1918: 1).
2 'the voices, languages and music of all peoples of the world'.
3 Cf. Hermann Urtel to Hugo Schuchardt, 31.10.1921, Hugo Schuchardt Archiv – Brief 47-12298: 'unser Rayonchef und phonographischer Weichensteller Doegen verspricht immer Berge von Gold oder Peseten – ich glaube ihm stets nur 1/3, aber auch das ist noch zu viel' ('our supervisor and phonographic pointsman Doegen always promises mountains of gold or pesetas – I always believe one-third of what he says, but that is still too much').
4 'My plates are based on photographs that I organized personally and independently of the sound recordings in the POW camps without state funds.'
5 Cf. Hermann Urtel to Friedrich Carl Andreas, 12.12.1916, Cod. Ms. F.C. Andreas 1:442.
6 His presence in the camps is attested only in fourteen minutes related to as many French dialectal recordings produced in Dyrotz POW camp between 4 and 16 February 1916.
7 In June 1916, he suffered from gallbladder (cf. Hermann Urtel to Hugo Schuchardt, 29.06.1916, Hugo Schuchardt Archiv – Brief 24-122275), and in the first months of 1917 he suffered from disorders related to diabetes (cf. Heinrich Morf to Hugo Schuchardt, 07.02.1917, Hugo Schuchardt Archiv – Brief 28-07519) and fractured a foot (cf. Heinrich Morf to Hugo Schuchardt, 18.03.1917, Hugo Schuchardt Archiv – Brief 30-07521). Furthermore, Morf had fallen into depression after the criticism he had received for signing – despite his Swiss nationality – the Manifesto of the Ninety-Three (*Aufruf an die Kulturwelt*, 1914), in support of the German military actions after the infringement of the neutrality of Belgium (Baggio 2018: 291–304).
8 Cf. Heinrich Morf to Hugo Schuchardt, 29.12.1915, Hugo Schuchardt Archiv – Brief 24-07515.
9 Cf. Hermann Urtel to Hugo Schuchardt, 03.03.1915, Hugo Schuchardt Archiv – Postkarte 16-12267 and Hermann Urtel to Hugo Schuchardt, 31.05.1915, Hugo Schuchardt Archiv – Brief 17-12268.
10 Cf. Hermann Urtel to Hugo Schuchardt, 21.11.1915, Hugo Schuchardt Archiv – Ansichtkarte 19-12270 and Hermann Urtel to Friedrich Carl Andreas, 12.12.1916, Cod. Ms. F.C. Andreas 1:442.
11 Cf. Hermann Urtel to Hugo Schuchardt, 01.02.1916, Hugo Schuchardt Archiv – Brief 20-12271.
12 Cf. Heinrich Morf to Hugo Schuchardt, 15.07.1916, Hugo Schuchardt Archiv – Postkarte 25-07516.
13 'The creation of living cultural studies that last for millennia'.
14 Cf. Doegen (1925b: 12): 'Zu Beginn der Revolution wurde mir durch das Vertrauen des damaligen Kultusministers Exzellenz Schmidt-Ott die fachmännische Leitung und Verwaltung des gesamten Lautmaterials übertragen, um es vor Schädigungen jeglicher

Art zu bewahren' ('At the beginning of the revolution, the Minister of Culture, Excellence Schmidt-Ott, entrusted me with the professional management and administration of the entire sound material in order to protect it from damage of any kind').

15 For example, the linguist Max Förster invited his Indianist colleague Johannes Hertel to an exhibition of the sound and photographic material collected in the prison camps that would be held by Doegen on 25 May 1921 in Leipzig. (cf. Max Förster to Johannes Hertel, 24.05.1921, Nachlass Johannes Hertel). These exhibitions took place not only in Germany, but also abroad: in the summer of 1925, Doegen was invited by the universities of London and Birmingham (cf. 'Library of Sounds' (1925), *World's News*, 18 June: 2).

16 The enthusiasm with which an American newspaper communicated the news can make us smile today: 'Every language and dialect spoken in the world is being recorded on copper phonograph discs in Berlin by Prof. Wilhelm Doegen. He says the records will last 10,000 years. If they do, and are played in the year 11922, will anyone except scholars be able to understand them? Ten thousand years from now speech may be a lost art, with people conversing by mental telepathy' ('Voices' (1922), *The Rock Island Argus and Daily Union*, 2 September: 1).

17 A text published in the same year offers and interesting overview of the war literature published between June and September 1915. A short section is dedicated to dictionaries for the troops (VV.AA. 1915: 76–7).

18 Cf. Doegen (1909: 1): 'Die englische Sprache wird gelehrt mit hilfe einer Lautschrift, deren Lautschriftzeichen nicht deutschen Buchstaben (weil kein englischer Sprachlaut in Wirklichkeit denjenigen der deutschen Sprache entspricht), sondern der Lautsprache des berühmten englischen Phonetikers Prof. Sweet enlehnt find' ('The English language is taught with the help of a phonetic notation, whose phonetic symbols are not derived from German letters (because no English sound actually corresponds to the sounds of the German language), but from the phonetic notation of the famous English phonetician Prof. Sweet').

19 Cf. Doegen (1909: 15–6).

20 Note that the phonetic transcription system of the *Association Phonétique Internationale* was published for the first time in 1888, when the association was still called *Phonetic Teachers' Association* (cf. Passy 1888: 58–9). Also Sweet, as a member of the association, had participated in the creation of the transcription method.

21 Cf. Schürr (1917: 16): 'Ursprünglich hatte ich die Absicht, mich einem der großen, gebräuchlichsten phonetischen Systeme anzuschließen, und zwar dem des "Maître phonétique". Typographische Gründe zwangen mich aber, davon abzugehen und mich soeit als möglich vorhandener Zeichen zu bedienen. So möge man entschuldigen, daß ich, obwohl schon etliche mehr oder minder gut ausgebaute bestehen, wieder mit einem eigenen Transkriptionssystem hervortrete. Es ist ja kein völlig eigenes, denn so wie ich die vorhandenen Zeichen verwendete, schließt sich meine Transkription doch in den Hauptsachen den unter Romanisten gebräuchlichsten Systemen an. Nur in einigen Punkten mußte ich zu Abweichungen greifen' ('I originally intended to employ one of the greatest, most common phonetic notation systems, the "Maître phonétique". Typographical reasons, however, forced me to avoid it and to use available symbols as far as possible. So I apologize for the fact that, although there are already a number of more or less well-developed ones, I am again using my own transcription system. It is not a completely original one: since I used the available characters, my transcription essentially follows the most common systems among Romanists. I only had to make some detours in some points').

22 Cf. Friedrich Schürr to Ernst Kuhn, 03.03.1919, Nachl. Kuhn 2.
23 Cf. Friedrich Schürr to Ernst Kuhn, 25.03.1919, Nachl. Kuhn 2.
24 Cf. Hermann Urtel to Heinrich Morf, 13.06.1916, Morf Archive.
25 Cf. Hermann Urtel to Heinrich Morf, 19.02.1915, Morf Archive.
26 Cf. Hermann Urtel to Heinrich Morf, 15.03.1918, Morf Archive.
27 Among all the texts of the Italian section, one precious dialectal version of Novella IX of Giornata I of *Decameron* stands out.
28 The prisoner Paolo Maretti (PK1315, PK1321 and PK1322) from Romagna.
29 It is the method employed by Max Leopold Wagner in two recordings of the Sardinian prisoner Enrico Spiga (PK1639 and PK1640), although he was able to read and write.
30 I analysed the elicitation systems used during the Italian recording sessions in Bannò (2018: 171–96).
31 Cf. Diodati (1822: 96–7).
32 Cf. Boccaccio (1857: 70–1).

References

Amersdorffer, A. and W. Doegen (1915), *Kriegsdolmetscher. Deutsch – Französisch – Italienisch – Englisch*, Berlin and Schöneberg: Saatz.

Baggio, S. (2018), 'Alternative al questionario. Inchieste nei campi di prigionia della prima guerra mondiale', in G. Ligi, G. Pedrini and F. Tamisari (eds), *L'accademico impaziente. Miscellanea di studi in onore di Glauco Sanga per il suo settantesimo compleanno*, 291–304, Alessandria: Edizioni dell'Orso.

Bannò, S. (2016–2017), 'Un corpus inedito: le registrazioni fonografiche di parlati dialettali italiani nei campi di prigionia tedeschi della Grande Guerra. Scritture di prigionieri e trascrizioni di linguisti al Lautarchiv di Berlino', MA diss., Facoltà di Lettere e Filosofia, Università degli Studi di Trento, Trento.

Bannò, S. (2017), 'Voci vive. Riaffiorano dagli archivi le prime registrazioni di voci dialettali italiane', *Studi Trentini. Storia*, 1: 275–8.

Bannò, S. (2018), 'Voci e scritture di prigionieri italiani della Prima guerra mondiale', *RID – Rivista Italiana di Dialettologia*, 41: 171–96.

Bannò, S. (2018–2019), 'Si sonus cadit, tota scientia vadit: Friedrich Schürr alle prese con il vocalismo nel dialetto di Nimis', *Quaderni di Filologia Romanza*, 26–7: 177–205.

Boccaccio, G. (1857), *Il Decameron*, edited by P. Fanfani, Firenze: Le Monnier.

Diodati, G., ed. (1822), *La Sacra Bibbia: contenente l'Antico ed il Nuovo Testamento*, Basel: Thurneysen.

Doegen, W. (1909), *Doegens Unterrichtshefte für die selbständige Erlernung fremder Sprachen mit Hilfe der Lautschrift und der Sprechmaschine. Englisch*. Band I, Berlin: Schwartz.

Doegen, W. (1918), *Denkschrift über die Errichtung eines "Deutschen Lautamtes" in Berlin*, Berlin: n.p.

Doegen, W. (1921a), 'Die Lautabteilung', in *Fünfzehn Jahre Königliche und Staatsbibliothek*, Berlin: Preußische Staatsbibliothek.

Doegen, W. (1921b), *Kriegsgefangene Völker, vol. 1: Der Kriegsgefangenen Haltung und Schicksal in Deutschland*, Berlin: Verlag für Politik und Wirtschaft.

Doegen, W. (1925a), 'Einleitung', in W. Doegen (ed.), *Unter fremden Völkern: eine neue Völkerkunde*, 5–6, Berlin: Stollberg.

Doegen, W. (1925b), 'Einleitung', in W. Doegen (ed.), *Unter fremden Völkern: eine neue Völkerkunde*, 9–17, Berlin: Stollberg.

Evans, A. D. (2006), *Anthropology at War: World War I and the Science of Race in Germany*, Chicago and London: University of Chicago Press.

Lange, B. (2015), 'Poste Restante and Messages in Bottles; Sound Recordings of Indian Prisoners in the First World War', *Social Dynamics: A Journal of African Studies*, 41: 1–17.

Lechleitner, G. and C. Liebl, eds (2019), *Sound Documents from the Phonogrammarchiv of the Austrian Academy of Sciences. The Complete Historical Collections 1899–1950. Series 17/6: Recordings from Prisoner-of-War Camps, World War I – Italian Recordings*, Vienna: Austrian Academy of Sciences Press.

Macchiarella, I. and E. Tamburini (2018), *Le voci ritrovate: canti e narrazioni di prigionieri italiani della Grande Guerra negli archivi sonori di Berlino*, Udine: Nota.

Passy, P. (1888), 'Our Revised Alphabet', *The Phonetic Teacher*, 7–8: 57–60.

Scheer, M. (2010), 'Captive Voices: Phonographic Recordings in the German and Austrian Prisoner-of-War Camps of World War I', in R. Johler, C. Marchetti and M. Scheer (eds), *Doing Anthropology in Wartime and War Zones*, 279–309, Bielefeld: Transcript.

Schürr, F. (1917), *Romagnolische Mundarten: Sprachproben in phonetischer Transkription auf Grund phonographischer Aufnahmen*, Wien: Hölder.

Schürr, F. (1930), 'Phonetische Proben der friaulischen Mundart von Nimis', *Zeitschrift für romanische Philologie*, 50: 319–26.

Sweet, H. (1899), *The Practical Study of Languages: A Guide for Teachers and Learners: A Guide for Teachers and Learners*, London: Dent & Co.

Urtel, H. (1897), *Beiträge zur Kenntis des neuchateller Patois*, Darmstadt: Otto's Hof-Buchdruckerei.

Urtel, H. (1925), 'Romanische Völker', in W. Doegen (ed.), *Unter fremden Völkern: eine neue Völkerkunde*, 338–50, Berlin: Stollberg.

VV.AA. (1915), *Deutsche Kriegsliteratur*, Leipzig: Hinrichs'schen Buchhandlung.

Ziegler, S. (2000), '«Stimmen der Völker»: Das Berlin Lautarchiv', in H. Bredekamp, J. Brüning and C. Weber (eds), *Theater der Natur und Kunst. Katalog. Eine Ausstellung der Humboldt-Universität zu Berlin 10. Dezember 2000 bis 4. März 2001*, 117–28, Berlin: Humboldt University and Henschel Verlag.

2

The French army and Russian interpreting and translating in France and Macedonia during the First World War

Gwendal Piégais

Languages were a daily issue for the Entente Cordiale. It was more than a problem of translating reports from one general headquarters to another. Languages were the bridge through which the allies could implement cooperation in the field, or even in unexpected theatres. Some recent studies developed the interest in the study of the coalition through this linguistic angle. Franziska Heimburger, for instance, demonstrated that the invention of collaboration mechanisms by interpreters in the field were a determining aspect of the coalition-building between French and British armies on the Western Front (Heimburger 2014a). The study of the interpreters' role in the coalition might also bring some insights if we have a look at the role of French interpreters working with Russian troops. Contrary to the French-British relationship, the French-Russian ties went through a particular deterioration: from the side of the allies' distrust developed between France and Russia, until the October revolution and the separate peace of Brest Litovsk, and then the French intervention in Ukraine and the Polish-Soviet War. The efforts of the French army to find men with linguistic skills in the Russian language and how their assignments developed over time give us an interesting observation point of the evolution of the French strategy in Eastern Europe.

Also, the task of the French army to constitute a substantial group of French-Russian interpreters or translators tells a lot about the relationship between the two countries, and more broadly about the relationship between France and Central and Eastern Europe at the end of the war. This chapter will try to describe how the French army managed to work with, at least linguistically, the Russian army during the operations, and in doing so, elements of the functions these men had in the French-Russian military cooperation will be examined.

The Eastern front comes to the West

Going back to the years before the Great War, military cooperation between France and Russia was not new. All throughout the nineteenth century, there were exchanges between French and Russian officers, even if these encounters varied greatly according to the context: there are records of the brief occupation of France by the Sixth Coalition in 1814, or of the contacts established at the end of the Crimean War (1853–6) or during the Boxer rebellion (1899–1901). Institutionalized cooperation only started in 1894, after the signing and ratification of a convention of cooperation which would be the start of the *Alliance Franco-Russe*. In the context of this French-Russian treaty, military cooperation was launched, which led to many encounters between officers and soldiers on a regular basis, such as the naval *revues* in *Toulon* or in *Brest*, and in Russia the *revue* of Cronstadt (Rey 2017: 25–32). But these remained officers' business. Cooperation and information exchange were conducted mainly in French, a language spoken or at least understood by the majority of Russian elites (Baker and Saldanha 2019: 364; Offord, Rjéoutski and Argent 2018: 242).

French-Russian cooperation was pursued at the level of inter-allied conferences, as seen in Chantilly in December of 1915. During events like this, Russian representatives conveyed quite a good knowledge of French, that is, good enough to work and exchange in this language without any need for interpreters. And on each side of Europe – in Paris as in Petrograd, French and Russian military attachés were working mainly in French or were helped, in the case of the French, by officers who were either able to converse in Russian or provide expertise about the Russian Empire and culture (Guelton and Pavlov 2019: 7–53).

But during the summer of 1915, Russia went through one of the most devastating setbacks of the war for the Empire; after the successful German-Austrian offensive of Gorlice-Tarnow, the Russian army retreated from Warsaw to the Riga-Jakobstadt-Bara novichi-Pinsk-Ternopil line (July–September 1915). The first consequence of what is known as the Great Retreat was the loss of a third of the Russian industrial capacity, notably the Warsaw Salient. This setback accentuated the dependence of the Empire on Allied aid and supply (Sanborn 2014: 73–87; Kappeler 1994: 261). In exchange for an intensification of delivery of French ammunition and weapons, France asked for the direct help of the Russian army on the Western Front, literally requesting Russian troops to support the French army.

After negotiations in Petrograd from December 1915 to May 1916, Russia and France agreed to the loan of 40,000 Russian soldiers who were to come to France to fight under the orders of the French command. This operation is also known as *Corps Expéditionnaire Russe en France,* the Russian Expeditionary force in France and Macedonia. Four Brigades of 10,000 men commanded by Russian officers came to fight in two theatres: in France, they operated around Rheims and Craonne, and in Macedonia they took part in the battles of Monastir (Bitola today) and stationed themselves along the Tcherna River or around the Prespa Lakes, in a region which is now Northern Greece and the south of Northern Macedonia (Former Republic of Skopje). These two different fronts generated two distinct kinds of cooperation, because in France it was mainly a French-Russian cooperation, whereas in Macedonia it was a French-Russian-Serbian cooperation in a post-Ottoman region with inhabitants speaking different Balkan languages (Cockfield 1998; Piégais 2018).

How were these Russian soldiers integrated into the war effort of the French? The French army created bases on the French and the Greek grounds in Macedonia. These bases and camps were of various sizes: from large-scale military camps in cities like Laval, Mailly or Le Courneau, to small leave centres in little French parishes, like Lesneven in Brittany (SHD: 17N663, 23 October 1918). In Macedonia, the soldiers shared their space with other troops in allied camps, like Zeitenlik, or in cities closer to the front, like Florina.

In France, these Russian Brigades fought until the summer of 1917, in Macedonia until the early winter of 1917. In France, the troubles started just after the disastrous offensive of the Chemin des Dames, where the 1st and 3rd Brigades fought, and when strikes and mutinies occurred in the Russian camp of La Courtine. A few weeks later, in Macedonia, Russian soldiers refused to fight when they heard the news about the Brest-Litovsk armistice (15 December 1917). The Russian soldiers had to be removed from the frontline, as fraternization with the Bulgarian soldiers became dangerous for the French positions. In France and in Macedonia, after these events, the French army proposed that these soldiers resume the fighting or join working battalions. Some accepted the order to keep on fighting for France in a newly created Russian section of the French Legion (the *Légion Russe*), some preferred to become workers paid by the French army in these labour battalions. They were sent in factories, in the fields or the woods in the military regions which needed manpower. But some others wanted nothing else than go back to Russia. These unwilling men were sent to labour

Figure 2.1 Russian soldiers in France in 1917. Source: Collection Marie Bellegou-Mamontov.

camps in Northern Africa or on the Greek islands. Whatever the choices made by the soldiers, or the destination where the French army sent them – every working place, every camp where these soldiers stayed – was regularly inspected by French officers. These were assisted by interpreters, to ensure that the Russians behaved well and duly accomplished their tasks (Piégais 2018: 23–9).

This situation meant that Russian detention centres were maintained on French and Greek soil until 1920. Moreover, these camps also accommodated Russian prisoners of war (POWs) freed from Germany in the winter of 1918. At this point, France had to deal with 65,000 Russian POWs. The role of the Russian bases increasingly grew from military camps to welcoming bases for workers and, later, gathering points for POWs waiting for their repatriation to Russia or to other states that had emerged from the fall of the Russian Empire (Poland, Baltic States, Georgia or Armenia, etc.). The presence and role of Russian soldiers in French military camps and bases evolved substantially between 1916 and 1920, but the need to create structures to welcome these men and the necessity to gather competent men – including linguistically skilled ones – to handle these soldiers was an ongoing task for the French army until the last Russian soldier left French soil (Konyaeva 2017: 145–51)

How to linguistically manage the Russian troops?

All throughout the 1916–20 period, the main problem for the French Army on the Western Front as on the Eastern front was as much linguistic as it was material: how to communicate with these men, especially when the soldiers who don't speak a word of French composed the vast majority of the troops, as French was spoken mainly by officers or aristocrats? How do you manage soldiers who come to a country where not a great number of people speak Russian? Because Russian troops were not numerous enough and did not have enough staff or even administration at the rear, so that they would be able to operate more autonomously, the Russian soldiers had been integrated into the French Divisions and had to rely on the French administration for every material aspect of their daily life.

To find competent men able to play a role in these inter-allied interactions between Russian soldiers and officers and the French army, the first option would have been to ask for French-speaking officers from the Russian army, but all of these officers were already engaged in the Brigades *états-majors* or commanding different units of this Russian expeditionary force and could not be appointed to administrative duties for the French army. The other option would have been to appoint the French officers of the *Ministère de la Guerre* or the *Mission Militaire Française en Russie*, who were already familiar with French-Russian cooperation. For example, in Petrograd as in Paris, the French army had quite a substantial number of qualified personnel dealing with Russian matters before and during the war. For example, among them we could find Jules Legras and Jacques Sadoul. Commandant Jules Legras, who had graduated from the École Normale Supérieure in Paris and had been dean of the Faculté des Lettres in Dijon, was one of the best specialists of the Slavic world and languages in France. He had spent part of the war with the Siberian army corps, then later served in the French 2ᵉᵐᵉ Bureau, the intelligence section of the French État-Major. This section oversaw all the French military missions abroad besides collecting intelligence for the Ministère de la Guerre and the Grand Quartier Général. We can also mention Captain Jacques Sadoul, lawyer and close adviser to Albert Thomas, the French minister of the Armament, and also a member of the French mission militaire in Russia (Laurent 2019: IV–3; Bourlet 2006: 33). Captain Jacques Sadoul was a lawyer and close adviser to Albert Thomas, the French minister of the Armament. Sadoul was also a member of the French mission militaire in Russia. Qualified and competent officers such as Legras and Sadoul could not leave their duties because their service in Russia was much appreciated and valued (Chabot 1940: 65; Delauney ed. 2008: 209–27).

So, if all the French experts of Russian language and culture were abroad and all qualified Russian-speaking French personnel were already mobilized in headquarters and ministry cabinets, what could the French army do in relation to the Russian soldiers and officers? From 1916 until the end of the war, the French army sent dispatches to every division of its army to make soldiers and officers aware that the headquarters were looking for men who could understand and speak Russian fluently. These calls were renewed regularly to the men among the ranks who might have a good knowledge of the Russian language, but with mitigated success (SHD: 7N144, 2 September 1916). Despite the difficulties of finding such profiles, the French army managed to maintain high standards. Even in 1919, requirements remained clear: only 'interpreters who speak perfectly the Russian language can really offer their services' (SHD: 7N634, 'Personnel français'). As demonstrated by Franziska Heimburger, these calls were not as efficient as they could have been (Heimburger 2014b: 166–8). So, to complete this strategy, the French army made several calls to other ministries or institutions such as the Ministry of Foreign Affairs. They also contacted the Jesuit Company, who gave the names of members who were former missionaries fluent in rare languages and who were serving in the French army or went to look for French merchants or bankers who had been active abroad (Heimburger 2014b: 167).

This strategy was not new. During the oriental and colonial expeditions organized by France in the nineteenth century (from the Campaign of Egypt to the Tonkin expedition, as well as the Crimean war), this strategy brought forth first professionals from the academic world or teachers who were mobilized or judged able for a service in headquarters. Joseph Duchêne, an officers' liaison interpreter with the Russian Brigades in France, is an example of this. Before the war, he had been a teacher in Eastern Europe and lived in the Russian Empire. After he graduated in 1898 (*licence de lettres*) from Grenoble University, he became a teacher in 1902 in the *Lycée français de Kielce* (in Russian Poland). There, in 1905, he married a Polish woman and stayed in Poland until the First World War. In August 1914, he was mobilized by France and fought in Northeast France (on the *Front de Meurthe et Moselle*). He was subsequently assigned tasks related to his Eastern European background in April 1916 when he became *officier-interprète auprès de la 1ᵉʳᵉ Brigade Russe* in France. During his service, he followed the Russian troops all throughout the battles on the Western Front and in their daily life in the camp of Mailly, in the Aube, also in the northeast of France. His notebook gives many examples of the role and the status of a French interpreter on the Western Front: '*April 5, 1916. Am designated to copy the documents concerning us, in the Office of Colonel Army Commander. Evening; visit of colonel Ignatieff and other Russian mission officers, as well as Commander Marchal from the GHQ's 2nd Bureau.'* When serving with high-ranking officers, the interpreters' duty is almost a diplomatic one. But on the field as in the ministries, intelligence tasks are a daily practice: '*23 March, 1917: At the General Staff, while preparing the offensive manoeuvre of the BRS on Courcy – le canal – Brimont – we follow the withdrawal of Germans on the Hindenburg line. Evacuees and plane photos [makes us believe they] pass through the S.. d'Arras – Cambrai –Saint Quentin – La Fère – Laon*' (Duchêne 2016: 8–22).

After his service at the French front, Joseph Duchêne was assigned to different *Missions militaires françaises* in Poland and Southern Russia and was sent to the Paris Peace Conference as an interpreter, all of which took place between 1918 and 1920. After the long end of the First World War, when France maintained an intense military activity to support their new allies in the East, Joseph Duchêne went to occupy a function that encapsulates his Eastern European background, the several connections he created with the *Missions militaires* and the influence that France tried to implement in Eastern Europe in the interwar period: in 1922, he became director of the *Office du Commerce Extérieur pour la Russie et les Pays Limitrophes* and then, in 1927, delegate for the *Groupement des Industriels Français en Pologne*. He remained in Poland until his death in 1932 (Duchêne 2016: 8–22).

But was it possible to find enough men of this kind to solve the issue of a shortage of interpreters? At some point, during the war, there were about twenty camps with Russian troops in France. Moreover, Algeria (where many Russian workers were sent) can be added to the list of 'host' nations, as well as Macedonia, where translators or interpreters with proficient skills in Russian were much also in demand.

The camps of Mailly, Laval, La Courtine and Le Courneau were the biggest ones to accommodate Russian troops in France. In these camps, interpreters were requested to help the camp police, the phone services, the treasury, supply and the medical services. Ideally at least twenty-five people with good skills in Russian were needed, but that figure never materialized (SHD: 7N634, 'Personnel français de la Base russe à la date du 1ᵉʳ avril 1919'). But it remained very difficult to find people with interpreting skills like Joseph Duchene during the 1916–18 period. The situation worsened when the French army started to demobilize men, including interpreters, whilst thousands of Russian POWs were sent to the Russian bases.

In order to find additional interpreters, the French army looked for more people with an Eastern European or Russian background. For example, in December 1918, the French *Ministère de la Guerre* received a letter from a soldier called Lemarchand, who had responded to one of these calls: 'I have the honor to let you know the name of Léon Lemarchand, born in Petrograd, from French parents who, after having served in the Russian army as a sous-lieutenant, then lieutenant, since August 1914 until January 1918, has left Russia to come to France . . . Léon LEMARCHAND [*sic*] speaks the Russian language very well and could advantageously be employed as an interpreter assigned to General Brulard' (SHD: 7N634, 'Personnel français', 20 December 1918). Over the few next months, the Russian base in Laval also received letters from more officers or soldiers who were looking forward to demobilization and were trying, at the very least, to find a service post at the rear, as in the case of the soldier Leloup, who was recommended for translation service in March 1919. Such a post permitted him to avoid service in the occupying divisions in Germany or Central Europe. In a recommendation letter, this soldier is presented as 'Soldier Leloup Marius, 2° class, born in Moscow the 12 of August 1895, presently assigned to the 26ᵉ bataillon de Chasseurs à Pied.' He 'knows the Russian languages very well and is willing to serve at the Russian Base' in Laval (SHD: 7N634, 'Personnel français', 20 December 1918).

The phrase 'Russian Background' also implied those Eastern Europeans who were living in France or serving in the French army. For instance, soldiers from the Czechoslovak Division who volunteered in the French army to fight against the Central Powers were keen to apply. In June 1919, the soldier Alexandre Eck who 'speaks perfectly Polish, Czech, Slovak, Russian, Bulgarian and other languages with a decent level' was recommended by the *Bureau Slave* to serve as an *Officier interprète* in the *État-Major* of the Czechoslovak Division or to be an interpreter in the Russian base at Laval (SHD: 7N634, 'Personnel français', 20 December 1918). The *Bureau Slave* had been established early 1918, at the 1ᵉʳᵉ section of the État-Major, in order to deal with all matters relating to Russian soldiers quartered in France, Northern Africa and Macedonia, but also to Polish, Czech, Slovak and Serbian soldiers (Nicot 1968: 535–42).

According to the archives of the Bureau Slave or the Russian Base (SHD: 7N634, 'Personnel français', Note pour la section du Personnel, 14 June 1919), it is not always easy to assess precisely the level of proficiency of the men trying to join the services of the Russian bases, especially when this level was not attested by a diploma but just by the mention of a professional stay or experience in Russia. Nevertheless, more cases provide further insights into the diversity of non-academic profiles and the French soldiers who became interpreters.

For instance, in 1916 a soldier named Paul Le Flem, who had served in the French army as a simple stretcher bearer, was appointed as a translator to the Russian Brigades in France. Before the war, Paul Le Flem had successfully concluded his philosophy studies at the Sorbonne in 1902. Although his studies were far from any discipline related to the Slavic languages and culture, upon completion he decided to go to Moscow to join a French family living in Russia, the Brocards. They had been looking for a tutor for their twelve-year-old son Sacha. During his studies, Le Flem had spent some time in the Conservatoire and he had become intrigued by the Russian music he encountered there. As soon as he arrived in Moscow in 1902, he had the occasion to learn the Russian language of his pupils whilst teaching them French in exchange (Mussat 1997: 45–57).

When the First World War started in 1914, Paul Le Flem served first as a simple stretcher bearer. Then, in May 1916, he was directed to the Mailly camp. The military hierarchy, which was looking for interpreters, had been informed that he spoke Russian and made great use of his skills. Le Flem was assigned to the first special Russian regiment commanded by Colonel Nietchvolodof. Moreover, having learned that Le Flem was a composer, Nietchvolodof asked him to form an orchestra for the Brigade (Le Flem 1960: 45–6).

In 1918, the Russian officers and soldiers serving in the French army perceived that there would be no return to Russia in the months or maybe even years after the

October revolution (7–8 November, according to the Western calendar). They also identified the fact that language skills could be a key to be more institutionalized in entities like the French army. After November 1917, several Russians applied to join the French army and emphasized their language skills as much as their ability as horsemen or officers (SHD: 7N616, 'Officiers russes pour armée française', October 1917–May 1919). Here the multiple languages some Russian officers spoke – English or German as much as French – became a way to find a new position. In earlier times of the Russian Empire, language skills were seen as belonging to a sphere to which also belonged music for instance. Language skills – be it translation, interpreting or both – had been considered solely as signs of distinction among a highly stratified society, but towards the end of the war and during its immediate aftermath, language skills became a vehicle of social advancement in foreign spheres.

More than interpreters: Mediating roles in Russian camps daily life

Most functions Russian interpreters carried out in the French army related to daily life in the bases, but also to postal control. Daily life activities included administrative work like translating military documentation, composing of orders given by the French army, but also the daily orders (*prikaz*) published regularly and addressed by the Russian generals to their soldiers. Although any exchange of information was carefully watched over by their French allies on site, interpreters remained the ultimate transmission belt between one military administration and another.

The other time-consuming activity was postal control. In France, there were two main postal centres controlling letters going from France to Russia. In every postal control centre, there were about a dozen Russian interpreters or translators, who among them rendered in total between 7,000 and 10,000 letters every month. This work was seen as very important because the French army became increasingly worried about the views and the morale of the Russian troops, particularly after the February Revolution (8–16 March 1917). Officers and interpreters wrote extensive reports about the content of the letters exchanged between the Russian soldiers and their relatives in the Russian Empire (SHD: Vincennes, 7N633, Contrôle postal de Dieppe).

In the case of the POWs, the Russian interpreters were even more necessary once the French army tried putting these former soldiers to work in different regions of France. So, interpreters were sent to inspect the state of affairs in camps and in companies, in farms, in factories where Russian soldiers were sent to work. Conditions for Russian soldiers in French camps were not always the same as for the French soldiers. Abuse by employers (typically munition-related) and camp personnel was reported and had to be dealt with (Mussat 1997).

Due to this evolution, interpreters, who had been translating orders or instructions in the camps and who took part in the daily life of these soldiers, found themselves in a new kind of role. Once these soldiers had decided to become workers in France because of the insurrections of 1917, an interpreter like Paul Le Flem was to re-encounter soldiers he had known in Mailly. Through Paul Le Flem's inspections notebook, a clear image transpires of how the interpreters had a real role as mediators between the Russian workers, the employers and the French army. In the 4th Military Region, he was, in fact, responsible for inspecting the Russians sent to work in Mayenne, Sarthe, Orne and Eure-et-Loir, and assigned to companies or agricultural work there. More rarely, Russians worked in craftsmanship (as shoemakers and seed producers), and more often in small businesses (wood operations, sawmills and glassware), or even in public utility work (track maintenance goods-handling at Laval station where the Russian base was located). Because these Russians were employed outside the confines of the military but were still soldiers, Le Flem also helped endorse military decisions and even enforce discipline. During this period, Paul Le Flem inspected and visited around 350 individual Russians or groups of Russians. He was responsible for settling or resolving conflicts either between the Russians and their employers or between the Russians themselves (Mussat 1997).

Le Flem's interpreted negotiations helped influence many aspects of the Russian workers' daily life, and he also actively contributed by asking authorities for improvements to their living conditions. Le Flem listened, discussed and negotiated for the improvement of their diet (such as the inclusion of fresh vegetables, especially cabbage) and the application of quantitative standards due to the shortage of stocks from early May 1918. When he found out how low pay for Russian workers was, he even protested on the issue of wages. Le Flem, even as a mere interpreter, threatened to have workers withdrawn from the employment scheme, and where pay rise demands were not met, he gave orders to do so several times (Mussat 1997).

Le Flem's whereabouts and actions were not needless: in some camps with Russian workers, tensions built up so much that riots occurred. In the village of Bruyères, in the Vosges, a grave inscription still bears the memory of this troubled situation: 'To the under-lieutenant Vassilitchenko, 2nd Russian Special Battalion, cowardly assassinated by a soldier of his section on the 10th of December 1918'. The officer Karp Vassilitchenko, to whom the plaque is dedicated, was at the head of a group of Russian workers of the same kind that were inspected by Paul Le Flem. These few examples give us to see many functions going beyond the simple tasks of translating: interpreters were both mediators in daily life issues and watchful controllers of the soldier's mood.

During the winter of 1918–19, when the number of former Russian soldiers coming to France and its military bases increased, the task of interpreters and translators became even more difficult. They acted as the main interlocutors of these former Russian soldiers arriving in the camps. And as such these interpreters faced the multi-ethnic aspect of the former Russian Empire when these prisoners addressed their requests for repatriation to the French authorities not only in the Russian language, but in Georgian, Armenian, Latvian, and so on (SHD: Vincennes, 7N652, Base russe – Lettons et lituaniens). Interpreters helped maintain order in the camps, in the context of the increase of numbers of prisoners in the middle of food shortages. Fighting between soldiers were daily issues and the Russians had to work hard to make a better living in these overcrowded camps. A Russian soldier recalls: 'There are not enough beds. We sleep on straw. We are only given water and horse meat, no potatoes, nothing. We are fed like German prisoners of war. We are not given tobacco or sugar. We are forbidden to go out and read' (GARF: Moscow, fond. 6117, op. 1, del. 5, Nikifor Kozachuk to his family, January 1919). This precarious situation was maintained until an agreement was signed concerning the POWs. The Russian language remained the key tool to deal with these issues for Russian prisoners, but life in camps was tense, and more and more translators had to maintain order, prevent mobs and help the military police in their duties. In big bases like Laval as in little ones in the French provinces, incidents erupted every day, whether it be about food, work or politics (SHD: 17N663, 12 mars 1918).

Implementing the alliance: Interpreters as transmitting belts

The Macedonian front gives us an interesting comparison point of the interpreters tasks during the First World War. Observing the French interpreters' serving with Russian troops, we can see they had functions that were not solely bilateral, for they took a great part in putting in place a large range of military practices inside a coalition that the French command was trying to unify. In Macedonia, the French and British army found themselves in a situation they had not foreseen: they were occupying Northern Greece after a failed attempt to rescue the Serbian army in October 1915, in a territory they did not know quite well. They had to manage a coalition of several nationalities fighting against the Central Powers and to maintain peaceful relations with the occupied populations and the neutral forces still present in Northern Greece. In this context, the linguistic skills of the interpreters were highly valuable. Moreover, in this theatre, as the Allies were fighting Bulgarian and Ottoman troops more than Germans or Austrians, dealing with the prisoners of the Central Powers caught on the battlefields was also a Babelesque problem (Fantauzzo and Nelson 2019: 157). These soldiers were seen as a valuable source of intelligence for the Armées Alliées d'Orient, and so interpreters had a key role in their interrogation process.

The situation has been eloquently described by Jérôme Carcopino, who was at the head of the 2e Bureau on the Macedonian front and gives an account of the academic origins of the interpreters serving in the Armée d'Orient: to correspond with its neighbours and friends, the Armée d'Orient 'had to speak Serbian, English, Italian, Russian and Greek. To stand up to his adversaries . . . needed to know Bulgarian, German, Hungarian, Turkish, Albanian. In total, [the *Armée d'Orient*] was condemned to the use of ten foreign languages and he appeared as a Babelian whose defenders were the interpreters, mostly academics' (Carcopino 1970: 80). Among these interpreters were the *agrégés de lettres*, who were in charge of the German and English languages, as well as professors from the *École des langues orientales* who were dealing with Bulgarian or Albanian translations. There were also Russian journalists, professors and former diplomats who were reinforcing them, and so on (Carcopino 1970: 80). According to Carcopino, to sum up, the French intelligence services had 'the figure of a Berlitz school' (Carcopino 1970: 79).

During these much-valued tasks, the presence of Russian speakers among interpreters was seen as a very good asset for a particularly technical reason. It was very difficult to find useful interpreters for each language spoken on this front, languages such as Serbian or Bulgarian. The French army guessed that it would not be that difficult for someone who had already learnt Russian or who was speaking it fluently to learn another Slavic language (Heimburger 2014b: 169). Otherwise, as in France, in the case of the Russian bases, the interpreters had a strong role in handling soldiers from the Allied armies like the Russians or the Serbians. For example, they were often moved to the allied camps or assigned to help the French Gendarmerie who had to deal with the multiple disorders and troubles caused by these troops when they were arrested for theft, drunkenness or violence perpetrated on other troops as much as on civilians (SHD: 20N912, 'Registre de correspondance de la Force publique de Salonique', 1 February 1916).

In the context of the Russian revolution and the mutinies in the armies on the Macedonian front, especially among the Russian troops, the interpreters found themselves with very extensive functions. First of all, they dedicated a lot of time to translating orders and documents and making clear hierarchical equivalences between the French and the Russian troops, but also between Serbian and Russian officers, or also with the other allies. This work included translations of many operational handbooks (artillery, infantry manoeuvres, etc.) and taking part in the instruction of soldiers and officers from the coalition (SHD: 7N612, 31 August 1917 and 11 September 1917).

But as we can see when we read the notebooks and diaries of interpreter Sous-Lieutenant Albert Ohl des Marais, who was with the 2nd and 4th Russian Brigades in Macedonia, interpreters also had to be mediators between the mutineers and the French authority. They took an important part in the negotiations (RGVIA: fond. 15230, op. 1, del 12, lis 95, lis. 107). But before, during and after the mutinies, these men were gathering important information about the morale of the troops and about their revindications or ability to self-organize against the French command (BibSDdV, Ms. 328. Ohl des Marais, Albert, f. 10-36).

On this front, more than on the Western one, interpreters of Russian language were to comply with duties related to more than two belligerents or allies. Their role was not only to help integrate a foreign body into the French army but to take part in the unification of a constellation of armies and military practices in a foreign occupied land. On the field, they still accomplished some duties quite similar to mediating tasks performed in France but also instructions, handbook translations, intelligence services and other duties that put them at the centre of the coalition warfare.

Conclusion

In 1916, the French army found itself in an unforeseen situation when it had to welcome among its ranks more than 40,000 Russian soldiers. To include these men in the French war effort, it mobilized the strengths of all the Russian speakers it could find among its ranks. Through several individual cases, it transpires that after having searched among the ranks of soldiers already serving in the French army or in the ministries, the academic world was the first place where the French army found suitable men to constitute a sufficient body of capable interpreters. The French army also received applications from people who had acquired a decent knowledge of the Russian language due to their jobs or background in Russia. They had sometimes eclectic profiles, like

Paul Le Flem, and became interpreters and composers for the Russian Brigade. In this recruitment policy, linguistic competence prevailed, but the interpreters did not remain simple translators. At different levels, either in headquarters or on the field, with officers as much as with soldiers, the interpreters – even in their mediating tasks – were fully fledged actors of the complex relationship between France and Russia during the First World War.

After one of the first diplomatic agreements between France and the Bolsheviks, the repatriation of Russians willing to go back to Russia was organized, and by 1921 the vast majority of these men were gone. Was it the end of a role for interpreters like Joseph Duchêne, for example? A lot of these wartime Russian-language interpreters received new responsibilities in Eastern Europe. Moreover, as the responsibility of France in the East grew, so did the need for interpreters who quite often became experts or actors of the French military and diplomatic game in countries like Poland, Czechoslovakia and Romania. After the war, Joseph Duchêne remained an interpreter of Russian and Polish for the missions of General Niessel in Poland and General Mangin in Russia. He then became director of the French Office of Foreign Trade for Russia; in 1929, in Poland, he was a delegate of the French industrialists' group. He died in Warsaw in March 1932.

This general overview of the efforts to create a 'linguistic space' for Russian soldiers in the French army during and after the First World War to respond to the needs of military effectiveness also shows us that even for this single issue, there are as many roles of interpreters as situations of interpretation. The tasks entrusted by the army vary from one coalition situation to another: interpreters like those of the Armée d'Orient took an important part in unifying the Allies' art of war in the Macedonian theatre as much as dealing with Russian or Serbian soldiers. This variety of interpreting situation enables us to see interpreters not only as go-betweens or gatekeepers (Heimburger 2012) but also as a transmitting belt of coalition warfare under construction and consolidation.

References

Archives

Bibliothèque intercommunal de Saint-Dié-des-Vosges (BibSDdV).
Russian State Military History Archive (RGVIA), Moscow.
Service Historique de la Défense (SHD), Vincennes.
State Archive of the Russian Federation (GARF), Moscow.

Secondary sources

Baker, M. and G. Saldanha (2019), *Routledge Encyclopedia of Translation Studies*, London: Routledge.
Bourlet, M. (2006), 'Le deuxième bureau et la diplomatie secrète: les négociations Armand-Revertera de 1917', *Guerres mondiales et conflits contemporains*, 221 (1), 33–49.
Carcopino, J. (1970), *Souvenirs de la guerre en Orient*, Paris: Hachette.

Chabot, G. (1940), 'Jules Legras (1867–1939)', *Annales de géographie*, 277: 65.

Cockfield, J. (1998), *With Snow on their Boots: The Tragic Odyssey of the Russian Expeditionary Force in France during World War I*, New York: Macmillan.

Delmas, J. (2008), 'La paix de Brest-Litovsk et le maintien en Russie de la mission militaire française', in J.-M. Delaunay (ed.), *Aux vents des puissances*, 209–27, Paris: Presse Sorbonne Nouvelle.

Duchêne, J. (2016), 'Carnets de Guerre', *La Gazette de l'ours Michka*, 14: 8–22. Available online: http://ascerf.fr/wp-content/uploads/2016/05/Gazette-de-Michka-N%C2%B01 4-.compressed.pdf (accessed 5 June 2020).

Fantauzzo, J. and R. L. Nelson (2019), 'Expeditionary Forces in the Shatterzone: German, British and French Soldiers on the Macedonian Front, 1915–1918', in A. Beyerchen and E. Sencer (eds), *Expeditionary Forces in the First World War*, 149–76, London: Palgrave-Macmillan.

Guelton, F. and A. Pavlov (2019), *V kabinetah i okopah. Francuskie voennye missii v Rossii v gody Pervoj mirovoj vojny*, Saint Petersburg: Izdatel'stvo RKhGA.

Heimburger, F. (2012), 'Of Go-Betweens and Gatekeepers: Considering Disciplinary Biases in Interpreting History through Exemplary Metaphors: Military Interpreters in the Allied Coalition during the First World War', in B. Fischer and M. N. Jensen (eds), *Translation and the Reconfiguration of Power Relations: Revisiting Role and Context of Translation and Interpreting*, Graz: LIT Verlag.

Heimburger, F. (2014a), *Mésentente cordiale ? Langues et coalition alliée sur le front de l'ouest de la Grande Guerre*, EHESS Paris: unpublished doctoral thesis.

Heimburger, F. (2014b), 'Mobiliser les compétences linguistiques et culturelles. L'organisation du service de langues dans l'armée française en Orient pendant la Première Guerre mondiale', in *Turcs et Français. Une histoire culturelle 1860–1960*, 163–71, Rennes: Presses universitaires de Rennes.

Kappeler, A. (1994), *La Russie, empire multiethnique*, Paris: Institut d'études slaves.

Konyaeva, J. (2017), 'Prisonniers de guerre russes en Alsace pendant la Grande Guerre', in F. Guelton (ed.), *L'alliance franco-russe à l'épreuve de la Grande Guerre*, Châlons-en-Champagne: Département de la Marne.

Laurent, S. (2009), *Politiques de l'ombre: L'État et le renseignement en France*, Paris: Fayard.

Le Flem, P. (1960), 'Je forme une fanfare chez les Russes', *Musica*, 27: 45–6.

Mussat M.-C. (1997), 'Le compositeur Paul Le Flem et les Russes: de Moscou en Mayenne et dans la Sarthe', in M. Lagréé and J. Sainclivier (eds), *L'Ouest et le politique*, 45–57, Rennes: Presses universitaires de Rennes.

Nicot, J. (1968), 'L'histoire de la première guerre mondiale: l'apport des Archives de l'Armée', *Revue d'histoire moderne et contemporaine*, 15 (3): 535–42.

Offord, D., V. Rjéoutski and G. Argent (2018), *The French Language in Russia. A Social, Political, Cultural, and Literary History*, Cambridge: Cambridge University Press.

Piégais, G. (2018), 'Le corps expéditionnaire russe en Macédoine, 1916–1920. Combats et mutineries sur un front périphérique', in *En Envor, revue d'histoire contemporaine en Bretagne*. Available online: http://enenvor.fr/eeo_revue/numero_12/le_corps_expediti onnaire_russe_en_macedoine_1916_1920_combats_et_mutineries_sur_un_front_per ipherique.html (accessed 5 June 2020).

Rey, M.-P. (2017), 'Les relations franco-russes à la veille de la Première Guerre mondiale. Grands traits, enjeux et problèmes', in F. Guelton (ed.), *L'alliance franco-russe à l'épreuve de la Grande Guerre*, Châlons-en-Champagne: Département de la Marne.

Sanborn, J. S. (2014), *Imperial Apocalypse. The Great War and the Destruction of the Russian Empire*, Oxford: Oxford University Press.

3

Language in East Africa during the First World War

Anne Samson

In a theatre such as East Africa, where approximately 177 ethnic or tribal groupings were involved, each with their own language or dialect, an analysis of the language(s) used opens new avenues to explore aspects of command and cultural relations. As little, if any, work has been done on language in the East Africa campaign, this chapter aims to provide an initial overview of the range of languages encountered and what insights they provide concerning the campaign.

The territory under discussion is today's Tanzania, Rwanda and Burundi, which together formed German East Africa, where the Germans trained their local forces, known as Askari, in German and were developing the use of Kiswahili, a locally devised trade language, as a standard alternative.[1] To the north was Kenya, then British East Africa, Uganda, then the Uganda Protectorate, and in the south, Malawi or Nyasaland and the two Rhodesias, Zambia and Zimbabwe, which were all British. The official language was English and the King's African Rifles, a local force with white British officers, was instructed in English. When war broke out, the settlers in the various territories enlisted into units with a number forming scouting parties which undertook intelligence work and acted as frontline troops. The scouts used local inhabitants to assist them, invariably because they knew the terrain, spoke the language and understood the culture. For example, Lord Delamere worked with Masai, Archibald Wavell with Arabs and Ross led a contingent of Somalis.

Range of languages

In 1914, the main administrative languages in East Africa were English, German, French, Dutch and Portuguese. In addition, reference is made to Danish, Norwegian, Greek, Swedish and Italian. The Belgian army had officers of Scandinavian background such as Olsen and Sorrensen, whilst German forces were supplemented with Danish speakers when the blockade runners, *Marie* and *Kronberg*, broke through. The author, Karen Blixen, a Dane, having befriended Paul von Lettow-Vorbeck on route to Africa, was believed to be a German spy, the German commander enlisting her to source horses for him in British territory. Greeks and Swedes were traders and farmers, and Italians generally missionaries, such as Verbi, who joined the British Intelligence Corps in the north.

The various African black tribal groupings had their own languages often with a common Bantu base. This had been influenced by the Arab slave trade and other economic encounters as people moved and migrated. The arrival of Christian missionaries and the introduction of Islamic schools resulted in local inhabitants becoming literate in ways recognized by the west. However, written records remain scarce. What we have are transcriptions and translations of interviews conducted with individuals in the post-war years: Melvin Page recorded veterans in Malawi as did Geoffrey Hodges and Gerald Rillings in Kenya.

Interpreters and clerks

Interpreters play an important role in our accessing accounts in languages not our own. On Discovery, the catalogue of The National Archives of the United Kingdom, for Africa only 1,917 interpreters are listed as having received Medal Cards during the First World War. Of these, 183 served in Egyptian forces and 123 in sub-Saharan African contingents. Of the 123 interpreters, 31 are directly linked to labour, supply or transport and 3 to marine defence.[2] The low number of interpreters reflects those employed for their English abilities within the imperial military system where commanding officers were not competent in the local language of their rank and file. Many medal cards are in names clearly not of English heritage, but there is no indication on the card as to the language(s) they spoke. One can assume the eight from Zanzibar were Arab or Kiswahili speakers, whilst the one from Sierra Leone was Kroo. Interpreters from Seychelles and Mauritius likely only spoke one language, whilst those accompanying South African labourers could have spoken one of a number of languages such as Xhosa, Zulu and Sotho, the same for those from Gold Coast and Nigeria: Fanti, Twi, Ga and so forth.

Mission-schooled Goans and Africans were often employed as clerks in preference to British-schooled clerks for reasons of cost and to relieve more senior administrators from the tedium of routine writing. Allan Chelemu, a Yao from Nyasaland and clerk in Fife at the outbreak of war, was left in charge of the Boma to notify outlying troops by firing a single shot if Germans invaded on a particular night in 1915 (Chelemu 1960). Many government-employed clerks despite having undertaken war-related work did not receive military medals unless, like Chelemu, they were employed to fulfil a military function. The same applied to British white Colonial Office employees, these men being expected to be conversant in various languages as set out by British East Africa Governor Henry Belfield on 13 August 1914: Swahili to a 'High Standard', Somali, Kamba, Kikuyu, Masai, Nilotic Kavirondo and Nandi. Five other languages, not listed, had been removed from the list (TNA 1914: CO 533/139 36047).

Learning the language

The policy of having administrators speak the language of the people they were responsible for helped build trust through a common understanding of cultural beliefs and practice. During the campaign, as the need for officers increased, and the local supply of men who could be seconded decreased, so British white officers and NCOs were sourced in Europe. Those selected had to be even better than officers of white battalions as the black soldier was a shrewd judge of character. Fendall explained: 'An officer, or non-commissioned officer, is not much good in the bush, where the platoon commanders are often obliged to act on their own initiative, unless he can understand reports brought to him by his company scouts' (Fendall 1921: 199–200). The officer who could speak the local language and understand the customs achieved more than others (Fendall 1921: 43).

The Colonial Office felt it imperative that officers learn Kiswahili (TNA 1917: CO 534/23/10 58745), the commandant reinforcing the 'great importance that British ranks should be acquainted with Swahili as quickly as possible and [given the] length of time occupied in voyage', should continue learning on board supported by 'administrative officers returning from leave' (TNA 1917: CO 534/22/3 50108). To assist with language learning, a training school was opened in London to teach officers the rudimentaries in Kiswahili. The appointment of Sabin bin Resasi to the King's African Rifles (KAR) provides insight into how interpreters were employed and the complexities of having civilians in military employ. On 28 August 1917, the Colonial Office supported Sabin being paid £5 per month and a third class passage to East Africa to 'assist Major Rigby in teaching Swahili to officers and n.c.o.'s at the K.A.R. school of instruction.' Employed by the War Office whilst in England, he would be on military rations. Additionally, Salim was to be employed by Rigby as his personal servant, Rigby assuming responsibility for him until arrival in East Africa where he would then enlist in the KAR. 'Mombasa steward boy' Salim had been recommended in March 1917 by Acting Governor AR Slater in Accra, where he had been a personal servant for ten years to Mr Justice Porter and was wanting to serve HM Forces in some capacity. It was noted that he spoke 'English – well; Arabic – perfectly; Swahili – perfectly; Modern Greek – well; Turkish – perfectly; Hindustani – fairly well'. He was also noted to be able to read and write: 'English – reads well writes indifferently; Arabic – perfectly; Swahili – perfectly; Turkish – well'. He was of a 'good well known Mombasa family' and a British citizen (TNA 1917: CO 534/24/3 40062).

That men continued to learn Kiswahili on board ship is diarized by Lieutenant John Bruce Cairnie, posted to the KAR. On 17 October 1917, 'I have put in a fairly useful day – Swahili in the morning . . .' On Sunday 21 October, 'Took a day off as far as Swahili etc are concerned'. On Wednesday 28 November, 'We have had a native interpreter up on deck for an hour at nights & are making some progress with Swahili.' A few days later, interviewing potential 'personal boys' or servants, Cairnie 'came to a complete misunderstanding with them, We didn't know that they were rationed by the Q.M. [quarter master] so we said they wd. have to buy their own posho [grain/food]. That was the bone of contention. My Swahili came in useful but leaves a great deal to be understood'. On 3 December, 'From 12 – 1 there is a Swahili class in the captain's *banda*, but it will probably stop after tomorrow when their exam. comes off. At 2 o'clock a tribal return had to be made out and the company was fallen in by tribes – 13 in all. As far as I could make out there was very little conformity to type within each tribe: tribal distinctions apparently consist in artificialities mainly, e.g. pulling out the lower incisors, scars etc.' Having gone through the process of learning Kiswahili, Cairnie discovered on 15 December 'that about 20 of my platoon don't understand Swahili and can't have even the slightest idea of what I am talking about' (Cairnie 1917). Given that in East Africa a platoon consisted of about thirty men, it is a significant proportion who did not speak Swahili.[3] Melvin Page in his well-researched historical novel setting out the life of KAR Sergeant Chimwera Juma explains that Juma learnt Kiswahili whilst he learnt military manoeuvres: learning to count as they marched and other terms as they developed military discipline (Page 2019).

Twenty-year-old Grahame Munro, who was to die in East Africa in December 1916, wrote home earlier, pleased with himself for, 'I have become quite a linguist being able to make myself understood as well as understanding them. When they start talking to you they rattle it off like a maxim so I can tell you it takes some following' (Satchwell 2014: 143). In November 1916, he had 'become quite an expert on speaking Swakeelli. When we first came here I was interpreting for an officer of the Pioneer Corps and on asking what sort of road ran between Trollo and Ladells I was told it was very good. I then asked whether it was passable during the rains. "Yes" Could a motor go along it? There was a roar of laughter and I was informed the only way to go along it was by boat' (Satchwell 2014: 140).

Whilst Kiswahili was the main language in East Africa, other African languages were also prevalent. From late 1916 into 1917, forces were brought into East Africa from West Africa. Gold Coast and Nigerian Regiments served in an armed capacity whilst labour was sourced in Sierra Leone. Men from Gambia and West Indies were also brought into the theatre along with Seychelloise and Chinese labour. The medal cards show only one interpreter from Sierra Leone and one from Gold Coast, whilst Hugh Clifford, governor and war historian, records five interpreters with the Sierra Leone Carriers attached to the Gold Coast Regiment, although he does not mention which language(s) they spoke. On arrival in East Africa, the contingent was given Captain H.C.C. de la Poer, a special services officer resident in East Africa and fluent in Kiswahili (Clifford 1920: 8, 92).

Another significant force in East Africa was Indian, from today's India, Pakistan and Bangladesh. Alec Kerr, a Captain attached to the Kashmir Rifles, who were noted to have performed impressively at Tanga in November 1914, missed the battle as he was on route to join the 2nd Battalion. Alec's attestation form records that he spoke Urdu to a high standard, and Punjabi and Pushtu to a lesser extent. The ability to speak one of the Indian languages was a necessity as evidenced by both Alec's father's and his son's records, all in Indian military units. Another officer to join the Kashmirs, Cooke, recorded that he was learning Urdu for an examination whilst on the Tsavo River defence line.[4]

In January 1917, Francis Brett Young, a British novelist and doctor in East Africa, wrote home: 'I do nothing much. I have started to learn a new language this time Pakhtu (Pushtu) because I like Pathans so a deal, especially the savage transfrontiersmen . . . It is very unusual for them to meet any British Officers who understand their language, and they love it' (Young 1917b: 106). Later he was having fun playing with Kiswahili (Young 1917a).

In the Nyasaland Volunteer Reserve of twenty-four white men listed, eighteen could speak Chinyanga, whilst six could speak Chinyanga and Kiswahili. Hector Duff, the chief political officer in Nyasaland, spoke Chinyanga and Kiswahili and was also fluent in German (Charlton 2018: 43). The additional languages were important for handling porters and for trading food stuffs with the chiefs (Charlton 2018: 105–6). According to Moyse Bartlett, historian of the King's African Rifles, it had been decided in 1902 that all officers should be able to speak the local language. The first examination in Chinyanga was held in August 1903 with the first in Swahili in 1905 (Bartlett 2004: 133–4). Before that, non-commissioned officers had been Sikh, which saw various Indian words introduced into the military lexicon – terms such as 'safari', which means 'journey'. In the neighbouring Rhodesias, Alfred James Tomlinson, British South African Police, noted that he had passed an exam in Sindebele in 1905, the language of the Matabele, who eventually formed a unit of the Rhodesian Native Regiment during the war.

Communicating

However, not all officers were able to speak a local language. Aibu Chikwenga on safari with General Llewellyn recalled: 'General Llewellyn a well-mannered man was quite kind, but because we could not understand his language, English, he used to shout at us and repeat himself to make sure that we understood what he was saying, and this gave him the appearance of being a fierce man' (Chikwenga 1972: 16).

Some officers, mainly South African, had Dutch or Afrikaans as their first language. In May 1917, General Jacob van Deventer, an Afrikaans/Dutch-speaking South African, was appointed commander-in-chief East Africa. 'On first arrival he was very shy of talking English, and all business with his English speaking staff had to be carried on through an interpreter' (Fendall 1921: 102–3, 129). Van Deventer refused to speak English because of an English bullet which went through his throat during the Southern Africa War of 1899–1902, causing him to speak with a rasp. He took great glee in reminding his English staff of this (Reitz 2012). His personal diary is written in a mix of English and Dutch/Afrikaans, the more secret information in the latter (Van Deventer n.d.). It makes for an interesting situation where the commander-in-chief needs a translator to conduct a campaign.

Similarly, but with less military impact, was German Governor Heinrich Schnee's wife, Ada. An Australian, she wrote her memoirs in German, refusing to speak English after her house in Dar es Salaam was destroyed. She led the resistance in Tabora arranging that the women and wounded be surrendered to the Belgians to increase pressure on the invading forces and relieve that on the mobile Germans (Fendall 1921: 227).

In the field

Despite all the preparation and learning of languages, practicalities in the field threw up their own challenges and insights.

There were occasions when local truces needed to be declared and discussions undertaken over the removal of wounded and other concerns. After the Battle of Tanga in November 1914, it was found the Germans could speak English quite fluently, the German commander Paul von Lettow-Vorbeck having 'extremely good English', but the British Admiral noted that none in his force could speak German (Fendall 1921: 128). Similarly, in the south, the commander of the *Hermann von Wissmann* on Lake Nyasa could speak English, whilst Tomlinson of 1st Rhodesian Native Regiment took Sergeant Kerckove with him on an intelligence safari because he spoke German (NAM 1999: 10). This was important for interrogating potential prisoners.

The nature of the campaign meant distinguishing between friend and foe became more difficult as clothing deteriorated and was appropriated by the stronger side. At Mpepo, a German officer called out in English 'Retire Retire!' to confuse the enemy who were a little too close (Wright 2001: 92). The use of English by German officers was nothing new. In 1911, the British had disbanded 2nd King's African Rifles, many of whom had enlisted with the German Askari at Neu Langenburg. 'So many ex-KAR askaris were serving there that English bugle-calls and words of command were in regular use' (Bartlett 2004: 265).[5] The British used the same ruse to disrupt German supply convoys by calling them from behind to halt (Wienholt 1922).

Two entries in Tomlinson's diary are revealing. On 21 November 1916, the Germans had sent a letter in Kiswahili to Chief, or Sultan, Lamenti Fusi inviting him to a talk (Tomlinson in Berry, Rogers and Stock n.d.: 71). The letter had been given to British runners returning from a neighbouring force, demonstrating the ease with which opposing forces could con each other. It further suggests that Chief Fusi could read Kiswahili, which accords with Jack Rollins, who noted that by 1914 the Germans had introduced the '*akida* and *jumbe* system of headmen . . . functioning through the medium of both spoken and written Swahili' (Rollins 1989: 5). A month later, 23 December, Tomlinson tells of capturing German askari believed to be in a specific village along the Buhora Road. Having blown a whistle as a ruse, they came across nine askari 'when they rounded the huts and shouted "hands up", making signs for them to do so' (Tomlinson in Berry, Rogers and Stock n.d.: 82). The use of demonstration is hinted at by Charles Barton when training carriers in Nyasaland to tie knots. Every two carriers had one European to support them. This suggests that either the European could speak their language and/or he was doing intensive demonstration. A similar picture is painted for the process of enlistment, where men were commanded by Nubians (IWM 1/3 KAR). Alongside demonstration were the trumpet calls drilled into the men during training (IWM 4/2 KAR).

Authors such as Fred Ashley recite basic conversations they had with local people they encountered. Ashley on having his bike come to a sudden stop in the bush encountered 'three grinning natives!' '"Jambo!" I said, laughing. "Jambo sana, bwana!" they replied, with grins that split their faces'. He wanted to know where Malangali was (Ashley 1938: 84). From the remainder of his encounter, it is clear that the men he encountered could tell the difference between British and German forces (Ashley 1938: 35). One assumes this was based on the spoken word, although it is known that the two forces dressed differently: the Germans wore long trousers and the British shorts.

As the war progressed, the Germans moved into Portuguese East Africa where Erroll McDonnel was liaison for the British forces. Fluent in Portuguese and having been in the territory since 1911, he was aware of the politics and relationships between the Portuguese administrators and German businessmen. When not in post, from the British perspective, things went awry. Liaison officers were also appointed to the Belgian forces in Congo where French was the main language. Indications from reading French and German accounts of the time suggest language experiences were similar. Max Poppe, a hunter who served in the German forces, recounted his encounters with Kiswahili, whilst the translated German war diaries talk of interrogations of captured soldiers of African, Indian and European background (IWM 49538). The Germans therefore had men who could speak various languages or make themselves understood.

Fraternization between ethnicities was discouraged. However, the nature of the war made this difficult to enforce with the result that men began learning other languages. Many porters thus learnt Kiswahili and hence about the wider world (Hodges 1999: 189). Shackleton noted that some porters could speak 'broken English' (Shackleton 1940: 85). Barton and Tomlinson speak of single-language units at the start of the war, for example Angoni, Atonga, Yao and Matabele. Later they are referred to as 1st Nyasaland Regiment, 1st Rhodesian Native Regiment and so forth, language and cultural identity having given way to broader categorizations.

From interviews, we get insight into daily life. Muthei Uvito, a herdsman of cattle and labourer, tells us:

> There was a little man who used to wake us up in the camp. He would call me in Kiswahili 'mtu wa ng'ombe' meaning the person in charge of cows and ask me to go herd the cattle while the rest were allocated other duties. . . . My boss was a Kavirondo a Luo named Kongoni. We never talked to the white soldiers and other personnel. They talked only to our leaders. The only place we interacted with them was while we were taking a shower in the river, all of us naked, as we crossed from Nguruman. We also lived in separate areas in the camp. (IWM 4/2 KAR)

Daudi Musyimi Muthwa (4/2 KAR Headquarters, No. 22) could not read but 'found out what was going on in the war through those who were injured because they would be returned to base after being taken to the hospital. They would give us stories about the war and how it was going' (IWM 4/2 KAR). Norman Kimomo Kitui recounted joining 1KAR:

> 'the Nubian lieutenant said that all his soldiers would go home with him . . . he said the captain had escaped and left him and his men had to fight alone. So, him and his soldiers left for Nairobi. They then brought a large group of Kamba soldiers with a few Gikuyus, Luos and others. Ngomoli (Montgomery?), who came with them, had said he did not want soldiers from another ethnic group, only Kambas

were needed. Montgomery had lived in Kangundo, spoke Kikamba and often sang songs in the Kikamba language with other Kamba young men . . .

In our company, we spoke in Kiswahili. The last time we spoke Kikamba was in Nairobi before we boarded our vehicle. We would speak Kikamba individually to each other but not to other people. Our orders came in Kiswahili. The whites would speak it within a month of joining us.' He also commented on how they enjoyed singing songs as a means to relax. (IWM 4/2 KAR)

Diversity was prevalent, especially in the medical environment. An East African Medical Corps stretcher bearer noted:

We were a mixed group. There were Nubians, Gikuyus, Luos, Embus, even cannibals from northern Tanzania. Others from Tanganyika. Everybody was there. There were also Indians and whites. We ate different types of food. There was meat, rice, Ugali and other foods like dates. The food was brought by white people. We would all cook together. That was not a celebration. . . . When we picked [up] wounded Germans, we treated them just like everyone else. We did not have a problem with them. We would treat them. After they had been captured, they were treated the same way as everybody. We only had a problem with them when they were fighting. . . . There was no time for newspapers in the war. Maybe the British received them but I did not see that. Times weren't that good. We didn't know what was going on at home. We did not receive letters either. Maybe the white people received information from where they were from but not us. (IWM 4/2 KAR)

It is the white participants who distinguish between their various ethnicities. Brett Young records a patient who was a 'very nice Boer (English speaking) who is on Brits' staff'(Young 1917b: 83). Barton distinguishes between going to 'English church' and 'Scotch church' in his diaries. In contrast, Mbuvi Thyaka, Nyasaland Company at Embakasi, recalled: 'Only white soldiers and visitors visited the mess. . . . We also had a white supervisor in the mess. We used to take orders from him. I did not see any Indians. It was only whites coming from Europe. We didn't know whether they were Boers or not. If they were white then they were Europeans' (IWM 4/2 KAR).

Literacy

Of the carrier corps, one that was raised on Zanzibar by Bishop Weston was thought to be the most literate, to the extent that the Bishop organized postcards for the men to use on the march. Hodges notes that Weston was able, because of the trust he had imbued, to get the real names of those who served with him (Hodges 1999: 115). Apart from officials not necessarily recording names correctly, the men themselves gave incorrect names for various reasons.

Africans, of all ethnicities, who were literate and who could speak English were in great demand and therefore able to do well. Corporal Tanganyika, who could write

English was sent with a patrol to Kitanda to report back (Tomlinson in Berry, Rogers and Stock n.d.: 16). Three native scouts were chosen who could read and write, not to fight but to get news (Charlton 2018: 124). And Allan Chelemu, the clerk interpreter, has already been discussed. German Max Wintgen's servant Serufugi defected to the Belgians using the opportunity of the vacuum created by the removal of Chief Musinga to increase his wealth. This he was able to do by speaking the language(s) of the rulers (Samson 2016).

Musyoki Nzyima, working for a Scottish mission in Nairobi, could read Kiswahili, Gikuyu and Kikamba but not English. During the war, he supervised the building of a school at Mboon near where fighting occurred: 'The German gun sounded like ndokuni ndokuni ndokuni and the one from here (the British side) sounded like tututu tututu.' He continued:

> We prayed for the war, not the sick or wounded. We prayed for the war to end and for the British to win. I told you that Ngomoli was the one waiting in the Coast, he had a black wire like your shoes that extended to Nairobi. The wire was on the ground, you couldn't see it and it went to every white person and talked to them from the ground. So when the war was over, those in Nairobi and us knew at the same time. (IWM 4/2 KAR)

Whilst most African blacks were taken to be illiterate, some whites also fell into this category: General Brits, the South African commander, could 'scarcely read or write, let alone read a map' (Young 1917b: 86)

Conclusion

Unravelling language in the East African campaign is complex given the great number of ethnic groups involved and the range of function and experience. An outcome of the interactions, some started pre-war, was the progress in dictionary compilation. George Sanderson, who served on the *Guendolen* on Lake Nyasa in August 1914, published an English-Yao Dictionary in 1922. Having lived in Nyasaland since 1910, he was also fluent in Chinyanga, writing an introduction to that language with a Mr Bithrey in 1939 (Goodall 1962: 149–50). The YMCA published *First Aid to the Swahili Language* in February 1915, whilst in August 1915 Captains H.B. Owen and J.G. Keane published *An abbreviated Vocabulary in Hindustani, Luganda, Lunyoro, Swahli, Nubi designed for the use of the Uganda Medical Service*. In 1916, the Church Missionary Societies was updating Bible translations alongside compiling a Swahili hymnbook (National Army Museum 8205/103/3; Cadbury Library YMCA and CMS 1915).

Whilst few oral accounts exist, scouring diaries and memoirs provides an insight into the extent and range of language use. However, all is not lost even with all the veterans having now died; engagement with local populations should allow aspects of the war in Africa to be recorded. A 2011 East African publication records the history of ten Luo clans recalling some aspect of the First World War. The richness can be seen in the account by the Kagwa, a clan in Tanzania. Ogo went up to Nyabange Musoma to see the Germans, who had a fort there, saying:

> there is this man, Mzee Kan, he is a spy for the British, they came from Kenya to this country to find out how you Germans are living here so that they can come and fight you. . . . After a while the war between the Germans and the British broke down around Kisii Kenya, and even the Germans were hunted down in the grass like guinea fowl by the British. In the end the Germans fled and all of the people who were imprisoned because of personal quarrels were left free. (Oloo Siso and Shetler 2010: 185–7)

Exploring languages, in context, mentioned in texts of the First World War, Africa has allowed insight into vertical and horizontal relationships of the time. With greater numbers of diaries and memoirs coming to light as a result of the centenary of the Great War, more comprehensive studies will be possible. However, an important question remains: To what extent has the variety of language been responsible for the apparent lack of memory of the campaign?

Notes

1   Kiswahili: 'a mixed language, which bears a somewhat similar relation to Arabic as that borne by Urdu (Hindustani) the lingua franca of Northern and other parts of India. Urdu is the language of the camps, Swahili is the language of trade.' It originated from the Swahili, a coastal tribe influenced by the Arab slave trade and other cultural encounters, resulting in the language moving along trade/slave routes into the interior. When the Germans and British arrived, it seemed logical to develop a local national language already found in pockets across the territory. The initial use of Kiswahili was linked to status and class, and was eventually adopted by Christian missionaries as a 'church language' (Fendall 1921: 200). More on the development of the language can be found in Maganda (2014); Rollins (1983, 2020).
2   8 Zanzibar, 1 Dodoma, 2 Uganda Transport, 4 Togoland, 7 Nyasaland, 2 Northern Rhodesia, 2 Southern Rhodesia, 8 SANLC, 1 Sierra Leone,32 Nigeria (6 carriers), 20 East Africa (8 labour, supply), 2 Gambia, 1 Gold Coast, 24 King's African Rifles, 6 Mauritius, 3 Mombasa Marine defence. The remainder served in Europe, with the Royal Navy, in the Middle East and 112 with the Macedonian Mule or Labour Corps.
3   Harry Fecitt on military terminology, and The Long Long Trail, 'What was a battalion of infantry?'.
4   Thanks to Andrew Kerr for the info. Kerr (2012).
5   Bartlett's source for this is 'Notes on Neu Langenburg, 23 Dec 1908, 1911 and 1913 in the Central African Archives, KAR, 3/1/1.

References

Archival sources

(Cadbury Library) Cadbury Library (1915) CMS Section IV Africa Missions, Part 17: Kenya Mission 1880-1934 G3 A5 L10 Letter books.

(Cadbury Library) Cadbury Library (1915) CMS Section IV Africa Missions, Part 17: Kenya Mission 1880-1934 G3 A5 L10 Letter books.
(Cadbury Library) Cadbury Library (1915) YMCA/K/2/8, YM 26 February 1915, p 164.
(Cadbury Library) Cadbury Library (1915) YMCA/K/2/8, YM 26 February 1915, p 164.
IWM: 49538 German War Diaries, Max Poppe memoirs.
IWM: Gerald Rillings interviews translated by Solomon Maingi; original recordings and translations available at IWM, copy supplied to author: Norman Kimomo Kitui, private, 1/3 KAR.
IWM: Rillings interviews: Daudi Musyimi Muthwa (4/2 KAR Headquarters, No. 22).
NAM: 1999-12-44 AJ Tomlinson, history of 1RNR.
National Army Museum, Templar Study Centre: 8205/103/3.
TNA: CO 533/139 36047, Language bonuses, 13 August 1914.
TNA: CO 534/22/3 50108, Officers and NCOs for KAR, instructions in Swahili on voyage out, Oct 1917.
TNA: CO 534/23/10 58745, Officers and NCOs of KAR, instruction in Swahili during outward voyage, Nov 1917.
TNA: CO 534/24/3 40062, Sabin [Salim] bin Resasi, KAR, Aug 1917.

Secondary sources

Ashley, F. J. (1938), *With a Motor-Bike in the Bush*, London: Blackie & Son.
Bartlett, H. M. (2004), *The King's African Rifles: A Study in the Military History of East and Central Africa, 1890–1945*, Uckfield: Naval and Military Press.
Berry, J., C. Rogers and A. Stock (n.d.), *The British South African Police: Military Operations Outside Southern Rhodesia during World War One and World War Two*, British South Africa Police Association.
Cairnie, J. B. (1917), *Diary, King's African Rifles*. Available online: https://wwi.lib.byu.edu/index.php/The_Great_War_Diaries_-_1917_(King%27s_African_Rifles) (accessed 29 January 2020).
Charlton, P. (2018), *Cinderella's Soldiers: Nyasaland Volunteer Reserve*, Rickmansworth: TSL.
Chelemu, A. (1960), 'Memories of Abandoned Bomas No. 15: Chinungu A 1914–18 War Time Boma', *Northern Rhodesia Journal*, 4 (4): 347–50.
Chikwenga, A. (1972), 'Aibu Chikwenga: An Autobiography', translated and edited by C. A. Baker, *Society of Malawi Journal*, 25 (2): 11–21.
Clifford, H. C. (1920), *The Gold Coast Regiment in East Africa*, London: J Murray.
Reitz, D. (2012), *On Commando*, Edinburgh: The House of Emslie.
Fendall, C. P. (1921), *The East African Force*, London: HF and G Witherby.
Goodall, J. (1962), 'Obituary: Dr George Meredith Sanderson', *Central African Journal of Medicine*, 38: 149–50.
Hodges, G. (1999), *Kariakor: The Carrier Corps*, Nairobi: Nairobi University Press.
Kerr, A. (2012), *I Can Never Say Enough about the Men*, Gloucestershire: PCM Management Consultants.
Maganda, D. M. (2014), *Swahili People and their Language*, London: Adonis & Abbey.
Oloo Siso, Z. and J. B. Shetler, eds (2010), *Grasp the Shield Firmly the Journey Is Hard: A History of Luo and Bantu Migrations to North Mara, (Tanzania) 1850–1950* / Shikilia ngao vizuri safari ni ngumu: Historia ya Waluo na Wabantu kuhamia kaskazini mwa Mara (Tanzania) 1850–1950, 185–7, Dar es Salaam: Mkuki Na Nyota.
Page, M. (2019), *Distinguished Conduct: An African Life in Colonial Malawi*, Malawi: Mzuni Press.

Rollins, J. D. (1983), *A History of Swahili Prose, Part 1: From Earliest Times to the End of the Nineteenth Century*, Leiden: Brill.

Rollins, J. (1989), 'Early Twentieth Century Published Swahili Prose Texts and Europeanization of Swahili Prose Genres', unpublished paper. Available online: https://www.researchgate.net/publication/47554044 (accessed 5 June 2020).

Rollins, J. D. (2020), *Early Twentieth Century Swahili Prose*, unpublished paper (available ResearchGate, accessed 5 June 2020).

Samson, A. (2016) 'Ruanda and Urundi', in U. Daniel et al. (eds), *1914–1918-Online: International Encyclopedia of the First World War*. Available online: https://encyclopedia.1914-1918-online.net/article/ruanda_and_urundi (accessed 5 June 2020).

Satchwell, K., ed. (2014), *Your Loving Son*, Yum: The letters of Grahame Alexander Munro to his family 1915–1916 (privately published).

Shackleton, C. W. (1940), *East African Experiences, 1916, from the Diary of a South African Infantryman in the German East African Campaign*, Durban: The Knox Publishing Company.

van Deventer (n.d.), *Diary*, Ditsong National Museum of Military History: Ditsong Military Archive.

Wienholt, A. (1922), *The Story of a Lion Hunt; with Some of the Hunter's Military Adventures during the War*, London: Andrew Melrose.

Wright, T. B. (2001), 'The History of the Northern Rhodesia Police', London: British Empire and Commonwealth Press.

Young, F. B. (1917a), FBY 552 letter 17 Jan 1917, Francis Brett Young collection.

Young, F. B. (1917b), Tanga Letters to Jessie, Francis Brett Young Society.

4

Pioneers of internationalism

Esperanto and the First World War

Javier Alcalde

The state of the art

Esperanto is a planned language, with the aim of becoming an international auxiliary language. Accordingly, scholars have generally studied it from a linguistic perspective within a subdiscipline called interlinguistics (Jespersen 1931; Wandruszka 1982; Kuznetsov 1987; Schubert 1989; Barandovskà-Frank 1995; Gobbo 2015; Blanke 2018; Tonkin 1997).[1] Exceptions to this trend are Peter Forster's solid *The Esperanto Movement* (1982), based on the sociology of the British case, and Andrew Large's *The Artificial Language Movement* (1985), which included as well other linguistic proposals, apart from Esperanto.

Nevertheless, in recent years social scientists have rediscovered Esperanto as a social movement. Partially because of the commercial success of Akira Okrent's *In the land of invented languages* (2009) and the popularity of the so-called Hollywood languages such as those of *Star Trek* and *Game of Thrones*, a reimpression of Forster's book (2012) was followed by a number of remarkable new contributions. Among them, Roberto Garvía' *Esperanto and Its Rivals* (2015) convincingly explains the victory of Esperanto over its rival language movements (mainly Volapük and Ido) at the turn of the twentieth century.

In fact, since the Middle Ages there have been hundreds of attempts to create an international language. Umberto Eco (1993) called this process *The search for the perfect language*.[2] However, only Esperanto became a living language and created a community of speakers, able to survive the death of its creator. By analysing the field of chemistry, Michael Gordin showed in *Scientific Babel* that Esperanto, and also its reformed version Ido, played a non-negligible role in the history of science (Gordin 2015). Meanwhile, Esther Schor presented in *Bridge of Words* the relationship between Esperanto and Jewish cultural and intellectual history, as well as the vitality of the current social movement (Schor 2016). This last aspect is also the topic of a recent PhD research project in anthropology: *Of Revolutionaries and Geeks* (Fians 2019).

Whereas the Esperanto movement flourished mainly in Europe, it was also a cultural bridge between Western modernity and Asian progressive individuals, as shown in *Green Star Japan* (Rapley 2013). And it played a relevant role in Russia during the first decades of the twentieth century, as explained in *Tongues of Fire* (O'Keeffe forthcoming). Its diffusion in the Soviet Union would end in Stalin's Purges, coincident in time with the persecution suffered by its supporters in Nazi Germany. Such persecutions are the focus of Ulrich Lins' work *Dangerous Language* (2020), published in Esperanto in 1989. In fact, this is one of the reasons that research on the Esperanto movement is not always well known in academia, as most of it is written and published in Esperanto. Another example is a collective volume by forty authors, coordinated by José Salguero and myself, published in 2018, *Antaŭ unu jarcento. Esperanto kaj la granda milito* [A century ago. Esperanto and the Great War]. One of the contributions to this book is a detailed and amusing war (and travel) journal written by Robert Murray, a Scottish soldier who described – in Esperanto – his adventures during the four years of the war.

The creation of Esperanto

By the end of the nineteenth century, revolutions in transport and communications facilitated international contacts like never before. Moreover, the belief in progress and rationality had stimulated agreements on standards in a number of issues, such as weights and measures, but also an international prime meridian to make it easier for worldwide travelling and trading across countries. That is, crossing and passing at Greenwich, the initial meridian was linked to a universal day, beginning at its mean midnight. From this perspective, a rational language was seen as a scientific tool, necessary in a world without an international *lingua franca*.

Since Latin ceased to play such a role, different powers had been struggling for their national language to take its place. To some extent, the diffusion of each language mirrored each country's power; consequently, the international equilibrium between 1870 and 1914 was translated into the field of language. French was dominant in the realm of diplomacy, English was gaining terrain particularly in economy and trade, German was strong in science, and Russian was also expanding its influence. In this context, the debates around an auxiliary neutral language arose naturally.

European ethnolinguistic diversity was particularly evident in places such as Białystok, today in Poland and then part of the Russian Empire. In that city there were communities of Poles, Russians, Germans, Belarusians, Tatars, Ukrainians, Lithuanians and Chuvash, but the Jews formed the majority of the population. One of them, Lejzer Zamenhof, was born in 1857 and adopted as well a Christian name in the Polish language, Ludwig. As a child he observed tensions between the different groups, the Jews often being those who bore the brunt. Sensitive and polyglot, he soon realized that they were all more alike than they thought, but they lacked a common language to communicate with each other.

Still a teenager, Zamenhof took on the exciting task of creating an interlanguage, not to replace other languages, but to use it among people with different mother tongues.

On 26 July 1887 he published in Warsaw the grammar of the new language. First in Russian, then in a quadrilingual edition: Polish, German, French and Russian. The following year, in English and in other languages, always with the same desire: to help achieve a fairer and more peaceful world. As he used the pseudonym Dr Esperanto, 'he who has hope', his work would be known as 'the international language of Dr. Esperanto', which would later lead to 'Esperanto'. In a few years dozens of clubs and publications in the new language had been created, mainly in Europe.

At the beginning, those interested in Esperanto were predominantly Jews from the Zone of Residence, many of them speakers of Yiddish variants and aware of the importance of neutral communication between different language groups. Secondly, those who had studied a previous project (Volapük) also switched to the new language, more democratic and easier to learn than the one created by the German priest Schleyer, who considered it as personal property. A third group was formed by the followers of the pacifist writer Lev Tolstoy, who had openly expressed his support for Esperanto.

In fact, many will be the links between Esperanto and pacifism (Lins 2000; Alcalde 2021). For example, most of the winners of the Nobel Peace Prize between 1901 and 1914 were related to the international language, such as Alfred Fried and Henri La Fontaine. Zamenhof himself would be a candidate for this prize eight times. As far as other Nobel recipients of this period are concerned, worth mentioning are Wilhelm Ostwald (chemistry), Romain Rolland (literature) and Charles Richet (medicine).[3] Meanwhile, Jules Verne imagined in his last (unfinished) book a not-too-distant future in which Esperanto is effectively used as an international auxiliary language.

Esperanto conquered intellectuals because of its rationality, with sixteen grammar rules easy to assimilate. Nouns ended in -o, adjectives in -a and adverbs in -e. It was a phonetic language, to each spelling corresponded one phoneme and to each phoneme a single spelling. There were no exceptions. Most of the roots were taken from the Romance languages, but they were also present in Germanic and Slavic languages. The idea was that a person with knowledge of an Indo-European language could intuitively understand the meaning of *lingvo*, *internacia* or *demokratio*. The use of the derivation made it easier for words to be learned, not through memory, but through logic. Thus, the prefix mal- created antonyms, so that the adjectives *granda* and *alta* were transformed into *malgranda* and *malalta* to mean small and low. This gave the language a great expressive capacity, developed through a remarkable literary production, first as translations and then as original creation.

Pioneers of internationalism

At the turn of the twentieth century, the centre of the Esperanto movement moved to Paris, the city of light. In 1905, the first international Esperanto congress took place in France, with 688 participants from all over the world. Without interpreters, they carried out all kinds of activities. Zamenhof was appointed Knight of the Legion of Honour, and Esperanto, until then a written language, became a spoken language. Since then, annual meetings brought together people aiming to contact other people from different countries, with whom they shared interests.

One of the groups interested in an international language was the railway workers. Because of their profession, they travelled frequently and experienced limitations in communicating with the local population. At the Barcelona congress in 1909, they created the *Internacia Asocio de Esperantistaj Fervojistoj*, with the following objectives: to promote Esperanto among railwaymen, to create a specialized dictionary, to promote international relations within the framework of their profession, to publish a list of addresses for their members, to facilitate exchanges for children in the non-school period and to help the participation of railway workers in Esperanto congresses. At that time, no other international railway association existed.

The Barcelona meeting also went down in history because it was the first in which there were international floral games. That is, an international literary contest – in Esperanto – which took its name from a medieval Occitan-Catalan event. The jury praised the German poet Marie Hankel, and among the winners there was also a young Carles Riba, who would later become famous as a poet in the Catalan language.

Also in 1909, a mass exercise was held by the Red Cross to see how humanitarian workers could deal with wounded soldiers in a foreign territory during war. A few days later, in Valencia, an accident in which several participants in the congress were involved served to test the practical utility of Esperanto. Afterwards, the magazine of the *Société Française Esperanto-Croix Rouge* would dedicate six pages to this event, describing the relief experience as very satisfactory. Such exercises by the Red Cross had already been tested the previous year in Dresden. Concerned about the growing tensions between the various powers, the international community was preparing itself to face the next war.

In 1908, new professional associations were formed in Dresden. Among them, the one for pharmacists, *Internacia Esperantista Farmaciista Asocio*. Also the association of doctors, *Universala Medicina Esperanto-Asocio*, aware of the vital importance of communication between doctor and patient. In addition, vegetarians used the congress to establish two associations. The fact that the International Vegetarian Union was created in an Esperanto congress shows the close connection between both social movements. As an anecdote, the Esperantist vegetarian association was created two days before the international one.

The *Internacia Scienca Asocio Esperanta* had been created in 1906 at the Geneva congress. There the *Internacia Societo de Esperantistaj Juristoj* was also founded. The latter had three objectives: to facilitate international contacts between jurists, to work through Esperanto to develop international and comparative law, and to write a legal terminology in Esperanto. At that time, there was no other association that put in contact lawyers from different countries.

Meanwhile, different religious groups were also interested in the possibilities offered by an international language. Following an ecumenical perspective well advanced for its time, in 1902 *Espero Katolika* appeared, a publication which would soon collide with the hierarchy of the church. Since then, several associations not only of Catholic Esperantists and of Protestants, but also within other religions, have been created. Worth noting are the cases of spiritualism in Brazil, the Japanese religion Oomoto and an Islamic faith known as Baha'i. All three had prophets who had spoken about the need for a neutral language of communication, and had some Esperantists among their most prominent members.

In fact, already at the first Esperanto congress in 1905 in Boulogne-sur-Mer there were groups that launched international associations. For example, the Freemasons at the time founded an international lodge, *Espero Framasona*, whose working language was Esperanto. Known Esperantists who were also Freemasons are Alfred Fried (Nobel Peace Prize Laureate), Charles Richet (Nobel Prize Laureate for Medicine), Henri La Fontaine (Nobel Peace Prize Laureate), Wilhelm Oswald (Nobel Prize Laureate for Chemistry), Wilhelm Molly (future founder of an Esperanto micro-state) and Gaston Moch. All of them were also convinced pacifists. Such a strong relationship between Esperanto and pacifism was embodied in the *Internacia Societo Esperantista by Paco*. Established by the French serviceman Gaston Moch, this association sought to promote Esperanto among pacifists, as well as pacifism among Esperanto speakers. Many of the leaders of the Esperanto movement were members of this association, such as Hector Hodler and Edmond Privat (founders of *Universala Esperanto-Asocio* (UEA)), the eminent mathematician Carlo Bourlet, Professor Théophile Cart (future president of the *Akademio de Esperanto*) and the writers Antoni Grabowski, Marie Hankel and Henri Valienne, initiators of the Esperanto literature.

In 1914, war broke out, a hard blow to all internationalist ideals. But it also evidenced the need to increase friendly contacts between people from different countries, with the aim of avoiding future wars. Multiple initiatives proliferated. In 1918, Alexander William Thompson and Norman Booth, two young British soldiers in a French battlefield, created the *Skolta Esperanto-Ligo*. Until then there was no international association to unite Boy Scouts. Their founder Baden-Powell also recommended them to learn Esperanto.[4]

A world to discover

The emergence of Esperanto in 1887 made it possible for people to consider having international contacts, thus overcoming linguistic barriers. Two years later, the first *adresaro* [the suffix -aro indicates 'set of'] was published with 1,000 addresses, 919 of them in the vast Russian Empire and the rest in Germany, Austria-Hungary, England, the United Kingdom, France, Sweden, the United States, Turkey, China, Spain and Romania. Successively more complete versions of this Esperanto agenda would be published. It was a useful tool for correspondence between people from different countries, who often achieved some local popularity. Exhibitions of letters and postcards from the most diverse places were common, a practice that would continue until the arrival of the internet.

Once the usefulness of Esperanto for international correspondence was established, a wide range of options opened up, such as travelling. The first Esperanto traveller was probably the Swedish Valdemar Langlet, who in 1895 began a series of long horseback crossings through Russia, Turkey, Romania, Austro-Hungary and Germany. Esperanto allowed him to meet Lev Tolstoy, whom he visited on several occasions at his residence in Yásnaia Poliana. Langlet described these trips in several books (see Langlet 2004 and 1935), but also in *Lingvo Internacia*, the most important magazine of the Esperanto movement until 1914, published monthly in Odessa – then in the Russian Empire and now in Ukraine.

The reading of these texts revealed fraternal contacts through the international language and encouraged other people to cross borders and meet their correspondents. For most of them, it was the first time that they practised Esperanto in a spoken way and they too wanted to write about their own experiences in *Lingvo Internacia* and in other publications. These writings are emotional and enthusiastic, halfway between surprise and admiration. Even those who visited the land of their ancestral enemies (Russians/Swedes, French/Germans, etc.) often pointed out that they had been treated with affection and generosity, understanding each other superbly through Esperanto. With an anthropological curiosity, they showed the customs of their hosts and highlighted the attractions of the places visited.

On another front, Langlet was a pioneer in another type of internationalism of a more intimate nature. In 1899, he married the Finnish Esperantist Signe Blomberg, thus forming the first international marriage between Esperanto speakers. The wedding trip was to the exotic Samarkand, combining again Esperanto and adventure. After Signe's death, in 1925 Langlet married another Esperantist, Nina Borovko, the daughter of his Ukrainian friends Nikolai and Antonina Szalko-Czajkovska. Nikolai had learned the language in Siberia as a soldier in exile and had subsequently met Antonina at the Yalta Esperanto club. As far as Antonina was concerned, she had been the Esperanto guide in Crimea for Langlet and his colleague Erik Etzel, beginning a friendship that would last a lifetime.

Meanwhile, Esperanto flourished in Paris. The local association, with more than 1,000 members, was divided into different sections, and groups existed in all the districts of the city. Every year more than a hundred courses took place, and every day it was possible to attend an Esperanto evening, in which foreign visitors often participated. In 1911, one of the usual comrades was the Russian Vasilij Nikolajević Devjatnin, who was then living in Paris. In the summer of 1912, Devjatnin would achieve notoriety by walking nearly 2,000 kilometres with Romano, a Turkish fellow-Esperantist, to participate in the Esperanto congress in Krakow. His experiences during these forty-two days of the journey were published shortly afterwards in *Propaganda piedvojaĝo al la Oka Internacia Esperantista Kongreso*, a book that also included photos of the author with the Esperantists he met along the way. As the title indicated, the purpose of the trip was to promote the international language. For this reason, Devjatnin and Romano gave conferences in the cities they visited, and also held interviews with the local press. After the congress, Devjatnin stayed in Germany working on different Esperanto projects. However, in 1914 he became an enemy overnight and he would spend the entire war as a prisoner of war near Leipzig, where he taught the Zamenhof language to German officers, earning a salary for it.

Other famous travellers at this time were the Dutch Abraham Mossel and Gerard Perfors. They were young socialists, pacifists, vegetarians, atheists and radical teetotallers. With light luggage and great ideals they intended to travel the world for eight years, learning about different cultures from a humanistic perspective. In Amsterdam, they enrolled in an Esperanto course, the instrument that would allow them to carry out their plan. Inspired by their enthusiasm, the teacher of the course, Frans van der Hoorn, decided to sign up for the trip also. All three departed in July 1911, with great public attention. After crossing the Alps, they were joined in Vienna by Marie, Gerard's fiancée. In 1912, the Balkan War surprised them, but they continued their way. They crossed into Egypt and walked through the Ottoman Empire until they reached Palestine. There they worked in the Jewish colonies and continued to explore the Middle East. When the Great War broke out, Gerard and Marie Perfors decided to return to the Netherlands. Meanwhile, Mossel continued to walk through Egypt and Sudan to the border with Eritrea. Back in Amsterdam, he published two books: one about his trip through Europe and the other about his time in the Jewish colonies in Palestine, in which he anticipated the tensions that would end up leading to the current Palestinian-Israeli conflict. Van der Hoorn remained in Palestine, where he created a family.[5]

The Great War (1914–18)

The nationalist rise of the European powers on the one hand and the need for the internationalization of scientific research on the other had placed the debate about the auxiliary language among the main issues on the international agenda. It was linked to the intellectual dilemmas of the time, ranging from technological to spiritual issues, from ethnic identities to the so-called Jewish problem and, above all, to the possibility of peace in international relations. Therefore, if there was something that characterized a large part of a social movement as diverse and plural as the Esperanto movement, it was its pacifist vocation. In this sense, it has been argued that, if it had taken place, the World Congress in Paris – scheduled for 2–9 August 1914 – would have been the largest concentration of pacifists in all of history (see Alcalde 2015). But the war broke out and the Esperantists had to adapt to the new situation (Alcalde and Salguero 2018).

There were numerous supporters of the international language among the leaders of the main pacifist currents: scientific pacifism, feminist pacifism, religious pacifism and workers' internationalism. Moreover, anti-war associations such as the International League of Women for Peace and Freedom or the International Office for Peace supported the use of Esperanto for their correspondence and international meetings. In addition, the German priest Josef Metzger created in 1916 the World League for Peace of the White Cross, an international Catholic association that used Esperanto as its working language.

Zamenhof's language was also widely spread among conscientious objectors. For this reason, prominent promoters of the language spent the years of war behind bars, such as the Slovak doctor and writer Albert Škarvan, follower and friend of Lev Tolstoy. For his opposition to military service, Škarvan was arrested several times, the last time in 1915; he would remain in prison until the end of the war. These periods of captivity were conducive to the spread of Esperanto, because this language allowed people who did not have a common language to understand each other in a very short period of time. There were even Esperanto magazines published in prison camps, such as in Rennbahn, Germany. Among those who learned the language as prisoners in Siberia, there were two Hungarians who would play a fundamental role in Esperanto literature: Tivadar Soros – father of the financier George Soros – and Julio Baghy.

Due to the war, many Esperanto periodicals ran into difficulties and some stopped publication. Those that were published, often (although not always) reported events from positions close to pacifism. In 1915, Zamenhof published his 'After the Great War: Appeal to the Diplomats' in *The British Esperantist*.[6] In this text, the initiator of Esperanto proposed the creation of something similar to a United States of Europe, as well as a Permanent European Court established by agreement between all the states. Meanwhile, *Internacia Bulteno* was a bulletin born in November 1914 to report on the war from the official perspective of the German government. Its objective was to counter English, French and Russian propaganda about the cruelty of the Germans and, using their own propaganda, to criticize the enemy.[7]

At another type of frontline, the humanitarian action carried out by UEA is worth mentioning.[8] At that time, it was based in Geneva and from neutral Switzerland reported on the dead Esperanto speakers or prisoners on both sides. In this role as a mediator between citizens of competing countries, UEA collected hundreds of letters daily through their network of local representatives and forwarded them to their recipients. Moreover, in collaboration with the International Red Cross, they tracked people whose whereabouts were unknown, distributed food, clothing and medicine, and helped to repatriate prisoners of war. It is estimated that the total number of this

Internacia Bulteno

Duonmonata informilo pri la milito

La Bulteno estas senpage sendata al interesuloj kaj gazetoj en ekstergermanaj landoj. En Germanujo kaj Aŭstrio-Hungarujo ĝi estas abonebla por 4 M (24 numeroj); unu numero kostas 20 Pf.

Zur Vermeidung der Herausgabe in mehreren Sprachen erscheint dieses Blatt nur in der neutralen Welthilfssprache Esperanto. Dolmetscher für diese Sprache gibt es in jedem größeren Orte aller Kulturländer.

To avoid the edition in different languages, this bulletin appears only in the neutral universal auxiliary language of »Esperanto«. There are interpreters for this language in every place of any importance in the whole civilized world.

Pour éviter l'édition dans plusieurs langues, ce bulletin ne paraît qu'en »Espéranto«, langue auxiliaire universelle neutre. Des interprètes de cette langue se trouvent dans toutes les places de quelque importance de tous les pays civilisés.

Per evitare l'edizione in più lingue, questo giornale verrà pubblicato nei paesi neutrali in lingua »Esperanto«. Interpreti per questa lingua si trovano facilmente nelle città di qualcuno importanza dei paesi civili.

Con et fin de extender la publicación en muchos idiomas aparece esta hoja solamente en los paises neutrales en el nuevo lenguaje »Esperanto«. En todas las ciudades de alguien importancia de los paises cultos, hay interpretes para este idioma.

Redakcio: Friedrich Ellersiek, Berlin S 59, Wissmannstrasse 46
Administracio: Esperanto-Zentrale, Dresden-A. 1, Struvestr. 40

N°j 1—3   1a de Novembro   1914

Enhavo: Kion ni volas — La radikoj de la milito — Anglujo deziris la militon — Anglujo kiel protektanto de neŭtralaj ŝtatoj — La germana imperiestro al prezidanto Wilson — La imperia kanceliero von Bethmann-Hollweg al Ameriko — La stato de Belgujo komence de Septembro — La tragedio de Loewen — La vero pri Loewen — La kanonpafadon sur la katedralon de Reims — La katedralo kiel artileria apogilo — „Times" kontraŭ „Times" — Milita kroniko — Diversaĵoj — Diversaj bildoj intermetitaj

Figure 4.1 *Internacia Bulteno* was an Esperanto-language periodical published in Berlin between November 1914 and January 1919, which reported on the war from the official perspective of the German government and was sent internationally free of charge.

Figure 4.2 Postcard sent to an Italian POW at Theresienstadt, December 1917.

type of services could have exceeded 100,000 annually. Meanwhile, the Red Cross distributed thousands of copies of a detailed vocabulary with a translation into the international language of the main health lexicon in different languages, designed for those who in times of war had to give or receive help in ambulances and hospitals. The YMCA Christian youth association also distributed thousands of books for learning Esperanto among the imprisoned soldiers of both sides.

Among all the human losses suffered during the war, Zamenhof's death, on 14 April, 1917, stands out for obvious reasons. Affected by the consequences of a militaristic evolution that touched him very closely – a few months earlier his younger brother Alexander had died at the front – he would not live to see most of his descendants perish in the Holocaust.

What if there had been no war?

By studying the evolution of the Esperanto movement, it is possible to imagine situations that could have changed the course of history. What would have happened if the First World War had not broken out? Up until the summer of 1914, Esperanto had gained in relevance and its future looked promising. The scheduled Paris congress had more than 3,500 registered participants, and this was not the only Esperanto project that was cut short by the war. Another one was a micro-state located between Belgium, Germany and the Netherlands.

Following Napoleon's defeat at Waterloo, the European powers met in Vienna in 1815 to redraw the borders more aligned with the new distribution of power. One of the hot spots was a valuable zinc mine between the Netherlands and Prussia. Failing to reach an agreement, they decided that Neutral Moresnet would be a neutral territory jointly administered by both kingdoms, and, since the independence of Belgium in 1830, by Prussia and Belgium. When the mine was exhausted in 1885, various initiatives were presented to revitalize it. The most successful one came from the mine doctor, Wilhelm Molly, inspired by the French Esperantist Gustave Roy. They wanted to create *Amikejo*, the first Esperanto state. Both being Freemasons, the proposal had humanistic roots, close to pacifism and the search for international brotherhood. As a consequence, the language began to gain support among the 4,000 inhabitants of Neutral Moresnet, the number of 135 speakers was soon reached, the press echoed the idea, and the creation of the Esperanto micro-state was considered imminent. Finally, in August 1908 the birth of *Amikejo* was proclaimed. However, neither Belgium nor Prussia renounced their rights and both refused to recognize the new state. Despite this, its promoters continued to defend its existence. During the war, Germany invaded Belgium and the neutral territory was annexed. Subsequently, the Treaty of Versailles decided that it belonged to Belgium, and it has been this way since then, with the exception of a brief period during the Second World War, in which Germany annexed the territory again.

Among the Esperanto projects of these years, worth mentioning is *Parkurbo Esperanto*, a garden city near Munich. The aim was to harmonize the urban world and nature, following the ideas of the English urban planner and musician Ebenezer Howard, who himself was an advocate of Esperanto. As a reaction to the poor quality of life and high rental prices in industrial cities, the proposal was to create small cities, structured around neighbourhoods surrounded by countryside, close enough to each other to enjoy a wide range of services and with affordable prices for all social classes. Each neighbourhood would be economically self-sufficient and governed by its own inhabitants. In addition, it would protect itself from speculation by non-construction land of communal property. In different periods, Howard's ideas would be put into practice and some garden cities were created, most of them as suburbs or administrative districts added to existing cities. But the case at hand never came to fruition.

According to its promoters, *Parkurbo Esperanto* would have a library, school, theatre, casino, business centre, church, restaurant, summer residence, youth centre for the teaching of Esperanto, a monument to Zamenhof, and many green spaces. It would be a cosmopolitan and innovative city that would go beyond racial, national, religious, political and socio-economic conditions, in which everyone would have the same rights and in which Esperanto would play a structuring role. Thus, in each family there should be at least one Esperanto speaker. Behind the project were lawyers, architects, doctors and even nobles, but also teachers, such as Vasilij Devjatnin – who worked in Munich after his Paris-Warsaw walking journey – and workers such as Leopold Schlaf, founder of the German Labor Party Esperanto-Association. In 1912, the banker Bernhard Wilhelm Schuler financed the purchase of land similar in size to hundred soccer fields. Soon after, forty houses had already been sold. The plan was to use an international lottery to complete the financing. However, when Schuler's brother (and partner) died in 1914, Schuler decided not to continue his economic activities. Furthermore, enmities between nations made international transactions increasingly difficult. And the project collapsed.

On another front, the economic potential of the language had become evident and Esperanto was taught in many chambers of commerce. In this context, an international currency was created: the *speso*. Proposed in 1907 by Genevan mathematician René de Saussure,[9] it was intentionally designed small to avoid the use of fractions. 1,000 *spesoj* (or 1 *spesmilo*) was equivalent to 0.5 dollars, 2 shillings, 1 rouble, 2.5 francs and 2.5 pesetas. Payments were made by cheque. Two banks that issued international cheques with their value indicated in this currency were the banking group *Schweizeriche Bankverein* (Society of Swiss Banks) and the Genevan bank Pictet.[10] Similarly, postcards printed by UEA stated that the shipping costs were four *spesdekoj*. Also the catalogues of the specialized bookstores, the subscription to the magazines and the price of membership of the Esperanto associations were priced in *spesmiloj*. During international conferences, these cheques were paid, including restaurant bills. The main supporter of this currency was the *Ĉekbanko Esperantista*, founded in London by Herbert F. Hoveler, an Esperantist patron of German origin, known for having published in a score of languages a pocket edition of the keys or *ŝlosiloj* of Esperanto grammar. On 30 April 1914, this bank had 730 clients in 320 cities in 43 countries. However, the war made its activities impossible and in 1918, after Höveler's death, the bank stopped trading. All the creditors were repaid, but the *speso*, *spesdeko*, *spescento* and *spesmilo* stopped being used.

Summary and conclusions

At the turn of the twentieth century, debates surrounding the possibility of an auxiliary language were a main topic of international discussion, including the support of various Nobel Prize winners. Esperanto became an essential part of internationalism. In the absence of other types of transnational associations, Esperantists provided direct contact to different groups. Railway workers, doctors, vegetarians, Freemasons, Catholics, scientists, scouts, lawyers and pacifists of different nations took advantage of the Esperanto congresses to meet and debate. Their dimension as pioneers is highlighted by the fact that in some cases they created associations in absence of any other means of international contact between them. Moreover, encouraged by the possibilities offered by the neutral language, audacious individuals decided to embark on adventurous trips on foot, on horseback or by bicycle.

Esperanto's expansion finished because of the war, a traumatic experience for all ideals of brotherhood and solidarity. Mostly pacifists, Esperantists had to adapt to the new context. They performed humanitarian acts in collaboration with the Red Cross, and they carried out information services via Esperanto publications. But what would have happened if there had been no war? Would diplomatic relations have been fraternized? Would a network of friendly cities have spread? Could a more humane economic system have been achieved?

Violence shakes consciences and new projects can also emerge from the ashes of destruction. In fact, the interwar years were a golden age for the supporters of the international language, which spread among the elites (e.g. in the League of Nations), but also in the labour movement in countries such as Germany, Russia and Spain. Then came the persecutions by dictatorships under a different sign, but this is another story, which will be told another time.

Last but not least, we saw that scholars such as Garvía or Gordin provided groundbreaking findings about events that happened more than a hundred years ago. Paradoxically, this has only been possible because other researchers overlooked the relevance of Esperanto in particular moments of history. Arguably, we are faced with a case of presentism. That is, as a common perception today is that the language and its community play a marginal role in the current society, many historians have projected such perception into the past, neglecting in this way its relevance in multiple dimensions of social, cultural and intellectual history. To a certain extent, this chapter also has benefited from such academic myopia.

Notes

1 A similar perspective is followed in other academic environments, such as the Special Chair of Interlinguistics and Esperanto at the University of Amsterdam, the post-graduate programme in Interlinguistic Studies at the University of Poznan (which came into being at the Institute of Linguistics), the *Gesellschaft für Interlinguistik* or Society for Interlinguistics in Germany, and the Interlinguistics' section of the peer-reviewed journal *Language Problems and Language Planning*.

2 Eco (1995).

3 More recent Nobel recipients who spoke Esperanto include Linus Pauling (chemistry and peace), Daniel Bovet (medicine), Isaac Bashevis Singer (literature) and Reinhard Selten (economics).

4 After the war, teachers and professors founded *Tutmonda Asocio de Geinstruistoj Esperantistaj*, and blind people created *Universala Asocio de Blindaj Esperantistoj*, the first international association to put them in contact with each other. Both associations were born in 1924 during the Vienna Esperanto congress. Also in 1924 the *Internacia Radio-Asocio* was founded, which dealt with radio applications and reached a high level of popularity, since it allowed people to exploit the potential of Esperanto as a remote communication tool.

5 After the war, Esperanto travellers proliferated again. Some examples are as follows: the Belgian libertarian Gassy Marin, who travelled the world for ten years; the French Lucien Péraire, who travelled the Eurasian continent by bicycle for four years; the Swiss-American Joseph R. Scherer, who visited forty-one countries in three years; the Frisian-Dutchman Sipke Stuit, who travelled on foot throughout Europe with his wagon; the Indian Sinha Laksmiswar, who taught the international language in Sweden, Estonia, Latvia and Poland. All of them described their experiences in a number of books. Meanwhile, the talented blind violinist and writer Vassili Eroshenko spent a decade in India, China and Japan, where he met the American Agnes B. Alexander, who was promoting Esperanto and Bahaism in Eastern Asia. It is precisely these two passions that Lidia Zamenhof, the youngest daughter of the creator of Esperanto, would foster in her travels through Europe and the United States.

6 vol. 11 (123): 51–5.

7 There were also multilingual war documents, such as *Germany's first crime in France, before the declaration of war. The Joncherey Affair (Belfort territory) of Sunday, August*

Second 1914. Written by Julien Mauveaux, secretary of the Committee for the Erection to the monument of Corporal Peugeot, it was published in Latin, French, English, Esperanto and Ido. I thank Julian Walker, who kindly sent me a copy of this valuable document.

8 Apart from UEA, other Esperanto associations participated in humanitarian work. One example is *Itala Katedro de Esperanto* (IKE), who edited postcards to be sent to prisoners of war, such as the one reproduced here, which was sent to an inmate in Therezienstadt in December 1917. IKE had been founded in 1912 by Achille Tellini, a naturalist, geologist and linguist from Udine, and it was the first body officially dedicated to promoting the teaching of Esperanto in Italy. With the entry of Italy into the war, the Italian Esperanto movement underwent a strong downsizing. In 1915, *Federazione esperantista italiana* (FEI) was established temporarily at the Bologna headquarters of IKE. Thus began a strong collaboration between the two associations. Meanwhile, during the war Tellini made numerous propaganda speeches in Venice and Emilia-Romagna, as well as organized dozens of fast Esperanto courses.

9 René de Saussure, brother of the linguist Ferdinand, was a fundamental figure in the Esperanto movement. Among other contributions, he offered the basic principles of creating Esperanto words: necessity and sufficiency.

10 The first has been part of USB, a Swiss financial services company based in Zurich, since 1998. The second also continues to exist today, as a major private bank.

References

Alcalde, J. (2015), 'The Practical Internationalism of Esperanto', special issue on *Pacifists during the First World War, Peace in Progress*, 24: 1–8.
Alcalde, J. (2021), 'The Esperanto Movement and Pacifism in Zamenhof's Time: A Special Relationship', in V. Beckmann and L. R. Feierste (eds), *Language as Hope: L. L. Zamenhof and the Dream of a Cosmopolitan Wor(l)d*, Berlin: Hentrich & Hentrich.
Alcalde, J. and J. M. Salguero, eds (2018), *Antaŭ jarcento. Esperanto kaj la unua mondmilito*, Paris: SAT.
Barandovskà-Frank, V. (1995), *Úvod do interlingvistiky*, Nitra: SAIS.
Blanke, D. (2018), *International Planned Languages: Essays on Interlinguistics and Esperantology*, edited by S. Fiedler and H. Tonkin, New York: Mondial.
Eco, U. (1995), *The Search for the Perfect Language*, translated by J. Fentress, Oxford: Basil Blackwell.
Fians, G. (2019), *Of Revolutionaries and Geeks: Mediation, Space and Time among Esperanto Speakers*, University of Manchester: unpublished doctoral thesis.
Forster P. G. ([1985] 2012), *The Esperanto Movement*, De Gruyter Mouton.
Garvía, R. (2015), *Esperanto and Its Rivals. The Struggle for an International Language*, Philadelphia: University of Pennsylvania Press.
Gobbo, F. (2015), *Interlinguïstiek, een vak voor meertaligheid*, Oratie 532, Amsterdam: Amsterdam University Press.
Gordin, M. (2015), *Scientific Babel*, Chicago: The University of Chicago Press.
Jespersen, O. (1931), 'Interlinguistics', *Psyche* 11: 57–67.
Kuznetsov, N. (1987), *Теоретические основы интерлингвистики*, Moscow: University of peoples friendship.
Langlet, V. ([1898] 2004), *Till häst genom Ryssland*, London: The Long Riders' Guild Press.

Langlet, V. (1935), *On Horseback through Hungary*, London: Hutchinson and Co. [First published in 1934 as *Till häst genom Ungern*. Stockholm: Wahlström & Widstrand].

Lins, U. (2000), 'The Work of the Universal Esperanto Association for a more Peaceful World', *Esperanto Documents* 45 (A), Rotterdam: Universala Esperanto-Asocio.

Lins, U. (2020), *Dangerous Language*, London: Palgrave Macmillan.

O'Keeffe, B. (forthcoming), *Tongues of Fire: Esperanto and Languages of Internationalism in Revolutionary Russia*, London: Bloomsbury.

Rapley, I. (2013), *Green Star Japan: Internationalism and Language in the Japanese Esperanto Movement, 1906–1944*, Universty of Manchester: unpublished doctoral dissertation.

Schor, E. (2016), *Bridge of Words. Esperanto and the Dream of a Universal Language*, Princeton: Metropolitan Books.

Schubert, K., ed. (1989), *Interlinguistics: Aspects of the Science of Planned Languages*, Berlin and New York: Mouton de Gruyter.

Tonkin, H., ed. (1997), *Esperanto, Interlinguistics, and Planned Languages*, Lanham: University Press of America.

UEA, Jarlibro (1908), *Jarlibro de Universala Esperanto-Asocio*, Geneva: Universala Esperanto-Asocio.

Wandruszka, M. (1982), *Interlinguistik: Umrisse einer neuen Sprachwissenschaft*, Munich: Piper Verlag.

5

Scenarios and projections in First World War phrasebooks

Julian Walker

The structure of First World War phrasebooks came from different directions, including language teaching books, travellers' phrasebooks, civilian engagement aids and military manuals. Many of these frequently offered constructed conversations, as a structure for teaching specific constructions or vocabulary, as an aid for travellers to use and understand appropriate phrases, or as imagined scripts for interrogating suspects. A general structure of difference emerges from examination of phrasebooks published in France, Britain, Germany and the United States, suggesting a range of motivations.

British concerns about German militarism influenced the view that German phrasebooks were creating scenarios that encouraged belligerence, even facilitating atrocities, and were seen as indicating Germany's preparedness for an offensive war (Heimberger and Horne 2013; Constantine 2011); they also offered potential for satire (Graves 1915). But this was not exclusive to German phrasebooks: two English-French phrasebooks prepared under crown copyright and printed by HMSO in Britain also offered phrases for threatening locals with death.

A culture of increasingly affordable travel to the continent from Britain, mostly starting in French-speaking countries, meant that by 1914 there was a ready market for English-French phrasebooks for travellers. Opportunist publishing, especially in 1914–15, used conversations and phrases lifted out of peacetime phrasebooks, which, though apparently absurd, had some use for troops behind the lines. In linking the past experiences to potential scenarios in wartime, these texts look both backwards and forwards. In contrast, there were officially published phrasebooks that were more focused on the military experience. A series of French phrasebooks were derived from a tradition dating to Napoleonic campaigns of military interpreters facilitating the accommodation of troops in foreign territory; HMSO-published British publications included phrasebook material in manuals of information about enemy or allied armies and theatres of war.

A range of motivations and sources guided the publication of phrasebooks for soldiers published in Britain. For the most part, these were guides to the use of French, this being the language for which there was seen to be most need, since it quickly became apparent that the majority of British soldiers would be fighting in France or Belgium. For the latter, it was assumed that French was the local language. Some publishers affected to ignore the war entirely: right up to 1918 *The Briton in France* (Rees, D.) was offering details of the boat train from Harwich to Antwerp and Brussels. Many of the phrasebooks published for soldiers were little more than convenient travel-based phrasebooks with additional military glossaries; whilst the pages on buying stamps, ordering tea and getting collars ironed look absurd in the context of industrialized warfare, this was the reality for many junior officers, nurses, staff officers and logistics personnel not many miles back from the trenches, in an environment where tea, clothes and entertainment were symptomatic of the incongruous geographical and physical hiatus. No primary evidence has been found to indicate that this directly proposed a way of behaving behind the lines, but it provided both a model for and a reflection of countless anecdotes of junior officers having tea twenty miles from the fighting, in quiet French gardens, or taking a nurse to the theatre. 'We want to see the Zoological Gardens . . . Is there a good music hall? Can one take a lady there?' asked *What You Want to Say in French and How to Say it*, by W.J. Hernan in May 1915 ('War Edition'). This book had been originally published in 1909, but had supposedly undergone 'a complete reconstruction and amplification by a vocabulary of military words and phrases' with suggestions from the War Office.

Editorial decisions by publishers of phrasebooks might show personal political positions, might be arbitrary or the result of rushed publication, might indicate underlying feelings or be a directive towards military actions and attitudes. Whilst a booklet for children to learn French (Palmer, E., *L'Entente Cordiale*, 1916), sponsored by Bostock's Circus, gives prominence to the Entente Cordiale, *Uncle Jack's Travel Talk* (Stomm, M., 1915), a phrasebook in English, French and German, had been published in Bristol by the *Bristol Times and Mirror* in twelve editions by the time they decided in 1915 to drop German in favour of Italian; however, the military glossary in this publication appears only in English and French. The discovery and republication of the *Tornister Wörterbuch Englisch* (actually *Englisches Tornisterwörterbuch mit genauer Angabe der Aussprache, English knapsack dictionary with precise pronunciation*, as reproduced on page 4 of the British republication), allegedly found in the possession of a captured German soldier in January 1915, provoked both outrage and ridicule, outrage at the cold-blooded material for implementing a plan for invading England and ridicule for its inappropriateness, its clumsiness and its hubris. It was republished by *The Echo & Evening Chronicle* as *The Hun's Handbook* in 1915, with cartoons by Charles Graves (of *Punch*) of short-sighted Germans slowly reading out 'The mayor will certainly be shot', or in a shop holding up the book and asking the indignant assistant, 'Have you got socks?' Graves' version successfully demotes the invasion plan cum phrasebook to caricature, whilst the reality of most German phrasebooks was more complex. Certainly some of the material provided military personnel with the linguistic means to conduct an invasion. The preface to *The Huns' Handbook* proposed that the description in the text of British Army uniforms as those in use in 1912 proved a pre-war publication date, and thus a pre-war invasion plan – 'its publication does set up a strong presumption that it was authorized for the use of a German expeditionary force destined for the invasion of England'; the captured phrasebook thus became part of British propaganda. *The Echo & Evening Chronicle* either did not or pretended not to know that the German book had been published in 1914.

The preface to *The Huns' Handbook* begins with the words 'Still another testimonial to the thoroughness of the German preparations for war with Great Britain is to be found in the shape of . . .', and later states that 'we now know that there exists an English-German war lexicon intended for one purpose and for one purpose only, viz. as a guide for a German Army of occupation in Great Britain when the "Tag" comes'. Yet this intention was supposedly not only for British circumstances, since versions in German-French and German-Russian proposed that 'one may assume that Germany held in readiness three striking forces with which to take each of the Entente Powers by surprise when the hours should sound'. Whilst there were indeed German-French and German-Russian phrasebooks published in 1914, it is not known whether these were published after August; what is noticeable is that ahead of the Schlieffen plan no German-Dutch phrasebooks were published to facilitate communication in Flanders, nor were any phrasebooks mentioned in the Report of the Committee on Alleged German Outrages (The Bryce Report), published in May 1915.

A more balanced set of scenarios appears in *Franzosich für Offiziere und Manschaften* (*French for Officers and Men*, Stuttgart, 1916), which offers a course in French as well as specimen conversations: 'Pardon, monsieur, voudriez-vous avoir la bonté de m'indiquer un salon de coiffure/Bitte, würden Sie die Freundlichkeit haben, mir anzugeben, wo ein Barbierladen ist?' (Please sir, would you be so kind as to direct me to a hairdressers'). Following are typical examples of more military conversations:

> Est-ce que des troupes enemies ont passé par ici? Oui, hier, beaucoup d'infanterie et d'artillerie a passé. Quelle direction ces troupes ont-elles prise?
>
> Sind hier feindliche Truppen durchgezogen? Ja, gestern kam viel Infanterie und Artillerie hier durch. Nach welcher Richtung zogen sie weiter?

> (Have any enemy troops passed by here? Yes, yesterday, lots of infantry and artillery passed by. Which direction did they go?).

Or, under the heading 'Cantonnement/Einquartierung' (Billeting):

> Eh bien! Préparez tout, dans environ trois heures, les troupes seront ici. Encore quelque chose, gardez-vous bien de ne rien entreprendre contre nos soldats. La population civile n'a rien à craindre; mais si elle prend part à la guerre, toute la commune en sera rigoureusement puni.
>
> Nun, gut, richten Sie darauf ein, in ungefähr drei Stunden sind die Truppen da. Noch eins. Hüten Sie sich, irgend etwas gegen unsere Leute zu unternehmen. Der Zivilbevölferung wird von uns fein Haar gefrümmt; sehen wir aber, daß sich die Bevölferung am Krieg beteiligt, so wird es der ganze Ort aufs Schwerte zu büßen haben.

> (Well! Prepare everything, in about three hours the troops will be here. One more thing, be careful not to do anything against our soldiers. The civilian population has nothing to fear; but if it takes part in the war, the whole commune will be rigorously punished.)

The threat of reprisal and execution against non-compliant civilians has become a long-term trope of this aspect of German phrasebooks, from *The Hun's Handbook* to *Si Vous Mentez Vous Serez Fusillé*, a reprint of a German-French phrasebook published in 2013. It derives from entries in phrasebooks such as the *Kriegs-Dolmetscher für Soldaten* (1914) series by Franz Wolfson, such as 'Lügen Sie nicht oder Sie werden erschoffen/ne mantez pas ou vous serez fusillé' (Do not lie or you will be shot), which appears under the subject heading 'Spione' (Spies), or 'Wenn Sie lügen werden Sie erschoffen/If you tell a lie you will be shot', in the *Soldaten-Sprachführer* series (1914) by Siegfried Haasmann. Further phrases give an impression of officiousness and a sense that the Germans had a clear idea of how to conduct an invasion: 'Lugen Sie nicht, das Dorf scheint sehr wohlhabend zu sein/Don't tell a lie the village seems to be a wealthy one', 'Wenn Sie alles zeigen, haben Sie nichts zu befürchten/If you show us everything, you have nothing to fear'. German memories of *francs-tireurs* from the 1870--1 war have been seen as motivational for the nervousness and extreme violence against civilians in the invasion of Belgium in 1914, and here we see the process scripted before the event. In contrast, in July 1916 German soldiers facing the British on the Somme were given a list of expressions in transcribed form to use when taking prisoners – 'Hands opp ju fohl', 'Arms ewa', 'Is anibodi inseid?' [inside a dugout], 'Kom ohl aut, quick, quick', 'Honds opp, kom on Tomy' and 'Go on, go on' (quoted in Duffy, C, *Through German Eyes*, 2007: 38). Given that by this stage there would have been fewer of the German troops who had returned from migration to English-speaking countries, such transcriptions were probably necessary; however, they indicate a lack of aggression and fear as regards the fighting enemy that is absent in the earlier 'invasion' phrasebooks.

The preface to *The Hun's Handbook* makes a point that the book could not be attributed to the German government; nor were there official imprimaturs to Wolfson or Haasmann's publications, which were formulaic in their use of the same phrases for publications across a range of languages including Russian, English, French and Polish. However, there was no lack of officialdom in the publication of *Short Vocabulary of French Words and Phrases With English Pronunciation* issued with Crown Copyright, and printed 'under the authority of His Majesty's Stationery Office' in 1915; quite distinct from the travel-oriented books, this publication offers 'Have any troops passed through here? Have German troops been quartered here lately? What numbers had they on their shoulder straps?' However, it also explicitly envisages a situation where local civilians might be hostile: 'Take care; take the shortest road, and if you lead me wrong you will be shot.' Just as the German publications envisaged sabotage from Belgian and French civilians, the British military authorities had direct experience of dealing with people suspected of being or satisfactorily proved to have been spies and passers of information, and phrasebooks provided for such scenarios.

Official publications in Britain by HMSO included phrasebook sections as part of the information provided to assist troops to understand their situation. Thus, *Notes on the Turkish Army, with a short Vocabulary of Turkish Words and Phrases* contains sections on parts of the army and its organization, uniforms, weapons, logistics, titles and ranks, and the civil administration. The linguistic section of the book, arranged by themes followed by lists of adjectives, verbs, adverbs, prepositions and conjunctions, shows a typical mix of tourist and language-learner material. The questions and phrases cover time and place, weather, introductions and simple statements, and then deal with moving about the countryside, including rivers, forests, hills, billets, inns and railways, indications of the envisaging of a war of movement, as had been envisaged for the campaign in Europe in the summer of 1914. More realistic advice appeared in *Notes on the Italian Theatre of War and Short Vocabulary*, published by HMSO in 1917; the text offers material 'prepared as likely to be of use to men proceeding to the Italian theatre of war' and begins with advice on flies and mosquitoes and how not to annoy local people. A brief history of the war as it involved Italy is supported with a pull-out map. The vocabulary is extensive and military in nature, but the section of phrases translated run alphabetically rather than thematically; this proposes that the book would have been used for learning at leisure rather than resorted to in real life, but it also creates sequences of absurdly unrelated statements:

Bring us coffee with milk	Portateci del caffé e del latte
Bring us the bill	Porateci il conto
Carry this	Portate questo
Clear those houses; we are going to quarter our men in them	Sbarazzate quelle casa; vi vogliamo allogiare I nostri uomini.

Scenario projection was part of marketing the importance of phrasebooks; two versions of *The Soldiers' Language Manual* by 'Ajax' were published in early 1915, one for French and the other for German. The preface to the French edition offered two scenarios, claimed to be true, where knowledge of French either would have or did aid British soldiers cut off from their comrades and fired on by the French, whilst the preface to the German edition proposed the necessity of learning German in order to see through false orders given to advancing German troops by their officers – 'some ruse of the enemy'. The selection of words and phrases translated is almost identical in both volumes, presenting to the soldier about to go to France the idea that he had better be prepared for trouble from both friend and foe. Similar publications, for example those attributed to Captain Keyworth, offered the same set of words and phrases in a range of languages, in Keyworth's case French, Italian, Serbian and German, reinforcing the idea that once across the Channel the British soldier was going to have to face up to talking 'foreign'. Foreign languages reflected the foreignness of people abroad, allies included. Less well-known languages, or less predictable foreign-language scenarios, were likely to revert to the polite suspicion of the European in non-European territory: in *Notes on the Turkish Army with a short vocabulary* (1915) the conversational phrases either defer to local conversational customs – 'How is your honourable health?' ('Mizaj-I sherifiniz nasil dir?') – or expect the deference due from a local – 'Innkeeper, we want a meal. . . . Hurry up, we haven't much time' ('Lokandaji, yemek istiyoriz . . . Chabúk, waktimiz kalmadi').

Despite being Britain's most immediate allies, the French were still liable to stereotyping: the introduction to *How To Speak French* (1914) includes categorizations of race typical of the period, such as 'The French are a Latin race, and quite unlike ourselves . . . the Latin temperament is very different from the Saxon: the Latin peoples are more excitable, more spontaneous, and more easily roused'. This view of French people is reinforced further on, as an inevitable breakdown in comprehension is proposed: 'A Frenchman talks louder and faster, and gets more and more excited, seemingly, the less you understand him.' The solutions offered emphasize this: 'Speak slowly', 'Don't talk so loud', 'Not so loud please', 'Not so fast'. A later-proposed conversation is introduced with 'Supposing that you were accosted by a French soldier, he would probably grip you by the hand, possibly embrace you, and say *Bonjour mon camarade! Comment ça va?* Your conversation would depend on the extent of your vocabulary'. The vocabulary offered next consists of a list of nationalities and the terms for 'the colours', 'the bombardment', 'a bomb', rather than a cordial expression of friendship.

Scenarios in phrasebooks both reflected repeated and expected situations, and, in giving the language, allowed and projected situations; in this, the quality of language to make things real can be compared to the reluctance of soldiers to discuss their experiences with civilians whilst on home leave. At the time, it was widely believed that retelling the experience of being under bombardment could reinvigorate a mental experience, which would be better served by refusing to talk about it; many soldiers suffering from shellshock were advised not to talk about their experiences, as a way of suppressing the trauma (Walker 2017: 285). This sets up the corollary that the creation in words of an experience, a conversation, could act as an encouragement to act within the model of words given. Scenarios should thus provide a key for the use of the book, by whom and to whom; though this is often given in a preface, proposed conversations frequently act primarily in one direction, asking questions and giving instructions. *Franzosich für Offiziere und Manschaften* is an exception, but a more typical example would be Volume 2 of the *Handy Black Cat English-French* series published for Carreras Cigarettes in 1915, which contains a list of around 200 conversational sentences and questions, of which no more than 15 would be spoken by a local. A more pragmatic phrasebook, the *Vade Mecum for the Use of Officers and Interpreters in the Present Campaign* by Eugene Plumon (1915), in the preface to the first edition, given in English in the third edition, states that it is directed at 'Interpreters attached to the British Forces', which by the third edition was extended to include 'even . . . the Officers of the British and Indian Expeditionary Forces'. The direction of the translation, and the languages used, changes frequently in the book, suggesting a range of scenarios of usage. This extensive text, with its stated intention to be of practical application, might be expected to offer the user help in understanding the person he is speaking to, but the four pages of 'Summons to surrender' and 'Questions to be put to prisoners or wounded', which appear only in English and German, offer no answers. The 'various terms and expressions for the examination of a suspect' and the 'Words used to describe a man', which include 'cunning, false, deceitful, hypocritical, frank, loyal, etc.' as well as physical characteristics, are given in French and then English; the book ends with a scenario of the 'Examination of a suspect', given in French and then English, followed by 'Model of report about a suspect, with a short description of same', given entirely in English, as if written by a French interpreter attached to a British regiment.

The interrogation of prisoners or suspects provides a useful scenario for comparison: *Notes on the Turkish Army with a short vocabulary* (1915) offers a few short phrases, no questions that actually interrogate the prisoner, but just orders, warnings and threats. *English-Flemish Military Guide*, published in Poperinghe, Belgium, in 1915, ends with 'Examination of a suspect', including questions such as 'Are you liable to military service?' and 'Are you in touch with anybody of this district?', but offers no possible responses. It is unlikely that many British interrogators would have found such answers easy to recognize, even if phonetic transcriptions had been included, which rather questions the point of the section; it may have served to help the interrogator show some authority, though without any phonetic transcription the interrogator would have been left like Graves' cartoon soldiers in *The Hun's Handbook*, struggling to ask for a pair of socks. However, the fact that the *English-Flemish Military Guide* was published within range of German artillery might explain that it carries a single page of phrases to do with shopping, among the forty of military expressions and questions. It was perhaps inevitable that phrasebooks published away from the Front should be less pragmatic.

Of the less well-known languages, Esperanto had an uncomfortable position in this environment; largely carrying a reputation of international fraternity pre-war, Esperanto in wartime was associated with the Red Cross and communication with prisoners of war. *An Esperanto/English/French/Dutch Phrasebook*, published in Britain in 1916, written by A.J. Witteryck, carried an overpaper on its front cover stating that it was 'designed to help the growth [of Esperanto] and to bring us into close touch with our French and Belgian Allies'. Witteryck was the president of the Belgian Esperanto Association, and involved with Belgian refugee aid in Hastings, so unsurprisingly the book facilitates the Belgian experience in Britain, with guides to passing through customs and asking for a train to London, showing a similarity to pre-war tourist phrasebooks.

In the first months of the war, the accommodating of Belgian refugees in Britain created the need for a Flemish-English phrasebook. E.V. Bisschop's *Dagelyksche Hulp Voor Belgen in Engeland* was published in London in October 1914, and marketed as being the only one of its kind, and thus essential for British hosts. 'Do you want to help the Belgians?' asked an advertisement for the book in *The Daily Mail* (19 October 1914), and an advertisement in *The Manchester Guardian* (7 November 1914) claimed that 'To help the Belgian refugees you must be able to converse with them in their own language, and to enable you to do this you must have a copy'. Bisschop's preface states the book is 'to help during the first days of [the refugees'] stay in England' with words chosen that the 'traveler in a foreign land invariably meets with'; the selection of terms appeared to recreate a tourists' book complete with pronunciation guide, with sections on food and drink, and 'engaging apartments' ('*y ri-grett Y kan not tee-ke zhis apaartmeunt*'); but it ends incongruously with a bilingual list of military terms, as if needing to acknowledge the overarching presence of war as its raison d'être. Bisschop's publisher, Leopold Hill, also published a Flemish-English/English-Flemish pocket dictionary and a *Shops and Shopping Phrase Book*, together advertised to help purchasers 'Converse with our allies the Belgians' (advertisement, *The Manchester Guardian*, 12 December 1914). The context of shopping and supposed foreign travel attempted to normalize the situation, with the military glossary, and the conflict itself, put into parenthesis; deference to the refugees' situation and good manners create a different story from the atrocity stories flooding the newspapers at the time. *Le Ménage belge en Angleterre/Belgisch huishouden in Engeland/Belgian House-keeping in England*, by Mary Margaret Clapham (1915) attempted to further normalize the situation by concentrating on food and household management; designed for households where Belgians and locals would have to get on together, recipes for scones and cottage pie, as well as instructions on how to clean the flue of an English stove, offered the picture of mutual learning through cooperation in the domestic sphere, ignoring the reality of increasing separation, suspicion and resentment. A similar avoidance is seen in *Useful Flemish phrases for Red Cross Work*, published by November 1914, which contained phrases relating only to physical conditions, reflecting the lack of awareness at this stage of the war of how sustained shelling affected the minds of soldiers; one of the absurd rhymes in E.F. Harris' *Active Service French Book* (1915a) trivializes shellshock as 'Vous avez Les nerfs maladies, Il faut vous Prendre du repos' ('Your nerves Are wrong, You must Rest').

In October 1914, Abbé H. Delépine's *What a British Soldier Wants to Say in French and How to Pronounce it* was published in both France and London, with a later edition published only in France; its preface instructed the soldier reader to 'learn a few sentences in this booklet, and ask some French people how to pronounce correctly the words between parentheses'. The second edition advertised *Familiar French*, 'an indispensable pocket guide' to terms 'commonly used in French conversation, the Slang of the French and British Armies, etc', furthering the idea that in this environment English and French speakers could be brought together by language learning. The preface declares that this book would 'provide that confident touch to your French, and supply the right word in the right place every time', and offer access to language 'in common use by the French, but never to be found in the books'. Delépine suggests then that the phrasebook itself is a basis for starting conversations, which could move into the comfortable use of slang, a novel idea, but one based on correspondences that were uneven; linking 'bully beef' with '*singe*', for example, missed the contempt of the French term, and the whole idea missed the reality that the appropriate use of slang is very delicate and based on the recognition of social nuances. Delépine presents scenarios between two privates (with stage directions), and a dialogue between two officers, all with class-appropriate slang. The agenda of the closer relation between soldiers of the two nations, manifested in easy use of each other's slang, is seen in the desire for a happy ending: 'let me hope that when the war is over you will come to see us in England; everyone at home will give you a hearty welcome'. A later American phrasebook, the *Oxford English and French Conversation Book for Army and Navy Men* (1917), also gave a glossary of slang expressions, recognizing that 'nearly all men use slang', but that it was 'to be used only . . . among men'; again the problem of the appropriate use of slang between speakers of different languages is not addressed. There is an implicit agenda in both books though, that the trying out of each other's slang as an act of sharing and respect could bring people closer together.

By 1917, those responsible for composing phrasebooks for American soldiers appeared to have learned from earlier publications that tourist material was probably unlikely to give a good impression. As in Britain, commercial sponsors found the soldiers' phrasebook a good area for self-promotion under an act of patriotism. *The Soldiers' French Phrase Book*, sponsored by Felt and Tarrant Manufacturing of

Chicago, starts with general salutations, including the rather formal 'Madam, permit me to introduce Mr X', which must have raised a smile for most American soldiers in its attempt, stated in the preface, to 'communicate the common wants, wishes and desires of everyday military and social life'. After some stilted attempts to fix English to fit French constructions – 'I have not his canteen/Je n'ai pas son bidon', 'Why have you two uniforms?/Pourquoi avez-vous deux uniformes?' – the average soldier would have felt more comfortable with 'I am ravenous/Je meurs de faim' and 'We stayed downtown last night/Nous sommes restés en ville hier soir'. 'Practical French and German phrases' were on offer in the *Kolynos 'Parley Voo Booklet'* (Maude, F., and F. Scudamore, F., n.d.), sponsored by a well-known toothpaste company. Exhortations in the booklet to keep the teeth clean whilst on active service place the idea of competence in both French and German in the wider field of soldiers' health, embracing the social with the physical. The jokey title was no doubt a good sweetener, but every entry in the booklet could have been used, from 'he is blinded' and 'the bandage has shifted' to 'a sparking plug' and 'God save the King, and the Republic, and the Allies'. *Speak French – A Book for the Soldiers* published in Cleveland, Ohio, in 1917, also gives realistic sets of questions and answers, not just for asking and showing the way, and for shopping, but for asking about a shot-down German aeroplane. The book goes on to give two quite poignant texts, part monologue, part dialogue, in which a soldier talks about not being able to see, but having to keep moving in the rain.

Rapid-Fire English : French : German, published in 1917 by Harper & Brothers, offered little in the way of scenario beyond what might be gleaned from a sequence of statements and questions: 'an aeroplane', 'an airship', 'a biplane', 'an aviator', 'the engine', 'the propeller', 'she is ascending', 'she is descending', 'I hear the engine', 'she has fallen', 'she is in rage' [*sic*], 'she is out of range', 'is it a zeppelin?', 'I want some gasoline', 'my machine is damaged', 'my engine is missfiring'. A sequence on slang is a glossary of French slang, presumably with the intention of aiding recognition. The book's intention is stoutly declared on the front cover – 'For the soldier going to the Front', and 'How to Make Yourself Understood Anywhere in France, Belgium or in the enemy's country' – and the title page states that the book has been 'compiled by a committee of well-known teachers from actual experience of soldiers' needs'. The back of the research copy used for this chapter contains a different scenario, handwritten by the then book's owner:

Vous pas venir hier soir
Vous me ne rencontrez hier soir

Je vous aime	I love you
Je vous aime avec/de tout mon coeur	I love you from all my heart
Je vous aimerai toujour ma Cherie	I you shall love forever my darling
Ou allerons nous?	Where shall we go?
Ou rencontrerons nous?	Where shall we meet?
Attendé ici pour moi.	Wait here for me.
Quelle est le signification de . . .?	What is the meaning of . . .?
Voulez vous aller a la theatre avec moi?	Will you go to the theatre with me?
Asseyé vous.	Sit down.

For all the errors, the scenario planned for here is clear, and quite possibly realized; it was also one which few phrasebooks wished to address. The non-American spelling of 'theatre' here suggests that the book may have passed into non-American hands; the desired scenario was one which did not observe national boundaries. A more cynical corresponding view in *La Vie Parisienne* (October 1917) shows a young woman half-wearing a nightdress, reclining with a French-English dictionary, from which she selects the words 'Goodbye', 'to bed', 'love' and 'dollar'.

Where one might least expect to find a scripted romantic encounter between local and soldier would be in the Eastern Mediterranean theatre of war, but this is where two appear in phrasebooks prepared by Egyptian writers. A reviewer in the *Londonderry Sentinel*, 11 March 1916, clearly enjoyed reading these scenarios between Egyptian women and British soldiers, 'marked by all the impetuous fury which is supposed to characterise passion in these climes': 'Come here girl'; 'Yes, sir'; 'What is your name?'; 'My name is Hanem'; 'You are pretty and gentle, and sympathetic, too; I love you so much'; 'I love you too, sir.' At this point, the writer plans for things to go quickly sour: 'You are a liar'; 'You are a cunning' [*sic*]; 'You love me for my money.' A reversal of mood – 'Your cheek is rosy' – is followed by the offer of money for a kiss. Zaki's text begins with 'You are a pretty girl. Give me a kiss' and 'I love you very much', followed by 'Good-bye my darling' and 'I hope to see you again'; there is melancholy written into this encounter – 'Give me your address', 'Write me always', 'Forget me not', 'I never forget you', 'My heart is always for you', and 'God keeps you', in the style of sentimental wartime postcards.[1] There is a lot in these that is disturbing, their acceptance, offering, and promotion of colonial and gender power relations, their scripted mix of aggression and tenderness, and overwhelmingly the sense of a moment and a chance of romance, or sex, to be grasped. Both texts also offer scripts for getting away from persistent demands for money, including 'I have spent all my money on beer' and 'Get away, donkey'. Aside from the attitudes expressed here, the phrasebook treatment of languages within colonial environments, as distinct from trained officers' proficiency in languages in the areas they were stationed in, would have caused further problems. Liesbeth Zack points out that failures in translation, grammar and transcribing dog Frank Scudamore's *Arabic for our Armies* (1915), which begins with an unexplained disparaging reference to Egyptian Arabic as 'bastard Arabic': 'It is clear that the many problems of this booklet, such as faulty translations, incorrect grammar, and botched transcriptions, cannot have done anything to improve communication between the British and the Egyptians, and must even have complicated it further' (Zack 2016: 20).

The apparent pragmatism of the interrogation of prisoners in phrasebooks or the American soldier's own scenario planning contrasts strongly with the projection of war almost as an opportunity for language learning rather than the reverse, implicit in one of the anecdotes in the preface to E.F. Harris' *French For The Front*, incorporated within the *Active Service French Book* (1915); the anecdote concerns a British soldier who was detached from his unit and fought alongside the French, the experience determining him to learn their language. This sense that learning a foreign language might be a beneficial outcome of service abroad is evident too in *Speak French – A Book for the Soldiers*. The imperative of the title underlines the book's hope that 'the student who has mastered the contents of this book, though knowing quite a little French, will no doubt desire to perfect himself'. Harris taught French to service personnel by means of rhymes, which in his phrasebook descend at times into doggerel, where the war resembles a pantomime script:

Aidez-moi,	Help me,
Je vais	I am going
Creuser	To dig
Une tranchée	A trench

Or

Il y a des tirailleurs dans le jardin,	There are sharpshooters in the garden,
Derrière les haies;	Behind the hedges;
Ils sont là, depuis le matin;	They have been there all the morning!
Tirez, ou prenez les!	Fire, or take them!

Harris' preface begins with the idea that this book would be wanted by soldiers 'returning to the Front', who had already experienced the lack of French, and presumably the reality of being under shellfire; despite rhymes that describe being in trenches and wearing gas respirators, Harris sometimes imagines, and thus projects, a war of movement, of Germans arriving and leaving towns, which was perhaps the case in the summer and autumn of 1914, but not in November 1915, when the title was registered at the British Museum.

If Harris' take on the war through rhymed scenarios seems absurd, this was also the case in phrasebooks which provided unintentional humour, through either the sequence of phrases or the sequences that happened through avoiding creating a scenario. H Buller's *The Soldiers' English–German Conversation Book* (1915) offered a sequence that ran as follows:

I am an airman
I have an aeroplane
There goes an airship
It is ascending
It is descending
I wish to make a flight
My aeroplane is damaged
Is the engine damaged?
No, a wing is broken

The British Soldiers' Anglo-French Pocket Dictionary (1915) offers two pages of phrases in alphabetical order, the inevitable jumping between subject matter creating a bizarre apparent sequence of thought:

Can you put a button on my coat?
Cease fire
Come in

Do you know?
Do you know where the enemy has gone to?
Do you speak English?
Entrance forbidden
Give me . . .
Give me something to drink
Give me two boiled eggs if you please
He is German

Other absurdities were inherent in the pattern of the multilingual phrasebook itself. What set of circumstances would occasion a British soldier to say in German, 'Help me to dig a trench' (*The Soldier's Word and Phrase Book*, 1915), or any Allied personnel to say in Turkish 'Will you take a hand at piquet? With pleasure, but I very seldom play' (*Manuel de la Conversation Française, Anglaise, Turque & Russe*, 1917)? The inclusion of occasional exhortations or toasts at the end of phrasebooks might usefully provide the Serbian for 'Long live the King of Serbia' (*Easy Serbian for Our Men Abroad*, 1915), or the French for 'Let us hope peace will soon be declared' (*How to Say it in French*, 1914), but what governed the selection for translation of 'It's a long long way to Tipperary' into Swahili (*First Aid to the Swahili Language, for the Use of His Majesty's Forces in East Africa*, n.d.)?

Despite the chaotic and bizarre editorial choices, most phrasebooks gave sentences indicating careful treatment of the wounds in the language of the opposing forces. Sentences expressing the reality of combat are rare, and often unrealistic, reflecting the point that most phrasebooks would be used in calmer situations – Ajax's scenarios of soldiers under fire from their allies proposes that the remedy would have been to learn French beforehand. The most resolved scenario offered is that in Buller's 1915 *The Soldiers' English–German Conversation Book*, which ends with a section 'Tommy in friendly talk':

After the fight	Nach dem kampf
Enemies must be friends	Feinde mussen freunde warden
Here is a restaurant	Hier ist ein speisehaus
Let us dine together	Essen wir zusammen
This is my chum	Dies ist mein kamerad
A table by the window	Ein tisch am fenster
German beer is good	Deutsch bier ist gut
Your good health!	Auf Ihr wohl!
A happy return home!	Auf eine glueckliche heim kehr

Such a scenario was easier to imagine away from the Front; indeed, phrasebooks may have been published with an awareness that they provided a vicarious experience of campaigning for a civilian market – Leopold B Hill publishers advertised two phrasebooks and a war information book pointing out that 'the three following books are being eagerly bought by Officers and Men, Belgian Refugees, French People, and the General Public'[2] just as much as they provided soldiers in training with 'norms of conduct for the engagement with civilian populations'.[3] Certainly, the publication of the phrasebooks away from the Front proposed a circumstance of civilian awareness of the need for soldiers' linguistic preparation, of soldiers being gifted phrasebooks in order to derive some benefit, even enjoyment, from campaigning as well as to survive it. In Buller's text, a pulling back from the entrenched positions of patriotism and the mindset of killing indicates that phrasebooks were a space for considering the wider nature of what was happening. Rather than the caricature of the scripted Hun preparing to invade England, a German soldier might learn in Haasmann's *Soldaten-Sprachführer* 'We are no barbarians, as people often say in France and in Belgium'.

Notes

1 From a review of *British Soldiers' Colloquial Arabic Pocket Guide* by Mohammed Hammam and *The Pocket Book of English-Arabic-French Self Study for the British Soldiers in Egypt* by A.H. Zaki in *The Londonderry Sentinel* 11 March 1916.
2 *Publishers' Circular*, 19 September 1914, p. 250.
3 Constantine (2012: 154).

References

Constantine, S. (2011), 'War of Words: Bridging the Language Divide in the Great War', *War in History*, 18 (4): 515–29.

Constantine, S. (2012), '"If an Inhabitant Attacks, Wounds or Kills a Soldier, the Whole Village Will Be Destroyed": Communication and Rehearsal in Soldiers' Phrasebooks 1914–1918', *Journal of War & Culture Studies*, 6 (2): 154–68.

Duffy, C. (2007), *Through German Eyes*, London: Weidenfeld & Nicolson.

Graves, C. (1915), *The Huns' Handbook*, London: The Echo and Evening Chronicle.

Heimburger, F. and J. Horne, eds (2013), *Si Vous Mentez Vous Serez Fusillé : Manuel de conversation à l'usage du soldat allemande*, Paris: Vendemiaire.

Zack, L. (2016), 'Arabic Language Guides Written for the British Army during the British Occupation of Egypt, 1882–1922', in D. Schmidt-Brücken, S. Schuster and M. Wienberg (eds), *Aspects of (post)Colonial Linguistics: Current Perspectives and New Approaches*, 1–26. (Koloniale und Postkoloniale *Linguistik/Colonial and Postcolonial Linguistics*; No. 9), Berlin: Walter de Gruyter.

Primary sources

'Ajax' (1915), *The* Soldiers' Language Manual by 'Ajax', London: Marlborough.

Biolet, W. (1916), *Französisch für Offiziere und Manschaften*, Stuttgart: Violet.

Bisschop, E. V. (1914), *Dagelyksche Hulp Voor Belgen in Engeland*, London: Leopold B Hill.

Buller, H. (1915), *The Soldiers' English–German Conversation Book*, London: T Werner Laurie.

Clapham, M. M. (1915), *Le Ménage belge en Angleterre / Belgisch huishouden in Engeland / Belgian House-keeping in England*, Cambridge: W. Heffer & Sons.

David-Bey, M. (1917), *Manuel de la Conversation Française, Anglaise, Turque & Russe*, Paris: Albin Michel.

Delépine, H. (1914a), *Familiar French*, Wimereux: Delépine.

Delépine, H. (1914b), *What a British Soldier Wants to Say in French and How to Pronounce It*, Wimereux: Delépine.

English-Flemish Military Guide (1915), Poperinghe: Sansen-Vanneste.

First Aid to the Swahili Language, for the Use of His Majesty's Forces in East Africa (n.d.), Nairobi: YMCA.

Forbes, N. (1915), *Easy Serbian for Our Men Abroad*, London: Kegan Paul, Trench, Trübner & Co.

Fursdon, F. (1914), *How To Speak French*, London: Simpkin, Marshall, Hamilton, Kent.

Haasmann, S. (1914), *Soldaten-Sprachführer* (series), Leipzig: Hachmeister.

Hammam, M. (n.d.), *British Soldiers' Colloquial Arabic Pocket Guide*, Cairo: Matar.

Harris, E. F. (1915a), *Active Service French Book*, London: Marlborough.

Harris, E. F. (1915b), *French For The Front*, incorporated within *Active Service French Book*, London: Marlborough.

Hernan, W. J. (1915), *What You Want to Say in French and How to Say It (War Edition)*, London: W J Hernan.

How to Say it in French (1914), Bristol. Arrowsmith.

Maude, F. and F. Scudamore (n.d.), *Kolynos 'Parley Voo Booklet'*, Connecticut: Kolynos.

Notes on the Italian Theatre of War and Short Vocabulary (1917), London: HMSO.

Notes on the Turkish Army, with a Short Vocabulary of Turkish Words and Phrases (1915), London: War Office.

Palmer, E. (1916), *L'Entente Cordiale*, Hythe: Bostock's Circus.

Plumon, E. (1915), *Vade Mecum for the Use of Officers and Interpreters in the Present Campaign*, Paris: Hachette.

Rapid-Fire English: French: German (1917), New York: Harper & Brothers.

Rees, D. (1918), *The Briton in France*, London: Siegle, Hill & Co.

Scudamore, F. (1915), *Arabic for Our Armies*, London: Forster Groom & Co.

Sherman Kidd, R. (1917), *Oxford English and French Conversation Book for Army and Navy Men*, Chicago: Stanton & Vanvliet.

Short Vocabulary of French Words and Phrases With English Pronunciation (1915), London: HMSO.

Speak French – A Book for the Soldiers (1917), Cleveland: Goldsmith.

Stomm, M. (1915), *Uncle Jack's Travel Talk*, Bristol: Bristol Times and Mirror.

The Handy Black Cat English-FrenchDictionary & Phrasebooks (series) (1915), London: Carreras.

The Soldiers' French Phrase Book (1917), Chicago: Felt and Tarrant Manufacturing of Chicago.

The Soldier's Word and Phrase Book (1915), London: G G Harrap & Co.

Useful Flemish Phrases for Red Cross Work (1914), London: Hugo's Language Institute.

Vertongen, E. (1915), *The British Soldiers' Anglo-French Pocket Dictionary*, Aldershot: Pickance.

Walker, J. (2017), *Words and the First World War*, London: Bloomsbury.

Witteryck, A.-J. (1916), *An Esperanto/English/French/Dutch Phrasebook*, London: Simpkin, Marshall, Hamilton, Kent.

Wolfson, F. (1914), *Kriegs-Dolmetscher für Soldaten*, Leipzig: Helios.

Zaki, A. H. (n.d.), *The Pocket Book of English-Arabic-French Self Study for the British Soldiers in Egypt*, Cairo.

Part II

Language and identity

Introduction to Part II

Constance Ruzich

The First World War brought together languages, dialects and idiolects previously separated by space and social distance; the chapters in this part look beneath the literal surfaces of verbal texts to explore the significance of writers' and speakers' language use. As Declercq and Walker have noted, language choices not only reflect and shape perceptions of war, but can themselves 'become battleground and weapon' (Declercq and Walker 2016: 6). Far more than a tool of communication, language may also function as a tool of oppression, a symbol of resistance, an expression of status, an instrument of persuasion, a sign of affiliation or a mark of otherness. Language both provides and denies access to power, community and culture.

War zones (both spatial and temporal) are contact zones, and two chapters in this part examine autoethnographic texts 'in which people undertake to describe themselves in ways that engage with representations others have made of them' (Pratt 1991: 35). Julia Ribeiro S. C. Thomaz's chapter, '"*O belo dizem que é beau*": The choice of poetic language, performed identities and imagined communities in the First World War', explores the language choices of bilingual authors and their insertion of other languages into poetic texts. Thomaz asserts that the choice of language(s) in which texts are written reveals significant markers of identity and affiliation. The chapter notes that for authors such as the bilingual Breton soldier Yan-Ber Calloc'h the decision to write war poetry in the Vannetais dialect of Brittany was a political act in support of Breton identity and autonomy, as well as an attempt to shape political recognition and French national policy after the war. In '"Authentic Histories" and racial insults: Memoirs on African-American soldiers in the First World War', Chris Kempshall examines competing written portrayals of African-American soldiers and their military service. Kempshall compares and contrasts Arthur W. Little's *From Harlem to the Rhine: The Story of New York's Colored Volunteers*, a book authored by a white veteran and aimed at white readers, with histories of the war written by African Americans: W. Allison Sweeney's *History of the American Negro in the Great War* (1919) and Kelly Miller's *Authentic History of the Negro in the World War* (1920). Little's memoir, written from the perspective of a white military officer, purports to provide an account 'of a race that I have learned to understand and respect' (Little 1936: vi), yet it reproduces negative stereotypes of African Americans as unintelligent, irresponsible children. The accounts authored by black historians, however, although including similar representations of African-American dialect, stress the heroism and sacrifice of black troops. These histories of the war argue that the sacrifice and service of African Americans have earned them more equitable treatment: African Americans' participation in the war fought 'to make the world safe for democracy' entitles them to the full rights of US citizenship.

As Julian Walker has stated in *Words and the First World War,* 'Language . . . operated as a major determinant in the making of national identities' despite the fact that 'several of the states involved in the Great War had many languages' (Walker 2017: 148). Chapters authored by Kuldkepp, Ilea and Hutečka examine divisions that were marked by language differences, many of which had existed prior to the war but were exacerbated and/or highlighted by the global conflict. Jiri Hutečka's chapter 'Politics of words: Language and loyalty of Czech-speaking soldiers in the Austro-Hungarian army' examines language diversity within the Austro-Hungarian Empire. At the start of the war, military policy accepted and ensured the rights of various language speakers within the Empire, but as the war progressed, language use became increasingly politicized, and language became a tool of identification rather than communication, linked to regional and ethnic identities and loyalties. The newly recruited officer corps of the Austro-Hungarian army were over-represented by German speakers, many of whom came to view Czech-speaking soldiers as disloyal and cowardly. As Czech-speaking troops became targets of humiliation and insult, they began to question their loyalty to institutions that degraded them. Thus, the Austro-Hungarian military's response to the use of the Czech language inflamed separatist feeling and unintentionally encouraged the Czech nationalist movement. In 'Romanian writers who fought in the First World War and how the Great War shaped their works', Cristina Ileana Ilea focuses on the post-war writing of three Romanian authors, two of whom were soldiers and the other who wrote of his brother's experience in the Austro-Hungarian army and of that brother's execution when he deserted after being ordered to fight against fellow Romanians. Ilea examines proper nouns in three novels and argues that the names given to characters (and withheld from others) offer symbolic commentary on ethnic loyalties, religious affiliations, status and influence. Finally, Mart Kuldkepp in 'The 1915 German-Estonian phrasebook as an interface of German-Estonian language contact and a vehicle of annexationist propaganda' argues that phrasebooks are not neutral texts, but rather predictive ones that anticipate contact and social relations between groups. In the case of the 1915 Estonian-German phrasebook (with three print runs totalling 35,000 copies by 1916), the primary aim of the phrasebook was not to assist German troops – who did not occupy the Baltic provinces until 1917–18 – but rather to influence German public opinion and policies. The introduction to the phrasebook and its translated conversational exchanges work to assert Germany history, affiliations and political rights in the Baltic provinces and to promote the agenda of those who sought the reunification and annexation of the Russian-held provinces with Germany.

Together, the five chapters in this part offer fresh insights on the ways in which language, as it represents both allegiances and alliances as well as otherness and outsider status, was a critical marker of individual, communal and national identities in the First World War.

References

Declercq, C. and J. Walker (2016), 'Introduction: Meetings between Languages', in J. Walker and C. Declercq (eds), *Languages and the First World War: Communicating in a Transnational War*, 6, London: Palgrave Macmillan.

Little, A. W. (1936), *From Harlem to the Rhine: The Story of New York's Colored Volunteers*, New York: Covici Friede.

Pratt, M. L. (1991), 'Arts of the Contact Zone', in *Profession 91*, 35, New York: MLA.

Walker, J. (2017), *Words and the First World War*, London: Bloomsbury.

6

'O belo dizem que é beau'

The choice of poetic language, performed identities and imagined communities in the First World War

Julia Ribeiro S. C. Thomaz

Introduction and theoretical framework

As the commemorations of the centenary of the First World War end, the transnational scientific efforts of these years have shed light on the asymmetry between the ubiquity of poetry in Anglophone commemorative culture and the relative omission of poetic texts elsewhere (Winter 1995). This raises broader questions surrounding the nature of the relationships between poetics, historiography and memory. This chapter aims to contribute to this debate by looking at poems as multilingual environments where languages are mobilized not only to represent but also to build identities. By focusing on the primordial choice made by poets – that of which language to write in – and its impacts on identification, this chapter proposes the view of poems neither as purely contextual and transparent historical documents, nor as decontextualized idiosyncratic creations, but as symbolic systems denoting the internalization of cultural patterns and capable of bestowing meaning upon the war itself. Poetry, due to its intrinsically prosodic nature, is at the frontier between the public and private spheres, between cultural and lyrical realities, and is therefore a privileged environment to assess the relationships between languages and identities. The chapter will therefore examine how poets, often bilingual, incorporate different languages into their poetry and how the choices they operate echo imagined communities and performances of the self, investigating links between poetic language and the multifaceted identities of combatant poets.

Two theoretical presuppositions outline this view of the poems of the First World War. The first one is that the war gave rise to a cultural system shared by those who experienced it (Audoin-Rouzeau and Becker 2000). This places poetry within the dialectics of general and individual, as poets internalize, linguistically rearrange and then communicate this cultural system via their poetry. The second presupposition, derived from the first one, is that poems work as cultural patterns, as Clifford Geertz (1973: 93) defines them: 'sets of symbols whose relations to one another "model" relations' between entities or processes 'in physical, organic, social or psychological systems'. This is replicated in a poem, where the relationship not only between symbols but also between the signifier and the signified within the symbols themselves models the experience of war, particularly in terms of the poets' identifications. Geertz claims that the word 'model' in intrinsically polysemic: it can mean both a model of reality, which makes it apprehensible, and a model for reality, capable of organizing social relations. On these grounds, this chapter presupposes that poems should be read as both models of wartime identities, representing them to readers and to the poet himself (the male pronoun is used because the focus on combatant identity excludes women poets from this chapter, and it would be interesting to see whether these conclusions are valid when applied to poems written by women) and models for wartime identities, since the act of writing is a constructive performance of identity.

The idea of a performance of combatant identity is not new. Martin Van Creveld (2008) shows how this is constructed and performed through war games and drills in his *The Culture of War*, whilst in *Combattre* Stéphane Audoin-Rouzeau (2008) looks at the combatant body (as well as the objects extending it and the landscape surrounding it) from an anthropological perspective that includes the embodiment of identity. The performance of a combatant's identity, especially when done through poetry, can also be read using an analogy with Judith Butler's theory about performative gender roles: 'Because there is neither an "essence" that gender expresses or externalizes nor an objective ideal to which gender aspires, and because gender is not a fact, the various acts of gender create the idea of gender and without those acts there would be no gender at all' (Butler 1990: 190). There is a clear difference, however, between Butler's theory and this chapter's argument: Butler posits that the performance of gender roles happens unconsciously and is the product of socializing institutions, whilst the performance through poetry of the different identities discussed in this chapter implies a certain level of consciousness. Nonetheless, it is important to consider poetry as an act of combat analogous to acts of gender, even for anti-war poetry, as these poems construct the identity of a disillusioned combatant forced to fight. Though we presuppose the culture of war exists, the multiple identities performed by a combatant are not given facts, and therefore these acts of combat, amongst which is poetry, construct the combatant's self. Moreover, Butler's vision of the way in which one inscribes the expected essence of an identity on and through one's body as creating the identity itself is based on the post-structuralist premise that utterances and acts of communication should be seen as both word and deed (Butler 2005). This chapter looks at poems as both language and a wartime practice, involving bodies writing whilst fighting (and furthermore writing poetry whilst fighting, which involves different material and cognitive constraints to prose). Looking at poems as a wartime practice also involves being aware of their material existence and of the networks of publishers and intermediates responsible for their publication.

Finally, Judith Butler also draws attention to the difficulty of expressing oneself within the constraints of language and grammar, as this grammar is the framework that offers the individual a possibility of existing, but the individual's existence is not fully determined by language and therefore cannot fully be expressed by it. The poetic work on language can provide a solution for this apparent *aporia*. Jêrome Thélot

(2013) argues that, because poetic work is intrinsically prosodic, poets create their own language. In other words, whilst the code used may be English or French, each poem is written in the poet's own semantics. According to Thélot, this linguistic creation ensures that the poetic gesture is the gesture of a subjective and lyrical self resisting against the external world. This chapter argues that the relationship between this self and the world constructed through the 'combat act' of writing poetry is not one of antagonism, as Thélot suggests, but rather dialectical: the subjective self is trying to understand, bestow sense upon and therefore shape the world around it and, in this case, its experience of war. How does the preliminary choice of this *travail vivant de la poésie* [living work of poetry] described by Thélot, that of which language to write in, intervene in the modelling of and for the world by the poem? Why did Alan Seeger choose the French word to express the rendezvous with death he should not fail? Why did the Italian poets Giuseppe Ungaretti and Auguste Conti choose to publish *La Guerre. Une poésie* and *Guerre Franco-Allemande. Apostrophe d'un Italien à Guillaume II* in French, for example? By examining the incorporation of different languages into poetry in relation to regional, national and allied identities, this chapter aims to shed light on the dynamics between language and identity and on poetry as a privileged source to interrogate it due to its explicitly prosodic nature.

Poetic language and sacrifice: Hernando de Bengoechea

The first case this chapter examines is that of the French-Colombian poet Hernando de Bengoechea, whose choice to write in French was interpreted and used to construct a mythology around the figure of the dead poet. Born in France to Colombian poets in 1889, Bengoechea spent his childhood in Colombia, before moving to Paris in his late adolescence (Achury Valenzuela 1973). Upon reaching adulthood, he had to choose between French and Colombian nationalities, and chose the latter. Nonetheless, he vowed to his friend and biographer Léon-Paul Fargue to fight for France in case a war with Germany broke out (Fargue 1948). This promise allegedly took place in 1910. Were the tensions so high that Bengoechea anticipated the war four years before it was declared? It is also possible that Fargue wrote this promise (by writing about it) in hindsight, to help shape the myth of the young Latin-American poet *mort pour la France*. Whether the promise was real or not, Bengoechea tried to enlist as soon as the conflict broke out, and was assigned to the French Foreign Legion on 21 August 1914. Nine months later, he died in Berthonval on 9 May 1915. Though only his war letters remain and there is no evidence that he wrote poetry during his time as a soldier, his previous poetic work, which had circulated among the Parisian intelligentsia since his return from Colombia, resurfaced after his death : *Les Crépuscules du Matin* was published in 1921 and *Le Sourire de l'Île de France* (prose poetry) in 1924.

His letters offer a sanitized view of life at the front to reassure his loved ones. In them, Bengoechea does not equate the sword and the pen and never establishes an association between combat experience and poetic activity. Though he claims to be fighting for *civilisation* and against *Kultur*, he believes the war entailed a loss of the French language, since the social composition of the Foreign Legion is perceived as rendering it an unfit environment for someone of his class and a place where the beautiful French language is constantly misused. For Bengoechea, there is, therefore, a dissociation between language, especially the prosodic use of language in poetry, and the war. Nonetheless, one year after his death, Marie Heredia, another exponent of the Latin-American literary movement in 1910s Paris, under the pseudonym Gérard d'Houville (1916) , praises his poem *Le Sourire de l'Ile de France* by saying,

> *Bien avant la guerre, il fut conçu, il fut écrit, ce poème tendre et prophétique ; le jeune homme épris de rythme et de beauté qui en mesurait les cadences harmonieuses ne connaissait pas encore les signes précurseurs de son destin. Mais déjà, à cette contrée qu'il choisit comme une femme bien aimée, à ce pays qu'il choisit dans son cœur, il offre sa jeunesse, son ardeur, ses élans, ses espoirs.* (603)

[Well before the war, it was conceived, it was written, this tender and prophetic poem. The young man filled with rhythm and beauty who measures the poem's harmonic cadences did not yet see the signs foretelling his fate. But since then, to this country which he chose as a well-beloved woman, to this country he chose in his heart, he offers his youth, his warmth, his élan, his hopes.]

Another of Bengoechea's biographers, the Colombian Dario Achury Valenzuela (1973), raises an important point about the poet's use of language. He was a bilingual writer, educated in Spanish, who was seemingly able to bend French words to his will and who was sensitive to all the nuances of a very complex second language. The implication is similar to the one in Heredia's homage: if Bengoechea was able to write beautifully in French, it must be because of his love for France, and therefore writing in French and dying for France are two aspects of the same engagement for his adopted country. Neither the fact that Bengoechea's pre-war poetry was filled with tropical imagery and longing for Colombia, that he was born in France and therefore fought for his own land, nor that he did not write poetry during the war have prevented the construction of a myth around Hernando de Bengoechea as a war poet of the Foreign Legion. This myth relies largely on his choice to write in French, though this was unrelated to the conflict itself but rather dates back to Bengoechea's years amidst the Parisian avant-garde. Nonetheless, the war fogs temporalities, and the conclusion to which his friends and biographers come is that he was capable of writing in French because he was capable of dying for France, the insistence being on the poetry as a prolongation of the experience of combat and the ultimate sacrifice, not the other way around. The first example used to illustrate how the choice of poetic language works as a model of and a model for identity is therefore of a bilingual poet who did not choose the language in which he wrote in order to construct and reflect his affiliations, but rather had this choice made for him a posteriori, after his death, in order to construct a myth around his Francophile engagement, prophesized by his previous work. Nonetheless, looking at the relationship between poetry and identity as it is shaped in hindsight and via an external identification renders the constructed nature of this link clearer and more comprehensible before moving on to more complex cases where poets consciously manipulate language in order to assert their own identities.

Poetic language and national history: Edmond Adam

Dismissed from military obligations in 1913 due to muscular weakness, Edmond Adam enlisted as a volunteer in August 1914 and is successively incorporated into different regiments of the engineering corps (*2e Régiment de Génie, 1er Régiment de Génie, 6e Régiment de Génie*). He fights in the Champagne, Artois, Aisne and Marne regions (Archives départementales . . . 1889). During the conflict, he continues to write and study poetry. His poems, mainly written in fixed form, often resort to an archaic language, and were published for the most part in the pacifist revue *Les Humbles*. Two of them bear the title *Rondeau*, in reference to medieval fixed form poems with three stanzas, two rhymes and refrain. They are written in old French, inspired by seventeenth-century compositions (one century after the golden era of the *rondeau*, and this mixture of different poetic traditions is an evidence of how Adam wants his identity as a French poet to be perceived as well rounded). The first one, published in *Soi-même* on 15 June 1918, contains a dedication to French and German powerful men:

> *À trop puissants et trop félons messires tant François que Germains de nostre siècle qui, gardant cul mollement fourré en leur curule, crachent sur nous moult belles et sophisticques parolles, ce pendant que laissent périr povres et honestes copaignons, leurs subjects, pas maschies horrificques, infectes fumées et aultres diabolicques inventions de nouvelle industrie.*

> *Cil qui pourra mieulx que moi dire*
> *De nostre eage grand martyre,*
> *Laschetez de nostre raison,*
> *Et plours en chascune maison,*
> *Que desjà résonne sa lyre.*

> *Lors, qu'il crye treshaut son ire*
> *Si n'est vaine ceste oraison –*
> *Contre coulpables grands messires,*
> *Cil qui pourra*

> *Si n'a paour de pendaison,*
> *Géhenne ou aultre rançon,*
> *Qu'il donne à Diable, qui n'a pire,*
> *Toutes maschines à occire,*
> *Et die à chascun sa chanson*
> *Cil qui pourra.*

[To the powerful and very perfidious sirs, both French and German of our time who, keeping their asses flabbily hidden by their curule seats, spit on us beautiful and sophistic words, as they let poor and honest companions, their subjects, die in horrible combats, in infectious fumes and in other diabolical inventions newly created.// He, who can speak better than me,/Of the great martyrdom of our age,/The cowardice of our time,/and the cries in each house/May his lyre sound immediately.//Thenceforth, may he loudly shout his anger/ – If this prayer is not in vain – /Against the Great who are guilty,/He, who can.//If he is not afraid of hanging,/Of torture or other ransom,/May he give to the Devil, who has nothing worse,/All of the killing machines,/And may he say to each their song,/He, who can.][1]

In this poem, Adam directly attacks both French and German political classes for avoiding danger whilst trying to express combat through a sophisticated rhetoric. The poem is based on an opposition between the beautiful discourse of the powerful and their consent to the deaths of their people by 'horrific machinery' and 'infectious fumes', and can therefore be considered metadiscursive. This metadiscourse is reinforced by Adam's choice of language: by claiming he is the one best suited to communicate the 'great martyrdom' (first stanza) in *ancien français*, he is not only avoiding censorship but also proving his point by showing he is a true Frenchman, capable of using the ancestral language. The choice of poetic language is therefore reinforcing Adam's national identity and legitimizing the act of writing and the text itself.

The same tactic is used one month later, in another *Rondeau*, published in *Les Humbles* in July 1918, one month before the author's death. In the previous issue (June 1918), *Les Humbles* had published Adam's *Poèmes de Tranchées*, three of which, written in German, had been censored. Adam then writes his *Rondeau*, in *ancien français* once again, to assert his French identity and his legitimacy as a French poet fighting for France, and dedicates it to his censor:

Ou mien censeur, qui ès 'Humbles' m'escarbouilla sans aucune raison trois meschants poemes, germains par le seul langage.

Ou mien censeur, ces humbles piès dédie,
Qui tresdoulx mots que chantoye à m'amie,
Sans grand raison durement a beschés,
Pour seullement ce qu'ilz feurent leschés
En pur jargon de la gent ennemie.

Eusse cuidé, si eussent trebuché,
Que de ces pipes feust la coulpe punie,
Et pardonné lors de s'estre fasché
Ou mien censeur !

Ains ne disoient haine ne vilenie ;
Amour chantoient, pudeur, cueur escorché,
Et aultres fleurs en mon ame épanies,
Or' si ces piés icy me veult faulcher,
Les luy mettray où ne fault que je die,
Ou mien censeur !

[To my censor, who, in *Les Humbles*, crushed without reason three poor poems, German but in language./To my censor, I dedicate these humble feet,/Which are very sweet words I sang to my friend,/And which he has without reason harshly injured/For no reason other than their being composed/In the language of the enemy people.//I would have thought, had they been faulty,/That the shame of these bad verses should be punished,/And I would have forgiven the anger/Of my censor!//Yet they speak not of hatred nor of villainy,/They sing of love, modesty, lashed hearts,/And other flowers blooming in my heart./Oh, if he wants to scythe my feet, I will put them where I shall not say,/ On my censor!]][2]

By claiming, in old French, that the poems in the 'enemy tongue' are German but in language, that they are in fact love poems, Adam is proving to the censor that he is a legitimate Frenchman and that the censorship agent's concerns are not only unfounded but also insulting. The choice of poetic language, in Edmond Adam's case, is therefore a matter of national identity, but also one of legitimacy. By writing in *ancien français* whilst opposing his position as a combatant to that of two classes involved in the war but not necessarily physically threatened by it (political classes and censors), Adam equates the legitimacy of first-hand experience of the fighting front and the legitimacy of being a poet inscribed in a long tradition of French poetry, who understands French poetic and linguistic history. His verse is composed in the manner of the baroque poet Théodore Agrippa d'Aubigné (1552–1630), one of the first examples of a French warrior-poet, therefore confirming the heritage into which Adam writes himself. The particularities of the First World War are nonetheless present, especially the hatred of the 'Great' commanding elites, which was increasingly common after the 1917 mutinies. However, this self-writing into French poetic history implies a view of a unified France and an essentialized view of French identity and a continuity between past and present, which does not necessarily resonate with all of the French *poilus*, especially those coming from regions with a history of fighting for autonomy.

Poetic language and regional dynamics: Yan-Ber Calloc'h

Identity politics had always been an important issue in Jean-Pierre or Yan-Ber Calloc'h's life. He was a defender of Brittany's autonomy and of the Breton language. Despite his attachment to his native region, he worked as a teacher in Paris and Reims, and at the start of the mobilization, he did not know whether he should present himself at the recruitment office in Paris or in Lorient (Lagadec 2018). A poet before the conflict, he had published in both French and Breton, under the pseudonym of Bleimor, and the legitimacy of his defence of the Breton language was based on his perfect bilingualism, so, whilst campaigning for autonomy and publishing in regionalist revues, he was also integrated into French society. Yet the war accentuated his Breton identity, and the dialectics that had been formative in his early years, understood in terms of belonging to both the *petite patrie* [little homeland] and the *grande patrie* [big homeland], started presenting itself in terms of the *grande patrie* being indebted towards the *petite patrie*: Brittany's men were dying for France. According to Calloc'h, the war had been responsible for reviving Breton pride, which had been dormant for 120 years. During his combat experience, Calloc'h wrote one poem in French, *Le P'tit Poilu de 1915*, but most of his wartime verse was written in his region's dialect, inspired by his Breton and Catholic upbringing. In 1915, he sent this material to his friend, Pierre Mocaer, asking him to publish this *poésie bretonne* [Breton poetry] in case he died in combat, and these poems form the collection *Ar en Deulin* (Calloc'h 1921). Though he had written in French before the war, Calloc'h's choice of abandoning French verse altogether is a way of exaggerating, whether consciously or not, the performance of his Breton identity, whilst fighting for the French army despite not identifying as a Frenchman. In the case of Yan-Ber Calloc'h, the poetry corroborates Jérôme Thélot's hypothesis of prosody as a means for the poet's intimate 'me' to defy the world, and furthermore of affirming his Breton identity and highlighting the fact that he was not a Frenchman fighting for France but a Breton offering his life for France. The implication is that there must be some kind of compensation for this sacrifice and that the region should benefit from the martyrdom of its men.

Calloc'h sent one of his poems, in Breton along with the French translation, to the daily newspaper *L'Echo de Paris*, which published it on 7 January 1917, three months before Calloc'h's death by shell fragment. This is, to our knowledge, the only poem definitely translated by Calloc'h himself. *L'Echo de Paris* published only the French version of the poem, along with an introduction (Calloc'h 1917):

Les ténèbres pesantes s'épaissirent autour de moi ;
Sur l'étendue de la plaine la couleur de la nuit s'épandait,
Et j'entendis une voix qui priait sur la tranchée :
Ô la prière du soldat quand tombe la lumière du jour !

Le soleil malade des cieux d'hiver, voici qu'il s'est couché ;
Les cloches de l'Angélus ont sonné dans la Bretagne,
Les foyers sont éteints et les étoiles luisent :
Mettez un cœur fort, ô mon Dieu, dans ma poitrine.

Je me recommande à Vous et à votre Mère Marie ;
Préservez-moi, mon Dieu, des épouvantes de la nuit aveugle,
Car mon travail est grand et lourde ma chaîne :
Mon tour est venu de veiller au front de la France,
. . .
Dors, ô patrie, dors en paix. Je veillerai pour toi,
Et si vient à s'enfler, ce soir, la mer germaine,
Nous sommes frères des rochers qui défendent le rivage de la Bretagne douce.
Dors, ô France ! Tu ne seras pas submergée encore cette fois-ci.

Pour être ici, j'ai abandonné ma maison, mes parents;
Plus haut est le devoir auquel je me suis attaché :
Ni fils, ni frère! Je suis le guetteur sombre et muet,
Aux frontières de l'est, je suis le rocher breton.

. . .

(Calloc'h, *L'Écho de Paris*, 7 January 1917)

[The heavy shadows grow thicker around me;/Over the whole plain the night's colour spread/And I heard a voice praying over the trench:/Oh, the prayer of the soldier when daylight falls!//The sickly sun of winter skies, this is what is asleep;/ The Angelus bells are chiming in Brittany,/The homes' lights are out and the stars are shining:/Put a strong heart, oh God, in my chest.//I command myself to You and to your Mother Mary;/Keep me, God, from the horrors of the blind night,/ Because my work is great and my chains are heavy:/It is my turn to watch over France's frontline.//Sleep, oh homeland, sleep in peace. I will watch for your, / And if the German sea swells tonight,/ We are the brothers of the rocks which defend sweet Brittany's shore./Sleep, oh France! Thou shalt not be submerged once again.//To be here, I left my house, my parents;/Higher is the duty I am committed to:/Neither son nor brother! I am the sombre and mute watchman/At the eastern border, I am the rock from Brittany.] [translation by the author]

In the second stanza, Calloc'h describes the evening prayer in Brittany, and his region is associated with the word *foyer* [home]. In the next stanza, France is associated with the front line and with the heavy burden of the watch's sleepless nights, in opposition to the home front of the previous stanza. Another verse reads, 'Sleep, oh homeland, sleep in peace. I will watch for you', and the use of the preposition 'for' instead of 'over' suggests a utilitarian approach to the watch, as well as a dissociation between the land the watchman has under his eyes and the one orienting this utility: in other words, whilst he is watching over French land, he is watching for Brittany. This dissociation is reinforced three verses later, with the repetition of the first verse formula ('Sleep, oh homeland'): 'Sleep, oh France!' The similarities between both verses accentuate the separation between France and the poet's homeland. Despite being initially published only in French, without the original poem in Breton, and therefore not allowing for a direct interrogation of how the choice of poetic language creates and reflects regional identity in the context of the *Union Sacrée* (the ideology of a united French nation fighting against the German invasions despite political, regional and religious divisions), this poem reinforces the affirmation of Calloc'h's Breton identity through the abandonment of French verse in favour of Breton verse in the native dialect of the Vannes region. By choosing to write in Breton whilst fighting for France, Yan-Ber Calloc'h transforms his war experience into the continuation of his political combat for Breton autonomy. This is confirmed by the prosody of *La Prière du Guetteur*, and this contrast between regional and national identity affiliations is reproduced on an international level, especially in the context of Expeditionary Corps fighting for and on territories different from those they consider home.

Poetic language and allied relations: José Alagoinha

José Alagoinha, 2nd Sergeant of the Portuguese Expeditionary Corps, kept a journal (Alagoinha, s.d.) throughout his war experience, and the entry for 20 August 1918 is a poem about his attempts at learning French, written in Brest (Brittany). The poem incorporates French words along with their Portuguese translation in a simple, binary structure:

Dire dizem que é dizer
Voir dizem que é ver
Joli dizem que é bonito
Palavreado tão esquisito
Não consigo compreender

Água chamam-lhe de l'eau
Conquistador conquerant
Não faz mal ça ne fait rien
O belo dizem que é beau
Ao novo chamam nouveau
Être arrivé ser chegado
Boire dizem que é beber
E não consigo compreender
Porque tudo está mudado

(Alagoinha 1918)

[*Dire* they say is 'to say'/*Voir* they say is 'to see'/*Joli* they say is 'pretty'/Such weird vocabulary/I cannot understand// 'Water' is called *l'eau*/ 'Conqueror' *conquerant*/'It's alright' *ça ne fait rien*/The 'beautiful' they say is *beau*/The 'new' is called *nouveau*/ *Être arrive* is 'to have come'/*Boire* they say is to drink/And I cannot understand/Because it all seems to have changed] [translation by the author]

By including French words to highlight the difference between Allied languages and the linguistic barriers faced by the expeditionary forces, dialect-speaking soldiers and colonial troops fighting in France, the poet also highlights the similarities between Latin languages. Having chosen to include French words that are phonetically similar to their Portuguese counterparts, he nuances his argument about how hard it is to understand the French language and draws attention to the Latin identity of allied nations Portugal and France. The same identitarian construction is operated by Guillaume Apollinaire in his poem *À L'Italie*, written when Italy joined the allied cause in April 1915. Apollinaire celebrates the common origins of French and Italian, praising both countries, linguistically and culturally united, as the cradle of *civilisation* in opposition to German and barbaric *Kultur*. By placing two Latin languages side by side, Alagoinha reminds us that whilst the Portuguese are fighting in and for a foreign land, they share a history and values with this land and these are the values for which the war is being fought. The relation established between words in both languages in the poem is a model of and a model for the relationship between Portugal and France, and a model of as well as for the dialectics of Portuguese and allied identities.

Conclusion

Recent historiography of the First World War has been in constant dialogue with other disciplines, especially literature and anthropology, and this has enabled poetry to be appropriated as a source, not in the condition of a transparent historical document, which seems to replace historiography, as Santanu Das (2013) argues, but as a system of symbols and ways of bestowing meaning upon the conflict. These systems should be interpreted as models of and models for identity both representing and constructing imagined communities, as defined by Benedict Anderson (2006), where members do not know each other but within their minds lives the idea of their communion. This cultural and communitarian interpretation of poems could focus on many aspects of poetic creation. However, the choice of incorporating multiple languages into one poem or of writing in a language different to that of the poet's main communication gives particular insight into the multi-layered identity systems operating during the conflict. The very act of choosing to write in one language rather than in another not only represents but also builds identities and inscribes the poet within these imagined communities.

Contrary to Anderson's arguments, which pertain exclusively to 'nation-ness', the cases examined in this chapter serve as evidence of the multiplicity of identities and affiliations the poets were subject to and actors of, both at the infra-national (e.g. regional) and at the supranational (e.g. within the allied forces) levels. Furthermore, they attest to how identity was dependant on a strong sense of temporality, whether within national literary traditions or as a resignification of a poet's biography. Identities are built, performed and inscribed on bodies through poems, as through other wartime gestures, from the moment the poetic creation is conceived and set in motion, and the first and most rudimentary choice operated by poets, that of which language to write in, should be the starting point of any historical anthropology regarding how the experience of combat is modelled in and through poetry. Poems written by bilingual poets or incorporating a language different to that in which the poet usually communicates, or communicated prior to the reality of war, are one of the many multilingual environments of the First World War, and this reflects and helps create the multiple identity constraints combatants were subjected to during the conflict.

Notes

1   Thank you to Marine Charpentier de Ribes, who translated these verses from *ancien français* to modern French. The translation to English is by the author. Marine's expertise in seventeenth-century French verse was also fundamental for the interpretation of the poems and their inspiration.

2   *Idem.*

References

Achury Valenzuela, D. (1973), *Cita En La Trinchera Con La Muerte. Vida y Muerte Del Poeta-Legionario Colombiano Hernando de Bengoechea Muerto En Acción de Guerra Pour La Causa de Francia (1889 -1915)*, Bogotá: Instituto Colombiano de Cultura.

Alagoinha, J. (s.d.), *Caderneta Militar*, https://portugal1914.org/portal/pt/inicio-pt/item/7184-caderneta-de-jose-alagoinha (accessed 13 July 2018).

Alagoinha, J. (s.d.), *Caderno de memórias de José Alagoina*, https://www.portugal1914.org/portal/pt/item/7450-caderno-de-memorias-de-jose-alagoinha#!prettyPhoto (accessed 13 July 2018).

Anderson, B. (2006), *Imagined Communities: Reflections on the Origin and Spread of Nationalism*, Revised edn, London and New York: Verso.

Audoin-Rouzeau, S. (2008), *Combattre. Une Anthropologie Historique de La Guerre Moderne (XIXe - XXIe Siècle)*, Paris: Éditions du Seuil.

Audoin-Rouzeau, S. and A. Becker (2000), *14 - 18. Retrouver La Guerre*, Paris: Gallimard.

Butler, J. (1990), *Gender Trouble: Feminism and the Subversion of Identity*, New York and London: Routledge.

Butler, J. (2005), *Giving an Account of Oneself*, New York: Fordham University Press.

Calloc'h, J. (1917), 'La prière du guetteur', *L'Écho de Paris*, 7 January 1917.

Calloc'h, J. (1921), *A Genoux: Lais Bretons ; Accompagnés d'une Traduction Française de Pierre Mocaër; Introduction de René Bazin, de l'Académie Française; Préface Bilingue de Joseph Loth, de l'Institut*, Paris: Plon-Nourrit et Cie.

D'Houville, G. (1916), 'Hernando de Bengoechea. Un poète soldat au "1er Étranger"', *Revue Des Deux Mondes*, Octobre 1916: 602–15.

Das, S. ([2006] 2013), 'Reframing Frist World War Poetry : An Introduction', in S. Das (ed.), *The Cambridge Companion to the Poetry of the First World War*, 3–34, New York: Cambridge University Press.

Fargue, L. (1948), *Hernando de Bengoechea ou l'Ame d'un poète*, Paris: Amiot-Dumont.

Geertz, C. (1973), 'Religion As a Cultural System', in *The Interpretation of Cultures: Selected Essays*, 87–125, New York: Basic Books Inc.

Lagadec, Y. (2018), 'La Banale Grande Guerre Du Sous-Lieutenant Calloc'h', in S. Carney (ed.), *Comment Devient-on Jean-Pierre Calloc'h?*, 47–77, Brest: Centre de Recherche Bretonne et Celtique, Université de Bretagne Occidentale.

Registre Matricule d'Edmond Adam 1889, Archives départamentales de la Gironde, 1 R 1425 573 –1889-09-04..

Thélot, J. (2013), *Le Travail Vivant de La Poésie*, Paris: Éditions Les Belles Lettres.

Van Creveld, M. (2008), *The Culture of War*, Stroud: Spellmount.

Winter, J. (1995), *Sites of Memory, Sites of Mourning: The Great War in European Cultural History*, Cambridge: Cambridge University Press, especially the chapter 'War poetry, romanticism, and the return of the sacred'.

7

'Authentic Histories' and racial insults

Memoirs on African-American soldiers in the First World War

Chris Kemsphall

After the Negro has proved his value and worth in all of these trying ways, when after this he asks for a full measure of equal rights what American will have the heart or the hardihood to say him nay?

(Miller 1919: 552–4)

In many ways, the experiences of black soldiers in the American Expeditionary Forces (AEF) during the latter years of the First World War greatly mirrored their experiences in American society before and after the conflict. The racial hierarchies, segregations, stereotypes and restrictions that had governed aspects of their civilian lives were swiftly reproduced by the US military to ensure that contact between white and black soldiers was kept to a minimum and that the upper echelons of command remained out of reach.

The notion of utilizing black soldiers within the American Expeditionary Forces (AEF) at all had been the subject of pre-war debate within the United States government and army. Their training was often marked by racial stereotyping and prejudices, and no sooner had the recruited men arrived in France than they discovered they had been traded away to the French. However, their time within the army, both during training and on active service in France, and the aftermath of the war were notable for competing written portrayals of the experience by white American officers, African-American soldiers, and black historians and writers. The use of language by African-American and black writers to explore and reclaim their own experiences and histories often contradicts starkly with the language used by white officers to describe the men under their command, even if those same writers would likely have described themselves as having affection towards their men.

Within this dichotomy lies a profoundly different understanding towards humanity, masculinity and democracy as expressed through spoken and written words. This chapter will endeavour to highlight the nature of this difference, explore how it manifested itself within different written sources and the impact it had on the post-war period.

Recruitment, segregation and African-American voices

African-Americans within the United States at the beginning of the twentieth century inhabited a dual existence, between being 'free' people and also heavily segregated. Whilst the American Civil War had seen the Confederate States amalgamated back into the Union and the end of the institution of slavery, racism in America did not die in the 1860s and would play a significant part in how the US military viewed the make-up of its new army in the lead up to the declaration of war in 1917. As noted by Woodward, 'whilst never voted on' proposals had been placed before Congress 'every year from 1906 to 1916' that aimed to 'prevent blacks from joining the military' (Woodward 2014: 11). Although the necessity of building an American army from, effectively, nothing would see black recruits admitted after war was declared in 1917, there was little effort placed on pretending they were viewed equally or welcomed into uniform.

Whilst General Pershing had been resolute in his desire for the American Expeditionary Forces to serve together as a cohesive army, this desire was soon found not to extend to the black soldiers within the 92nd and 93rd Divisions. The arrival in training camps of the men who would make up the 93rd Division, in fact an incomplete division that would lack supporting or service troops, had initially been delayed in 1917 so that they could complete the picking of South Carolina's cotton crop (Woodward 2014: 180–1). As explained by Chad Williams in *Torchbearers of Democracy*, upon entering the army 'segregation defined many of their experiences, from the quarters they slept in to participation in the Young Men's Christian Association (YMCA) recreational activities' (Williams 2010: 2).

Whilst the spaces provided for black participation were heavily policed, so were the spaces permitted for black voices. Black authors of the period were presented with what James Weldon Johnson described as the 'the material dissemination of black letters in a white supremacist society' as 'a special problem which the plain American author knows nothing about – the problem of the double audience' (Hutchinson and Young 2013: 4–5). The issue with how to write on African-American experiences in a manner that also appeased white readers was further complicated by the American determination to maintain a unified morale on the home front war and the ongoing black struggle for something approaching civil rights. The author Kelly Miller had fallen foul of American censorship during the war when publishing a pamphlet against the lynching of black men whilst the government turned a blind eye. After this pamphlet began circulating in training camps, it was banned in October 1918 on the grounds that it threatened morale and army unity because it 'tended to make the soldier who read [it] a less effective fighter against the German' (*The Chicago Defender*, 19 October 1918). Whilst the war provided an opportunity for black soldiers to accrue new experiences, their opportunity to voice these experiences was effectively restricted.

Simultaneously, white authors who reported on their time with black soldiers would present their work predominantly to a white audience who bore no understanding of general black experience.

Furthermore, the desire to ensure these men avoided contact with white soldiers other than their officers led to African-American soldiers effectively being isolated and then given away by the AEF. When they were moved to France, the African-American soldiers were presented to the French without being required to return to the main American army. Although most served in labour units at docks, along railroads and at other support locations, some 40,000 of the approximately 200,000 of these soldiers who served in France saw combat in the 92nd and 93rd Infantry Divisions. The latter became the only American division to be permanently assigned to a foreign power for the duration of the war. Such was the manner of this transfer that many of the men in these divisions were unaware it was happening until after the deal had been struck (Heywood 1928: 32–3).

If the American military had hoped that this would provide a solution to black soldiers developing a degree of autonomy and confidence, they would, as will be discussed in greater detail below, be sorely mistaken. At the same time, as Richard Fogarty has argued in his excellent book *Race & War in France*, France was not a colour-blind or post-racial society. However, the manner in which France interacted with its black citizens and colonial subjects was a world away from that which African-Americans had routinely encountered back home (Fogarty 2008: 2–6).

Child soldiers

Works created by African-American authors of black experience during the First World War were often politically insistent as an expression of the agency of the writer and draw heavily on the moments of triumph experienced by black soldiers in the AEF and how participation in the war should lead to further emancipation in the peace. As a result, whilst grappling with the aforementioned 'double audience problem', they are often written specifically for black audiences. The inside cover of W. Allison Sweeney's 1919 book *History of the American Negro in the Great War* gives instructions on how best to sell this book to the 'more than 12 million negroes in the United States'. Sweeney's book is, in his own words, 'a thorough race book' which should be sold to 'members of the race first'. Whilst some of the language can be considered publishing hyperbole, the same selling instructions also claimed that the book's publication meant that 'a new era of liberty, progress, and opportunity dawns for every Negro in America' (Sweeney 1919: n.p.). As a result, the audience and readers became an integral part of the author's message.

In even greater detail, Kelly Miller's *Authentic History of the Negro in the World War* is best described not as purely a history of African-American involvement but rather a history of the war designed for African-American audiences. The 'authenticity' of this account came from the fact that it was not simply a retelling of actual black experience but, similarly to Sweeney's book, that it was produced to fulfil the desires of a black audience. To achieve these goals, Miller's 'Authentic History' stretched beyond 700 pages in length. Given the nature of this account, Miller and Sweeney's potential audience was likely expanded by those black soldiers who had entered military service in 1917 and then taken advantage of the educational opportunities offered to them by groups such as the YMCA, something that had also caused consternation among serving white soldiers as will be discussed later in the chapter (Williams 2010: 96–9).

As previously mentioned, Miller was effectively censored in 1918 for using his writing to stoke political activism among the black population. However, upon publishing his 1919 book, Miller used it as an opportunity to not only amplify the successes of black soldiers in the war but to posit what their participation should mean. These achievements and experiences were not inconsiderable. Black soldiers within the regiments and divisions now loaned to the French rapidly discovered that the norms of segregation back home did not apply to French units who 'knew no colour line' and black American soldiers were instructed in the necessity of ensuring that no such line was introduced (Little 1936: 128–30). African-Americans in the 92nd Division came to have excellent relations with their new French allies, and one man reported that he was treated far better by French civilians than he ever had been by men in his own army (Robinson n.d.: n.p.). The 369th Infantry Regiment, composed of black soldiers, was permanently assigned to the French army in April 1918. During their first tour in the trenches, they were paired with the 131ᵉ R.I., and even the white commanding officers noted how the French honoured their new allies by allowing them to fire the first American rounds in their sector before the French commandant declared that 'for many months we have toasted the Americans as our friends. Tonight we shall toast them as our allies!' (Little 1936: 168–71). French commanders would later state their increasing confidence in the black American soldiers under their command upon hearing that they had stood their ground under artillery attack at the end of June (Heywood 1928: 76).

The stories that these men wrote for a predominantly black audience were of achievement, heroism and victory. They were feats to be marvelled at and portrayed a level of acceptance from white Europeans which they had never seen at home. In a lengthy passage in Kelly Miller's book, he declared that after black men had travelled to fight for humanity, no American would now stand before them and declare them as 'a subspecies of mankind' and having 'proved his value and worth in all of these trying ways, when after this he asks for a full measure of equal rights', were these men not deserving of it? (Miller 1919: 552–4). The answer to this question can be found in the memoirs and accounts written by white officers in charge of black soldiers.

In the opening dedication to *From Harlem to the Rhine – The Story of New York's Colored Volunteers*, Arthur W. Little, at the time a major, wrote about how he aimed to add this book and his stories to 'the sagas of a race that I have learned to understand and respect' (Little 1936: vi). But it is important to note that the word used here is indicative of wider trends and racial contexts in these memoirs and accounts. Key here is that 'understand and respect' are not synonymous with 'love' or 'view equally' but might be with 'tolerate'. If anything, it is the language of anthropology; Major Little and other white officers effectively studied black men as objects of scrutiny and then delivered the results of these studies to a white audience. The content of the stories

Major Little tells share similar themes, with the main similarity within them being the apparent childlike stupidity of black men. The notion that there were 'innate mental differences' between the races, with African-Americans viewed as being at the lower end of the scale, was popularized by the 'specious intelligence testing' carried out by 'army-employed psychologists' who conveniently overlooked that the 'illiteracy rates of white soldiers from the Southern states almost equalled those of black soldiers' (Williams 2010: 96–7). With Southern States harbouring ongoing concerns about the use of African-Americans in the AEF the men of the 92nd and 93rd Divisions found themselves heavily mocked throughout their training by white soldiers, and rumours that some had been lynched by white residents of nearby towns often spread through the ranks (Miller 1919: 539; Little 1936: 57–62). In response to one such rumour, black soldiers in a training camp nearly rioted before the two missing soldiers reappeared safe and well. The given explanation for their absence is as follows:

> Suh, Cap'n, Suh, Privates Blank and and So-and-so, A.W.O.L. at *Reveille* Roll Call has Jest reported. Day saiz as how dey turned left instaid of ter der rahght, w'en dey waz er-comin' comin home las' nahght, and dey gits loast, and goes ter sleep in der fiel's, and dey's jest now cum in, Sah, Cap'n, Say. (Little 1936: 62)

The seemingly childlike nature of these men acts to both emasculate them and also strip them of any intellectual agency. Discipline within armed forces has long been rooted in the notion that the men need to be led to ensure order, but this is a step away from that. These soldiers need to be led because they are not truly considered to be men at all. At best they are children, naïve in a manner that hints at a lack of racial maturity as well as intellectual shortcomings. In the eyes of white officers, these men need to be led because they cannot be trusted to take adequate care of themselves.

The written language of these accounts also consistently provides something rarely seen in similar publications. Accounts by British, French and other nationalities only rarely, if ever, reproduce a spoken style in the way that these American publications do. Memoirs like Major Little's are often written by men who appear sympathetic to the experiences of black soldiers, but they are simultaneously written in a manner that suggests that they are to be read out loud and further infantilize the subjects. There is, for example, a noticeable difference in how Major Little, a white officer, in comparison to how Chester D. Heywood, a black soldier, reproduces the speaking style of black southern men in his book *Negro Combat Troops in the World War*. Whilst the men in Major Little's accounts are often portrayed as the butt of a joke they do not understand, those men in Heywood's account are shown as being more worldly wise in examples such as the following where some men had missing equipment during an inspection:

> 'Privitt William Scriggs, sah reports de loss ub two tent-pins, an' a toof brush.'
>> 'Do you want to be left behind when we start for France, Scriggs?'
>> 'No, sah, Cap'n I'se done set ma mine on carvin' up some o'dem Bushes' [Our men always called the Boche 'The Bushes.']
>> 'Ah recon ah kin fine dem missin' equipments somewhere, sah.'
>> 'Don't borrow them from anyone in *this* company, Scriggs.'

'No, Sah,' replies Scriggs, with a smile and a knowing look that bodes ill for some luckless private or N.C.O. in an adjoining unit. (Heywood 1928: 22–3)

The situation of black soldiers making a mistake and being held to account by a white officer is not overwhelmingly different to that seen in Major Little's book, but whilst the same manner of speaking is on show, the black soldiers here are not portrayed anywhere near as childlike or stupid and instead seem to have some of the slightly 'rough around the edges' aspects to their character that the Americans had prized in their white soldiers (Dickman 1927: 164).

Whilst Major Lewis would purport to support the men under his command, there were those who viewed the black soldiers with far less affection. At Camp Merritt in New Jersey, a letter signed by 'Southern Volunteers' threatened to 'clean this place out' if the assigned YMCA continued to pay 'entirely too much attention to the niggers' whilst the 'white men are neglected' (Williams 2010: 92). This creates a notion that there is a finite amount of attention or care on offer within the military and any spent on a black soldier is an amount deprived from one of the whites. The use of racial insults directly towards black soldiers, who are effectively described as an infestation, should not be overly surprising, but, in addition to this type of declaration, race-based slang was also noticeable within white units. The authors of the 115th Infantry described the training regime their recruits undertook as producing men who were 'as dexterous with a bayonet as a negro with a razor' (Reynolds and McLaughlin 1920: 37–9). The image conjured within this statement owes much to Jim Crow-esque understanding of African-Americans.

The language and actions of white American soldiers and military leaders presented an image of white supremacy which did not sit well with their French ally. Blaise Diagne, a black African deputy from Senegal (the very existence of such a man holding a place of office would have been an aberration in America), vehemently complained to President Georges Clemenceau about the recommendations of Colonel J.A. Linard, a French liaison officer embedded with Pershing's staff. Colonel Linard had drafted a memorandum explaining American racial prejudices and recommending a series of actions to avoid insulting the sensibilities of their trans-atlantic allies which included avoiding treating black Americans with any semblance of equality or praising them too heavily in front of white Americans as it would 'deeply offend the latter'. In Diagne's eyes, such recommendations were 'outrageous prejudices' and an affront to the virtues of French civilization (Fogarty 2008: 6). Matters would become worse at the end of the war.

A world safe for democracy

In many ways, the American military would have been quite content for the hegemonic structure of American racial dynamics to remain exactly as it was during the war, but by first permitting black soldiers to join the military at all and then gifting these soldiers to the French, they themselves introduced a serious problem. What may have initially been thought an ideal short-term fix to this racial issue posed a long-term problem. Not only had black soldiers been exposed to a level of social interaction with the French population that, if not truly equal, was far more progressive than what had been the norm in America, they had also seen active combat and gained pride and confidence from their victories. A culturally enriched African-American male population was one thing, an emboldened one was quite another.

After arriving in Brest in January 1919, the men of the 369th Infantry Regiment were in a jubilant mood; however, within a few minutes of their arrival, one private had his head split open by the club of a military policeman (MP). Major Little questioned the MP as to his actions towards a man who had simply been asking for directions towards the latrines and it was in response to this that the situation became complicated. Initially the MP announced that they had been instructed not to answer questions or accept orders from the officers in charge of these soldiers. Despite this, Major Little was able to get the man to reveal that 'they had been warned that our "Niggers" were feeling their oats a bit and that instruction had been given to "take it out of them quickly just as soon as they arrived, so as not to have trouble later on"' (Little 1936: 351–4).[1]

Little's reaction through his writing to this incident is an instinctive, but not instructive, one. It is clear that he believes the situation to be wrong and, effectively, an injustice. But what aspect of it is he truly objecting to? It is more likely that it is the violence used rather than the racial language, but, even within this, is the MP wrong because these are human beings and they should not be treated like this? Is it wrong because these are war heroes and they should not be treated like this? Is it wrong because, based on his previous writing about the men under his command, Major Little considers them to be children who should not be treated like this? Is it wrong because these are another officer's soldiers and they should not be treated like this? There is no clear answer to these questions, and Little's inability or unwillingness to elucidate further on why he objects to this action highlights a problem in deconstructing this material. It lies in the disjunction between Little's own actions and his confusion at what he has witnessed. This sort of violent treatment of soon to be demobilized African-American soldiers was not reserved for those under the command of Major Little and nor would violence towards black people be reserved solely to France, either.

The 'Red Summer' of 1919 saw attacks against black Americans across the United States. Returning African-American soldiers in particular were targeted for having 'physically and symbolically disrupted the southern color line', and a number of black veterans were attacked in different manners including being beaten, shot, burned alive and lynched (Williams 2010). Having returned to America in 1919, Private Malcolm Aitken, a white soldier, recalled being part of a casual company utilized to put down race riots in Washington and Baltimore. On one occasion, after a member of the company, a man who had been all through the war in France, was shot and killed from an upstairs window, Aitken and his men became 'terrible'. After a 'pitched battle' for a minute or two in which they used all of their ammunition, Aitken and his men 'proceeded to finish the war'. Aitken 'did not care to report the number killed on the other side' but referred to this incident as 'Special Duty with the Blacks' (Aitken n.d.: n.p.).

Following their efforts in the First World War, black veterans utilized the same language of freedom and democracy that President Woodrow Wilson had deployed to justify the American entry into the conflict. Having been attacked in the street by a white man in April 1919, Daniel Mack retaliated and was arrested. At his trial, Mack declared, 'I fought for you in France to make the world safe for democracy. I don't think you treated me right in putting me in jail and keeping me there, because I've got as much right as anybody else to walk on the sidewalk'. As he was sentenced to thirty days in 'a chain gang', the presiding judge reminded him that 'this is a white man's country and you don't want to forget it'. Mack would not forget; whilst in prison he was seized by a white mob in cooperation with the local police chief and beaten nearly to death on the outskirts of the town (Williams 2010: 239–40).

At the end of his book, W.A. Sweeny, in a chapter entitled 'The New Negro and the New America', declares that the war brought about new nations and new ideas and that 'if the conflict has been a just one, waged for exalted ideals and imperishable principles . . . a new character, a broader national vision' would be formed (Sweeney 1919: 301). In his 'authentic history', whilst reflecting on the successes and service of black Americans in the war, Kelly Miller asked, 'After the Negro has proved his value and worth in all of these trying ways, when after this he asks for a full measure of equal rights what American will have the heart or the hardihood to say him nay?' (Miller 1919: 552–4). The reality was stark; many were prepared to say exactly that. Black soldiers who had participated in the First World War viewed themselves not only as contributors to the new world made safe for democracy but also as rightful beneficiaries of this better world for which they had fought and died. From the 'authentic histories' of noted writers to the courtroom pleas of soon to be incarcerated and assaulted men, language was used to express black achievements, experiences and desires for more. The language of white lawmakers, army authorities and even the officers of men they professed to admire was far more reductive and, effectively, violent. For them, a black soldier's having seen service in France swiftly became a problem to be solved rather than a feat to be admired. Black military service became a point of rupture in status quo racial politics, and, if left unchecked, many seemed to fear that it could destabilize the maintained order. As a result, the participation in a war for the advancement of democracy was not enough either to stop crowds shouting 'let's get the niggers!' or to stop white authors using similar language in their writing (Williams 2010: 552).

The language of black wartime experience, both during and after the conflict, existed within this racially constructed paradigm. Whilst one group sought to use their newly emboldened voices to rise from where they had been, others reached for historic and contemporary terms to force them back. Evolution and revolution met indefatigable racial conservatism. The heavy imbalance in both political and acceptable power meant that black veterans were regularly the victims of their own earned successes. When faced with interlinking institutions built on white racial status and white mobs wielding both the language and tools of violent oppression, what black American could say them nay?

Note

1   The regiment would have ongoing issues with American MPs during their time at Brest, all of whom seemed to be under similar instructions towards the treatment of black soldiers but also to disregard the intrusions of the regiment's commanding officers.

References

Aitken, M. D. (n.d.), 'Personal Experiences of the War', USAHEC WWI 273 (2nd Division – Folder 3), U.S. Army Heritage and Education Centre.

'Bar Miller's Book from Camp Libraries', *The Chicago Defender*, 19 October 1918.

Dickman, J. T. (1927), *The Great Crusade – A Narrative of the World War*, New York: D. Appleton and Co.

Fogarty, R. (2008), *Race and War in France: Colonial Subjects in the French Army, 1914–1918*, War, Society, Culture, Baltimore: Johns Hopkins University Press.

Heywood, C. D. (1928), *Negro Combat Troops in the World War – The Story of the 371st Infantry*, Worcester: Commonwealth Press.

Hutchinson, G. and J. K. Young, eds (2013), *Publishing Blackness: Textual Constructions of Race since 1850*, Editorial Theory and Literary Criticism, Ann Arbor: University of Michigan Press.

Little, A. W. (1936), *From Harlem to the Rhine – The Story of New York's Colored Volunteers*, New York: Covici Friede.

Miller, K. (1919), *Authentic History of the Negro and the World War*, Virginia: National Publishing Co.

Reynolds, C. F. C. and C. W. M. F. McLaughlin (1920), *115th U.S. Infantry – The World War*, Baltimore: The Read Taylor Co.

Robinson, W. (n.d.), 'Veteran Survey Questionnaire', USAHEC WWI 2380 (92nd Division), U.S. Army Heritage and Education Centre.

Sweeney, W. A. (1919), *History of the American Negro in the Great World War*, G. G. Sapp.

Williams, C. L. (2010), *Torchbearers of Democracy: African American Soldiers in the World War I Era*, The John Hope Franklin Series in African American History and Culture, Chapel Hill: University of North Carolina Press.

Woodward, D. R. (2014), *The American Army and the First World War*, Armies of the Great War, New York: Cambridge University Press.

8

Romanian writers who fought in the First World War and how the 'Great War' shaped their works

Cristina Ileana Ilea (Rogojină)

The First World War started on the 28th of July 1914 and lasted until the 11th of November 1918, and involved two opposing coalitions: the Triple Entente (French Third Republic, Russian and British Empires) against the Central Powers (Germany, Austria-Hungary), both of these factions bolstered by a number of allies. Romania chose neutrality when the war started, but circumstances forced it to choose a side two years after the decision of neutrality. Therefore, on 15 August 1916, Romania joined the fray alongside the Entente, fighting simultaneously on three battlefronts. The decision to break neutrality was swayed by the stipulated conditions of the Treaty of Bucharest, which promised the (post-war victory) reunification of Transylvania with the then Romanian Kingdom of Wallachia and Moldavia. The start of the First World War put Romania in a difficult situation. Whilst King Carol I of Hohenzollern favoured an alliance with the Triple Alliance, the public and political power of Romania favoured the Triple Entente. Ultimately, Carol I's death, followed by Ferdinand's crowning, ensured the pact with the Entente.

The sociopolitical and economic interests of the nation revolved around the Great Unification of the Romanian Kingdom. Before the First World War, Romania secured the southern part of Dobrogea ('Dobruja') under the Treaty of Bucharest (1913), which inaugurated the end of the Second Balkan War. The treaty stipulated that Bulgaria would cede Cadrilater (the Southern Dobrogea), including the city of Turtucaia. Following the Second Balkan War (in which it entered to ensure Bulgaria's defeat), Romania confirmed its dominant position in South-eastern Europe, and there arose the question regarding the Balkan Vlachs (considered also Romanians) and Romanian people in Transylvania. The area populated by the Balkan Vlachs was too large to be annexed by the kingdom, so the Southern Dobrogea came as a concession.

Therefore, Romania entered the First World War in order to make territorial claims in Transylvania, a historical region with a Romanian-speaking majority. Although Romania suffered massive losses on the Turtucaia front and signed an armistice with Germany (Treaty of Bucharest, 1918) to escape annihilation, it re-entered the war alongside the Entente. The Great Kingdom of Romania was united when the representatives of Bukovina and Transylvania voted for union, respectively, on 28 November and on 1 December.

The ending of the war meant major changes to the world map: it disbanded four major empires and caused the emergence of new nation states such as Czechoslovakia, Finland, Greater Romania, Poland, Latvia, Lithuania, Estonia, Hungary and Austria. However, the changes brought by the Great War also left their imprint on culture, literature and language, bringing Romania ever closer to Western Europe, in a constant drive for harmonization with its Western siblings. The Romanian novel emerged relatively late on the European scene, exploiting historical and socio-economic subjects such as the decline of the aristocracy, the ascension of the bourgeoisie, the process of dehumanization the war inflicted and, at the same time, respect for the authentic spiritual values that society still encompassed.

The beginning of the twentieth century is not strong on these aspects. Most authors wrote short stories and tried to write novels, not with great success. However, this is a stepping stone period, more of a preparatory exercise for most authors, and outside its boundaries, the epic genre encompassed other types of writing such as essays, publishing, pamphlets, journals and published correspondence. Regarding theory and critique, we should not forget that in the reprise between wars synthesis and/or grand 'Magnus Opus' projects briefly shone. Several literary magazines, which promoted a large number of new writers, helped support the literature of the time (*Gândirea, Sburătorul*).

The Romanian novel thus expands its boundaries, and is finally unbound, arriving in a short time span to values on a par with its European peers. In this period, the novel goes through a remarkable development and is composed of two subtypes: the 'Creation novel', which represents characters through their behaviour, and the 'Analysis novel', which is more interested in the inner self and the psyche.

The novel is after all a form of metamorphic art. It is characterized by the lability of expression; the representation of the world differs according to the point of view of each author – being in constant link with reality, this has, as an effect, synchronization with the modern world. The Great War is now the focus of the novel and it is a 'profitable' topic. The metamorphosis of the novel takes place at an astounding pace. The propensity for authenticity surpasses aspects of realism, entwining fact and faction to create fascination. In Western literature, these types of novels succeeded one another but in Romanian literature they co-existed. Even the relationship between narrator, author and character varies wildly. The perspective and points of view are multiple, and the birth of parallel voices brings about the introduction of reflective character(s), or a reflective consciousness that perceives reality without the intervention of the author. Through the literature of Mircea Eliade, the Romanian novel gets a new and improved form, which melds elements of the scientific and fantastic with psychological observation and pages from journals. The literature of the period is diverse, but the novel is its uncrowned king.

The Romanian literary canon is formed in the interwar period, its advent and period of brilliance being the 1930s. Two major modern currents arise, folded under the wings of two important literary magazines: *Gândirea* and *Sburătorul*. Whilst *Gândirea* rallied the Anti-modernists, *Sburătorul*, led by Eugen Lovinescu, the father of the Romanian literary canon, rallied the Modernists. There was also a third group, the ultra-modernists, promoted by *Criterion* and other avant-garde literary magazines but none of its representatives are important for our aim. However, we should note that this period and its reflection in literary life is a constant struggle between *national literature* (anti-modern) and *literature as world literature* (modern).

Gândirea grouped writers such as Liviu Rebreanu and Mihail Sadoveanu, the critic George Călinescu, and the poets Lucian Blaga and George Topârceanu. This literary magazine represented the traditional direction, preserving the archetypal values of the Romanians, displaying an inclination towards traditionalism – agrarian and orthodox features. This direction is a reaction to modernity and to the modernists. However, authors that contributed to *Gândirea* are also included in the canon that Lovinescu shapes.

Modernism is promoted mainly by *Sburătorul*, and its group includes writers such as Camil Petrescu, Anton Holban and Hortensia Papadat-Bengescu, the critic Eugen Lovinescu, and the poet Tudor Arghezi. This current is more connected to modern city life, exploring the urban background and adopting French psychologism. The works are focused on an inward-glancing perspective in the manner of Proust and Gide.

It is necessary to begin with this division of literary life in distinct directions that indicates diversity in order to present the linguistic innovations this period brought about through the connexions of Romania with the Western world during the First World War. We chose the works of three major exponents (Liviu Rebreanu, Camil Petrescu and George Topârceanu) to display the degree in which the Romanian literature adopts modern features through linguistics means, employed in the fabric of the novel. We will respect the chronological order in which the novels appeared to prove our point. Therefore, the first novel analysed is *Forest of the Hanged* (1922), followed by *Last Night of Love and First Night of War* (1930) and *Memories from Battle of Turtucaia, Pirin-Planina, Tragic and Comical Episodes from Captivity* (1936). This chapter will discuss two main issues: the proper nouns and their function in the novel, identity and the use of language.

Liviu Rebreanu's work is in part derived from a personal trauma. Liviu Rebreanu's confessions tell us that the plot was born when a friend of his showed him a photograph in 1918 depicting a forest full of hanged Czech soldiers, close to the Italian front lines. The image haunted him and somehow, he knew that many Romanians suffered the same fate. The novel was stuck in manuscript limbo until 1919 when an acquaintance informed Liviu Rebreanu about his brother's fate. Emil Rebreanu (the younger brother of the novelist Liviu Rebreanu) was a Romanian artillery officer in the Austro-Hungarian army. Although he fought bravely on different fronts, he ended up fighting on the Romanian front, against Romanians, as part of the Austro-Hungarian army. Caught when crossing the border illegally and charged with desertion, he was executed by hanging at the age of twenty-two. Admitting that without his brother's tragedy the novel would not have seen the light of day or have had the same impact and form we know today, Liviu Rebreanu tries to synthetize in his main character – Apostol Bologa – the blood baptism of all Romanians in the Austro-Hungarian army who refused to fight against their brethren on the Romanian front.

As we stated before, we are interested in the proper names that appear in this novel. The first proper name we read in *Forest of the Hanged* is *Svoboda*. It is the name of a sub-lieutenant in the Austro-Hungarian army, Czech-born. He stands accused of treason. *Svoboda* is the reason for the execution described at the beginning of the novel and a revelation for events to come. The name is used to demonstrate that the characters aspire to the same ideal. *Svoboda*, as a proper name, is derived from the common abstract name that in some Slavic languages means 'freedom'. One may think that Liviu Rebreanu uses it because in Czech it is one of the most common surnames, to create the prototype of the oppressed Czechs during the war. In Slovak, Croatian and Serbian, the orthography is 'Sloboda'. On the other hand, in Romanian, because of its Slavic adstratum, we have the adjective 'slobod', which means 'free (man), liberated'. As in many other cases, the adjective became productive and changed its grammatical category, creating the verb 'a slobozi', with the meaning of 'to liberate, set free'. The use of this name comprises the essence of the story.

Since the liberation is mainly spiritual, the name of the main character is Apostol Bologa, 'apostle Bologa'. The author gives an explanation regarding the background of the character. His childhood was patronized by the presence of the orthodox God, although his father disapproved of the blind faith his wife exhibits through their only child. Nonetheless, whilst he is attending school, the process suffers a reversal, and Apostol Bologa loses his faith. His faith seems to return to him in moments of crisis, when his Romanian heart and the loving memory of his father turns him back to God.

It is important to take note that the lexical elements of the novel feature a fairly large number of religious terms and related imagery, denoting hierophanies or divine revelations. Liviu Rebreanu spent his childhood in Ardeal (Transylvania), and it was natural for him to employ strategies that exhibit the ideal held by most Romanians ethnics who lived in late nineteenth- and early twentieth-century Transylvanian society: religious unity (under the Orthodox Church) and union with the mother country Romania. The fate of Emil Rebreanu and the novel dedicated to him revolves around these tenets. Perhaps another observation is important: all Romanian names of the characters are the names of Orthodox Saints (such as 'Petre', 'Constantin', 'Marta', 'Maria'), whilst other characters, who are non-Romanians by descent, have general names, to imply their origin ('Ilona', 'Svoboda'). We observe in this novel a more traditional approach to denomination than in the next one chosen for analysis, since Liviu Rebreanu is one of the most influential writers at *Gândirea*.

The function of the proper name in the economy of the narrative texts became more and more important in interwar literature, since proper names can be invested with meaning which surpass their primary function: to identify and differentiate. In *The Last Night of Love, The First Night of War,* Camil Petrescu employs proper names to convey various meanings. Reading his journal notes, we understand that the writer made use of his personal war experience to build not only his main character (*Ştefan Gheorghidiu*), but the entire second part of the novel. From his journal and documents of the time, we learn that the author was drafted as a reserve soldier on the 1 August 1916 and mobilized as second lieutenant on 16 August 1916 in the 22nd Infantry Regiment. He participated in the frontline battles of Predeal-Braşov. The battle of Târgovişte left him wounded and hospitalized. Although he did not fully recover, he returned to the front, serving with the 41st D and 16th Infantry Corps of Suceava. Hurt again in battle and crippled for life (deaf in one ear), he was taken prisoner and held in a concentration camp in Hungary (Sopronyëk). This piece of biographical information is relevant in order to show that the path of his character, Ştefan Gheorghidiu, follows Camil Petrescu's memoirs up until one point. However, the author uses various proper names in his work, which will function differently throughout the novel.

Camil Petrescu is assigned to the 22nd Infantry Corps. In his novel, his character is assigned to the 'XX' Infantry Corps. Following the Roman numerals, we would be tempted to believe that Ştefan is enrolled in the 20th Infantry Regiment. Nonetheless, reading further, we come across information regarding another Regiment, this time called *XR*. Thus, we understand that *XX* does not stand for the Roman numeral 20th, but it is the description of another number, which only the careful reader will decipher. In a mathematical reasoning (which is called upon throughout the novel in Ştefan's claims), the repetition of 'X' means the repetition of the number which 'X' serves to represent. Therefore, *XX* can be read as 11, 22, 33, 44 and so on. Given that Camil Petrescu himself was assigned to the 22nd Infantry Regiment, we can safely assume the same for Ştefan, although Camil Petrescu never discloses the reason for which he prefers to keep the corps number a mystery.

Studying the function of the proper names in *The Last Night of Love, The First Night of War*, we conclude that the author distributes the anthroponyms in a circular radius of experience and interest, whose epicentre is Ştefan and his view of the world. For instance, we do not know the name of his wife ('Ela') until the characters have a serious fight, when the narrator recounts a dialogue with her. The novel starts with Ştefan's story about how he spends his time on the front on Prahova Valley, somewhere between Buşteni and Predeal, almost in the same location the author was sent into the front lines. However, the timeline is broken: the narrator sets aside the events that happen simultaneously with the story and starts recounting his past with Ela as in an intimate journal. The verbal time range shifts from past simple tense to present simple tense when describing the officers' mess and transports the reader inside the mind of the narrator. At dinner, he asks for permission to visit his wife. The request is denied, and the small talk of the officers triggers the recollection of his two years of marriage and the unbearable thought that Ela has been having extramarital affair. In all his memoirs, which comprise the first half of the novel, Ştefan's partner is referred to under the tag 'my wife', the definition highlighting the sense of possession he has over her. In one passage, he writes 'your destiny will change because of me' (referring to her destiny), which leads us to believe that avoiding the use of her name, 'Ela', and stressing her definition as 'my wife', reveals the connection between love and war and how these two experiences are seen and interact with each other. At the same time, the literary character is an element of the fictional world which organizes the entire structure of the novel. We can always see Ştefan's perspective of the world but this is not the case for Ela, since he is the one contemplating their relationship, a one-way introspection. War experience intertwined with Camil Petrescu's life, as he admitted multiple times in interviews. Şerban Cioculescu notes that 'As an individualist without escaping, Camil Petrescu can only create, in the masculine line, men in his face and likeness and, in the feminine line, only weak and females driven by instinct' (Cioculescu 1930: 1–2), as we can see in Ela's development throughout the narrative. This is why the main character, Ştefan Gheorghidiu, is strongly built whilst 'his wife' is more of a ghost of a lost love and her anonymity plays an important role in the form of the novel, not in the content. Deeply nested in the novel's structure, we find out that the experience of the war is a major source of knowledge about the world, surpassing the knowledge granted by love. Whilst his failed marriage, and therefore love, are not the highlights of this narrative, we understand why the narrator chooses to use only last names for his superiors, but full names for people on the same rank as himself or lower. Thus, we are introduced to characters such as Corabu, Floroiu, Dimiu (captains), Orişan, Dumitru and Popescu (second lieutenants). The experience of war marked Camil Petrescu, and he transferred the wounds to his characters. The fear of entering the war confuses the human brain, making it capable of retaining small and insignificant details such as the name of somebody's orderly ('Niculae Fira', who does not appear in the novel as a character). At the same time, the name of the colonel who died at the customs remains in capital letters: P.B., although the narrator notes down the name of the first prisoner, Bela Kiss. Another regiment is noted as *XR*, which means that the narrator dismisses the information regarding the name, since it is not in his radius of interest or influence. Ştefan's orderly is remembered by his full name, denoting his closeness to the narrator: 'Nicolae Zamfir'. The same goes for Mitică Rădulescu and Tudor Popescu, characters who saved Ştefan's life and waited for him in the trenches to go back together to safety, although they were under attack. Another name which provides the sense of authenticity is Maria Mănciulea, a real individual, a female hero who helped the Romanian regiments to safely cross the Olt River. The unnamed and, consequently, individualities fade in this tragedy. People melt under the tag of 'quantity' and fall into the 'stack' category when they die in battle.

As we stated earlier, war experience marked deeply Camil Petrescu's life and left him deaf in one ear. The deafness consumed him as he wrote in *'Daily Notes'* (*'Note zilnice'*):

> Deafness exhausted me, intoxicated me, gave me neurasthenia. I have to do killing efforts for things normal people do naturally . . . I am excluded from all life's possibilities. To walk the street, I have to spend an enormous capital of energy and attention that others use to read a book. Here, where everything is arranged <<in whispers>>, I am eternally absent. (Arhip 2009: 20)

The writer will always be obsessed with noise, which he massively employs in the discussed novel, although he portrays in a realist manner the life of confused, scared and puzzled soldiers on the front line, describing daily tedious activities. The noise of the exploding shells, a constant of the life at the front, it is compared to a collision between locomotives, haunting the author for the rest of his life (due to his infirmity caused by an exploding shell). Thus, he transposed this to his character and embedded it in the narrative: 'in this moment I had the impression that two locomotives collided, with a noise of hell, and I saw the two carts grown into a mountain of smoke. Orişan must have been crushed with his men' (Petrescu 1979: 275).

The prose style of Camil Petrescu was often characterized as 'anticalliphile', meaning little or not at all unnecessary stylistic embroidery to represent the almost artificial and useless life on the front line. This is why he describes with no pomposity the precarious state of the Romanian army. Ştefan's soldierly spirit is lacking as he comments caustically on the war strategy, disorganization and the missing weapons and modern war tactics. Exhausted and uncertain of his wife's fidelity, the character feels the need to demonstrate that the enemy uses, just like Romanian army, expired ammunition:

> A shell is not exploding. Bragging, I declare to my pissed comrades that Hungarian artillery is harmless and I take the shell in my arms to show them it has bad powder. All people shout at me . . . I throw it on the ground, just like you would throw a beetroot . . . and I freeze at my madness because, thrown on the ground, the projectile could have exploded. (Petrescu 1979: 258–9)

As we can see, the unadorned style of the author is often shadowed by his real trauma on the front line. In his novel, Camil Petrescu makes use of an intellectual image ('a finding of the mind' as Tudor Vianu calls this kind of image) rather than the pathetic allegories that we see in other works before and in the interwar period. He also employs the comparison when analysing Ştefan's love and war memories, with expanded explanations instead of epithets or other figures of speech.

An interesting fact, since the main character dissects the infidelity issue in his own marriage, is that Daiana Gârdan's study finds that the emotional spectrum of the novel comprises a vocabulary of grief, anger, lust, hatred but less of jealousy. The analysis reveals that 43.4 per cent are positive emotions whilst 56.6 per cent are negative emotions, which represents a balanced distribution between the two ends of the emotional spectrum, although the novel does not feature a 'happy ending'. The lexical negative elements incorporate a large spectrum of emotions, being extraordinarily expressive; thus, the need of figures of speech fades. This modern novel entered the canon because the formula used (Proustianism) was easily accepted. The Romanian literary terrain was already prepared by a significant number of previous literary attempts. This shows that Romanian literature was not only local as the process of finding a good novel formula was rather global: 'In the evolutionary process that began with *Elvira or the Endless Love, An Original Romance*' and culminating with Petrescu's and Holban's novels, foreign models, translations and theoretical discourses on universal literature contributed in equal measure to the aesthetic performance of the modern Romanian novel. The foundation of Romanian literature itself rests upon a complex dialogue and the circulation of foreign literary formulas' (Gârdan 2018: 108–9).

The third work we are going to discuss has fewer proper names but more interesting linguistic aspects, and it should not be treated as a novel but as a *memoir*. When Romania entered the First World War, George Topârceanu was drafted to the Turtucaia front line. The entire experience at the front is seen as a massacre, as events happen fast and there is no time to understand what is really going on.

In George Topârceanu's writing, we are more interested in the fragments that recount the time he spends as a prisoner in Bulgarian camps. The defeat of the Romanian army at Turtucaia starts on 24 August 1916. Although we are confronted with a description of the armies and the front, it is not very technical. The writing is characterized more by the presence of comparison and epithet as figures of speech, cultivated by George Topârceanu in his other forms of literature. Thus, his memoir can be considered more of a literary device through which he can express his views of the war, encampment and military training. We note similarities between this piece of writing and Camil Petrescu's prose. Although critics did not have detailed opinion on George Topârceanu's recollections of captivity, his account of the fall of Turtucaia and the days spent as a prisoner help us understand the reality of the events that happened.

The memoir of *Pirin-Planina* begins with a letter that explains why he writes about his captivity in various concentration camps in less than welcoming Bulgaria. It is a philosophical inquiry in which he debates whether war is necessary or not and whether people, in general, are good or evil.

What matters most in his writing is the language he employs to illustrate the survival of the not-so-lucky soldiers on the front line captured by the Bulgarian army. One of the first things that captures your attention is the Bulgarians' shouts, whether they are just villagers or soldiers: 'trinaisi godina', which is meant as an insult to Romanians. This is also recounted in Nicolae Balotă's study (*The War Seen by Soldiers, 1916-1919*). The phrase became a leitmotif and refers to the previous war in which Romania and Bulgaria fought as opposing armies.

George Topârceanu's story presents us with many Bulgarian words learnt from the front and made use of in his writing, even though they have proper translations in Romanian. For instance, when he refers to the sentries, he uses the Bulgarian word 'ciasovoi'; he proceeds in the same way when referring to second lieutenants, as he calls them 'starşi' or 'potporucic' not 'sublocotenenţi', in Romanian. For some phrases uttered in Bulgarian, he provides the translation in footnotes. However, the writer draws the reader's attention from time to time to show in footnotes that some of the words and phrases are not well written in Bulgarian. In some cases, we have phonetic transcriptions, adapted to the Romanian phonetic system ('Ciacă tucă, rumanski', later corrected in a footnote by the author as 'Ciacai tuka, rumanski', translated as 'wait here, Romanian'). This can be explained, perhaps, as an imperfection of the memory or how the words and phrases became fixed in his mind in his process of learning the new language in order to have a better chance of survival. When the writer does not know the word for a military rank in Bulgarian, he replaces it with the word in German (he talks about 'the German 'Feldwebel', not 'sergeant major'), stating the fact that the prisoners had to build railway lines under German leadership. The writer also reproduces some of his dialogues with French soldiers in their language ('Ces bougres-là! Sont-ils asses emmerdants avec leur ciaka et utre . . . nom de Dieu!', to which he provides the translation, usually in a footnote).

George Topârceanu also provides information on how people would learn the language during their captivity. The first step in acquiring vocabulary would be to point and show different objects in order to learn their name. When one would gather enough vocabulary, learning and singing songs provide a good exercise in learning a new language. Since the writer displays lyrics of Bulgarian and Serbian songs and their translations in footnotes, we understand that he had at least a basic knowledge of the captors' language. After the time spent in Pirin-Planina, the author confesses that he was reassigned as an assistant in a hospital in which he learnt to speak *Volapük*, a mix of language with Serbian, Russian, Bulgarian words and a mix of Greek and French terms.

In the first prisoner camp (Radomir) when he and what little is left of the Romanian army at the Turtucaia front arrive, he finds prisoners of allied armies: French, English, Serbian, Italian, Greek, Montenegran and Russian soldiers. Apart from all the linguistic information we can extract from George Topârceanu's recollection, it is also important to note his perspective of the other prisoners. Regarding free time, which characterized Sundays, he remembers that English soldiers were not very talkative, were smoking pipes and were the beneficiaries of a more comfortable encampment, whilst the rest were grouped together. A curious fragment depicts a fair called 'trampa', a kind of exotic bazaar in which soldiers exchanged few of the goods they still possessed (although valuable items such as soap, Gillette razors, cigarettes, money and even clothes were hoarded by the Bulgarian 'ciasovoi' and 'starși' in the first days of captivity). This, again, required linguistic competence in order to sell goods.

There are also references to what he ironically calls *culinary delights*. In one passage he reveals that French soldiers were eating cats, snakes and hedgehogs, whilst Italians were eating frog legs, since their captors were providing the prisoners only with old bread, bell peppers and, on very rare occasions, cheese. Of these, the Romanian soldier only tried the frog legs that gave him three days of nausea.

The denomination aspects have the same value as in Camil Petrescu's prose. George Topârceanu remembers few full names, and some first names of these reflect his prolonged interaction with them. For instance, 'Mieluș, the gypsy' is one of the first he remembers, and he portrays his tragic death on the front. He offers the full names of some men he spent time with at Pirin-Planina, a Macedonian prisoner-of-war camp: 'Toader Coban', 'Toader Căpuzaru', 'Gheorghe Andronic', 'Lazăr Ilie Drișcă' and 'Stan Ioan Boldișan'. Time spent at Pirin-Planina is described almost as Eden-like as the camp was surrounded by forest and pasture in a geographic region very closely related to Romania.

These three pieces of literature regard the First World War as a tragedy of the uncountable lost lives but also as life experience. During this study, we have observed multiple similarities between works of fiction and a memoir which reaffirm the new and improved form and strategies of the Romanian novel. Denomination plays an important role that goes beyond its primary function of identification and individualization. In these cases, proper names function as a compass for the main characters or narrators navigating through the seas of authenticity. We also must remember that both *The Forest of the Hanged* and *The Last Night of Love, The First Night of War* are not monographs but draw their narrative powers from the personal tragedies of the authors. Here, the war is just a condition for finding the true meaning of the existence in search of synchronicity with the Western world literature.

References

Arhip, C. (2009), *Altfel despre Camil Petrescu*, Iași: Junimea.

Cioculescu, Ș. (1930), 'Cronică literară', *Adevărul*, 43, no. 14386, 18 November.

Gârdan, D. (2018), 'Mapping Emotions in the Romanian Novel of the Interwar Period. Canonical Affect and Popular Sensibility', *Dacoromania Litteraria*, V: 101–14.

Petrescu, C. (1979), *Ultima noapte de dragoste, întâia noapte de război*, Bucharest: Minerva.

Bibliography

Balotă, N. (2019), *Războiul văzut de soldați*, Pitești: Tiparg.

Petrescu, C. (1975), *Note zilnice*, Bucharest: Cartea Românească.

Rebreanu, L. (1980), *Pădurea spânzuraților*, Bucharest: Minerva.

Topârceanu, G. (1983), *Scrieri*, vol. II, preface, notes, comments, chronology table and bibliography, edited by Al. Săndulescu, Bucharest: Minerva.

Vianu, T. (2010), *Arta prozatorilor români*, edited by G. Șerban, Bucharest: Orizonturi.

Vodă Căpușan, M. (1988), *Camil Petrescu – Realia*, Bucharest: Cartea Românească.

9

The 1915 German-Estonian phrasebook as an interface of German-Estonian language contact and a vehicle for annexationist propaganda

Mart Kuldkepp

The purpose of this chapter is to consider the ways in which the 1915 German-Estonian phrasebook (subsequently republished in 1916 and 1918) attempted to facilitate German-Estonian language contact while also functioning as a vehicle for German annexationist propaganda.[1] I will argue that by trying to convince its German-speaking audience of the natural 'Germanness' of Estonia and the Estonians in a political and cultural sense, the phrasebook made a contribution towards preparing the ground for a future German occupation of the northernmost part of the Baltic region, meant to be followed by a permanent annexation of the Estonian-speaking areas to Germany. The phrasebook's practical purpose as a language guide must have been limited, not least because the actual occupation of Estonian-speaking areas was delayed until the autumn and winter of 1917–18. This, however, did not stop the phrasebook from being printed in tens of thousands of copies already before any German troops managed to reach Estonia.

This short study hopes to add a new facet to the growing body of research on dictionaries, phrasebooks and primers as by-products or even tools of war (Constantine 2011; Constantine 2013; Footitt 2010; Footitt and Kelly 2012), while also contributing towards a better understanding of German occupation and annexation policy on the Eastern front – particularly relating to how it was shaped by Baltic German propaganda.

Phrasebooks as linguistic auxiliaries of war-making

The following discussion will be mostly limited to the 1915 German-Estonian phrasebook, but this does not mean that similar publications were not produced for other target audiences and by other belligerent powers, or that their production and use was particular only to the First World War. Indeed, there are significant similarities with other comparable cases, analyses of which have unveiled racist or colonialist agendas, clearly demarcating between the more and less 'civilised' halves of the language pair

(Hallett 2017; Sheldon 1998). At least for comparative purposes, it is useful to consider German annexationism also as a form of colonialism, even if it was expected to be realized first and foremost through military occupation, with other measures (such as economic coercion and industrial restructuring benefitting the motherland) following later. This means that insights gathered, for example, from analysis of modern Lonely Planet phrasebooks (Hallett 2017) are still broadly relevant for the current case study.

The role and provenance of what might be called 'occupation dictionaries', 'war phrasebooks' and so on is well documented in recent research. Most helpfully, Simon Constantine has conducted two thorough studies of such materials as used in the First World War (Constantine 2011, 2013), highlighting both the wide variety available and their impressive print runs (often in the hundreds of thousands) (Constantine 2011: 516, 2013: 155). He also points out that most such publications were not produced or even commissioned by government officials, but rather appeared on the initiative of private publishers looking to cash in on the enormous market that had opened through mass mobilization of overwhelmingly literate armies. Whole armies of soldiers were gifted these books, purchased them before being deployed, or did so later in field bookshops. In Germany, military authorities sometimes also bought such publications in bulk and took care of the distribution themselves (Constantine 2013: 155–6).

At least in Germany such books could also be commissioned by the authorities (see e.g. the German-Lithuanian phrasebook, mentioned later in the text), or even produced in-house. An example of the latter is the seven-language dictionary of German, Polish, Russian, Belorussian, Lithuanian, Latvian and Yiddish, which was published in early 1918 by the translation unit of the Supreme Commander of German Forces in the East (*Oberbefehlshaber Ost* or *Ober-Ost*) on the basis of a card catalogue that had been compiled for the purposes of translating official decrees and regulations. The compilers note that as a result, their book includes many expressions that might 'sound barbaric to a philologist', but nevertheless fulfil a practical purpose. In any case, the fundamental reason for the book's unevenness is explained to lie in the various languages' different stages of cultural development, in comparison both with each other and with German (Sieben-Sprachen-Wörterbuch 1918: 5–6). Thanks to such institutional and ideological framing, even a dictionary could acquire a distinctly colonialist flavour.

However, while dictionaries could be expected to have fulfilled a primarily practical purpose, Constantine argues that phrasebooks, for the most part, should not be viewed as guides to actual communication. This was partially because their authors often failed to foresee the actual circumstances of their use, with the books rather providing a 'source for the exaggerated expectations on both sides early in the war', and partially because most verbal exchanges would in any case not be sufficiently patterned to enable straightforward usage, with the possible exception of entirely ritualistic interactions, such as pro-forma interrogations of enemy prisoners (Constantine 2011: 516–18).

The actual importance of phrasebooks, Constantine argues, rather lies in the manner in which 'they helped to transmit to soldiers expected norms of conduct for the engagement with civilian populations'. He goes as far as to suggest that 'for German soldiers, the scenarios and dialogue of phrasebooks functioned as a kind of virtual-training, promoting the use of illegal methods of warfare in occupied Belgium and

France' (Constantine 2013: 154). These insights can be taken as the point of departure also for this inquiry about the expected norms governing German-Estonian relations. Furthermore, if, as argued by Kathleen Sheldon, 'phrase books offer a window into the world view of those who compile them, and might provide clues about society at large as well' (Sheldon 1998: 341), they can be assumed to say something about the aims of wartime propaganda, reflected in the paratexts attached to the phrasebook, but also in what the imaginary participants say and do in the depicted interactions, and in what sort of exchanges are expected to arise in the first place.

Estonians, Baltic Germans and Germany

Among other German-occupied territories in the First World War, the Baltic provinces (now Estonia and Latvia) were in some ways a unique case. Even though they had formed a part of the Russian Empire from 1721 onwards, they had for centuries both before and after been dominated by a German-speaking landed nobility, which traced its roots back to the crusading knights that had conquered these pagan lands back in the thirteenth century. Having secured a foothold in the Baltics and reduced the native Estonian- and Latvian-speaking populations to serfdom, they managed to maintain their privileges and a broad regional autonomy under the various states that went on to rule over the Baltics from the Middle Ages onwards.[2]

One result of the near-overlap of linguistic and social boundaries in the Baltic provinces was that the Estonian national awakening, beginning around the mid-nineteenth century, found in the Baltic Germans (less than 5 per cent of the total population) a natural target for both their national and social grievances. This gave the Estonian nationalist movement a strong inner cohesion, helped by the fact that the Baltic German leadership found it impossible to reach a political compromise even with the most moderate Estonian politicians. For a small community deathly afraid of any developments that could have led to their downfall from the status of the privileged elite to that of a disadvantaged national minority, the Estonian nationalist aspirations of putting the provincial system of governance on a more democratic grounding would have been acceptable only if there had been a simultaneous increase in the number and influence of German speakers – for example, through immigration from Germany or from other German-speaking communities in Russia. This, however, was something naturally opposed by even the most conservative Estonians (see Kuldkepp 2019).

Among other consequences, this state of tense inter-ethnic relations made the language question in the Baltic provinces a sensitive one, closely linking the use of German language to the Baltic German claim of cultural and political supremacy in these 'ancient German territories'. Conversely, the prospects of further spreading the use of German at the expense of Estonian and Latvian came to be seen by the Baltic German leadership as something on which the ultimate survival of the Baltic provinces' 'Germanness' depended – either in conjunction with colonization by German-speaking settlers or as a possible alternative to it.[3]

The beginning of the First World War sparked in Russia a wave of Germanophobia, directed not only against Germany, but also against Russia's own German-speaking population. The public persecution of Germans was welcomed many Estonians, and certainly contributed to the willingness of conscripted Estonian soldiers and officers to fight for Russia. For example, Juhan Tõrvand, the future chief of staff of the army of the independent Republic of Estonia, wrote in his diary on 22 April 1915: 'These [Germans] can't save themselves! And that's how it should be! Compared to the Russians, I as an Estonian feel the joy of victory over the Teutons a thousand times more. We have sucked in the feelings of historical hate against the Germans already with our mothers' milk. And this hate will only find satisfaction when the German might is destroyed' (Pajur 2009: 59).

The wartime German military and political leadership, for their part, was far from unanimous on the question of what to think of Russia's Baltic borderlands. The influential circles in Berlin that supported the conclusion of separate peace between Russia and Germany found it inexpedient to stake such claims on Russian territory, hurting Russian national pride and making the achievement of separate peace more difficult. At the same time, the more uncompromising German annexationists, especially the generals of the Supreme Army Command (*Oberste Heeresleitung*, OHL) who gained the upper hand in the latter part of the war, found in the Baltic provinces a natural target for German expansionism in the East (Kuldkepp 2015: 259–60).

In this, they were significantly encouraged and aided by exiled Baltic German propagandists in Germany. Soon after the beginning of the war, these men had taken up agitation for the conquest and annexation of the whole of the Baltic region by Germany. Well-connected and able to evoke feelings of German-national pride by referring to its 'cultural mission in the East', they eventually gained significant influence over German policy.[4]

The initial Baltic German efforts to lobby the German authorities soon led to the establishment of permanent organizations. The first of these, German People's Defence (*Deutscher Volksschutz*), which had the comparatively modest purpose of defending German economic and political interests in Finland and the Baltic States, was founded already in 1914 (Loit 2006: 53). Of course, as long as the relevant territories remained unoccupied by Germany, there was no land available to colonize or Estonians and Latvians to Germanize. Nevertheless, the conquest of Courland by German troops in April 1915 meant that the region came to attract more attention and Baltic German propaganda won a broader audience in Germany.

The guide through Livonia, Estonia and Courland with phrasebooks and a map

In May 1915, this new attention accorded to the Baltics led to the founding of a new and more ambitious Baltic German exile organization, The Confidential Baltic Council (*Baltischer Vertrauensrat*). It was centred around the figures of Otto von Veh, the head of *Vertrauensrat*, and its ideological leader Theodor Schiemann, previously the town archivist of Tallinn and later professor of Eastern European history at Berlin University, who acted as a close foreign policy adviser to Wilhelm II. During the 1918 German occupation of Estonia, Schiemann also briefly became the curator of the University of Tartu (Loit 2006: 53).

In their first *Denkschrift* published already before the organization had been formally founded, Veh and Schiemann stated the following in no unequivocal terms: 'The culture of the Baltic Sea provinces is German . . . still today. The culture of the Estonians and Latvians is also German. They owe it to the Germans . . . The three provinces constitute a single cultural area and therefore belong together. They have the same faith, the same language of culture (German), the same constitution with local differences. The circumstance that the Estonians live in the north and the Latvians in the south plays no role, as both peoples have only one culture: the German culture' (Lehmann 1994: 131).

Vertrauensrat's confidential statement of aims, formulated at its founding on 10 May 1915, furthermore explicitly stated that the purpose of the organization was to achieve the reunification of the Baltic provinces with Germany and to do all that was necessary to achieve that goal (Lehmann 1994: 131). The organization envisioned future Baltic provinces as '[a] great German Protestant land with blooming agriculture that is capable of further development, so that it can richly provide Germany with its surplus food production; an area of settlement that can receive Germany's surplus population or German colonists in the millions . . . a population that readily, and, in part, enthusiastically, will acquiesce to German dominance and has already for centuries been used to autonomy built after the German example; a healthy race that will provide able conscripts for the army and the navy' (Lehmann 1994: 132).

In addition to *Vertrauensrat*'s journal *Stimmen aus dem Osten*, which quickly became an important vehicle for annexationist propaganda (Loit 2006: 53), and the confidential printed memoranda that were distributed to prominent personalities in German political, military and academic circles, one of the first publications produced by *Vertrauensrat* was a book titled *Guide Through Estonia, Livonia and Courland. With German-Latvian and German-Estonian 'Phrase Books' and a Map* (*Führer durch Est-, Liv- und Kurland. Mit deutsch-lettischem und deutsch-estnischem 'Sprachführer' und einer Karte*). According to a note included in the first edition of the book, it had been published under the aegis of *Vertrauensrat* by August Löwis of Menar (*Führer durch*... 1915: n.p.), one of the two editors of *Stimmen aus dem Osten*.

It is not entirely clear whether the initiative for this publication came from *Vertrauensrat* itself or whether it had in some sense been commissioned by the German authorities. The latter possibility is supported by the fact that the compilation of a similar German-Lithuanian phrasebook had been initiated in 1914 by the *Generalkommando* of the I Army Corps, which commissioned one Rittmeister Wilhelm Steputat to undertake the task (Politisches Archiv [1914]: 33).[5] If the same was the case with *Vertrauensrat*'s phrasebook, this would be an interesting addition to the history of German policy development, since the publication of a German-Estonian phrasebook already in 1915, if officially sanctioned, would indicate preparations for an occupation of Estonia already in the early stages of the war – long before the actual occupation in 1917–18.

However, even if not outright commissioned by the military authorities, the book certainly was distributed by them. According to Veh's letter to other *Vertrauensrat* members from October 1915, the entire initial print run of 6,000 copies had been handed over to the Prussian Ministry of War and the Imperial Naval Office, which intended to bring 5,000 copies to the front (Bundesarchiv-a n.d.: n.p.). In a report written probably in the following spring, it was furthermore mentioned that the publication, which had 'aroused a lively interest in military circles', had by that point been printed altogether in 35,000 copies in three print runs (Bundesarchiv-b n.d.: n.p.).

The contents of the phrasebook

Whatever the degree of the military authorities' exact involvement in the book project, it is clear that as far as *Vertrauensrat* was concerned, the substance of the publication was in line with its aim of facilitating future German occupation of the whole of the Baltic region. As noted in the general foreword, the book was meant for 'our troops fighting hard in the north-east on land and on sea who would bring the book from Courland to Tallinn and Narva, but would be a trustworthy guide also for everyone else interested in learning about the "oldest colonies of the German Reich"' (*Führer durch*... 1915: 1). Furthermore, the introduction to the phrasebook section states that the phrasebook is meant to facilitate mutual understanding between the readers and the non-German population of the Baltic provinces, containing not just expressions and sentences immediately relevant for military purposes, but also such that would be used 'only in unforced, peaceful conversation' (*Führer durch*... 1915: 39).

Before the phrasebook itself, the volume includes a thorough historical overview (narrated, of course, from an entirely Baltic German point of view), a multifaceted description of the region covering geographical, political and cultural aspects, characterizations of the different national groups (Baltic Germans, Latvians and Estonians) and two Baltic German poems full of longing for Germany.[6] These earlier sections also give a somewhat paranoid framing to the phrasebook proper by urging the German invaders, if possible, to rely on the Baltic German population, whose mindset is described as thoroughly German-national (*deutschnational*). The Latvians and Estonians are also said to be longing for liberation from the Russian yoke, but the reader is warned that unlike the Germans some of them might be spies (*Führer durch*... 1915: 12–14). In the later editions, this warning was dropped, perhaps to not to undermine the central narrative that the Latvians and Estonians were already culturally German.

In terms of general principles of communication, the reader is advised that Latvians can be easily dealt with if one employs correct ('strict but human') methods, that is, more is achievable by patience and clarification than by sheer threats. In the case of Estonians as well, it was suggested that too strict, curt and sharp treatment was to be avoided as much as possible (*Führer durch*... 1915: 17–18). Such paternalism towards one's prospective conversation partners can be compared with Sheldon's observations about Mozambican phrasebooks, where 'Africans were perceived as potential converts who were equals before God and at the same time ... continued to hold "pagan" beliefs and practice "uncivilized" customs' (Sheldon 1998: 346). The Latvians and Estonians, likewise, are depicted as potential converts to full 'Germanness', but nevertheless in need of some guidance before they would be able to get there.

The bulk of the book consists of functionally identical introductions to Latvian and Estonian grammar, and German-Latvian and German-Estonian phrasebooks with their lists of words, phrases and dialogues. Finally, the book includes a list of conversion tables between German and Russian weights and measures, and a map of the region.[7]

The phrasebook proper includes lists of words for numbers, time determinants, various adjectives, prepositions, verbs and adjectives, words for people, animals and plants as well as vocabulary relating to army and navy.[8] While all this could be regarded as more or less neutral information, more loaded expressions pop up in the section about buying and selling, where phrases are worded as commands rather than requests ('I want to buy this!'). Even more remarkably, the section on 'general expressions' includes such supposedly everyday phrases as 'tell me what you have seen!', 'quiet!', 'idiot!' and 'answer me!', making it clear what the nature of the exchanges with Estonian-speaking civilians was expected to be.[9] More expressions that would be useful for ordering people around can also be found in the sections on food and eating ('I want to eat!', 'Make me a soup!'), on 'clothes and equipment' ('Brush my coat!', 'Clean my boots!') and on 'population', which includes sentences such as 'the corn has to be delivered by tonight!', 'if you do not comply, you will need to pay 100 roubles in fines!' and the ever-useful 'you must follow the orders!' (*Führer durch . . .* 1915: 71–2, 75).

The section 'on accommodation' is similarly rife with commands, but also includes questions related to intelligence gathering ('how many people are there in this village?', 'where does the pastor live?') (*Führer durch . . .* 1915: 76). The same holds true about the next sections 'on the move' ('give me a guide who knows the surroundings well!', 'how long is it to the nearest house, village, manor house?') and 'in the battle'. The latter section is again very much focused on questioning ('where are the enemies?', 'are there Russians on the top of this hill?'), but also includes commands ('hands up!', 'lay down all weapons!') and certain performative utterances ('you are my prisoner!') (*Führer durch . . .* 1915: 77–8, 81–2). As Constantine points out, sentences like these are found in most German phrasebooks, with nearly all authors anticipating in the need to question civilians and issue threats – that in spite of Germany's own commitments under the international law prohibiting such actions (Constantine 2013: 161, 163). In any case, the selection of phrases is fully in line with the likely expected needs of 'our troops, fighting hard from Courland to Tallinn and Narva'.

The predominance of imperative forms can also be compared to other similar examples more broadly, such as those found in the 1944 phrasebook for Allied occupation troops in Germany, about which Hilary Footitt and Michael Kelly note that '[t]roops were clearly expected to be meeting German civilians only to give them harsh and explicit orders' or the 1946 Portuguese-Mozambique phrasebook, about which Sheldon points out that '[t]he vast majority of the phrases are presented in the imperative verb form, rarely offering any of the polite versions' (Footitt and Kelly 2012: 344). Perhaps not unexpectedly, the contents of the 1915 Estonian-German phrasebook therefore mostly fail to bear out the stated purpose of facilitating 'unenforced, peaceful conversation', or to follow its own recommendation against using threats and acrimonious speech.

In terms of politeness, there is also disparity of expression between the two languages, with the German phrases appearing consistently more polite than their Estonian equivalents. To some extent, this could be due to lack of language skills (the Estonian used in the book is rife with grammatical errors), but it would not be far-fetched to interpret this as colonialist prejudice requiring one to be more straightforward in Estonian, whereas more 'civilised' wording would be employed in German. For example, the threat 'if you do not follow my commands, or give me false information, or attempt to betray us, I will immediately make use of my weapons!' (word-by-word from German) is rendered as 'if you do not do what I order, you lie or deceive us, you will immediately be shot!' in Estonian (*Führer durch . . .* 1915: 83).

The impact and the aftermath

As stated in the foreword and suggested by its distribution channels, the book was above all intended for military use, but at least this far I have failed to find sources that would tell more about its use on the front. However, it certainly did have some propagandistic impact on German civilian audiences. For example, it was praised at a January 1916 meeting of the German Folklore Society (*Verein für Volkskunde*), where its chairman Max Roediger read out some of the book's verses expressing longing for liberation by Germany (Brunner 1916: 221). In 1917, a reviewer remarked that 'when leafing through this book, one is touched by a certain sense of longing for the old German culture lands . . . just as Elsass-Lothringen after 1871, so will Courland after the end of the war become a new, desirable and frequently visited German travel destination' (Dehn 1917: 256).

Baltic German propaganda also found inroads into the higher echelon of German politics. In a *Reichstag* speech on 5 April 1916, Chancellor Theobald von Bethmann-Hollweg stated that Germany would not allow the people liberated by Germany and its allies to be returned to Russia, 'whether they be Poles, Lithuanians, Balts or Latvians'. The leadership of the *Vertrauensrat* took this to indicate that the conquest and colonization of Estonia and Livonia had been adopted as a German war aim (Lehmann 1994: 132–3). Possibly in connection with this belief, a second edition of the phrasebook was published in 1916, its foreword stating that the publication had in a short time found many friends and thankful users both on the front and at home. Now, the editors hoped, it would ease the way for the heroic German troops crossing the Düna River (i.e. the Daugava River dividing the southern part of the Baltic region from the northern provinces Livonia and Estonia) (*Führer durch . . .* 1916: 2).

Daugava would not be crossed for a while, but as OHL (Supreme Army Command), headed by generals Paul Hindenburg and Erich Ludendorff, rose to the position of the de facto military dictatorship of Germany in the last two years of the war, the outlooks of Baltic German propaganda rapidly improved. On 23 April 1917, OHL took the principal decision to attempt to conquer at least a part of the rest of the Baltic region, including the Estonian islands, in addition to Lithuania and Courland already under German occupation (Kuldkepp 2019: 373). This meant that serious political and military weight was now put behind the two-pronged annexationist solution to the Estonian-Latvian question propagated by *Vertrauensrat* and its sympathizers: mass colonization with German-speaking settlers and accelerated Germanization of the native population through propaganda and German-only education.

If anything, the leaders of *Vertrauensrat* now had to urge for more cautiousness. In yet another secret memorandum from May 1917, they stated once again that Estonia, Livonia and Courland are 'old, German, colonial lands' that had over the course of 700 years been Germanized thanks to the hard work of their Baltic German upper class. Now, however, they argued that it would be politically inexpedient to openly advocate for forceful Germanization of Estonians and Latvians, since this would provoke the centrist and radical forces that had arisen in German politics. Furthermore, it was advised, forceful Germanization would not even be necessary, as these small 'splinters of nations' would be unable to withstand the impact of German progress and would in a generation be anyway completely overrun by the settlement of two million German speakers from Russia with their high nativity rates (Lehmann 1994:133).

In autumn 1917 and winter 1917/18, the long-awaited German occupation of Livonia and Estonia finally began. The third, 1918 edition of the phrasebook includes a new, jubilant foreword by the editor (dated with 8 September 1917) beginning with the words 'Riga is ours!' and thanking the 8th Army and the German fleet for their new conquests in the Baltics (*Führer durch . . .* 1918: 37). The following occupation of the Estonian islands in October 1917 and the invasion of Estonian mainland in February 1918 were possibly the first time that the German-Estonian phrasebook saw actual use, as intended, by German soldiers to communicate with Estonian civilians.

However, any such use was probably limited, and it is more than likely that the eventual significance of this publication remained primarily propagandistic. This is also demonstrated by the fact that the Estonian phrases in the 1916 and 1918 editions repeat all the same typos and mistakes already found in the first edition – native Estonian input to correct them was either not forthcoming or not even sought. Indeed, the only Estonian opinion of this book that I have come across is a critical one: a copy of the 1918 edition in the University of Tartu library bears in its first page an exasperated scribble in Estonian: 'the author of this book is one of the stupidest people ever to be born.'

Conclusion

The 1915 German-Estonian phrasebook, subsequently republished in two more editions, was a product of *Baltischer Vertrauensrat*, a Baltic German lobby organization that was based in Berlin and spreading propaganda with the aim of achieving the occupation and annexation of all three Baltic provinces to Germany. Rather than fulfilling any immediate practical purpose, it seems that the Estonian part of phrasebook was primarily used as a work of propaganda, spreading the notion that the Baltic provinces – including their non-German majority population – were already culturally German, and should become politically German as well. This process of Germanization would be further facilitated by occupation, denationalization of the Latvians and Estonians, and colonization of their territories with German-speaking settlers.

The contents of the phrasebook follow the conventions of other similar German publications of the period, expecting the invading troops to issue threats and commands to the civilian population and to interrogate them for the purposes of intelligence gathering, thereby undermining its own narrative about the already basically German culture and sympathies of the Latvians and Estonians. As the time window when the German-Estonian phrasebook could have been used for its intended purpose was rather narrow, its practical application must have been limited. However, in conjunction with other propaganda initiatives of the Baltic German annexationists, it probably did have some impact on the public opinion and policies of the military leadership in Germany, especially during the last two years of the war that saw an annexationist swing in German policy towards the Baltics.

Notes

1 The research for this chapter has been supported by the project PHVAJ16908 'War after War: The War Experience of Estonian Servicemen in the Twentieth Century', funded by University of Tartu.
2 The best one-volume history of Estonia in English remains Raun (2001).
3 See, for example, the memoranda to that effect presented to the German military authorities during the 1918 German occupation of Estonia: Kruus (1920: 64–8).
4 About German colonialism in the Baltics, see Mann (1965).
5 Steputat's German-Lithuanian phrase book went on to be published in a number of editions: Steputat 1915. I would like to thank Vasilijus Satronovas for his help with establishing the identity of the author of this *Denkschrift*.
6 For the various sections, see *Führer durch . . .* 1915: 3–12, 13–19, 19–36, 37–8.
7 *Führer durch . . .* 1915: 39–83; 85–7.
8 *Führer durch . . .* 1915: 65–71, 79–81.
9 *Führer durch . . .* 1915: 65–6, 69–70.

References

Archives

(Bundesarchiv-a), Bundesarchiv Berlin-Lichterfelde, R 8054 (Baltischer Vertrauensrat), Vol. 2, Otto von Veh, *Meine verehrten Landsleute!*
(Bundesarchiv-b), Bundesarchiv Berlin-Lichterfelde, R 8054 (Baltischer Vertrauensrat), Vol. 9, *I Jahresbericht. Entwurf.*
Politisches Archiv des Auswärtigen Amtes, R 10199. Wilhelm Steputat, *Denkschrift über Litauen im Jahre 1914.*

Printed primary sources

Brunner, K. (1916), 'Aus den Sitzungs-Protokollen des Vereins für Volkskunde', *Zeitschrift des Vereins für Volkskunde*, 26: 221–4.

Dehn, P. (1917), 'Mitteilungen. Ein neues Reiseziel in Osteuropa', *Osteuropäische Zukunft. Zeitschrift für Deutschlands Aufgaben im Osten und Südosten*, 2 (17): 256.

Führer durch Est-, Liv- und Kurland. Mit deutsch-lettischem und deutsch-estnischem 'Sprachführer' und einer Karte (1915), Oldenburg: Gerhard Stalling, Verlag des Deutschen Offizierblattes.

Führer durch Est-, Liv- und Kurland. Mit deutsch-lettischem und deutsch-estnischem 'Sprachführer' und einer Karte. 2. Auflage (1916), Oldenburg: Gerhard Stalling, Verlag des Deutschen Offizierblattes.

Führer durch Est-, Liv- unwd Kurland. Mit deutsch-lettischem und deutsch-estnischem 'Sprachführer' und einer Karte. 39 Tausend (1918), Oldenburg: Gerhard Stalling, Verlag des Deutschen Offizierblattes.

Sieben-Sprachen-Wörterbuch. Deutsch/Polnisch/Russisch/Weissrussisch/Litauisch/Lettisch/Jidisch (1918), Herausgeben im Auftrage des Oberbefehlshabers Ost, Berlin: Presseabteilung des Oberbefehlshabers Ost.

Secondary literature

Constantine, S. (2011), 'War of Words: Bridging the Language Divide in the Great War', *War in History*, 18 (4): 515–29.

Constantine, S. (2013), '"If an Inhabitant Attacks, Wounds or Kills a Soldier, the Whole Village Will Be Destroyed": Communication and Rehearsal in Soldiers' Phrasebooks 1914–1918', *Journal of War & Culture Studies*, 6 (2): 154–68.

Footitt, H. (2010), 'Languages at War: Cultural Preparations for the Liberation of Western Europe', *Journal of War & Culture Studies*, 3 (1): 109–21.

Footitt, H. and M. Kelly (2012), *Languages at War: Policies and Practices of Language Contacts in Conflict*, Basingstoke: Macmillan.

Hallett, R. W. (2017), '"A Taste of This Lively Language": Attitudes Towards Languages Other than English in Lonely Planet Phrasebooks', *Journal of Multicultural Discourses*, 12 (3): 222–38.

Kruus, H. (1920), *Saksa okkupatsioon Eestis*, Tartu: Odamehe kirjastus.

Kuldkepp, M. (2015), 'Hegemony and Liberation in World War I: The Plans for New Mare Nostrum Balticum', *Ajalooline Ajakiri: The Estonian Historical Journal*, (3): 249–84.

Kuldkepp, M. (2019),'Eestlased ja "eestlase vaenlased." Survemeetmed baltisakslaste ja nende poolehoidjate vastu Eesti Vabadussõja ajal', in Tõnu Tannberg (ed.), *Vabadussõja mitu palet*, 365–421, Tartu: Rahvusarhiiv.

Lehmann, J. (1994), 'Der Baltische Vertrauensrat und die Unabhängigkeit der baltischen Staaten Ausgangs des ersten Weltkriegs', *Journal of Baltic Studies*, 25 (2): 131–8.

Loit, A. (2006), 'Baltisaksa rüütelkondade seisukohad ja tegevus Eesti iseseisvumisel 1918-1920', *Tuna: Ajalookultuuri ajakiri*, (4): 50–74.

Mann, B. (1965), *Die baltischen Länder in der deutschen Kriegszielpublizistik 1914-1918*, Tübingen: Mohr.

Pajur, A. (2009), 'Landeswehr'i sõja puhkemine. Eesti vaatenurk', *Tuna. Ajalookultuuri ajakiri*, (2): 58–64.

Raun, T. U. (2001), *Estonia and the Estonians*. Updated Second Edition. Stanford: Hoover Institution Press.

Sheldon, K. (1998), '"Rats Fell from the Ceiling and Pestered Me:" Phrase Books as
    Sources for Colonial Mozambican History', *History in Africa*, 25: 341–60.
Steputat, W. (1915), *Litauischer Sprachführer*. 2. bis 6. verbess. Aufl. Tilsit: Druck und
    Verlag Buchdruckerei 'Lithuania'.

10

Politics of words

Language and loyalty of Czech-speaking soldiers in the Austro-Hungarian army

Jiří Hutečka

In the morning of 19 October 1898, a yearly assembly of reservists of the k.u.k. (*kaiserlich und königlich*, i.e. Imperial and Royal) Infantry Regiment 28 took place in one of the meeting halls of the Prague suburb of Královské Vinohrady, its main purpose being to update important personal data on the men, such as their permanent address and status. The commanding officer *Oberleutnant* Danzer took a roll call, ordering the men to announce their presence by loudly proclaiming *hier*. Three of them, two university students and a journalist, all educated men of middle-class background with a strong affinity to radical Czech nationalism, responded instead by a proud *zde* ('here' in Czech). Oblt Danzer demonstrated remarkably little patience for such shenanigans. Seeing their behaviour as a provocation (which it most certainly was) and an affront to the notion of German being the universal command language of the Habsburg 'common army', he ordered the three offenders to be put under guard and escorted to the barracks, where they were sentenced to two days of arrest (Zuckert 2011: 209). 'This unbelievably offending and disrespectful treatment of the members of the Czech nation happened in the heart of Prague itself!', bellowed *Národní listy*, the primary outlet of Czech liberal nationalism. 'The whole of the nation must rise to defend its sons, whose right of using their mother tongue is denied to them with utmost impudence by all sorts of k.u.k. lieutenants, and when they exercise this right anyway, they are treated as the worst of criminals.'[1]

There is little doubt that the fierce reaction of the press was partially fuelled by the fact that one of the affected 'criminals' was one of their own. Václav Klofáč, who ended up serving the sentence in the barracks library, was not just a radical second lieutenant who decided to support his two junior colleagues (both one-year volunteers, i.e. aspiring reserve officers) in their act of defiance against military authorities; he was both a leading editor of *Národní listy* and a key figure in the recently established Czech National Socialist party, which emerged in reaction to Social Democrats severing their ties with some basic nationalist policies in favour of a more internationalist position in early 1897, creating a space for a party that would harvest the votes of the more nationally minded working-class electorate (Kelly 2006). As such, Klofáč clearly recognized the political value of public gestures made in the name of the nation, and thoroughly milked the opportunity for all it was worth to further the exposure of his young party, starting with joining the 'rebellion' in the first place; having an outlet of *Národní listy* at his disposal only helped to further a widespread promotion of his party as the only bulwark against both 'Austrian militarism' and 'German chauvinism', with language becoming the centrepiece of the whole affair.

The purpose of this chapter is to focus on the 'sons of the Czech nation' in uniform. In particular, we will leap in time a bit into the years of 1914 to 1918, using the abundance of personal accounts written by the soldiers during the First World War to answer a series of questions. First and foremost, was language use in the army really that much of an issue from their perspective? Can we trace the same hostility to the use of other languages than Czech in their accounts as we have apparently seen in the aforementioned example? What meaning did the army, the nationalist politicians and the men in uniform ascribe to the use of language in the army? Second, whatever the original attitude was, did it remain static throughout the war, or do we see any dynamics as the conflict goes on? And third, did the language issue play any role in the way Czech soldiers perceived their loyalty to the Habsburg cause?

Of course, the latter question in particular is already loaded with meaning, as loyalty of the Czech-speaking troops is one of the most discussed themes in any debate on the Austro-Hungarian military and its wartime combat record. According to the traditional consensus, Czech-speaking soldiers despised the war on the side of the Habsburgs, particularly one against their Serb and Russian Slavic brethren, and they spent their time in service either trying to desert or sabotaging the imperial war effort through decidedly lacklustre military performance. In general histories, they are often described as 'passive supporters of Russia' prone to 'mutinies' and 'large-scale desertions', or at least 'popular demonstrations' (Strachan 2001; Clark 2012). Two recent projects summarizing contemporary First World War scholarship similarly point to their disputable loyalty, 'mass surrenders' and 'national conflict' whenever Czechs in the service of the monarchy are mentioned.[2] As noted by recent research, this is basically a stereotyped image based not necessarily on the performance of Czech troops, but much more on its perception as it emerged among both German and Czech nationalists during and after the war, with both groups ironically agreeing on the same interpretation of disloyalty and betrayal for their own political reasons (Lein 2011; Hutečka 2020). However, as has been repeatedly shown, reality, while not necessarily the opposite, was decidedly different – while the Czech-speaking population was not keen on going to war, which it had a hard time understanding, it was anything but disloyal to begin with, and while many proudly self-identified as Czechs, this feeling did not get in the way of their loyalty to the state in 1914 (Hutečka 2020; Boisserie 2017).

Similarly misleading would be to see language practices in the Austro-Hungarian army as an effort to 'Germanize' the recruits, as the Czech nationalists would put it. In fact, the linguistic practice in the Habsburg military was defined by rules so bizarre that they quickly evoke the notion of the proverbial 'tower of Babel', along with serious doubts about its combat effectiveness. The language of command (*Kommandosprache*) in the Imperial or Common Army was – by tradition as well as by convenience from the point of view of the aristocratic top-ranking officers – German. It consisted of about 100 words or phrases every officer and soldier had to know to be able to operate effectively on the battlefield. The language of administration (*Dienstsprache*) in which all the paperwork was produced was German as well. The same applied to the Landwehr, that is, a separate territorial army of the Austrian part of the monarchy; Honvéd, the territorial army of Hungary, adhered to Hungarian. Both Landwehr and the Common Army operated under the framework of the Austrian Constitution of 1867, and therefore had to reflect the constitutional right of the citizens to use their native language while engaging with public institutions. And as the subsequent Conscription Law of 1868 made citizens into conscripts in the new mass army, they had the right to be trained in their respective languages – of which there were officially eleven throughout the empire (Scheer 2016: 63). The solution was ingenuous – if a given group of speakers constituted more than 20 per cent of manpower in a given regiment, their language became a regimental language (*Regimentssprache*) and they had the right to use it in everyday contact with the officers, who were obliged to learn it. If we look at the linguistic patchwork of the Habsburg monarchy and realize that regiments were conscripted regionally, it is hardly surprising that what resulted was an amazing variety of linguistic experiences – in 1914, 162 out of more than 300 regiments and independent battalions were bi- or even multilingual (Deák 1990: 99), and there was only so much their command could do to create linguistically homogenous companies or at least platoons in an effort to make everyday communication more efficient. As a result, 18 out of the 102 Infantry regiments included a contingent of anything between 20 and 95 per cent Czechs in their ranks (Broucek 2003).

Of course, numerous issues emerged under this scheme, especially with there never being enough bilingual officers or those willing (or able) to learn new languages quickly when assigned to a new unit, which led to the language skill requirements often being flouted or, especially in the case of reserve officers, practically ignored (Koldinská and Šedivý 2008). And as the new conscription law brought men of all kinds of class, educational, ethnic and linguistic backgrounds into the army, moments when commanders could not understand their men and vice versa became distressingly commonplace, sometimes leading both to bizarre moments of a k.u.k. company being commanded in English (as it was the only language in which a German-speaking officer and his Hungarian-speaking soldiers who used to work in the United States before the war could communicate), or to a widespread resort to *Armeeslawisch* or *Armeedeutsch*, a military slang mixing various languages, typical for anyone who went through the linguistic experience of the Habsburg army: 'It is because of *lénunk* [*Löhnung* – soldier's pay]', said Josef Švejk to his commander in Jaroslav Hašek's *The Fateful Adventures of the Good Soldier Švejk*, 'and signing me up for *frpflégunk* [*Verpflegung* – rations]' (Hašek 1921, I: 465).[3] These seemingly highly impractical solutions were widely accepted as being a matter of efficiency – the language of command was a practical necessity everyone had to follow in order for the army to be combat effective; the regimental languages were a solution to the issue of everyday communication with a multilingual mass of troops which the army went out of its way to implement, even if it was not necessarily successful in practice. As noted by Tamara Scheer, political dimension was added to it only by the outside forces mostly from the nationalist camp (2016: 64).

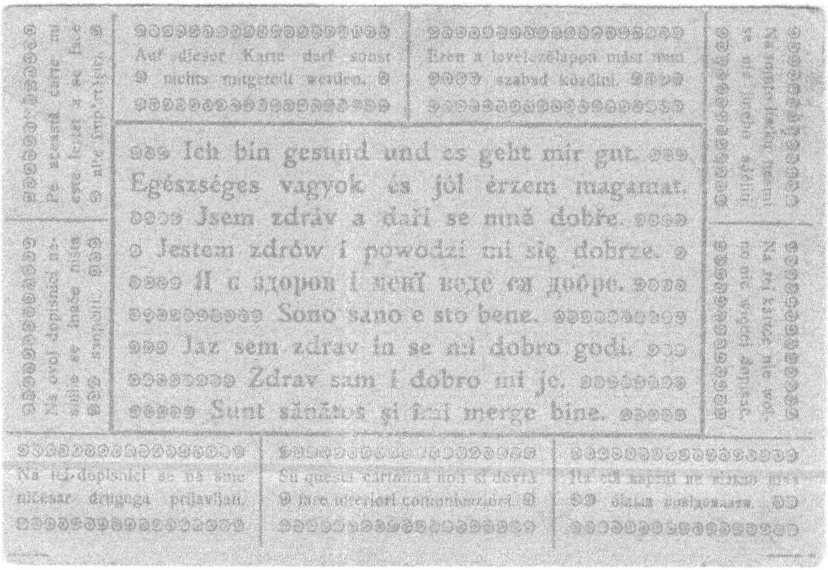

Figure 10.1 'I am in good health and doing well.' A military-issue postcard in nine languages of the monarchy, given to Austro-Hungarian soldiers when all other forms of correspondence were banned for operational reasons (*Military History Institute*, Prague).

It was indeed Tamara Scheer who brought us the most recent work on the language issues in the Austro-Hungarian army (2014; 2016). Building her research on the previous work of scholars such as István Deák and Christoph Allmayer-Beck, who analysed the topic from the point of view of the overwhelmingly German-speaking Habsburg officer class (Deák 1990; Allmayer-Beck 2003), she came to the conclusion that in wartime language use became increasingly politicized. Compared to other groups, German speakers were over-represented in the ranks of the reserve officer corps, and the fact that they often came from middle-class background made them often nationalist-minded and anti-Slavic in their attitudes (Deák 1990: 181–3; see also Schmitz 2016). They lacked experience and had a hard time communicating properly with their men, which contributed to a number of military disasters (some said mass desertions) involving Czech-dominated regiments from Bohemia in the spring of 1915 (Lein 2018). Subsequently, Czech troops were increasingly seen as disloyal and unreliable, their real performance notwithstanding – it was enough that they spoke Czech which made then to be seen as 'nationalist Czech', and therefore suspect. As a result, using Czech language in public or singing Czech patriotic songs became a red flag for many an officer. While before the war, language use in the army was seldom questioned in the mainstream thought, after 1915, many officers as well as the army command itself increasingly sorted languages according to political bias. Some were seen as 'loyal' (i.e. German or Hungarian), and some as 'disloyal' (i.e. Czech, Serb, Italian) (Scheer 2016).

This issue of loyalty vis-à-vis language is of course a potential key to unlock the language experience of Czech-speaking soldiers – the earlier-quoted story of the

Prague reservists may well show that at least some of them understood language in similarly politicized terms. However, was this attitude really that widespread in the ranks during 1890s? Before we start looking for answers, it is important to look into the meaning of language use in the army as it was officially understood by the military authorities and by the nationalists of all kinds, respectively.

Finishing the story of the three men arrested on 19 October 1898 may be of some help here. While it is difficult to establish the overall impact of the affair, the fact is that it kept the readership of most Bohemian newspapers, both Czech and German, entertained for several months. It brought radicals into the streets in public demonstrations, and, based on the reports of the press, it reverberated as far as Hungary, where some reservists took it as an inspiration and made a point of reporting for duty in Hungarian instead of German.[4] Throughout the Bohemian Lands, a number of assemblies of reservists were reported to demand the use of Czech in roll calls, some of them successfully, while the German-language press expressed disappointment at the rumblings that in order to quell the issue, the army was considering skipping the roll calls altogether, seemingly giving up the fight for its German-speaking nature.[5] While it appears that previous practice was highly dependent on the individual officer taking the roll call, with some demanding the use of German and some not, and soldiers just reporting as they were told for decades, it is clear that after November 1898 this seemingly unambiguous process joined the list of contentious issues picked up by the ever-more influential nationalist politicians.

Ultimately, the conflict in Bohemia bubbled over all the way up to the Emperor. Francis Joseph I joined the fray adamantly demanding respect for the 'language of command' according to the regulations, telling a Czech parliamentary deputy during a state dinner that 'on the *zde* issue I can see no compromise. If necessary I will proclaim martial law to settle this business, because I am very strict in military matters' (Rothenberg 1976: 130). After that, Czech radicals backed down and the whole conflict evaporated over the course of 1899. Even so, it was a godsend for Klofáč and his party (which he came to chair in 1899), because it enabled National Socialists to gain visibility as well as distance themselves from their established competitors for the Czech vote by presenting themselves as the most ardent defenders of national rights represented through the sanctity of free language use as guaranteed by the Constitution of 1867 (Kelly 2006: 72).

The choice of language use in the military as the battleground for the ever-radicalizing Czech nationalist movement is symptomatic, as language rights and the use of language in the public space, especially education and government business, became one of the most contested political issues in Bohemia and Moravia during the closing years of the nineteenth century. In recent years, a number of historians have shown how language as the most obvious and visible identifier of one's own identity became the key to the spread of nationalist agenda along with the 'notion that a separate language denotes a separate nation' (Stergar 2019, 2012; also Scheer 2017). Under this logic, complete separation of language groups with minimal overlap became the nationalist solution to the multilingual and multi-ethnic enigma of the Bohemian Lands (Zahra 2008; Judson 2006; King 2002). As in our case, language came to symbolize things far beyond the simple issue of communicating even just the simplest of messages, like one's presence. While we do not know if Oblt Danzer was in fact a 'German chauvinist', as Czech nationalist press defined him, or just a by-the-book pen-pusher, it is obvious that for many of his colleagues including the Emperor himself, the question was far from trivial. The unequivocal insistence on the use of German was not a product of Germanizing tendencies. The word '*hier*' was a symbol of the universal command language of the army which, by extent, was seen as a bulwark of unity of the monarchy besieged by the centrifugal forces of liberalism, nationalism and socialism. From the point of view of the Emperor, as long as these forces were kept out of the army, it would be able to represent the ultimately unified nature of the Habsburg power over its subjects, inoculating them with dynastic patriotism not only through the common experience of military service, but also by the commonly shared language experience connected to it. Without the single language of command, there would be no order, no unity, no patriotism and, at the end, no empire (Stergar 2019: 59–60).

Similarly, the words '*hier*' and '*zde*', respectively, carried even more charged symbolism for both German and Czech nationalist politicians. As accurately noted by Pieter Judson, the Constitution of 1867 inadvertently opened space which soon became a battleground of emerging nationalisms (Judson 2006). Nationalists readily applied the right to use their own language wherever it served the purpose of enlarging their power base, making language use at schools and in official correspondence a crucial issue of national survival (Zahra 2008). Language conflict represented a visible, easily understandable and relatable field where the national question could be played out in front of the widest possible audience defined by simple preference to one of the languages. When Count Badeni's cabinet introduced the so-called Badeni Language Ordinances in April 1897 to solve the ever-growing conflict by introducing language equality into all government business in Bohemia, German nationalists went apoplectic as they interpreted the measure as discrimination, as, while Czech speakers often learned German as part of the higher education, German speakers had little social incentive to learn Czech. The result was a series of street protests and riots throughout the Bohemian and Austrian Lands, with the army being deployed to quell them and martial law introduced in a number of cities (Wingfield 2007: 48–78). Besides ultimately bringing Badeni down along with his cabinet in November, the crisis showed clearly the inherent connection of nationalism to the issue of language use (Germans defending their prerogative, Czechs demanding a share in it and the government caught in the middle), as well as its destabilizing potential to the army – more than thirty reserve officers were stripped of their rank because of their participation in the anti-Czech riots in Graz (Deák 1990: 68).

Looking at the other side of the barricade right after the Emperor quelled another potential disruption to the army's unity in the *hier/zde* affair, we see Václav Klofáč, who, on being elected a deputy in the *Reichsrat* (Austrian Parliament), repeatedly insisted that 'we must bring a fundamental solution to the situation in the army ... We must put the Czech language on equal footing and make it a language of administration in the Bohemian Lands'. His preferred solution to the unsatisfactory situation in the Austro-Hungarian military was reforming it along local-based contingents of national militia, doing away with what he saw as the ultimately aristocratic, Germanizing and anti-democratic regular army. Tellingly, he also pointed out: 'All efforts in assimilation have to cease immediately' (Klofáč 1908: 17). As every nationalist, Klofáč saw assimilation into other social bodies, be it the German nation or a nation based on Austrian imperial patriotism, as by far the biggest threat. His understanding of the symbolic importance of language even became a target of his own party comrades from the radical socialist-pacifist wing, who wryly noted with regard to the ex-national liberals like him: 'The Czech public often holds anti-military attitudes, but the reasons for these are purely nationalist. It would be enough to introduce Czech as a universal regimental language in the army and many a Czech bourgeois townsman would quickly abandon his opposition to this "God-given" institution.'[6]

However, this criticism did not stop nationalists like Klofáč from disseminating their message both in speeches in the *Reichsrat* as well as on the streets of Bohemian and Moravian towns. Connected with an anti-militarist political position criticizing everything connected with the army, it made Czech-speaking soldiers natural targets for their vigorous campaigning. Looking at the history of Czech soldiers' behaviour prior to 1914, one may be tempted to admit their success. While the well-known incident when soldiers of k.u.k. Infantry Regiment 28 from Prague refused to accept catering services from the German-controlled city council in České Budějovice/ Budweis in 1905 (hence the 'sausage affair', as it became known) is a good example of how pressure from German nationalist elites turned relative national indifference into a nationalized protest, 'Czechifying both soldiers and Social Democrats in town' (King 2002: 126–7), numerous incidents during the mobilizations against Serbia in 1908 and 1912 indicated high levels of nationalist and panslavist indoctrination in the ranks (Plaschka 1985a and b). An alarming number of Czech-speaking units participated in anti-war demonstrations, clashed with their German-speaking counterparts during transport, refused to board trains and even briefly took over control of a train station in Pardubice (Pichlík 1961: 11). Based on this experience, the k.u.k. military authorities essentially gave up on Czech troops and ordered to add the Styrian III Corps to the partial mobilization plans in order to 'make up for the trouble' expected in Bohemia (Šedivý 2001: 30).

At the end, however, these fears did not materialize and the 1914 mobilization in Bohemia went surprisingly smoothly, the k.u.k. Ministry of the Interior reporting only nine cases of desertion here in August (Rauchensteiner 2014: 165). For the majority of Czech-speaking recruits, loyalty to the state and their duty did not create high enough tension with whatever other identity they harboured to discourage them from heeding the call (Hutečka 2020). Similarly, their attitude to the language question was apparently much more nuanced than what both nationalists and the military authorities would expect from would-be-traitors.

The war they were about to live through was indeed a 'linguistic experience' par excellence, as one would indeed expect in a multilingual army: 'In my štafl [*Staffel*], I have Poles, Germans, Ruthenes, Romanians, Hungarians, one Slovak and a Serb, and I am a Czech. Eight nationalities among 100 people, and everybody has to understand me and I have to understand them', a Czech reserve officer serving with a supply column noted in a letter to his wife in 1915. 'Sometimes it is difficult, but overall, it works and we all have found a new home with our štafl' (Michalec 2018: 89; 6 April 1915). Sometimes, language caused him more trouble than expected, such as when some Czechs arrived as replacements to his unit and soon took offence at some of their comrades using 'a not very nice phrase, which you know well from your visits and which is very common for Poles and Ruthenians, but carries a burden of serious offence for Czechs – and emotions flared up.' (Michalec 2018: 110, 26 April 1916). Besides that, however, his letters written during his almost four years of service are bereft of any mention of language conflicts. In that he differs little from dozens of his colleagues, including those of much lesser rank than *Oberleutnant*.

In fact, it seems that for many soldiers, language was generally a non-issue they only notice when it is directly affecting their present situation. Otherwise, in most diaries and letters, language goes unnoticed for months of the author's wartime existence, and the moment it gets mentioned, it often betrays a sort of language indifference that would be hardly comprehensible to most nationalists, as it seems to ignore any inherent political value in its use. After all, as one Czech-speaking recruit from Vienna described his comrades, 'they were mostly sons of peasants, people with little education and simple needs, used to obeying and working hard' (Tříska 2001: 23) Thus, an infantryman recorded in his diary that his unit, a battalion from Jihlava/ Iglau, was always enthusiastically singing a number of a bit vulgar songs in both Czech and German while on the march (Kubík 2005: 10). Similarly, many a description of Christmas Eve, especially early in the war, is rather similar to the following: 'There were also some Christmas trees along the road, with soldiers singing; they were singing all around the place, by the fires, in Polish, Hungarian, Italian, and a lot in Czech, too' (Michalec 2018: 38, 24 December 1914). Symptomatically, not only the language, but the songs themselves were still mostly outside of political scrutiny during the early

Figure 10.2 A postcard by 'Emil' sent on 1 April 1915. 'Easter Wishes from the Carpathians' in German is supplemented by the sender's additional 'Happy Easter' inscription in Czech (*Museum of Eastern Bohemia*, Hradec Králové).

months of the war, with numerous units leaving for the front to the accompaniment of 'patriotic songs' which would get the men arrested a year later: 'The band played "*Kde domov můj*" [Czech patriotic song, the future national anthem of Czechoslovakia] and the train started to move' (Svobodný 2019: 5, 19 March 1915; also Bouček 1998: 13, August 1914).

Of course, it would not be right to claim that no Czech soldier at the beginning of the war felt exasperation or even indignation at the language rules they encountered in the ranks. Especially those higher up the educational ladder, of middle-class origins and often from monolingual regions seem to be much more sensitive to which language are they expected to use. As noted by a reserve medical officer (and a future Czechoslovak legionnaire) serving in Galicia in the Fall of 1914, 'to speak Czech was not necessarily dangerous, but definitely suspicious' (Bouček 1998: 15). Another middle-class soldier found it difficult to stomach how he and his comrades were treated only because of their language skills: 'Hardly any of us spoke German, and even those who did were completely confounded by all the military drill. As a result, our report to the Lieutenant did not go well. . . . Already the first one of us, a comrade named Sokol, a civil engineer back home, had messed everything up immediately. The captain joined in: "Wie heissen Sie?" [What is your name?] "Sokol." "Was sind Sie in Zivil?" [What do you do as a civilian?] etc. Then the Captain noticed the difficulty Sokol had in expressing himself. "Why don't you know any German? What did you study? Where? In Prague? But Prague is a German town, only maids and *pepiks* [derisive term for Czech-speaking lower classes] speak Czech there. It must have been a nice company indeed you were in, not learning any German while in there!"' (Hodek 2004: 2). Also, the men who answered the call of radical politics during the pre-war years, protesting their deployment against their Slavic brothers in 1908 and 1912, violently clashing with their German compatriots in the process, did not disappear; they were still very much there, but it seems that the general mobilization of the masses left them a minority, drowned in social pressure: 'Tůma, who so often indulged in radical talk about the Czech nation and its hatred towards the government in Vienna, proposed that we should sing "*Hej Slované*" [a pan-Slavist anthem] on our departure from the barracks', noted one infantryman in his diary. '[He says] better to be shot now than to go against our Russian brothers. I wonder what's he up to.' A day later, he added: 'Departure from the barracks was quiet; Tůma didn't start any revolution; he walked in front of me, a bit drunk, quietly singing "No-one loves me anymore"' (Vaněk 2013: 33–4; 15 and 16 February 1915).

It seems that the early months of the war, with the immense expectations, anxieties and pressures, left many a would-be nationalist keeping to themselves and suffering what they thought to be a gross injustice perpetrated against their mother tongue and therefore their nation as well. In the sum of personal accounts available to us, however, they seem to represent a minority. For most Czech-speaking servicemen, language was primarily a tool of communication. Secondarily, they understood that use of language in the army was situational and reflected both the official directives (which situations, when and in what unit a certain language was required or allowed), social pressures in the case of the officers talking to other officers or the other ranks, or individual attitudes of those present at a given moment. There are numerous instances of soldiers or junior officers who, otherwise mostly silent vis-à-vis language use, happily report a moment when they were officially allowed to speak to their superiors in their native tongue, usually leading to otherwise impossible informal conversations: 'We hold Major Müller in high respect. . . . He is a regular, knows no danger for himself and takes care of his soldiers. He is sympathetic to everyone's concerns. He also openly proclaims to be of Czech nationality, even though his education was German. He often recalls his mother, saying: "Only that language is my mother tongue which my mother has taught me. . . . By the Christmas tree, the regulations are forgotten and we only speak Czech" (Skála 1937: 125–6). This diary entry shows us the oft-expressed preference of the men for regular officers who, in their eyes, were often less nationalist in their world view. It also brings us to the rather typical trope in Czech soldiers' discourse of their wartime experience, where language plays support role to the character of the given officer.

Indeed, language preference is often mentioned by the soldiers only to add colour to an already-established situation as well as to the feelings they express about it. The case of immediate superiors in instructive, as it is included in almost every diary and in many correspondence collections, too, at least to an extent allowed by censorship. Using this example, we see that even soldiers who expressed strong affinities towards national self-identification early in the war still preferred to judge officers by their character first, their language of preference second – Major Müller is first and foremost a brave soldier and a good leader caring for his men; his willingness to address other ranks in Czech is a bonus of sorts. '*Obrlajtnant* [*Oberleutnant*] Šátral . . . shot himself . . ', noted one soldier in his diary in 1914. 'He was young, handsome, really enjoyed war, tried to be the first in every skirmish. It was a shame to lose him, even though he was a German . . . or at least always spoke to us in German' (Prudil 1990: 18). In December 1915, another soldier went on to express similar attitude to the issue of language: 'The Colonel is an honest man. . . . He always says that he is not afraid of his men and does not care if they're Germans or Czechs, as he knows only soldiers. He is a German from Carinthia himself, can't speak a word in Czech' (Skála 1937: 122). Language is often mentioned only as a secondary qualifier with little potential to improve the image of those who did not pass the test of moral or soldiery qualities: 'Horzinek was the name/visit us he indeed did/In Czech he spoke, and tame/at first our fears grew thin. . . . But it was the only shtick/that good about him was/As we quickly learned/all of his crazy thoughts.'[7]

All these men thought it necessary to mention the language preferences of their officers, which makes them – as we have mentioned – somewhat exceptional. For them, language carried a symbolic value which was only loosely attached to their practical concerns regarding the way they communicated with the world around them. While for the Emperor and the army, the command language represented the unity of the empire, and for the nationalists, either a proof of dominance or a threat of assimilation and 'denationalization', for the soldiers it was the regimental languages and their use (or not use) which often underscored a character of the authority. Good officers are said to be tolerant to things Czech, including speech, or even encourage its use while being Czech or not themselves, this further showing respect for the men who feel they are treated as equals to an extent. In a similar example, the flourishing pre-war Czech veterans associations were not interested in joining their German-speaking counterparts in a common federation unless the Czech language was given equal status with German in the proceedings (Cole 2013: 291); the men who followed in their footsteps during the war may have felt the same, acknowledging every authority that gave them equal treatment in this regard. While for most of the men this issue apparently remained under their radar, as it had little effect upon their immediate well-being, those who took notice were often critical when things smelled to them like disrespect expressed through language use or abuse. For them, this was a sure sign of a character fault which disqualified the authorities in question completely: 'We divided the officer corps into two groups: the true officers, i.e. men who could be addressed *"Herr Leutnant"* as well as *"pane poručíku"* . . . and *"Die Herren Offiziere"*, who did not understand the Czech phrase, or did not want to, or did not tolerate it . . . These men, though, came to the trenches only when these were deep and solid, and that only once or twice.'[8] The extended logic of the argument that only a good character reflected in one's attitude to language equality led to the conclusion that those who made fuss about language regulations or even requested the Czech language not being used at all were cowardly characters in the first place. In this way, the more linguistically sensitive Czech soldiers applied a specific filter which 'helped' them, at least in their eyes, to identify who was a good commander and who was not.

The problem was that soon after the Austro-Hungarian war effort ran into trouble in the Fall of 1914 and some Czech-dominated units faltered and surrendered in April and May 1915 on the Eastern front, a perfect storm formed of the army command looking for scapegoats and the army being increasingly commanded by those who came from the background already mistrustful of anything Czech – the German- and Hungarian-speaking reserve officers (Schmitz 2016: 84–91). With everyone vividly remembering all those pre-war attacks by Václav Klofáč and other nationalists, the situation for Czech-speaking soldiers and officers turned increasingly sour. The previously more or less non-contentious language situation in the army may have brought its frustrations in practical situations to many and served some as a rough-and-ready tool to quickly identify the character of the military authorities, but it remained mostly without direct influence on the men's well-being. This changed with the reports of 'Czech treason' filling the pages German and Hungarian newspapers and spreading like fire. Suddenly, the relatively few and far between instances of language being seen as a politically charged issue became a widespread phenomenon. In a curious reversal of the soldiers' logic described earlier, the army authorities as well as the general public came to see use of Czech as a decidedly negative reflection on the soldiers' character.

As in this process *all* Czech speakers were lumped together, suddenly even those men who previously took no notice of the language issue were often painfully reminded of who they were – just because of what language they speak. Over the next three years of the war, an ever-increasing number of Czech-speaking soldiers had the opportunity to experience bad treatment in terms of harsh disciplinary measures and frequent application of collective guilt expressed in purely national terms, with language serving as a tool of identification, not communication. What was arguably an exception to the rule in 1914–15 became a pattern and later an outright policy reflected on by the men between 1915 and 1918: 'Our command took care to make life for all Czech people in uniform as miserable as possible, all the time', noted a university-

Figure 10.3 Officers and NCOs of the 3rd *Marschkompanie* (Replacement Company) of the infamous k.u.k. Infantry Regiment 28 from Prague posing for a group photo. The unit was dishonoured and disbanded in the spring of 1915, with only one battalion being kept intact and relocated to Hungary, and then Styria, and later deployed with great success in Italy. Notwithstanding, in a statement of esprit de corps, these men proudly showcase both their unit's title and its regimental language (Czech) on a placard with a telling and highly ironic inscription: '20 July 1917, k. u. k. Infantry Rgt. 28 in Bruck an der Mur, 3rd *Marschkompanie* of the "Children of Prague". Appreciate them now as they won't last!' (*Military History Institute*, Prague).

educated one-year volunteer in his diary as early as October 1914. 'It was just because of our nationality. They were saying that a lot of men were deserting to the Russians' (Opletal 1998: 13, 21 October 1914). Over the following years, the experience of public humiliation became a staple of the soldiers' war accounts, often connected to the use of language. Immediately after k.u.k. Infantry Regiment 28, the Czech-speaking unit which supposedly deserted to the Russians in April 1915, had been dishonoured and disbanded by the Emperor, a Czech-speaking officer serving with a Slavonian regiment recorded a 'nasty recollection' of a classmate in the officer training school in Obilin, Croatia, who 'had introduced himself to me with a derisive greeting of "hands up", just to let me know his offensive opinion of the Czechs. He considered us cowards, who would throw their arms up in the air the moment they saw the enemy.' (Šmída 2014: 24–5) From the way he recorded the experience, it is obvious that he regarded it as offensive, and felt even worse when he realized that it was just because he had expressed himself publicly in Czech. Similarly, in Szeged, Hungary, a Czech-speaking unit was greeted by nurses looking out of the windows of a hospital, 'mockingly raising their arms and laughing at us openly'. The only reaction the men could come up with was disgust at their own plight: 'Just look at those fucking Magyar bitches up there!' (Lirš 1936: 24). Of course, this sort of attitude left many a soldier doubting their loyalty to a system that failed to provide them with basic respect for their excruciating service. Even those who had previously shown little interest in nationalist agenda were left with feelings of increased exasperation and anger: 'The Corps commander . . . made a speech [that] was full of bile and hatred for everything Czech. He wanted to degrade and humiliate us. You could see the helpless, unbound anger in everyone's eyes' (Skála 1937: 15).

The most depressing part from the point of view of the soldiers was that the label, carried on the symbolical realignment and politicization of language, stuck. In December 1917, several German nationalist deputies presented the *Reichsrat* with a 400-page-long summary of the Czechs' betrayal (Lein 2011: 14). It soon got published and appeared in Prague bookstores along other similar titles (Cornwall 2000: 33). And it was still one's language which made one a target of this campaign: 'We cannot speak a word in Czech, otherwise they'll point at us and put their hands up in the air. . . . It's just tiresome, and there's no hope of it getting any better except for death' (Dolejší 2014: 258, 28 August 1918). The general feeling of an undeserved and increasingly institutionalized injustice generated, not surprisingly, a growing resentment among Czech-speaking servicemen. Many felt that while they sacrificed their lives in a war they hardly understood, the only thing they were getting in return was disrespect, scoff and accusations aimed at them just because of the language they spoke. Not surprisingly, many went on to accept the logic of such group identification and started to interpret all kinds of perceived mistreatments, injustices and offences, as well as increasingly catastrophic supply problems at the front and economic failures at home, in the same terms, that is, as a consequence of national conflict; what was a matter of class or general anti-war attitude before became a matter of national identity (Kučera 2013). Turning everyday use of language into a politicized act painfully reminded Czech soldiers of their 'suspect' status at every turn, giving them little choice: they could either stop using the language, which many did not want or simply could not do from a practical point of view, or they could just accept the 'disloyal' status ascribed to them collectively, thus internalizing the nationalist notion that language defines a group. Their group, as they were often told, was defined by disloyalty, which could hardly made them more loyal or enthusiastic.

Ultimately, it is an utmost irony that it was the Austro-Hungarian military authorities who, because of their nationalist-induced pre-war paranoia and subsequent dynamic changes brought by war, sowed disaffection which led many previously borderline indifferent men to realize that because of their preferred language, their political interests were not potentially similar to those of the Empire. While the soldiers were often as exasperated by the 'tower of Babel' of the Austro-Hungarian military as anyone, the process of politicizing language use had opened a can of worms by making the connection between language and loyalty. As a result, men increasingly understood the meaning of language in the similar terms pre-war nationalists tried to promote throughout their radical political campaigns, which was a consequence opposite to what the military authorities hoped to achieve by their crackdown on 'disloyal' behaviour. Nationalist discourse was becoming more and more acceptable and language moved from an issue picked up by a vocal nationalist minority to a matter of everyday experience of the many. This, of course, was not a preordained conclusion.

But it was the army itself which, at the end, made many Czech speakers into conscious Czechs by its policy of identifying one's loyalty through their use of speech. In doing so, it made nations out of language groups more efficiently than any pre-war nationalists could hope for. The wartime Austro-Hungarian military therefore became the best ally Václav Klofáč could hope for.

Notes

1   *Národní listy* 38, no. 289, 20 October 1898, p. 1.
2   See Ziemann (2014: 122); and Watson (2014: 194).
3   The diary of Bohuš Adamíra includes a similar example: '14 February [1916]. *Rast* [rest] the whole day, as there will be some night work. We will be building *Spanischereiter* [Spanish riders, a type of obstacle] in front of the Italian trenches from *Stickpunkt* [stick points] 37 to 40. Not a shot from a *kvér* [*gewehr* – a rifle]. . . . There are woods on fire somewhere. We took *kvérs*, *patrontaše* [*patrontasche* – pouches] and *holcvercajk* [*holzwehrzeig* – wood-cutting tools] and went . . . We dig *laufgraben* [communication trenches].' Adamíra (2014: 64 and 71).
4   *Národní listy* 39, no. 297, 26 October 1899, p. 1.
5   *Vaterland* 39, 2 November 1898, p. 1.
6   *Mladé proudy* 7, no. 8, 4 August 1907, p. 1.
7   Slezák (1961: 120).
8   Flaišer (1931: 104).

References

Adamíra, B. (2014), 'Deník Bohuše Adamíry', in Miloš Konečný (ed.), *Když naši dědové bojovali a umírali v 1. světové válce*, 61–75, Vlkov: Obecní úřad.

Allmayer-Beck, J. C. (2003), 'Die Führung vielsprachiger Streitkräfte: Die k.u.k. Armee als Beispiel', in P. Broucek and E. A. Schmidl (eds), *Militär, Geschichte und politische Bildung: Aus Anlass des 85. Geburtstages des Autors*, 370–84, Vienna: Böhlau.

Boisserie, E. (2017), *Les Tchèques dans l'Autriche-Hongrie en guerre (1914–1918)*. Paris: Eur'Orbem.

Bouček, B. (1998), *Prosím, aby zápisník byl odevzdán mé ženě jako pozůstalost*, edited by P. Payne, Prague: Medard.

Broucek, P. (2003), 'Die Mehrsprachigkeit und Sprachenpolitik in den Einheiten der k. und k. Armee in den böhmischen Ländern', in J. Ernst (ed.), *250 Jahre Fremdsprachenausbildung im österreichischen Militär am Beispiel des Tschechischen*, 16–21, Vienna: Landesverteidigungsakademie.

Clark, C. (2012), *Sleepwalkers: How Europe Went to War in 1914*, London: Penguin.

Cole, L. (2013), *Military Culture and Popular Patriotism in Late Imperial Austria*, Oxford: Oxford University Press.

Cornwall, M. (2000), *The Undermining of Austria-Hungary: The Battle for Hearts and Minds*, London: Palgrave.

Deák, I. (1990), *Beyond Nationalism: A Social and Political History of the Habsburg Officer Corps, 1848–1918*, Oxford: Oxford University Press.

Dolejší, A. (2014), *Válečné vzpomínky z první světové války vojína Dolejše z Nového Strašecí*, edited by D. Neprašová, Brno: unknown.

Flaišer, V. (1931), *Důstojníci a oficíři u 30. střel. pluku*, in A. Žipek (ed.), *Domov za války*, vol. 4, 104–8, Prague: Pokrok.

Hašek, J. (1921), *Osudy dobrého vojáka Švejka za světové války*, 4 vols, Prague: A. Sauer.

Hodek, J. (2004), *Hrst vzpomínek z první světové války*, Plzeň: Studijní a vědecká knihovna Plzeňského kraje.

Hutečka, J. (2020), *Men under Fire: Motivation, Morale and Masculinity among Czech Soldiers in the Great War, 1914–1918*, Oxford: Berghahn.

Judson, P. (2006), *Guardians of the Nation: Activists on the Language Frontiers of Imperial Austria*, Cambridge: Cambridge University Press.

Kelly, T. M. (2006), *Without Remorse: Czech National Socialism in Late-Habsburg Austria*, New York: Columbia University Press.

King, J. (2002), *Budweisers into Czechs and Germans*, Princeton: Princeton University Press.

Klofáč, V. (1908), *Armáda a český národ*, Prague: Ant. Hajn.

Koldinská, M. and I. Šedivý (2008), *Válka a armáda v českých dějinách: Sociohistorické črty*, Prague: Nakladatelství Lidové noviny.

Kubík, F. (2005), *Přežil jsem. Frontový deník z 1. světové války*, Nové Město na Moravě: Horácké muzeum.

Kučera, R. (2013), 'Entbehrung und Nationalismus: Die Erfahrung tschechischer Soldaten der österechisch-ungarischen Armee 1914–1918', in B. Bachinger and W. Dornik Innsbruck (eds), *Jenseits des Schützengrabens. Der Erste Weltkrieg im Osten: Erfahrung – Wahrnehmung – Kontext*, 121–38, Innsbruck: StudienVerlag.

Lein, R. (2011), *Pflichterfüllung oder Hochverrat? Die tschechischen Soldaten Österreich-Ungarns im Ersten Weltkrieg*, Vienna: LITVerlag.

Lein, R. (2018), 'Zwischen Pflichterfullung und Nationalgefiihl. Die tschechischen Soldaten der k.u.k. Armee', in O. Überegger (ed.), *Minderheiten-Soldaten. Ethnizität und Identität in den Armeen des Ersten Weltkriegs*, 25–43, Leiden: Ferdinand Schöningh.

Lirš, F. (1936), *S Osmadvacátníky za světové války*, Prague: František Rebec.

Michalec, L. (2018), *Pradědova válka. Dopisy z fronty (1914–1918)*, Prague: Triton.

Opletal, B. (1998), *Anabáze hanáckého medika, 1914–1920*, Prague: Paseka.

Pichlík, K. (1961), *Čeští vojáci proti válce (1914–1915)*, Praha: Naše vojsko.

Plaschka, R. G. (1985a), '"… a střílet nebudem!" Ein Modellfall zur Frage der Auswirkung der Balkankriege auf Österreich-Ungarn', in R. G. Plaschka and H. Haselsteiner (eds), *Nationalismus – Staatsgewalt – Widerstand: Aspekte nationaler und sozialer Entwicklung in Ostmittel- und Südeuropa*, 246–52, Vienna: Verlag für Gechichte und Politik.

Plaschka, R. G. (1985b), 'Serbien und die Balkankriege als Motivationselemente in der österreichisch-ungarischen Armee', in R. G. Plaschka and H. Haselsteiner (eds), *Nationalismus – Staatsgewalt – Widerstand: Aspekte nationaler und sozialer Entwicklung in Ostmittel- und Südeuropa*, 246–52, Vienna: Verlag für Gechichte und Politik.

Prudil, F. (1990), *Legionářská odyssea. Deník Františka Prudila*, edited by O. Jurman, Prague: Lucie.

Rauchensteiner, M. (2014), *The First World War and the End of the Habsburg Monarchy*, Vienna: Böhlau.

Rothenberg, G. E. (1976), *The Army of Francis Joseph*, West Lafayette: Purdue University Press.

Scheer, T. (2014), 'Die k.u.k. Regimentssprachen: Eine Institutionalisierung der Sprachenvielfalt in der Habsburgermonarchie (1867/8-1914)', in M. Niedhammer and M. Nekula (eds), *Sprache, Gesellschaft und Nation in Ostmitteleuropa. Institutionalisierung und Alltagspraxis*, 75–92, Göttingen: Vandenhoeck & Ruprecht.

Scheer, T. (2016), 'Habsburg Languages at War: "The Linguistic Confusion at the Tower of Babel Couldn't Have Been Much Worse"', in J. Walker and C. Declerq (eds), *Languages and the First World War: Communicating in a Transnational War*, 62–78, London: Palgrave.

Scheer, T. (2017), 'Konstruktionen von ethnischer Zugehörigkeit und Loyalität in der k.u.k. Armee der Habsburger Monarchie (1868–1914)', in A. Millner and K. Teller (eds), *Transdifferenz und Transkulturalität. Migration und Alterität in den Literaturen und Kulturen Österreich-Ungarns*, 155–74, Bielefeld: Transcript.

Schmitz, M. (2016), 'Als ob die Welt aus den Fugen ginge': *Kriegserfahrungen österreichisch-ungarischer Offiziere 1914–18*, Paderborn: Ferdinand Schöningh.

Šedivý, I. (2001), *Češi, české země a Velká válka 1914–1918*, Prague: Nakladatelství Lidové noviny.

Skála, F. (1937), *Válečný deník, 1914–1918*, Kyšperk: Alois Otava.

Slezák, J. (1961), *Paměti Josefa Slezáka k I. světové válce*, manuscript, 5 vols, Regional Museum in Dobruška – Archival Collections (unprocessed).

Šmída, F. (2014), *Vzpomínky z vojny 1914–1919*, edited by M. Kobza, Olomouc: Poznání.

Stergar, R. (2012), 'National Indifference in the Heyday of Nationalist Mobilization? Ljubljana Military Veterans and the Language of Command', *Austrian History Yearbook*, 43 (1): 45–58.

Stergar, R. (2019), 'The Evolution of Linguistic Policies and Practices of the Austro-Hungarian Armed Forces in the Era of Ethnic Nationalisms: The Case of Ljubljana-Laibach', in M. Prokopovych, C. Bethke and T. Scheer (eds), *Language Diversity in the Late Habsburg Empire*, Leiden: Brill.

Strachan, H. (2001), *The First World War*, Volume 1: *To Arms*, Oxford: Oxford University Press.

Svobodný, J. (2019), *Válečný deník*, Brno: Šimon Ryšavý.

Tříska, J. (2001), *Zapomenutá fronta: vojákův deník a úvahy jeho syna*, edited by J. F. Tříska, Prague: Ivo Železný.

Vaněk, K. (2013), *Charašó pán, da? Zápisky všelijakého vojáka, 1914–1919*, Prague: Dauphin.

Watson, A. (2014), 'Mutinies and Military Morale', in H. Strachan (ed.), *The Oxford Illustrated History of the First World War*, 191–203, Oxford: Oxford University Press.

Wingfield, N. M. (2007), *Flag Wars and Stone Saints: How the Bohemian Lands became Czech*, Cambridge, MA: Harvard University Press.

Zahra, T. (2008), *Kidnapped Souls: National Indifference and the Battle for Children in the Bohemian Lands, 1900–1948*, Ithaca: Cornell University Press.

Ziemann, B. (2014), 'Soldiers', in G. Hirschfeld, G. Krumeich and I. Renz (eds), *Brill's Encyclopedia of the First World War*, vol. 1, 118–28, Leiden: Brill.

Zückert, M. (2011), 'Antimilitarismus und soldatische Resistenz: Politischer Protest und armeefeindliches Verhalten in der tschechischen Gesellschaft bis 1918', in L. Cole, C. Hämmerle and M. Scheutz (eds), *Glanz – Gewalt – Gehorsam: Militär und Gesellschaft in der Habsburgermonarchie (1880 bis 1918)*, 199–220, Essen: Klartext.

Part III

Non-combatants

Introduction to Part III

Jane Potter

In total war, it is not only soldiers who are faced with linguistic challenges and a need for a new vocabulary to define their experiences. Non-combatants on what may loosely be called 'the home front' as well as those confined to prisoner-of-war (POW) camps also found themselves engaging with language in new ways and/or creating a vocabulary that would fit their day-to-day experiences. The chapters in this section take us to a POW camp on the outskirts of Berlin, to the streets of Russia, to the corridors of power and philanthropy in the United Kingdom. Each demonstrates a distinct experience, but all are linked by language, revealed in what Emily Hayman calls 'multilingual fragments' (Hayman 2014: 2) in hitherto neglected printed texts, contemporary memoirs and civic records. The scholars featured in the following pages draw our attention to charity books published and sold in Britain for the benefit of Belgian refugees, reminiscences of former internees at Ruhleben Camp, and the database of the Russian National Corpus.

In 'Translating charity for allied aliens: Belgian charity books in Britain', Christophe Declercq demonstrates how Victorian and Edwardian philanthropy informed the response to the waves of Belgian refugees who sought protection in Britain from the outset of the war in August 1914. Numbering in their tens of thousands, these often-traumatized exiles became a tool of propaganda, used not only to justify Britain's involvement in the conflict, but to reinforce ongoing support for the war effort. Charity gift books were produced to raise money for relief funds and a whole host of popular writers (some now forgotten) rallied to the effort, notably Hall Caine. Publishers such as Hodder and Stoughton, in funding the production and distribution of such gift books, made the book trade complicit in government propaganda, responding to both their own sense of duty to country and to the advantages that such worthy publicity would bring to their firms. Declercq focuses on six publications, which went to market between 1914 and 1916, and traces the trend in their linguistic and translational aspects: *Poems of the Great War* (Chatto and Windus, 1914); *Special Belgian Relief Number* (Everyman/JM Dent, 1914); *King Albert's Book* (*The Daily Telegraph*, 1914); *Princess Mary's Gift Book* (Hodder and Stoughton, 1914); *The Glory of Belgium* (Erskine MacDonald, 1915); and *A Book of Belgium's Gratitude* (John Lane, The Bodley Head, circa 1915/16). The 'cross-cultural, multilingual, transnational and translational aspects' of the charity books makes them one of the most fascinating outputs of the British cultural home front.

While non-combatants such as publishers and authors found a ready market for their wares among the home fronts, POWs were literally a captive audience. Not only were they the recipients of vast consignments of books, periodicals and other reading material sent to them by well-wishing citizens at home, but they were truly immersed in a multilingual environment. Jamie Calladine, in '"Berlitz Krieg": The development of a modern language pedagogy at Ruhleben civilian internment camp', highlights how prisoners devoted 'rigorous and passionate study' to what amounted to over ten modern languages. This was supported by the camp school and 'delivered by a diverse cohort of teachers, approximately a third of which had occupied positions as tutors in Britain and across Europe', especially with innovative schools such as Berlitz and Institut Tilly. Calladine 'uncovers how language impacted on the lived experience of internment and provided the relief and stimulation that comforted civilian internees through an unprecedented state of enforced inactivity'.

Lived experience also impacts on language, a fact that is borne out by Golubinov in his chapter entitled, '*Khvosty, meshochniki* and "internal Germans": The transformation of everyday life language in Russia during the First World War'. Here Golubinov hones in on 'practices of surviving' on the home front and how these were reflected, in addition to the Russian language, as 'old and rare terms became ubiquitous and found new significance'. Specifically, Iaroslav Golubinov concentrates on the practice of the queue *khvosty* (tails) for consumer goods, something which even today resonates as a feature of the Soviet system. In fact, the queue had a much longer history but found new meaning during 1914–18, and adjunct words were attached to it. Gradually, 'new elements of everyday life in the language (and, consequently, in the space of social practices)' emerged: *khvostetsy* Moscow 'line people'; *meshochnichestvo* ('literally, bagging, from word *meshok* – bag') denoted a 'type of public organization intended for the food supply of the urban population' with its own *meshochniki* (bag men); and *vnutrennie nemtsy*, 'internal Germans', profiteers who were thus both external and domestic enemies. Golubinov demonstrates how wartime brought out a particular resilience in the Russian language, 'an unprecedented adaptability' to invent new words to describe non-combatants' acute, everyday need for food.

The global war, which touched all aspects of day-to-day life, was by its very nature multilingual; the violence of 1914–18 had not only physical and mental consequences but cultural ones, a good of deal which was expressed – or tried to be expressed – through language. The three chapters that follow demonstrate just how varied that adaptation was among non-combatants and the degrees to which multilinguism was crucial to emotional and cultural, if not physical, survival.

References

Hayman, E. (2014), *Inimical Languages: Conflicts of Multilingualism in British Modernist Literature*, Columbia University: Unpublished doctoral dissertation.

11

Khvosty, meshochniki and 'internal Germans'

The transformation of everyday life language in Russia during the First World War

Iaroslav Golubinov

A period of upheaval is a time of formation of new social relations, new social groups, new social practices. Wars and revolutions make people of all social strata look for new ways of surviving in conditions of political and economic instability (Narskiy 2001). Adaptation to the new mode of existence is primarily reflected in everyday life and, of course, in everyday language.

It seems that this idea is also correct concerning the epoch of the First World War. The disappearance of habitual foodstuffs and consumer goods from the market (because of interruptions in supply), restrictions on work, leisure, movement and other changes in long-established social practices shook the life of Russian urban dwellers. It forced them to look for new 'tactics' of survival (in this case, I use Michel de Certeau's methodology (2002: 45–60)). This activity can be defined as 'the art of solving practical problems in a situation of uncertainty' (Volkov and Kharkhordin 2008: 15), and it has nothing to do with the political views of the citizens, but followed the simple task of self-preservation in the 'extreme era'. At the same time, the authorities imposed specific ways of behaviour on the citizens. They prescribed those types of activities that were necessary for the successful conduct of the war, such as rationing and issuing of food stamps, price restriction, the prohibition of alcohol or consumption of other products, and the banning of trade transportation between regions within a state and across state borders.

So, the main goal of this chapter is presenting some practices of surviving and their reflection in the Russian language in 1914–18 and also showing the image of the notorious social class of bourgeoisie that was created in the process of such practising.

Actually, the strategy of the authorities stumbled upon resistance in the form of survival tactics (the practice of surviving) by the citizens, who gave a hostile reception to the government's initiatives. One such type of practice was very familiar to all people in a time of war, a queue before a consumer goods store. Of course, it is impossible to say that the queue, as a social phenomenon, was entirely unfamiliar to Russian citizens, but it never became crucial to their daily routine before the First World War. A queue is usually perceived as 'an integral part of the Soviet experience' (Zemtsov 2017: 261–4). Sociologist Vladimir Nikolaev wrote that Soviet life 'in its entirety is impossible to imagine without constant standing in various queues. Such a long, regular, massive, significant experience could not have been lost without a trace. The habits formed in the queues have settled in our memory and continue to manifest themselves today in our behaviour, even if we do not realise it' (2005).

Researchers who have examined the queue in philology and folklore studies (Bogdanov 2012), history (Chapman 2013, 2017; Fishzon 2017; Golubinov 2016), sociology (Rukavishnikov 1990) and anthropology (Maunier 2014) share similar positions. They consider the phenomenon of queues, in any of the periods of Soviet history, as something invariable. It might appear genuinely invariable and inherent in the Soviet system, but it was born before the establishment of Soviet power and continued to grow as an image during Soviet times. Thus, Belovinskij (2015: 445–6) stated that the genesis of the Soviet queues (*khvosty* (tails) as they were usually named in Russia) as a social phenomenon should be attributed to the time of the First World War, but did not explain it broadly.

The queues of the wartime were not engaged in self-description; for this, they were too amorphous and unstable. There had always been an external observer who fixed the essence of this social phenomenon. However, for observers well over 100 years ago as well as more contemporary scholars, the queue itself seems to be something unimportant, and the information about queues, more precisely about their peculiarities, is scarce and fragmented in the sources.

Therefore, the sources used in this chapter are quite diverse. A significant part of them was taken from published texts as well as from the database of the Russian National Corpus (RNC).[1] The records in the latter were involved as they describe quite well the gradual process of entering new elements of everyday life in the language (and, consequently, in the space of social practices). It is necessary to say a few words about the word '*ochered*'' (queue) and its synonym *khvost* (line, literally 'tail'), which was widely used in the nineteenth and early twentieth centuries. The definition in 1909 edition of Vladimir Dahl's well-known 'Explanatory Dictionary of the Living Great Russian Language' indicated a similarity of meanings: the first one is the sequence, 'the accepted order of coming one after another' (Dal' 1909a: 2017); the second has a meaning 'the tail or trunk of the people (French "queue")' (Dal' 1909b: 1179).

So, the fact that the line (*khvost*) was familiar to the urban residents of Russia (at least in the big cities) before the Great War is undoubted. The press of the 1900s and 1910s preserved evidence not only of the existence of such a social phenomenon but also of its rather complicated structure. Examples of the use of the words *ochered*' and *khvost* from the RNC database confirm this. The newspaper *Russkoe Slovo* (Russian Word) of 24 October 1908, in connection with the stir around the opera premiere, had the following note: 'Today opens the sale of tickets for "Boris Godunov" with Feodor Chaliapin in the *Bolshoi* Theatre. Moreover, yesterday afternoon there was a "queue" at the theatre. In the afternoon, the places in the queue were resold for 3 roubles, about 10 p.m. they were "quoted" no lower than 5 roubles.'[2]

Another example (*Russkoe Slovo*, 15 December 1908) is also related to the activities of the theatres:

> in a long line of people waiting in the queue at the box office you may notice a dozen or one and a half [dozen] women also standing in the queue. From time to time, women go out into the corridor and come back from there with a lady or a gentleman, who replaces this woman in a queue for a small fee and depending on the number of people, and she gets a place at the end of the queue again, and when she gets closer to the cashier's office she sells her place again. . . . Judging by the pleasant attitude of the doorman towards them, we can conclude that these women are wives or sisters of the lower employees in the theatre.

The use of two terms simultaneously in one source is also available, as, for example (from the autobiographical 1912 novel *Tale of the Days of my Life* by Ivan Vol'nov's), in the phrase, 'in front of the wine shop, a long line existed, obeying the strict queue'. One cannot help noticing the similarities between some of the methods of queue functioning more than a century ago and Soviet-era signs.

> Due to regular reproduction of these meetings of people in the conditions of 'unity of place and time', they were formed into stable configurations of thoughts, mutual feelings and mutual behaviour. . . . This is a particular pattern of mutual behaviour of people in connection with the competition for access to one or another desired, but scarce goods, which is realized where the claims of some people for a particular benefit face the claims of others and where the hierarchical order of priority makes the chances of applicants unequal. (Nikolaev 2005)

Such behavioural patterns became a form of sustainable social practices during the First World War, which no longer aroused any surprise in the press that only recorded some particularly striking manifestations of this phenomenon.

The phenomenon was a problem first of all for those who stood in queues. Thus, for example, the author of an anonymous address to the governor of Samara (Middle Volga region) on July 1916 stated that 'people have to wait in line for seven hours and do not get sugar on the cards, women who left their children homeless come to the shop 2-3 am to occupy the line and stand for several days and have no opportunity to get two or three pounds of sugar' (Semenova 2011: 171). The customers tended to blame the merchants or the authorities, who did nothing to curb profiteers. Albeit some journalists considered this as a result of the passivity of the public itself, because 'the people, who are not accustomed and not taught the right social behaviour, cannot acquire the skill of it in a moment and therefore they are powerless' (Semenova 2011: 177). As a result, 'the Fast has come, lines have appeared' (Semenova 2011: 179). They, 'lines for bread, are invisibly born in the darkness of the night, and in the daytime, you will see neither buyers nor loaves' (Semenova 2011: 201).

The Moscow newspaper *Ranneje Utro* (Early Morning) summed up the following in January 1917: 'at the beginning of 1916, we had no idea about the lines and even did not have an idea of them at all. Goods were expensive, but there were no lines. The inhabitants came to the shop, to the bakery, to the dairy and got what they needed. By spring, the growth of prices for products and the first appearance of lines began to be noticed. At first, they were "moderate in size", but as they approached the fall, they began to grow and enlarge. Lines received titles. There were "meat", "milk", "bread", "egg" lines, and by the end of the year even "alcohol" lines. Residents took up "line duty"; receiving the necessities had turned into continuous torture. Standing in the lines led to an intensification of cold fever, and in December even a case of death in the lines was registered. Moreover, in the new year, we enter under the sign of lines' (Ruga and Kokorev 2011: 281).

The authorities, of course, paid attention to the situation and tried to cope with it, but success was variable. The governor of Samara, for example, in response to the appeal mentioned earlier, immediately pointed out the problem with sugar to the mayor of the city and instructed him to change the order of delivery of the deficit product (Semenova 2011: 173). Also, scholars noted that 'to facilitate the situation of Muscovites languishing in the lines in the cold, the mayor Shebeko ordered to allow them to warm themselves in the cafes and other facilities located near the bakeries' (Ruga and Kokorev 2011: 287). The main conversation topic among those standing in the queues, blaming officials and profiteers, in early 1917 became a bright detail in the novel *Road to Calvary* by Alexei Tolstoy, written in 1921–22, when memories of the military period were still very fresh:

'How much was that?'
  'Two and a half roubles a pint, my girl.'
  'What, for paraffin?'
  'That shopkeeper will not get away with it. We will remember him when the time comes.'
  'My sister told me there was a shopkeeper in Okhta and he had been carrying on like that, so they took him and pushed his head first into a barrel of pickle and drowned him, for all he begged hard to be let go.'
  'They let him off too easily at that – ought to have tortured him a bit first.'
  'And meanwhile, we can freeze out here.'
  . . .
  'Look what they are doing to the people, the blood-suckers (svolochi)!' (Tolstoy 1941: 158–9)

Unfortunately, it is not clear whether pre-war methods of selling a place in queues were in demand, as it was in the case with the theatres described earlier. Historians found something similar, pointing out that 'there were also professional buyers – mobs of boys and girls in "tails". They had studied the schedule of bakeries well and had managed to appear at the time of distribution and had been among the first customers. These tricksters then resold loaves for 25-30 kopecks [four times the official price] to the people standing at the end of the queue' (Ruga and Kokorev 2011: 283). However, it was simple black marketing, just adapted to the format of a queue. There has been no evidence so far of people in the wartime queues who would have sold their place. The shortage of goods and the increase in their prices made this phenomenon impossible since the sellers of the places had to stand in line for essentials themselves.

Also, some details related to queuing remain unclear. The available sources do not contain information, for example, on how the queue was set in the line: was there a registration of new people joining (each new person in a queue got a unique number, registered by the head of the queue), like in Soviet queues, or, maybe, a periodical headcount? The aforementioned quotes show that the queues gathered at night or early in the morning, so the people standing in them had to leave periodically. However, there is evidence that with the deepening of the sociopolitical and economic crisis, the practice of standing in queues became more and more sophisticated. Some Moscow 'line people' (*khvostetsy*), as Nikolaj Okunev testified in July 1917, had an agreement according to which they were alternated for 'feeding and the call of nature' (Okunev 1997: 60).

The composition of the queues was, at first sight, homogeneous; they were people of low income – workers, employees, servants. For many of them standing in queues and buying cheap food became a matter of survival. Women from these families made up the majority of the lines. Thus, newspaper reporters who examined the district of *Bolshaja Cherkizovskaja* Street in Moscow received an answer to the question about adults in houses everywhere: 'The mother went to the queue (*chered*)' (Ruga and Kokorev 2011: 497). The families who hired maids had the opportunity to send them to the lines. Professor of Moscow University Mikhail Bogoslovskij noted in his diary: 'In the morning [22 October 1916] during a walk, I visited A. P. Basistov [and his family]. It was already noon, but they were sleeping, and their maid had left to stand in line' (Bogoslovskij 2011).

The citizens acquired a peculiar habit for surviving. They began to join the first queue they found because every queue was a sign of some scarce product. Journalist and writer Mikhail Prishvin left in his diary a very remarkable illustration of such behaviour:

'Familiar ladies are standing in line for bread'.
  'How did you get here?'
  'We went to the exhibition of the Union of Artists, and we noticed the short queue and joined it immediately. We always stop and join, when we see a short queue, no matter what is distributed.' (Prishvin 2007: 368)

There were also queues in front of other places besides shops. Queues were noted in front of theatres, cinemas, newspaper kiosks and, finally, brothels. The latter case made a great impression on contemporaries. One of them, for example, noted that 'there is an endless line of soldiers waiting for the queue near these houses, just as there are waiting in the queues when sugar is distributed by rationing cards' (Anichkov 1998: 19). Writer Alexis Remizov was shocked and noticed that 'in Saratov on *Petina* street in early morning lines formed – a queue in front of brothels – public soldiers' lines' (Remizov 2000: 56–7). Indeed, a queue in these years pursued the citizens everywhere. The joke told about the old woman who 'saw the line of stopped trams' and shouted: 'How long must you live to see it! Even trams become lined up in a queue!' (Mel'nichenko 2014: 572). Moreover, children, equal in their observation to adults, remarked in their texts 'the maturation of the revolution in the queues' and played in them (Aksenov 2002:

150). One boy, who went abroad with his family, recalled in exile how once he and his brother had 'made a toy town of clay cubes and multi-coloured clay people', and 'the small toy town has the same excitement [as real one]: dolls are standing in queues for bread, and toy soldiers are rebelling' (Tsurikov [1925] 2001).

Thus, the queue firmly took its place among other practices of survival in wartime and beyond. Queues were similar in their organization with cooperatives and the system of rationing cards (Golubinov 2018). Both cooperatives and the card system became more and more sophisticated organizationally, and the queues also acquired new additional methods of self-organization and coordination. Moreover, cooperatives and cards were created as a means of fighting against queues, but they could not win them and were forced to adapt to them.

Another type of public organization intended for the food supply of the urban population was *meshochnichestvo* (literally, bagging, from word *meshok* – bag) (Davydov 2007). It had some similarities with the queue phenomenon. *Meshochniki* (bag men) went to peasant villages in their own or other regions which had food surpluses. Bag men tried to exchange different valuable things for bread. Authorities were inclined to consider such activity often as profiteering. Bagging seemed to have emerged as a natural continuation of the method of sending one or more inhabitants of an apartment house or a bunch of households to stand in line for bread and sugar. When shops in towns and cities had no bread, the mission of these people continued and led them to the countryside. Bag men from cities often met their colleagues from starving rural areas. Such *khodoki* (travellers) could cover vast territory in search of food,

Residents learned specific practices of the extraction of scarce products, and the queue gradually became a 'cultural focus', that is, a phenomenon 'which gives culture its special emphasis, allows outsiders to feel its special, distinctive flavour and characterize in a few words its essential orientation' (Nikolaev 2005). The queue became a peculiar place of memory inherited by Soviet society from the pre-revolutionary epoch. Jillian Porter noticed that 'from the immediate aftermath of the Revolution, queues of all sorts have served Soviet mythmakers as *topoi* of collective origins and cultural memory' (2017: 495). This aspect of the subject is emphasized in Golubinov 2016.

The queues became the catalysts of the most extreme way of self-supplying the urban masses, food pogroms, which resulted from the inefficient activity of queues and cooperatives, an introduction of rationing cards and operations of bag people as well as worsening of the food situation generally. In 1917–18, the queue simply ceased to obey any social rules and turned into crowds ready to loot. Paradoxically, the queue was also an effective way of social communication and, at the same time, a generator of various rumours. Conversations in the queues did not stop and touched upon the most discussed topics. Newspapers became alarmed in 1917, noting that 'the lines are not appropriate, not only because they make us lose much expensive time and make us freeze in vain, but because they are places of general discontent . . . In the lines, as one of the prominent socialists said, a counterrevolution is born' (Semenova 2011: 237).

The queues became a mechanism of rumours and gossips, which had as their protagonist a tradesman or shopkeeper. Such a situation had a natural explanation. At the beginning of the First World War, Russia faced a problem that was new for the government: the problem for creating a highly coordinated food supply of the army and numerous local communities in cities, towns and villages (Holquist 2002: 12–46). Of course, the government and provincial governors tried to solve this task using old bureaucratic methods. At the same time, cities and towns had to supply their dwellers themselves. Governors and police forces under their command just controlled the situation and punished the merchants who overpriced food products. The only competitor to the private commercial system was a decentralized and weak system of various consumers' cooperatives (at manufactories, villages, railroads junctions) (Golubinov 2018).

Customers were not satisfied with the work of shops and markets. Prices increased, and the diversity of products decreased (e.g. bread was baked using one sort of flour instead of four or five before the war). The number of food riots ('food pogroms', 'women's riots', 'market or food unrests') may measure the degree of dissatisfaction. In 1914, such riots were sporadic, but in 1915 there were 14 riots of workers and 8 of peasants, and in 1916 already there were 53 riots of workers and 253 of peasants (Kir'janov's 1993). Moreover, these were just the cases registered by the police. Many cases of unrest remained unknown because they hide under the words 'misapprehensions between merchants and customers' (quoted in Kir'janov's 1993: 10). The police often preferred to hide such cases and reported to the capital about the calm and patriotic public mood.

The most widespread cause of such 'misapprehensions' was challenging (typically with the use of obscene words) the high prices or poor condition of products, and the consequence of such debate was a scuffle first and then a riot. The crowds shouted slogans against profiteers and looted and demolished shops and stores, and police or even soldiers dispersed a demonstration after this. Sometimes crowds made merchants sell products (sugar in most cases) for a fair price (in this context, it meant prices which were established before the war).

Anxiety was very noticeable in a field of symbolical interpretation of war events. Vladislav Aksenov noted that 'the official propaganda made much easier the task for artists [of humorous magazines] who criticized the policy of the Russian authorities' to disguise Russian problems as a mockery of the Germans. Moreover, 'in the conditions of rising food prices, the establishing of a card system in several cities, and the disruption of the supply of essential goods to the Russian cities, the reports on the food crisis in Germany seemed to be a cruel joke'. (Aksenov 2017: 7)

Other people always suspected merchants because commercial trading was something sinful for many of them. Moral accusation against merchants may be found in classic Russian literature of the nineteenth century and the beginning of the twentieth century (e.g. in Maksim Gorkij's novels and stories). The diaries of wartime were also full of remarks about 'greedy merchants' who 'tried to fill their purse' and the 'madness of avarice'. Alternatively, retired general A.V. Zhirkevich wrote in his diary in mid-July 1916 that 'the middle class wastes its last money to purchase the essentials, but the shopkeepers prey on people's grief. The government has not yet worked out anything that would hold these bandits from robbery in broad daylight' (Zhirkevich 2007: 274).

Merchants in towns and cities became accused as well as wealthy peasants (*kulak*) in rural areas. Many urban dwellers suspected in 1914–16 that the countryside grew rich and made profits out of war (Gatrell 2005: 72–6). Later this perception became a crucial drive to begin the compulsory grain levy (*prodrazverstka*) in 1917–18.

Many wartime businessmen were people of adventurous, and sometimes even fraudulent, nature; they did not like questions about the origin of their capital; the purpose of these people was to search for 'happiness and money'. The mentality of the Russian bourgeoisie, including in the regions, changed gradually as well as the whole range of social behaviour and orientations of entrepreneurs, and, most importantly, their methods of management. The negative features of Russian entrepreneurship intensified. At the same time, merchants still conducted energetic altruistic activities; they helped the Russian Red Cross, the All-Russian Zemstvo Union of Aid to Sick and Wounded Warriors and the All-Russian Union of Cities, individual hospitals and charitable societies.

The attitude of state power towards merchants was ambiguous. On the one hand, many wealthy merchants joined the new bodies for the provision of the army or were intermediaries in the purchase of foodstuffs, and the merchants who 'behaved very suspiciously in 1905-1907, now generally satisfied with the existing system, especially now, making huge capital during the War', as the Simbirsk governor noted in his report of 10 September 1916 (Golubinov 2014: 197). On the other hand, merchants might well behave meanly with the government because of their traditional envy towards nobility. The message of the governor of Samara indicated that 'local merchants, selling groats and other food products, store vast reserves of thousands of tons in their barns , , . Furthermore, they sell only a small amount, firmly hoping for further growth in demand and for speculative inflation. The local merchant class dreams about the influx of profits and this class has shown already the same "patriotic" mood' (Golubinov 2014: 197). However, the authorities had no choice but to compromize with the merchant class, since it was not involved in political intrigues. In this context, the comprehensive collaboration between civil society, the state and merchants was uncertain.

Vladlen Izmozik, citing excerpts of censored letters from people of various social classes, concluded that none of the correspondents found a kind word in assessing the economic activity of the government and merchants. The tone of correspondence was extremely depressed, and a rise in prices, lack of products, and the greed of profiteers were the most common topics. A member of the Russian Monarchical Union, landowner of Tula province Paskhalov, claimed in mid-February 1917 that 'there is enough bread in Russia, but it is hidden due to firm prices that do not correspond to the rise in prices of other consumer goods, and it is impossible to take grain to the market except by violence. It is necessary to abandon the firm prices and give grain complete freedom of movement, destroy customs outposts between the provinces, but strictly . . . punish profiteers and banks hiding food items' (Izmozik 1999: 162).

Moreover, another correspondent, a few months before, in October 1916, prophesied the workers' riot 'because of hunger', and because 'day by day – the queues . . . we are all cold and hungry'. Izmozik emphasizes that 'regardless of how much all these statements corresponded to the real state of affairs, they transferred the essentially identical economic sense of people from different social, national and political groups' (Izmozik 1999: 163). On the eve of February 1917, no one in Russia doubted that the merchant class was the class of greedy predators who betrayed the country. In that case, the images of internal predators (profiteers) and external enemy (Germans) combined. The spectre of 'internal Germans' (*vnutrennie nemtsy*) appeared in Russia. Moreover, such attitude complemented a campaign against ethnic Germans (actual internal Germans) who had been living in Russia for a long time. After August 1914, Russian Emperor's subjects with German names and origins became suspicious persons and accused in spying (Gatrell 2005: 178–83).

Mikhail Prishvin wrote in August 1915 that 'the first enemies were at the front, then they became people with German family names, then merchants, and finally you are told: "You thought the inner German was outside, but he was sitting at the same table eating with you"' (Prishvin 2007: 211). Two years later, he continued speculation:

> All this is very clear: at the beginning of the war, the people imagined a German enemy outside the state. After a series of defeats, they felt that their enemy was an internal German. Furthermore, the first of these enemies, the Tsar, was overthrown. After the Tsar people overthrew the old rulers, and now overthrow all owners of the land. However, the manors are inseparable from capital. [People] overthrow the capitalists – the internal Germans. With them, their own [part] of the essential organizing power is swept aside: the bourgeois intellectuals. After the general destruction of property, a new era will come: the destroyers will understand and see with their own eyes that the internal German is personally in each of us. Then comes some last act of tragedy; and a particular servant, a cunning man, went in to his master's house and slew him, and ate what the lord eats, and slept in his bed [like a lord], but he did not get enough from his master's table and rest on his bed. So in the legends of the Bible, 'the lean and the ill-favoured cattle did eat up the first seven fat cattle' and 'they were still ill-favoured, as at the beginning'. (Prishvin 2007: 427)

A journalist from Astrakhan could agree and add that kine were lean because 'dangerous parasite nests in the belly of the people, and the name of this helminth is scarcity' (Semenova 2011: 148).

During the war, Russian everyday language demonstrated an unprecedented adaptability and invented new words and expressions for describing the situation with the food supply. Old and rare terms became ubiquitous and found new significance. This wartime practice continued in the 1920s because of the 1917 Revolution and the subsequent civil war. The everyday language gave birth not only to expressions for the evaluation of product scarcity but also to terms for the description of enemies. It is noteworthy that the success of the Bolsheviks became possible after their sanctioning and legalizing wartime 'immoralization' of certain social classes via political language.

Notes

1 http://www.ruscorpora.ru/
2 This and two following examples are derived from RNC database via search queries *khvost* and *ochered'*.

References

Aksenov, V. (2002), 'Povsednevnaja zhizn' Petrograda i Moskvy v 1917 godu' (Everyday Life of Petrograd and Moscow in 1917), PhD diss., Moscow State University, Moscow.

Aksenov, V. (2017), 'Zhurnal'naja karikatura kak zerkalo obshchestvennyh nastroenij v 1917 godu' (Magazine Caricature as a Mirror of Public Mood in 1917), *Vestnik TvGU. Serija 'Istorija'* 1: 4–16.

Anichkov, V. (1998), *Ekaterinburg – Vladivostok (1917–1922)*, Moscow: Russkij put'.

Belovinskij, L. (2015), *Enciklopedicheskij slovar'istorii sovetskoj povsednevnoj zhizni* (Encyclopaedic Dictionary of the History of Soviet Everyday Life), Moscow: Novoe Literaturnoe Obozrenie.

Bogdanov, K. (2012), 'The Queue as Narrative: A Soviet Case Study', in A. K. Baiburin, C. Kelly and N. B. Vakhtin (eds), *Russian Cultural Anthropology after the Collapse of Communism*, 77–102. Abingdon: Routledge.

Bogoslovskij, M. (2011), *Dnevniki, 1913–1919* (Diaries, 1913–1919), Moscow: Vremia. Available online: http://russiahistory.ru/download/library/memuaryx-vospominaniya/bogoslovskij-m.-dnevniki-1913-1919.pdf (accessed 17 March 2020).

Certeau, M. de (2002), *The Practice of Everyday Life*, translated by Steven Rendall, 2nd edn, Berkeley: University of California Press.

Chapman, A. (2013), 'Queuetopia: Second-World Modernity and the Soviet Culture of Allocation'. PhD diss., University of Pittsburgh, Pittsburgh. Available online: http://d-scholarship.pitt.edu/18446/ (accessed 16 March 2020).

Chapman, A. (2017), '"Let There Be Abundance! But Leave a Shortage of Something!" Distinction, Subjectivity, and Brezhnev's Culture of Scarcity', *Slavic & East European Journal*, 61 (3): 519 11.

Dal', V. (1909a), *Tolkovyj slovar'zhivogo velikoruskogo yazyka Vladimira Dalja. Tom vtoroj* (Explanatory Dictionary of the Living Great Russian Language. Second volume), Saint Petersburg: Tip. Tovarishchestva M.O. Vol'f.

Dal', V. (1909b), *Tolkovyj slovar'zhivogo velikorusskogo yazyka Vladimira Dalja. Tom chetvertyj* (Explanatory Dictionary of the Living Great Russian Language. Fourth volume), Saint Petersburg: Tip. Tovarishchestva M.O. Vol'f.

Davydov, A. (2007), *Meshochniki i diktatura v Rossii, 1917–1921 gg* (Bag-People and Dictatorship in Russia 1917–1921), Saint Petersburg: Aleteia.

Fishzon, A. (2017), 'Queue Time as Queer Time: An Occasion for Pleasure and Desire in the Brezhnev Era and Today', *Slavic & East European Journal*, 61 (3): 542–66.

Gatrell, P. (2005), *Russia's First World War: A Social and Economic History*, 1st edn, Harlow: Pearson/Longman.

Golubinov, I. (2014), '"Potrebnost' v samopomoshchi": reshenie prodovol'stvennogo voprosa v srednevolzhskih gorodah v 1914–1917 gg' (Need in Self-help: Food Issue in Middle Volga Region Towns in 1914–1917), in M. Mjagkov and K. Pahalyuk (eds), *Velikaja vojna: sto let*, 191–205, Saint Petersburg: Nestor-Istorija.

Golubinov, I. (2016), 'Ocheredi v rossijskih gorodah v 1914–1918 godah: k voprosu o skladyvanii novyh social'nyh praktik' (Queues in Russian cities in 1914–1918: On Evolution of New Social Practices), *Vestnik Baltijskogo federal'nogo universiteta im. I. Kanta. Serija: Gumanitarnye i obshhestvennye nauki*, 1: 48–57.

Golubinov, I. (2018), 'Food and Nutrition (Russian Empire)', in U. Daniel, P. Gatrell, O. Janz, H. Jones, J. Keene, A. Kramer and B. Nasson (eds), *1914–1918-Online International Encyclopedia of the First World War*, Berlin: Freie Universität Berlin.

Available online: https://encyclopedia.1914-1918-online.net/article/food_and_nutrit ion_russian_empire/ (accessed 16 March 2020).

Holquist, P. (2002), *Making War, Forging Revolution: Russia's Continuum of Crisis, 1914–1921*. Cambridge, MA: Harvard University Press.

Izmozik, V. (1999), 'K voprosu o politicheskih nastroenijah rossijskogo obschestva v kanun 1917 g' (On Problem of Political Climate in Russian Society in the Eve of 1917), in N. Smirnov, Z. Galili, R. Zelnik, B. Kolonitskij, S Potolov, W. Rosenberg and V. Cherniaev (eds), *Rossija i Pervaja mirovaja vojna*, 160–70, Saint Petersburg: Dmitrij Bulanin.

Kir'janov, Yu. (1993), 'Massovye vystuplenija na pochve dorogovizny v Rossii, 1914 – fevral'1917 g' (Mass Demonstrations on the Grounds of High Cost in Russia, 1914 – February 1917), *Otechestvennaja istorija*, 3: 3–18.

Maunier, R. (2014), 'Groupes et durée. La queue comme groupe social' (Groups and Duration. The Queue as a Social Group), *Terrain: Anthropologie & Sciences Humaines*, 63 (September): 12–21.

Mel'nichenko, M. (2014), *Sovetskij anekdot (Ukazatel'sjuzhetov)* (Soviet Anecdotes (Plot Index)), Moscow: Novoe literaturnoe obozrenie.

Narskiy, I. (2001), *Zhizn' v katastrofe: Budni naseleniia Urala v 1917–1922 gg* (Life in Catastrophe: Everyday Life of Ural People in 1917–1922), Moscow: ROSSPEN.

Nikolaev, V. (2005), '"Sovetskaja ochered": proshloe kak nastojashhee' (Soviet Queue: Past as Present), *Neprikosnovennyj Zapas*, 5 (43). Available online: http://magazines.russ.ru/nz/2005/43/ni11.html (accessed 16 March 2020).

Okunev, N. (1997), *Dnevnik Moskvicha: 1917–1920 (Diary of Muscovite 1917–1920)*, Vol. 1, Moscow: Voen. izd-vo.

Porter, J. (2017), 'Commemorative Queues: Bread, Lenin, Requiem', *Slavic & East European Journal*, 61 (3): 495–518.

Prishvin, M. (2007), *Dnevniki. 1914 -1917* (Diaries 1914–1917), Saint Petersburg: Rostok.

Remizov, A. (2000), *Sobranie sochinenij. Tom 5. Vzvihrjonnaja Rus'* (Collected Works. Volume 5. Whirled up Russia), Moscow: Russkaja kniga.

Ruga, V. and A. Kokorev (2011), *Povsednevnaja žizn' Moskvy: ocherki gorodskogo byta v period Pervoj mirovoj vojny* (Everyday Life of Moscow: Essays on Urban Life during the First World War), Moskva: AST.

Rukavishnikov, V. (1990), 'The Queue', *Soviet Sociology*, 29 (5): 20–36.

Semenova, E., ed. (2011), *Social'no-jekonomicheskie i obshhestvenno-politicheskie uslovija zhizni gorozhan Povolzh'ja v Pervuju mirovuju vojnu, 1914 – nachalo 1918 gg.: cbornik dokumentov i materialov* (Socio-economic and socio-political Conditions of Life of Volga Region Citizens in the First World War, 1914 – Beginning of 1918: Collection of Documents and Sources), Samara: ANO Izdatel'stvo SNC RAN.

Tolstoy A. ([1922] 1941), *Road To Calvary*, translated by E. Bone, London and New York: Hutchinson International Authors Ltd.

Tsurikov, N. ([1925] 2001), 'Deti emigracii' (Children of Emigration), in *Deti emigracii. Vospominanija*, Moscow: Agraf. Available online: http://rus-sky.com/history/library/vospominania/ (accessed 16 March 2020).

Volkov, V. and O. Kharkhordin (2008), *Teoriia Praktik* (Theory of Practices). Sankt-Peterburg: Izdatel'stvo Evropeiskogo universiteta.

Zemtsov, I. (2017), *Encyclopaedia of Soviet Life*, New York: Routledge.

Zhirkevich, A. (2007), *Potrevozhennye teni . . . Simbirskij dnevnik* (Worried Shadows . . . Simbirsk Diary), Moscow: Eterna-print.

12

'Berlitz Krieg'

The development of a modern language pedagogy at Ruhleben civilian internment camp

Jamie Calladine

It was not only the conglomeration of languages but the diversity of types that made Ruhleben a true cosmopolis.

(Cohen 1917: 114)

By the autumn of 1916, the camp school at Ruhleben camp had efficiently incorporated over a third of the camp's entire population with around 1,500 students assigned to some 300 classes led by more than 200 teachers (Cohen 1917: 150). This broad cohort of students and teachers reflected all elements of the camp's population. Oxbridge old boys and university lecturers studied alongside sailors, clerks and factory workers from the far-flung reaches of the British Empire. Education became an empowering activity and enabled the men to combat the most debilitating elements of the internment experience. Politician Alfred T Davies coined the phrase 'enforced inactivity' during the war to refer to the unique plight suffered by civilian internees (Potter 2007: 12). While internment shielded many from the unimaginable horrors of the front line, it placed prisoners of war in a constant battle to keep occupied and maintain psychological resilience. Civilian internees were exempted from the forced labour assigned to military POWs but their relief from physical plight was replaced by a novel predicament of 'mental starvation' (King 2013: 254). At Ruhleben, as in other camps, prisoners were encouraged to adopt new ways of keeping busy and remaining physically and mentally active. The camp school was just one of many concerted efforts by the prisoners to alleviate the monotony and repetition of their captivity.

Formal education was commonplace in First World War internment camps on both sides of the war and features prominently in contemporary civilian and military accounts. In recent years, studies have shown that the impact and legacy of education during internment extended far beyond the generation of 1914 to 1918. Heather Jones (2011) has identified that First World War internment camps were sites of experimental education, witnessing both the development of a progressive teaching pedagogy and the introduction of schemes and conventions that were adopted for prisoners in the next world war. The development of camp institutions was an intrinsic part of the internment experience (Vischer 1919: 22), and in Ruhleben this varied from the primarily utilitarian establishment of a postal service and police force to the explicitly cultural faculties of a camp school, theatre and orchestra. Enforced inactivity became the catalyst for an explosion of cultural and sporting endeavour in which prisoners sought to construct new meaning in their lives and combat the feeling of powerlessness perpetuated by their captivity. This vibrant 'culture of internment' has received increasing coverage in the years surrounding the war's centenary as First World War scholars have explored the legacy of this watershed moment in international history. Carr and Mytum's (2012: 13) edited collection, for example, has demonstrated the immediacy of creativity in various centres of captivity and its ability to encourage spiritual resistance to the depravity of internment.

Of these cultural responses to 'enforced inactivity' in Ruhleben, education was undoubtedly the most impactful – in terms of both participation and longevity – yet it remains one of the most understudied areas of camp life.[1] According to camp tutor Henry C Mahoney and Talbot (1917: 172), the school at Ruhleben 'attracted the greatest attention and achieved the most impressive success' of all the endeavours of the prisoners during the war. Formal education thrived in the camp, driven not only by the enthusiasm and demand of its students but by the passion and devotion of its tutors. Internment would be viewed by optimistic politicians back home as an opportunity for prisoners to exercise mental agency and make use of their ample time (King 2013: 254), though the prisoners at Ruhleben needed little encouragement. The development of a robust school structure accompanied a vast curriculum that was constantly expanding as demand for learning continued throughout the war. The camp boasted classes on core subjects such as mathematics and English literature alongside more obscure offerings like shipbuilding and agricultural chemistry. Surprisingly, however, the courses which provoked the most rigorous and passionate study were those dedicated to modern languages.

Language study was not entirely uncommon in First World War internment camps, though comparative studies suggest that Ruhleben was unparalleled in its participation and variety. Its preponderance is demonstrated quantitatively by language's dominance within the school administrative structure; of nine departments initially established to govern the camp school, a third were devoted entirely to the administration and delivery of modern language study (Cohen 1917: 150). Indeed, it is difficult to find a more dedicated faculty among its contemporaries. Language study in British-run camps, for example, was perhaps most resilient at Handforth Camp near Manchester. School records show that language study was on an equal footing with German literature, mathematics and electrical engineering with a surprisingly popular English course and smaller, fervently studied classes in French, Spanish and Italian (Bogenstätter and Zimmermann 1921: 163). This language offering is typical of the time and thoroughly impressive given the circumstances, yet ultimately it appears minimal in comparison to Ruhleben. There, the camp school boasted classes in over ten languages, ranging from the typical Latinate and Germanic courses of English, French, Spanish, Italian and German to the more advanced parlances of Mandarin,

Yiddish, Russian and Welsh. The classes were delivered by a diverse cohort of teachers, approximately a third of which had occupied positions as tutors in Britain and across Europe (Cohen 1917: 153).

The overwhelming popularity and breadth of language study at Ruhleben, combined with the tangible impact of education on the lived experience of internment, necessitates a comprehensive examination of the development of the camp's language school. This chapter seeks to explore the intricacies of language study at Ruhleben, identifying not only the practicalities and pedagogical methods in camp but the factors that were contributory to its success. This chapter argues that environmental factors, such as the development of a multilingual society and a professionally consummate faculty of tutors, created a fertile learning environment, characterized by respect for education and multiculturalism. This prolific environment was coupled with a progressive, multimethod pedagogy that rendered significant results for willing scholars. Drawing from both the vibrant publications produced by the prisoners in situ during the war and the plethora of post-war memoirs from former 'Ruhlebenites', this paper uncovers how language impacted on the lived experience of internment and provided the relief and stimulation that comforted civilian internees through an unprecedented state of enforced inactivity.

Ruhleben: A multicultural and multilingual environment

On 6 November 1918, the mass internment of all British males of military age in the German Reich began. The destination for most of these unfortunate men was a former trotting racecourse on the outer reaches of the Berlin metropolis, the *Ruhleben Trabrennbahn*. The order for mass internment came in response to the expiration of an ultimatum presented to the British government by the German authorities. The stipulation demanded the release of all German citizens interned in Britain, in exchange for reciprocity for the British in Germany. Mass internment at Ruhleben would precipitate the amalgamation of prisoners from various cultural, linguistic, and socio-economic backgrounds. This 'diversity of types' would create a heterogenous camp society, characterized by multilingualism and professional diversity, that would naturally determine the development of camp institutions. This diversity would foment an atmosphere in which language study was not only well respected but eagerly sought after, contributing to the insurmountable success of the camp school in contrast to its contemporaries.

Matthew Stibbe in his unprecedented study of Ruhleben likened the camp society to that of Edwardian London, home to a similarly diverse population with concomitant attitudes and values (Stibbe 2008: 81). It is clear, however, that the population of Ruhleben reflected not only the Eurocentric cultural diversity of the Imperial capital but the global diversity of the Empire itself. By 1914, the British Empire controlled almost a quarter of the world's population across six continents reaching the apex of its territorial swell at the end of the First World War (Maddison 2001: 97). By virtue of the size and influence of the British Empire, British citizenship was afforded not only to those born in Britain but also the citizens of its colonies and dominions, and men born in the British Empire but naturalized elsewhere. In prisoner memoirs, these groups are often categorized for ease of providing a detailed summary of the camp's population.[2]

The largest of the interned groups, unsurprisingly, were white British men of Britain and its colonies and dominions. This group, commonly referred to as *Stockengländer*, consisted of men from all classes, occupations and locales, reflecting the distinctions that prompted Stibbe's comparison. They hailed not only from the length and breadth of the British mainland but from Ireland, Australia, Canada, New Zealand, South Africa and beyond. Some had travelled to Germany in the days, weeks, and months before the outbreak of war for holidays or to visit family and friends residing on the continent. The vast majority, however, had lived, worked and studied in Germany for years, settling into life on the continent. Small British contingents were present in almost all of the Reich's major cities, most notably in Berlin and Hamburg, where some 2,247 British subjects resided. Many of these men were immersed in the city's commercial, insurance and banking sectors that had long-established relationships with British ports, and over 1,000 were merchant seamen stopping at the port en route to destinations across Britain and the Empire.[3]

'Enemy' status was also extended to the *Scheinengländer*, or those who were British merely by a technicality. This group included British subjects naturalized in Germany, Austria and Switzerland and later German-occupied territories in Europe such as France, Poland and Belgium. Around 600–800 were of German origin, largely German-born sons and grandchildren of British couples, or those of British men that had married German wives (Stibbe 2008: 28). German citizenship laws of 1870 and 1913 outlined that German women who married foreign nationals were stripped of their German citizenship along with their children and grandchildren. The fluidity of what defined nationality and citizenship, and ultimately what constituted 'British', meant that many of these men who were unable to speak English and had never set foot in Britain were extracted from German society and detained as enemy subjects. The internment of those who were born or lived much of their lives on the continent meant that a significant portion of this predominantly 'British' camp was able to speak a foreign language.

Owing to Britain's imperial influence, the camp also contained a small contingent of men from the Caribbean, Africa, the Middle East and South and East Asia. These *Kolonialengländer* represented around one in fifteen of the camp's population at its peak (Stanley 2019: 416). Most of these men were merchant seamen from colonial ports, captured in Hamburg on the outbreak of war (Ketchum 1965: 6). For some, it was their first expedition away from their homeland, and many suffered from poor literacy skills and an inability to speak fluent English. Despite their lack of agency and evident subordination in camp affairs, they are an important, if understudied, segment of the camp's population and contributory to the nature and form of language pedagogy within the camp. A recent exhibition at the Brunei Gallery at the University of London has shed light upon the experiences of these men, and an upcoming edited collection will examine them in greater detail.

In addition to the categorized groups mentioned, a fourth group existed that was perhaps the most diverse of all. Ruhleben's proximity to the German capital rendered it a convenient location as a holding camp for men waiting to be transferred to other sites throughout the Reich. Within the first few weeks of mass internment, and in the aftermath of German military success in the early months of the war, the camp witnessed an influx of prisoners from various different backgrounds including Russians, Poles, Dutch, Spanish, Chinese and Finns to name a few. These men were held at the camp impending transfer to a more appropriate prison in accordance with their circumstances, though some remained at Ruhleben for the duration of the war. Transfers out of the camp occurred sporadically throughout the conflict with the largest taking place over the first winter of 1914–15. This diverse contingent, while transient, helped to establish the 'cosmopolis' that became Ruhleben.

With the internment of such a globally diverse population, Ruhleben boasted not only native speakers of a plethora of languages, but also individuals who had acquired a second language through living and working abroad. Linguistic diversity precipitated an acceptance of foreign culture that for some, rather than accentuating the idiosyncrasy of internment, endowed a sense of 'romance' to an otherwise drab and depressing situation (Cohen 1917: 114). This presented a stark contrast to the experiences of those in Britain who had seen the Victorian exoticism and appreciation of foreign cultures replaced by a virulent insularity borne out of anti-German propaganda and jingoistic rhetoric (Panayi 2014). Exposure to foreign languages was unavoidable as many were unable to speak English, thus making multilingual dialogue a fundamental part of everyday life at Ruhleben.

Prisoner memoirs indicate that these cultural and linguistic distinctions were not only heartily accepted but also sparked curiosity and enquiry, as conversations between men of different backgrounds naturally progressed into the teaching of each other's language. An excerpt from Cohen's (1917: 114) memoirs gives us a vivid depiction:

> You could fancy yourself in some busy international resort, for you heard snatches of conversation not only in English, French and German, but also in Spanish and Italian, in Russian and Polish, in Dutch and Danish, in Yiddish and Esperanto. Many of those speaking these foreign tongues during their evening constitutional . . . were actually learning the languages by the conversational method.

The immediacy of this learning exchange suggests that language tuition was an innate response to the environmental conditions that existed in the camp. Interestingly, the organic development of conversational language tuition between interned men has also been evidenced elsewhere. Ruhlebenite Israel Cohen's account of the camp provides us with edifying observations of his brief internmwent in Berlin's *Stadtvogtei* prison in autumn 1914.[4] The account provides us with crucial evidence of a precedent of informal language learning that antedated its formalization and growth at Ruhleben. He details his brief internment at Berlin's municipal prison alongside a diverse 'little community' of enemy aliens including fellow Britishers, Americans, Russians and Poles. He observed that despite their short time behind bars, 'one or two Russians had already begun to teach their language in exchange for English' (Cohen 1917: 10). While anecdotal, this account demonstrates the immediacy with which language learning was introduced into social exchanges between culturally diverse prisoners. This gives us a clear indication of how this informal language exchange would be imitated on an even larger scale at Ruhleben, in accordance with its intrinsic heterogeneity.

Language behind barbed wire: The development of language study at Ruhleben

The greatest benefactor of the rich cultural and linguistic diversity that conglomerated in the camp was undoubtedly the camp school. The multicultural consensus in the camp engendered a learning environment that was inherently conducive to the successful delivery of a progressive language pedagogy. Diversity enabled the camp school to call upon native speakers and professional tutors of an array of different languages and created an environment in which their study was both welcomed and encouraged. The creation of this multilingual, self-styled 'cosmopolis' would ensure that modern language study was not only a valued part of the new curriculum but the dominant force in a new camp school that would involve over half of the camp's entire population.

From the very beginning of life at Ruhleben, language proficiency was power. On 8 November 1914, just two days after the order for mass internment, the prisoners were lined up on parade and informed of their requirement to elect 'captains' for each barrack to act as a go-between for the prisoners and military authorities. A criterion of successful candidates was that they were fluent in the German language to ensure that these transactions went as smoothly as possible. Given the camp's polyglot character, German speakers were well represented with approximately a third of the camp having some understanding of the language from living and working in the Reich (Ketchum 1965: 96). The election of captains bestowed influence on bilingual prisoners and elevated the candidates into a state of relative privilege with captains afforded distinct perks such as occasional visits to the US embassy in Berlin and exemption from fatigue duties. The creation of this meritocratic administrative structure based on German fluency would no doubt have polarized the camp population as a distinct few obtained power where others were resigned to the 'informed powerlessness' of their immersion in a multilingual environment of captivity (Constantine 2011: 259). Undoubtedly, this situation would have provided an immediate incentive for men to improve their language skills in order to alleviate their material plight.

Early developments in language study

Demand for language tuition in the first months of internment was overwhelming and would help to explain the eventual precedence that language would take in the affairs of the camp school. Almost immediately, the pattern of behaviour observed in the *Stadtvogtei* was replicated at Ruhleben with the development of an informal system of 'buddying'. Cohen describes early language study at Ruhleben as being 'conducted partly in exchange: English for German, Spanish for French, and so forth', much like how it had transpired at the *Stadtvogtei* (Cohen 1917: 149). Buddying was common at Ruhleben and continued throughout the war, becoming an important extracurricular activity after the development of the camp school. The extent of cultural diversity and multilingualism in the camp facilitated the organic growth of the buddying system and allowed it to thrive. It would prove instrumental in socializing prisoners during the first difficult months of internment and contribute to a widening appetite for language study.

For those unable to teach a language in exchange, competent tutors swiftly acted to meet their demand advertising their services on the walls of the camp boiler house: 'The hoarding was no sooner up than impecunious polyglots began to advertise on it for pupils. One specially interesting announcement, addressed by a pro-German to pro-Germans, ran as follows: "I give Englisch lesson very chepe. Also haircut or shave"' (Powell and Gribble 1919: 124).

The opportunism of these 'impecunious polyglots' indicates the presence of a willing clientele of prisoners committed to paying for language lessons in the same way they would a haircut or a shave. Private tuition would continue after the creation of the camp school as a means of procuring additional study outside of the classroom and as a valuable source of additional income for language tutors whose livelihoods were relinquished with the act of internment.

Soon enough, language study evolved from sporadic exchanges and private tuition to the creation of independent and largely improvised language classes. Their primitive beginnings present us with the stark reality of learning a language from behind barbed wire. Various efforts to organize classes are described by camp captain Joseph Powell in his post-war memoirs, including a Spanish class given by a tutor 'pacing up the yard between Barrack IV and V'; a course in colloquial German taken by men during 'route marches on the racecourse'; and an ill-fated Russian class taken on top of one of the grandstands (Powell and Gribble 1919: 124–5). These makeshift attempts at an organized language pedagogy coincided with the creation of a short-lived 'School of Languages' by Dr Cimino in December 1914, which would eventually be absorbed by the camp school proper. While largely unsuccessful, these efforts demonstrated the growing popularity of language study and the mandate for a regulated system of education that could bring teachers and learners together in a more coordinated environment.

The establishment of a camp school

Spring 1915 witnessed an unprecedented 'expansion' in cultural activity at Ruhleben (Ketchum 1965: 175). The visit of the American Ambassador, James W. Gerard, on 3 March 1915 had revealed the extent of the deplorable conditions in the camp to the outside world and sparked outrage in Britain. The ambassador made a series of recommendations to the German authorities that sought to address the poor sanitation, diet and accommodation of the prisoners. His visit combined with deflating news the following day from camp captain Joseph Powell, who notified the men of the breakdown in talks between their captors and the British government regarding a prisoner exchange. The inevitable blow triggered a palpable change in camp life as rumours gradually dissipated and the men succumbed to the realization of life at Ruhleben for the foreseeable future. The announcement set into motion the determination of the prisoners to improve life in the camp from within and give their lives new meaning (Ketchum 1965: 93).

Educational establishments at Ruhleben could be traced back to the first months of life in the camp with the development of the Arts & Sciences Union (ASU), the first explicitly educational organization in the camp after the development of a lending library. It was established in December 1914 by the so-called Ruhleben 'Supermen', a group of well-respected academics and university men in the camp. The ASU provided its learned members with a platform to exchange research and ideas and to debate different topics. From late 1914 until the end of the war, it organized lectures on a broad range of academic subjects ranging from the works of Goethe to advanced biochemistry. The ASU was largely inaccessible for the rank and file of Ruhleben and remained the domain of the well-educated, middle-class elite until April 1915 when membership was expanded to the rest of the camp. It became clear early on that the widespread enthusiasm for a formal education system would prohibit any monopoly on knowledge by the educated few, and in January 1915 the establishment of a camp school was announced as an offshoot of the ASU (*In Ruhleben Camp*, 15 August 1915: 25). The camp school would be at the forefront of the unprecedented 'spring expansion' that would determine life in the camp for the rest of the war.

Following the announcement of a formalized education system in Ruhleben, the camp school distributed forms asking prisoners to list subjects that they wished to study. In all, a quarter of the camp – some 1,100 prisoners – registered their interest in a variety of different subject areas (*In Ruhleben Camp*, 11 July 1915: 47). Quantitative records of these questionnaires no longer exist, though we can ascertain their results from the developments within the school during its formative months. A review of the departments established to administrate the camp school, for example, give us perhaps the clearest indication. From the initial nine departments that were established, three were dedicated to modern languages, three to the sciences and the remaining three to handicrafts, commercial subjects and the arts (*In Ruhleben Camp*, 15 August 1915: 44). The overwhelming response from the camp's population was a direct result of both the environmental conditions at Ruhleben and the development of informal language teaching that, while not always successful, had sustained its interest.

Teaching methods at Ruhleben

The orthodoxy in language pedagogy at the outbreak of war in 1914 was largely based on archaic principles that had governed the tuition of Latin and Ancient Greek for several decades (Michels 2004: 209). Lessons centred on direct translation from the target language to the student's native tongue and the memorization of grammatical rules. Typically, significant progress and competency were required before a student was encouraged to begin speaking the language (Musumeci 2009: 43). Over the latter half of the nineteenth century, attitudes towards modern languages shifted as pioneering linguists began to devise more conducive methods of learning languages that were appealing to the modern learner. By the turn of the century, professional language academies began to spring up in cities across Europe and subvert the pedagogical status quo (McLelland 2018: 12). Schools like Berlitz and Institut Tilly would revolutionize the teaching of modern languages and popularize the conversational methods with which we are familiar today. These schools advocated the 'direct method' of language teaching, an immersive approach that encourages oral exercises and the student's immediate exposure to the target language. Incidentally, the German branches of these language academies had provided employment and tutelage for a number of men who would later be interned at Ruhleben. This included the eponymous founder of the Institut Tilly, Australian phonetician William Tilly, who was interned at Ruhleben before his release in May 1916.[5] Tilly had initially studied the principles of the direct method under the supervision of linguist Wilhelm Viëtor at Marburg University, a world leader in language study (Collins and Mees 1999: 12–13).

The lingering influence of Tilly's ideas and principles manifested in the teachings of those men in the camp who had devoted their careers to his revolutionary methodology. It is difficult to establish the exact number of Tilly's pedagogues in the camp, though former employee Thomas Wyndham Richards' reference to a clique of 'Tilly's boys' in his diary indicates the presence of at least a small group of ex-tutors (Richards 2014: 16–17). They were joined by several Berlitz teachers including men like Robert Stoneham who had successfully taught English in Spain and Germany by the famed 'Berlitz method' (direct method) before settling in Cologne where he was later captured.[6] These men were remarkably well-travelled for their time and expressed the inquisitive acceptance of different cultures which would become characteristic of the camp. They would go on to have a profound effect on the way that language study was administered, transferring the progressive methods which they had developed in the leading language schools in Europe to the comparatively humble language department of Ruhleben. In the following sections, I will introduce some of the principal methods adopted by teachers in the camp's language school.

Formal language teaching

The establishment of a departmental school structure provided a democratic system for those experienced teachers and pedagogues to devise their own curricula and debate any changes to its schedule and delivery. This professional freedom not only allowed experienced tutors to adopt the tried and tested methods of language teaching they had followed throughout their careers, it also encouraged them to practise more experimental forms of tuition that were less accepted in the contemporary school environment. The innovative approaches of those who had worked in the specialist language academies would be instrumental to the success of the language school and ensure that the demand for language study continued until the end of the war.

It is important to note that language classes at Ruhleben still incorporated aspects of traditional pedagogy – such as the use of textbooks like Otto's *Conversational Grammar* – which were shipped in their hundreds by the Prisoner of War Book Scheme and housed in the camp's vast reference library.[7] While classes drew inspiration from the exercises and contents of the textbooks, a more progressive and keenly enjoyed component of formal study existed alongside the more traditional written methods as teachers emphasized the social aspect of lessons and the opportunity for discussion and dialogue, a value inherited by some from their prior exposure to innovative methods. The most progressive element of the school's pedagogy involved the deliberate immersion of students in the culture of their target language by way of lectures and exercises pertaining to cultural topics. This approach was incredibly innovative for the time and only widespread in the more distinguished language academies again indicating the significance of the tutors' professional experiences.

The men of Richard Roe's French class were encouraged to embrace 'French thought' to assist them with their studies and received guest lectures from other French speakers in the camp on various cultural topics such as the writings of Stendhal and the Touraine region (Sladen 1917: 163). Culture was a key frame of reference in language classes and provided the scholars with a viable context in which to develop their vocabulary in accordance with their own interests. This approach shows stark resemblances to principles of Content Based Instruction (CBI), a method of language tuition that is still commonly used in language institutions. CBI encourages the provision of stimulating content through which the learner can more effectively engage with the target language. The establishment of a French Dramatic Society and French and Italian periodicals in 1915 and 1916 were steps taken by the prisoners not only to cater for native speakers but also to provide learners with practical experience of using a foreign language within a wider cultural context. These associations were supplemented by the well-established 'language circles' that had first appeared in the camp during the winter of 1914–15. Language circles, much like class-based instruction, encouraged the use of spoken language within cultural contexts to further the student's understanding.

Language circles

Conversational language learning at Ruhleben had originated with the buddying system that had developed in the initial weeks of internment. Languages circles continued their oral emphasis but allowed them to expand and involve learners who were unable to offer a language in exchange. They were formed sporadically throughout the war and initially independent of other institutions until their affiliation with the ASU in September 1915 (Ketchum 1965: 197). Like buddying, language circles were an important feature of early life at Ruhleben and facilitated social interaction between prisoners with similar interests. Circles covered a variety of subjects ranging from primarily geographic interest societies, such as a Lancastrian and Irish circle, to the explicitly cultural and educational circles of languages, sciences and the arts. These organizations allowed internees to reconstruct identities that had been suppressed by the dehumanizing process of internment.

The language circles were among the most popular with associations established covering a variety of languages including English, Italian, French, Spanish, German and Scandinavian (Cohen 1917: 153). They were designed to be as informal as possible but still endowed a distinct set of expectations for its membership. Circles usually met once or twice a week, with the impassioned members of the Italian circle meeting thrice weekly (Cohen 1917: 153). Meetings followed a distinct structure that included the presentation of a paper or selected readings by a member of the group followed by a discussion and debate on the topics that arose. In accordance with CBI and the direct method, papers and readings largely concerned cultural, historical, and geographical topics and were delivered in the preferred language of the circle to optimize the development of spoken language. For the language circles to function, they required a minimum amount of fluency among the group to allow less experienced members to gradually develop speaking and listening skills. Richard Roe infers that the informal nature of the groups was imperative to their function and helped to instil confidence in those whose experience in conversational language was in its infancy (Sladen 1917: 222).

Ultimately, in order to fully understand the nature of language tuition at Ruhleben, we must respect that education within the camp was not an exclusively homogeneous experience. Much like today, the individual success and progression of the learner was largely determined by personal characteristics, such as their enthusiasm, ethnicity and even, in the case of Ruhleben, their cultural capital. For the most passionate and culturally aware learners, the school's progressive methods were instrumental to their swift development and would pave the way for exciting opportunities after their release. It would shape the lives of men like E R Vincent who would go on to edit the camp's Italian periodical *Il Messagero* and gain an Italian scholarship at Oxford immediately after his release, despite beginning tuition as a complete novice (Powell and Gribble 1919: 212).

While the admirable achievements of the most successful learners provide tangible evidence of the school's success, we must remember that not all learners viewed language study as a cultural activity that could be measured by prestigious qualifications. For the BAME population in the camp, for example, language tuition was a utilitarian activity that gave them an opportunity to learn the fundamental English language skills which many lacked through poor education and limited opportunities. Perhaps the most progressive aspect of all was that students were given the freedom and responsibility to personalize language learning in a way that was applicable to them. Men were permitted to be as dedicated or as casual as they liked, and it mattered little to the teachers if they viewed language learning as an immersive way to experience other cultures or whether it was a purely recreational activity that passed the time away until their release. Ultimately, it is the myriad of learner experiences which makes language study at Ruhleben so distinct and worthy of meticulous study.

Conclusion

In this chapter, I have presented an environmental framework through which we can understand the delivery and procurement of language study at Ruhleben. This developmental study is by no means exhaustive, but it is hoped that it provides a sufficient foundation for more in-depth studies of elements of the camp school which fall outside of the remit of this chapter. It would be enriching to discover the long-term impact of language learning upon these men and how it shaped their future careers. It is also important to consider, in response to this environmental study, how external factors contributed to the overall language pedagogy in Ruhleben. The work of Elisabeth Rotten and relief organizations such as the British Prisoners of War Book Scheme (Educational), for example, were instrumental in providing educational literature and examination for those wishing to gain qualifications and further study. Just how important were these to the overall success of the camp school in comparison to the environmental factors presented here. Such questions alas fall to another study and perhaps another writer.

Overall, the questions posed emphasize the demonstrable intricacy of the camp school and the Daedalian infrastructure that governed language study in this most unorthodox of environments. I have argued that the heterogenous nature of the camp's population created a conducive environment in which foreign culture and language were accepted and embraced by the majority. Progressive language teachers harnessed this cultural diversity, encouraging students to familiarize themselves with writers, artists and philosophers that they may never have heard of prior to their internment. Ruhleben allowed these men to expand their horizons and better their understanding of a world that was becoming increasingly divided and hostile. Juxtaposed with communities in the United States, who would later ban the tuition of German after the American entry into the war,[8] we can appreciate just how progressive Ruhleben was, both in its perception of foreign languages and in the methodology in which they were taught. The freedom to construct study according to the learner's needs and motivations was coupled with the liberty bestowed upon teachers to prescribe advanced learning techniques and utilize wider camp institutions in a way that, ironically, was simply not feasible for those outside of this micro-society of interned men.

Notes

1 Recent cultural history studies have dealt with theatre (see Hoenselaars 2011) and artwork and photography (see Ludewig 2016).
2 See Cohen (1917) and Powell and Gribble (1919) for a typical categorization of the prisoner community.
3 Bundesarchiv (Berlin-Lichterfelde), Reichsamt des Innern, R 1502/112376-77.
4 Located on the *Molkenmarkt* in the *Nikolai* district, the *Stadtvogtei* was a municipal prison that was used extensively throughout the early period of the war to monitor enemy aliens during registration. It would to be used to reprimand Ruhlebenites accused of offences deemed too serious for the camp's temporary holding cells, such as making anti-German remarks or attempting escape. The prison was demolished in 1934.
5 National Archives (London), FO 383/190.
6 Information retrieved from genealogist Chris Paton's website www.ruhleben.tripod .com which provides biographical details for men interned at Ruhleben.
7 By April 1916, the camp reference library held over 6,000 books in a variety of languages (Ketchum 1965: 200).
8 See Ramsey (2002) for further reading.

References

Bogenstätter, L. and H. Zimmermann (1921), *Die Welt hinter Stacheldraht*, München: Piloty & Loehle.

Bundesarchiv (Berlin-Lichterfelde), Reichsamt des Innern, R 1502/112376-77.

Carr, G. and H. Mytum, eds (2012), *Cultural Heritage and Prisoners of War: Creativity Behind Barbed Wire*, London: Routledge.

Cohen, I. (1917), *The Ruhleben Prison Camp: A Record of Nineteen Months' Internment*, London: Methuen.

Collins, B. and I. M. Mees (1999), *The Real Professor Higgins: The Life and Career of Daniel Jones*, Berlin: De Gruyter Mouton.

Constantine, S. (2011), 'War of Words: Bridging the Language Divide in the Great War', *War in History*, 18 (4): 259.

Hoenselaars, T. (2011), 'In Exile with Shakespeare: British Civilian Internee Theatre at Ruhleben Camp, 1914–1918', *Shakespeare in Southern Africa*, 23 (1): 1–10.

In Ruhleben Camp, 11 July 1915.

In Ruhleben Camp, 15 August 1915.

Jones, H. (2011), *Violence Against Prisoners of War in the First World War*, Cambridge: Cambridge University Press.

Ketchum, J. (1965), *Ruhleben: A Prison Camp Society*, Toronto: University of Toronto Press.

King, E. G. C. (2013), '"Books Are More to Me Than Food": British Prisoners of War as Readers, 1914–1918', *Book History*, 16 (1): 246–71.

Ludewig, A. (2016), 'Visualising a Community in Incarceration: Images from Civilian Internees on Rottnest Island and in Ruhleben during the First World War', *War & Society*, 35 (1): 54–74.

Maddison, A. (2001), *The World Economy: A Millennial Perspective*, Paris: OECD.

Mahoney, H. C. and F. A. Talbot (1917), *Sixteen Months in Four German Prisons: Wesel, Sennelager, Klingelputz, Ruhleben*, New York: R. M. McBride & Co.

McLelland, N. (2018), 'The History of Language Learning and Teaching in Britain', *The Language Learning Journal*, 46 (1): 6–16.

Michels, E. (2004), 'Deutsch als Weltsprache? Franz Thierfelder, the Deutsche Akademie in Munich and the Promotion of the German Language Abroad, 1923–1945', *German History* 22 (2): 206–28.

Musumeci, D. (2009), 'History of Language Teaching', in M. H. Long and C. J. Doughty (eds), *The Handbook of Language Teaching*, 42–62, Chichester: Wiley-Blackwell.

National Archives (London), FO 383/190.

Panayi, P. (2014), *The Enemy in Our Midst: Germans in Britain During the First World War*, Oxford: Berg.

Potter, J. (2007), 'For Country, Conscience and Commerce: Publishers and Publishing, 1914–18', in M. Hammond and S. Towheed (eds), *Publishing in the First World War: Essays in Book History*, 11–26, Basingstoke: Palgrave Macmillan.

Powell, J. and F. Gribble (1919), *The History of Ruhleben: A Record of British Organisation in a Prison Camp in Germany*, London: W. Collins Sons & Company Ltd.

Ramsey, P. J. (2002), 'The War against German-American Culture: The Removal of German-Language Instruction from the Indianapolis Schools, 1917–1919', *Indiana Magazine of History*, 98 (4): 285–303.

Richards, T. W. (2014), *Wyndham's War: Being the Diaries of Thomas Wyndham Richards of 85 Marion Street*, Cardiff and Newport: The Vine Press.

Sladen, D. B. W. (1917), *In Ruhleben: Letters from a Prisoner to His Mother*, London: Hurst and Blackett.

Stanley, J. (2019), 'Ruhleben 1914–1918: African Diaspora and Arab Civilians Interned in Germany', *The International Journal of Maritime History*, 31 (2): 416–22.

Stibbe, M. (2008), *British Civilian Internees in Germany: The Ruhleben Camp, 1914–1918*, Manchester: Manchester University Press.

Vischer, A. L. (1919), *The Barbed Wire Disease: A Psychological Study of the Prisoner of War*, London: John Bale Sons & Danielsson.

13

Translating charity for allied aliens

Belgian charity books in Britain

Christophe Declercq

Liberty is the best of all things
That can be sought in the whole world,
Because with liberty comes honour

Hjalmar Branting (*King Albert's Book*, 1914: 155)

By the time of the Battle of the Yser (16 October 1914) and the First Battle of Ypres started (19 October), Germans had occupied most of the territory of Belgium. More than one and a half million Belgian citizens – and soldiers – had fled and sought refuge elsewhere, and an unaccounted number were internally displaced. Ultimately about 600,000 Belgians were to spend the entirety of the war period abroad, mainly in the Netherlands, France and the United Kingdom (Amara 2008: 12). For Britain, figures vary between 225,000 and 265,000 – a figure that will remain fluid, to a large extent because of long-term convalescent soldiers employed in Belgian factories in Britain and overseen by local Belgian refugee committees affected statistics, but also because a considerable share of the relevant archives have been lost. *The Times History of the War* (THW 1915) stated that from early August 1914 until the beginning of June 1915, 265,000 Belgians had come to Britain, of whom 211,000 were still resident there in June 1915 (p. 459). It is estimated that between mid-September and mid-October 1914 over 140,000 Belgians had arrived in Folkestone alone, although, again, that figure does not distinguish between civilians and soldiers: 'I went among the crowds of refugees at Folkestone, and sat in the midst of sick Belgian soldiers' (*King Albert's Book* 1914: 105). By mid-1917, 172,298 Belgians were registered in Britain (COB 1917: 9). The duty of care that so characterized Victorian and Edwardian philanthropy (Freeman 2003; Grant 2012; Laybourn 2015) and that was carried through franchise fundraising (Roddy, Strange and Taithe 2019) instigated a multitude of charity organizations in support of Belgian relief. The main collaboration consisted of the War Refugees Committee and the Local Government Board, but up to 2,500 Belgian refugee committees were formed across Britain (RWU 1920: 9). Upon arrival the destitute Belgians were not only met by a wave of empathy and sympathy, they were used as a tool as well, as a vivid reminder of the cruelty of war and the barbarism of the enemy; they became a token representative of why Britain had gone to war (Declercq 2019: 9). Indeed, 'if the Belgian refugees had not existed, they would have had to be invented by agents recruiting labour for voracious munitions factories' (Cahalan 1977: 3).

The Belgian refugees in Britain became the face of a British propaganda campaign that maintained British popular support for the war effort. Moreover, with references to refugee stories in the British press as early as 8 August 1914 (*The Derby Daily Telegraph*) – four days into the war – attention to displacement because of the 'vile Hun' preceded an organized British response to the German propaganda machine by nearly a month. Under the instigation of David Lloyd George, the Chancellor of the Exchequer in the Asquith government, the Cabinet decided on 5 September 'to counteract the dissemination of German false news' (Sanders 1975: 119). Headed by Charles Masterman, the British War Propaganda Bureau (WPB) became known as Wellington House and formed the foundation of the later Ministry of Information (established March 1918). The WPB was involved in publishing two and a half million copies of pamphlets, books and other means of propaganda in seventeen languages in the first ten months of the war (Altenhöner 2017). Wellington House worked with the Belgian legation in London, and the combined effort virtually acted as the entire ministry of propaganda for Belgium, at least in the early months of the war (Messinger 1992: 40). The WPB at Wellington House was responsible for producing and disseminating books, pamphlets and periodicals (Prieto 2018: 90), published by private publishing houses to give the impression that British propaganda was the creation of private citizens (Buitenhuis 1989: xvii; Prieto 2018: 90).

As far as the Belgian refugees were concerned, the manoeuvres carried out by Masterman and his WPB were at their most renowned with the publication of the Bryce Report, an official investigation by the Committee on Alleged German Outrages into the atrocities committed by the Germans in Belgium, more particularly on Belgian civilians. The Bryce Report – translated into twenty-seven languages (Rankin 2008) and published mid-May 1915, literally days after the sinking of the Lusitania – was very influential in fuelling further antagonism towards the Germans (Doyle and Walker 2012: 24) and in shaping attitudes and morale in virtually all the countries affected by the conflict (Cunliffe 1974: 301). However, part of the legacy of the Bryce Report – already disputed during the war because of factuality becoming detached from empirical grounding (Wollaeger 2008: 132)[1] – was that it contributed to the history of the Belgian refugees disappearing from view after the war: the 'destitute Belgians had been used as a tool of warfare and when the war was finally over, those tools were hastily discarded, and all the stories that came with them suppressed' (Declercq 2019: 14).[2] However, the Bryce Report was not the sole publication that furthered the discarding of the Belgian refugee. On the back of the initial wave of empathy, gift books were produced for charitable purposes, the proceeds of which went partially or solely to distress relief for Belgians, typically for Belgian refugees in Britain. As these charity books constituted an important part of the primary material on the subject of Belgian refugees in Britain during the First World War and contributed to the reception and perception of those refugees, this chapter therefore aims to look into the charity books published during the First World War on behalf of the Belgians in Britain from a descriptive point of view.[3] To date, only some of the charity books concerned have been included in First World War historiography, but not all those listed here. Nor have they been organized so far as a specific wartime genre.

Gift books and charity

There is quite a distance between Hall Caine's fame as an author before, during and after the war. Caine was 'established throughout the English-speaking world' (*Inverness Courier*, 13 November 1896, p. 6.) with novels that became 'astonishingly popular' – Caine's novel *The Christian* (1897) was the first in Britain to sell over one million copies (Allen 2011). His renown was boosted further for being the 'Hommy-Beg' in the dedication of Bram Stoker's *Dracula* (1897, Archibald Constable), but his disappearance from public view in the immediate post-war years was a rapid one and occurred as part of the new realities of literary language and its modernist alienation and fragmentation. Despite the successful sales figures for his last two novels – *The Master of Man* (1921, Heinemann) and *The Woman of Knockaloe* (1923, Cassell) – critical reception was minimal: the literary world had moved on from Caine's old-fashioned style and melodramatic themes (*The North American Review* 1921). Yet, Hall Caine has several credits to his name in terms of First World War publications: other than the propaganda output for *The Daily Telegraph* and trying to rally support there, Caine helped Lord Cecil 'draft the document proposing a League of Nations after the war' (Allen 2011: n.p.). However, just as James Bryce's name and reputation lent weight to the Bryce Report on German atrocities in Belgium, the alignment with specific output proved pivotal for the fraught post-war legacy for Caine as well. A friend of the Prince of Wales, then Edward VIII, Hall Caine edited gift books on behalf of Queen Alexandra – *The Queen's Christmas Carol Book* (*The Daily Mail*, 1905) and *Queen Alexandra's Gift Book* (*The Daily Telegraph*, 1908) – and he did so again six years later in the early months of the First World War. During the First World War, Hall Caine – one of the early signatories to Masterman's Propaganda Bureau – was instrumental in reinvigorating a book genre that he himself knew well: the charity book or gift book. And, as he did so in support of relief for Belgians and in support of Belgian charity, Caine, and with him the institutionalized wartime genre of the charity gift book, contributed to the use of Belgians as a tool in support of the war effort.

The origins of the gift book tradition in England can be traced back to Rudolph Ackermann, a publisher of German origin. Born in Leipzig in 1764, he started to travel early on and established one of the first significant lithographic presses in England (Ford in Jefcoate 2020: 76). In 1822, he introduced the literary annual as a 'gift book' (Declercq 2015: 270). Ackermann's first gift book annual, *Forget-me-not*, sold 20,000 copies annually and is seen as the first literary annual (Harris 2012: 18). The genre soon mushroomed with varying contributions including poetry, short stories, letters and sheet music by various famous authors and artists, all in a lavish publication. The gift book was born as a concept and by name, 'loaded with values involving aesthetics, rituals, gender, and class', and was seen as a commodity that could be 'purchased, offered, possessed, displayed, contemplated, read, copied, admired, and praised' (Lehuu 2000: 79). However, by the mid-1850s, the gift book craze was over (Siemens 2011: 27). Soon though, the genre was revived in a slightly different appearance: a one-off publication, no longer an annual one, linked to a charitable initiative and preferably one with a royal alignment. Two important events helped charity and philanthropy initiatives mature, the first of which was the establishment of the International Committee of the Red Cross (ICRC) in 1863. Shortly after John Stuart Mill had advocated female suffrage and campaigned to include female suffrage in the Reform Act of 1865, John Sherer and Anna Maria Hall published *The Princess Alexandra Gift Book*. The 1868 book contained 152 pages of literary contributions by notable people such as Lord Lytton and W M Thackeray as well as twenty plates (Declercq 2015: 270). Later charity books were compiled along the same lines, including the 1905 and 1908 ones edited by Hall Caine. The template also proved popular in Britain, the United States, Australia and New Zealand during the Great War.

Hybrid purposes, diverse geographies

Any overview of gift books published during the First World War for charitable purposes is complicated because their features differed so widely and because of their inherent hybridity. They did not easily align themselves with specific genres or styles of writing. Although this chapter focuses on gift books that concern the Belgians in one way or another, with the proceeds from the sales of the books supporting charitable initiatives connected with the Belgians, at least in part, there are several levels of hybridity that are relevant. Two such examples are *The Land of My Fathers* and *The Queen's Gift Book*. Both were published in 1915, the former aiming for 'all profits on sale [to be] given to the National Fund for Welsh troops', whereas the latter was produced 'in aid of Queen Mary's Convalescent Auxiliary Hospitals for Soldiers'. Although there is no apparent link with Belgium or Belgian refugees, both were published by Hodder and Stoughton, a Masterman publisher who proved to be very keen to produce gift books during the First World War. Contributors to the two books also appeared in other books by Hodder and Stoughton aiming to raise funds for Belgian charity. Another example is *Melba's Gift Book of Australian Art and Literature*, which contained no contributions from the contributors who usually wrote for British gift books, but was published by Hodder and Stoughton on behalf of the Belgian Relief Fund. One last hybrid publication was *Told in the Huts: The YMCA Gift Book*, which aimed to promote the YMCA Active Service Campaign among soldiers, sailors and munitions workers. This last category also related to the many thousands of Belgian munitions workers in Britain.

Not only did gift books often operate at various levels, the blurring of categories also became inherent to the type of publication, typical of a pan-European and a global conflict of allies. For instance, *Pro Patria et Rege* included poems in aid of the Belgian Relief Fund from American and British sources. Although *The Lady Galway Belgium Book* was published in Adelaide, the gross proceeds from its sales were transferred to the Belgian War Relief Fund. Similarly, when MacMillan published its *Poems of the Great War*, the proceeds contributed to the American Belgian scholarship committee.

Table 13.1 Overview of the main gift books for charity that involved distress relief for Belgian refugees in Britain (based on Declercq 2015: 272)

Title	Publication	Publisher	Purpose
Poems of the Great War	1914, no month	Chatto and Windus	On behalf of the Prince of Wales' National Relief Fund.
Special Belgian Relief Number	1914, November	Everyman	On behalf of the Everyman Belgian Relief Fund.
King Albert's Book	1914, December	*The Daily Telegraph* and others	Sold for the benefit of *The Daily Telegraph* Belgian Fund. Between 50,000 and 100,000 sold.
Princess Mary's Gift Book	1914, no exact date	Hodder and Stoughton	On behalf of The Queen's Work for Women Fund, which acted in conjunction with the NRF. 600,000 sold.
The Glory of Belgium	1915, no exact date	Erskine MacDonald	Sold for the benefit of the Belgian Repatriation Fund.
A Book of Belgium's Gratitude	1915, no exact date[4]	John Lane, The Bodley Head	The profits derived from the publication of the book were placed at the disposal of Her Majesty Queen Mary.

Edith Wharton published her *The Book of the Homeless* for the benefit of the American Hostels for Refugees and the Children of Flanders Rescue Committee in France (Declercq 2015: 207–71).

With an explanatory preface dated All Souls Day 1914, *Pro Patria et Rege* (ΠΠΕR) is another early example of a charity book relating to the Belgian refugees, here the Belgian Relief Fund. The book included contributions from many American and British authors and was edited by William Angus Knight, a Scottish professor at St Andrews. In his preface, Knight reminisced about the origins of the book and how an earlier publication in response to an appeal by Queen Alexandra on behalf of her Soldiers' and Sailors' Fund was the immediate inspiration for organizing something around 'a need of a larger fund for a more stupendous cause' (Declercq 2015: 280). Because the publication included work by authors, some of whom had long been gone – such as William Blake, Emily Brontë and Robert Burns to name but a few – this gift book for charity was not included in the overview.

However, with respect to Belgians and gift books published in Britain, six publications have contributed specifically to Belgian identity in exile: a frame of refugeedom, in which Belgians were allowed to develop their own sense of belonging as well as an imminent discarding of the Belgian refugee card that was played with such empathy at the start of the war (Table 13.1).

Early gift books for Belgian charity

Published by Chatto and Windus in 1914, *Poems of the Great War* (PGW) was an early gift book. Although no specific date is included in the book, there are several advertisements relating to the publication in *The Times* between 6 September and 11 September. The otherwise uncertain publication date of PGW can therefore be safely attributed to early September 1914. Antwerp, the last stronghold in Belgium and safe haven for about half a million inhabitants and another half million refugees, had not even fallen yet.

The title of the volume was an early use of the expression 'The Great War' and also an indication of the association of the term with charity. The seventeen poems and forty-eight-page booklet must have sold well (for one penny) as the fourth imprint is still dated 1914. This collection of war poems was published to support the newly established 'The Prince of Wales's National Relief Fund'. Most poems had already appeared prior to being included in PGW. Of the seventeen poems, eight had been contributed by early signatories to Masterman's literary propaganda scheme, including Laurence Binyon, Robert Bridges, G K Chesterton and Rudyard Kipling. Others like Harold Begbie, Alfred Noyes and William Watson had been involved in supporting the war effort by publishing recruitment poems or by working with John Buchan. Some were closely connected to people like Rupert Brooke (in the case of John Drinkwater) and Edward Marsh (John Freeman). Even though the book was published with the specific aim that its proceeds should go to the National Relief Fund that also contributed to the distress relief for Belgian Refugees, there is hardly a mention of anything Belgian either in the contributions or in the opening pages. All was in English, no translation was involved, nor was any code switching included. Only G K Chesterton's poem 'The Wife of Flanders' related explicitly to the Belgians, although at this stage in the conflict the focus of attention still lay with the fighting and the atrocities being committed in Belgium. Even though PGW was a relatively modest publication, its success – measured by the speed of it selling out and by the number of reprints – was characteristic of the overall desire for mobilizing the population and building up momentum for the wave of empathy that swept society in the early days of the war. Very soon after PGW, a second publication for charity involved the Belgians much more fully (Declercq 2015: 273–5).

In November 1914, *Everyman* published a *Special Belgian Relief Number* (ESBRN). The publication was edited by the Belgian Charles Sarolea, who had come to Britain in 1894. By 1914 he was the Belgian honorary consul in Edinburgh and Professor of French at Edinburgh University. In 1912, the publisher J M Dent had asked Sarolea to start *Everyman*, a new literary weekly, which was associated with Everyman's Library, one of the greatest ventures in popular publishing. Proceeds from the ESBRN were to go in support of the Everyman Belgian Relief Fund (Declercq 2015: 276). Already, by the time of its printing the charity book had raised over £31,000 (roughly £2 million today).[5] Many thousands of people subscribing to the fund are listed over nineteen pages in very small print at the back of the issue. People paying £1 or less covered nearly seven pages, approximately 2,500 people in that category alone. The content contributors of ESBRN to the number included 'many famous Belgian, French and British names', even though some texts had been reproduced from newspapers like *The Daily Express* and *The Daily Mail* on the one hand and *The Times* and *The Manchester Guardian* on the other. Among the British authors were H A L Fisher, who had contributed to the Bryce Report, G B Shaw who would soon turn proto-pacifist, G K Chesterton and Hilaire Belloc, who were both on the steering committee of Everyman, and Lord Curzon, a friend of the Belgian King Albert and supervisor of the Belgian royal children in exile in Britain. Also on the board and contributing was Canon Barry, a renowned Catholic priest. Along with other Catholic priests, such as R H Benson and Conrad Noel, there was a clear interest in advocating specific Christian values, most of which were aligned with Christian socialism. Given the focus on the small financial contributions made by thousands of people, the inclusion of more than just famous names was not only deliberate but also unique to all charity gift books. Regarding contributions by British authors, the main focus was no longer on poems rapidly assembled from other publications, but on texts on topics that include more of a Belgian and/or Belgian refugee theme, like 'The Cry of the Refugee' (Brenda Murray Draper), 'Some Belgian Contributions to Human Progress' (Benjamin Seebohm Rowntree) and 'Ravaged Belgium' (John Howard Whitehouse) (Declercq 2015: 277). Among the Belgian authors were most of the renowned Belgians in Britain at the time: the playwright Maurice Maeterlinck (winner of the 1911 Nobel Prize for Literature), the poets Emile Verhaeren and Emile Cammaerts, Cardinal Mercier and, of course, Sarolea himself. Also included were Roland de Marès, the editor-in-chief of the main francophone Belgian exile newspaper in Britain, *L'Indépendance Belge*, and Count Goblet d'Alviella, who already sat on the board of *Everyman*. The inclusion of French authors and academics – such as Paul Henri Balluet d'Estournelles de Constant, the 1909 Nobel Peace Prize winner – was a logical one, since Sarolea was so intimately involved with French circles in Belgium, France and Britain. Hardly any of the texts were in French. The French letter by Mercier was translated, Cammaerts started his piece with a French quote, and Verhaeren contributed an English text and a poem in French. The only code switching from French into English appeared in an advertisement for typewriters. Jean E H Findlay was the sole translator mentioned, for the contribution by Paul de Saint-Victor.

The *Everyman Special Belgian Relief Number* claimed to have a contribution by 'a Belgian refugee' (p. 13). However, in line with the approach to text production like the Bryce Report later on in the war, his or her 'Thoughts of a Belgian refugee' appears to have been written by someone whose first language was English: 'The steel of Belgian makers, who started the first German steel works, has long been discarded in favour of Krupp's implements of warfare' (p. 14). The ESBRN also contained anonymous contributions such as that by 'the Englishman' writing about 'The Burgomaster of Brussels: heroism and humour' and one by a Belgian refugee who wrote 'Thoughts of a Belgian exile' (Declercq 2015: 277). Resembling a newspaper in form, with its use of relatively thin paper, cheap ink finish, articles of varying length and content, the ESBRN paved the way towards a much more stylized approach to gift books for charity.

Hodder and Stoughton's lush gift books for charity

A third Belgian charity book – and beyond any doubt the most renowned – is *King Albert's Book: a tribute to the Belgian king and people from representative men throughout the world* (KAB), which was published just before Christmas 1914. Along the lines of previous gift books, KAB was an anthology of prose and poetry written by famous authors and public figures – 227 contributions listed at the front of the volume – and was widely disseminated and sold for the benefit of *The Daily Telegraph* Belgian Fund.[6] It was published by *The Daily Telegraph* in conjunction with *The Daily Sketch* and *The Glasgow Herald*, and Hodder and Stoughton.[7] The presence of *The Daily Telegraph* and Hodder and Stoughton support the idea that the tentacles of Masterman's operations can be felt throughout the entire KAB, not least because it was edited by Hall Caine. The continued presence of War Propaganda Bureau (WPB) 'men of letters' is represented by William Archer, Arnold Bennett, A C Benson, G K Chesterton, John Galsworthy, Thomas Hardy, Maurice Hewlett, Rudyard Kipling, William J Locke, Gilbert Murray, Gilbert Parker and Israel Zangwill.[8] Prominent individuals other than literary figures also felt compelled to appear, including: PM H H Asquith, Robert Baden-Powell, Arthur Balfour, Lord Bryce, Arthur Carnegie, Lord Curzon, Edward Elgar, H A L Fisher, J L Garvin, Edmund Gosse, J A Spender and Sidney Webb – the list is well-nigh inexhaustible and providing labels for each would most certainly create an interesting research effort – not only for their respective possible links to Belgium, but also for the resulting rather repetitive reading resembling a 1914 *Who's Who in Britain*. Other than the listed contributors, KAB also included glossy colour plates by artists such as Arthur Rackham, Briton Rivière and W L Bruckman.

King Albert's Book, however, stands out in comparison with other charity gift books for its noted, albeit still limited, inclusion of women. Other than key suffragists and suffragettes such as Millicent Fawcett and Emmeline Pankhurst, nearly one contribution in ten was by a woman. Admittedly, some were equally attributed to Masterman's WPB, such as May Sinclair, Flora Annie Steel and Mary Augusta Ward. Lady Lugard, one of the founders of the War Refugees Committee – the main relief organization for Belgian refugees in Britain – was also included. Of the 227 contributions, only 5 contained a degree of code switching, always French language appearing in the English narrative. Intriguingly, four out of five inclinations towards openness towards the Other were by women: Mary Cholmondeley, Baroness Orczy, Flora Annie Steel and Edith Wharton. Wharton dedicated her poem 'Belgium' with *La Belgique ne regrette rien*, and declared solemnly that citizens of the Belgian nation, with its ruined infrastructure, shamed cities and burnt down villages, could go anywhere in the world and call that place their home.

Not with her ruined silver spires,
Not with her cities shamed and rent,
Perish the imperishable fires
That shape the homestead from the tent.

Wherever men are staunch and free,
There shall she keep her fearless state,
And homeless, to great nations be
The home of all that makes them great.

(Wharton in *King Albert's Book*, 1914: 165)

KAB was as a much more prominent example of international support for the war effort: other than the roughly two-thirds of entries in English, the languages on its pages were French, Spanish, Italian, Danish and Swedish, each of which came with a translation, some being abridged. KAB also included a note on its translations, thanking its translators.[9] Two people emerged with a certain level of prominence: Florence Simmonds, who had been translating the Belgian poet Emile Verhaeren in the years prior to the war, and Edmund Gosse, who had been publishing on Belgian poetry in the same period. It is most peculiar though that in this sphere of internationalism virtually no Belgians ranked among the 227 contributors. Other than Maurice Maeterlinck and Emile Verhaeren, only Emile Cammaerts appeared, even though he only provided the words of the short poem 'Carillon', which was put to music by Elgar. KAB includes nearly as many Dutch entries. The virtual bypassing of the Belgians, for whom the volume was established in the first place, was most significant in the inclusion of the music 'Pour la Patrie', based on a poem by Victor Hugo, which most certainly could not be more French.

When he was finalizing the order of contributions and layout, Hall Caine acted rather immodestly by putting his own poem alongside that of a Nobel Prize Winner for Literature, in much the same way as Charles Sarolea had turned the spotlight on himself with the special relief issue for Everyman. More substantial criticism was also levelled against KAB. The rather lush and luxurious edition was published in times of paper rationing. The perception of favouritism was justified by the fact that Hall Caine's son Ralph provided the paper on which KAB was printed. What did not help KAB to last long after the war was a contribution by the British scientist James Barr, who went as far as attributing eugenic ideals to his appraisal of the Belgian King: 'In King Albert we have a worthy ruler of an imperial race' (p. 178).

A final note on *King Albert's Book* goes to another gift book for charity that is often named alongside KAB (Potter 2007; Towheed and King 2015): like *King Albert's Book*, *Princess Mary's Gift Book* (PMGB) was published at the end of 1914. The book was a major success and sold over 600,000 copies (Potter 2007: 16). Profits from the sale went to the Queen's 'Work For Women' Fund (QWWF), which Queen Mary had inaugurated on 20 August. Technically, the QWWF was a branch of the National Relief Fund – which also supported distress relief for Belgians in Britain – and was established to create a framework in which employment could be provided for those women who had lost their jobs because of the war. PMGB was published – again – by Hodder and Stoughton.[10] Although the finish of PMGB was much less luxurious than KAB – size of the book, cover and font finish – the volume still included colour plates by artists such as Edmund Dulac and Arthur Rackham.[11] PMGB was a collection of short stories and poems, a few of which had been published before. Among the twenty contributions were work by J M Barrie, Hall Caine, A C Doyle and Rudyard Kipling, all of whom featured on Masterman's WPB watch. No fewer than six stories were written by women: Ellen Thorneycroft Fowler, Lady Sybil Grant, Beatrice Harraden, Baroness Orczy, Annie S Swan and Kate Douglas Wiggin, nearly one-third of the overall total. This not only followed on from KAB, but also suited a gift book under the patronage of a female royal. However, other than some shared authors and artists on the one hand and some common features on the other, PMGB barely covered anything Belgian: no naming a Belgian relief charity, no Belgian identity of a contributor and no Belgian theme in the stories and poems. Only a few entries contained remote references to the French culture. Moreover, the renowned *francs-tireurs*, the Belgian snipers who caused so much grievance among German soldiers that real atrocities were committed on Belgian civilians, were transposed to France in the story by A E W Mason. 'The Ant-Lion' by J H Fabre could not be further removed from wartime stories, but was translated by the English-Dutch literary figure, Alexander Teixeira de Mattos, who had translated most of Maurice Maeterlinck's work into English in the period 1904–19. 'The Escape' by Annie S Swan was set in Belgium during the war and describes how one of the main characters ultimately made it to Britain, becoming a refugee there:

> Julie and her charges were driven for hours and miles of tortuous ways which kept them out of danger, until they reached Ghent, where it was still possible to get a train for Ostend. Two days later, she landed in England with Rose and Biddy, herself utterly ruined, her home gone, one of the most pitiful of the refugees. (Swan in *Princess Mary's Gift Book*, 1914: 129)

A shift from British/Britain to Belgian/Belgians

One year into the war, the gift book *The Glory of Belgium, a Tribute and Chronicle* (GOB) was published. With a preface by the Belgian poet Emile Cammaerts, the volume included a collection of poetry edited by Russell Markland.[12] The book was divided into two parts. The first half included poetry composed since the start of the war and, the second, poetry about things Belgian, but written before the war.[13] Most poems had been published elsewhere. The first part, more than half the volume, included contributions by poets such as Laurence Binyon and John Drinkwater. G K Chesterton, for instance, contributed a poem called 'The Wife of Flanders',[14] which had previously been published in *The New Witness*, the magazine founded by Hilaire Belloc and owned by G K's brother, Cecil Chesterton. Even though all the proceeds from the sales of the book were devoted to the Belgian Repatriation Fund, the repatriation itself did not feature in any of the contributions and neither did the theme of going back to Belgium. Most poems covered the bloodshed and posed dramatic questions about guilt. In his preface, Emile Cammaerts elaborated on the purpose of a Fund concerned solely with repatriation and explained how it simply made sense to prolong the support derived from distress relief to refugees in Britain to the point where they had returned to their home soil and resumed work as normal (Declercq 2015: 297–9). However, the GOB and its equally Anglo-Belgian editor signalled a move by gifts books away from Masterman's propaganda machine and saw charity publications move closer to the Belgians themselves.

A Book of Belgium's Gratitude (BBG) was published 'in recognition of the help and hospitality given by the British Empire and the relief bestowed by the United States during the Great War'. For the purpose of the charity, the book should not even feature in the list that drives this chapter. Neither did BBG run along the lines typical of publications like *King Albert's Book* and *Princess Mary's Gift Book*. However, combining the fact that the profits from the book were placed at the disposal of the Queen Mary Fund – part of which did support Belgian charity – with the fact that many of the contributors were Belgian, *A Book of Belgium's Gratitude* certainly deserves a place here. This is stressed even more by the fact that many of the British contributors to other charity books acted as translators, including such figures as Lord Curzon, Hall Caine, Laurence Binyon and William J Locke. The *Book of Belgium's Gratitude* is divided into two parts. The first part contains contributions from politicians and members of the Belgian royal family. The first piece, a letter from King Albert himself, was (officially) translated into English by his friend Lord Curzon. Comte de Lalaing contributed the text on 'Le Belgian Relief Fund' in French and translated it himself. It was thanks to the translators that the published 'tribute, however incomplete and imperfect, can find wider scope and can reach the vast expanses of the earth where the English language is spoken' (p. viii). The second part contains contributions of a more literary nature by Belgian authors such as Maurice Maeterlinck, Emile Verhaeren and Emile Cammaerts. Several non-literary figures feature as well, such as Jules Destrée, Henri Davignon and the spouses of Carton de Wiart and Biermé (Declercq 2015: 281–2). Among the contributions was a piece on the Belgian Relief Fund by Le Comte de Lalaing, translated by himself. In it the Belgian diplomat made the case for Belgians being able to support themselves in Britain through a Belgian operation but supported by British resources. By the time of publication of BBG, in late 1915, this depletion of resources of relief organizations was quite a reality. The British authorities had to support the British War Refugees Committee through the Local Government Board, had to rely on local support from many hundreds of local committees and had to liaise with Belgian organizations in Britain.

The fact that a gift book for charity relied less on British contributors as well as WPB mediation was testament to two wartime developments regarding Belgian refugees in Britain: (a) the initial wave of empathy and the tool of the Belgian refugee in support of the war had waned substantially, and (b) Belgians in Britain had been allowed a space in which to develop their own identity in exile.

Conclusion

With the *Book of Belgium's Gratitude*, a trend emerged: as attention for Belgian refugees in the British press declined during the war period (Declercq 2015; Hughes 2016), books published for charity, the proceeds of which went to Belgian refugee relief in Britain, shifted from glossy bestsellers to smaller standard print books. The Belgians themselves became increasingly more present in charity publications, and the focus on Masterman or WPB authors moved elsewhere. Whereas *King Albert's Book* hardly contained a Belgian author, the *Book of Belgium's Gratitude* had Belgian authors only. In the latter, the Belgian contribution was printed first, in French only, and translated into English next. The British people involved acted as translators and added to the linguistic accommodation of the Belgians that was part of the Belgian refugeedom in Britain. Translating issues relating to the Belgians in Britain, and by extension the wider Belgian community, had become a clearly visible trait in publishing in Britain during the war (Declercq 2015: 282). This feeds into a second point of view on charity books on behalf of Belgians in Britain: the cross-cultural, multilingual, transnational and translational aspects. Many of the contributors to gift books for charity acted as translators. Other than Belgian sections in British newspapers, British attention to some of the most defining features of the Belgians, their linguistic differences, took the form of translated sections of non-English contributions in charity books, and this grew into a Belgian identity represented in the editing of, and contributing to, gift books for Belgian charity in Britain.

Other than translating between cultures, switching between codes also took place on several other levels. Code switching took place at prime interlingual level: within the confinements of a textual entity in one language another occurred. Interlingual code switching also took place on the level of documents and publications, so that monolingual contributions in one language appeared alongside contributions in another language. These different forms of otherlingual representation – often fragmented or fragmentary – make up the core identity of gift books for Belgian charity during the First World War: the multilingual fragments of translated and untranslated foreign language in the charity gift books reveal the close involvement of the contributions with the conflict of their time, resulting in a seemingly harmonious publishing exercise.

This corresponds to Hayman's position on conflicts concerning multilingualism in British modernist literature: 'these fragments' inherent contrast between foreign language and English context interlace the text with points of rupture, exposing authorial manipulations of language and disrupting any single-minded ideology to reveal ambivalence, ambiguity, and nuance' (Hayman 2014: n.p.). In the same way, the multilingual fragments of the charity gift books support this volume's view of multilinguism proper.

Notes

1 For a more objective analysis of the atrocities of the time, see Horne and Kramer 2001.
2 Whatever Bryce did next. Even though the validity of the testimonies on which the Bryce Report was built was already disputed during the war, Masterman was urged to work around the subject of the Armenian genocide (Tusan 2012: 126), resulting in a second Bryce Report, this time co-written with Arnold Toynbee: *The Treatment of Armenians in the Ottoman Empire* (Hodder and Stoughton 1916).
3 The author's PhD dissertation – from which several chapters and articles have been drawn – used an entire chapter on 'Publications and exile' (2015: 265–89), of which the gift books for charity were a substantial part 268–82). This chapter builds on those sections. Reused material has been referenced, but most of those sections have been substantially reworked.
4 Adverts in English local newspapers on 16 and 17 December 1915 (*Globe*, 16 December 1915, p. 3; *Westminster Gazette*, 17 December 1915, p. 8).
5 The conversion was based on the historic currency converter from The National Archives (https://www.nationalarchives.gov.uk/currency-converter/#).
6 *The Daily Telegraph* Belgian Fund was an addition to the already-existing Daily Telegraph Fund, which had collected £28,000 for those affected by the Titanic disaster

only a few years earlier. This sum was in fact less than the overall total obtained by the ESBRN!

7   There is a hint of the speed in which the volume was compiled in that Hjalmar Branting, the Danish politician, was not listed at the start of the volume and on page 155 appeared with the wrong spelling, Barnting [*sic*].

8   Caine had to give in to pressure from *The Daily Telegraph*. He had initially scheduled G B Shaw to be included among the authors of the KAB, but *The Daily Telegraph* refused to include a pacifist and anti-war author like Shaw (Waller 2006: 750).

9   KAB also appeared in several other languages, although records never quite match the supposed number of translations. The author owns a French edition in which all the contributions are translated into French, even the note on the translators who worked into English.

10   Hodder and Stoughton had co-published *King Albert's Book* in 1914 as well as publishing *Melba's Gift Book of Australian Art and Literature* in 1915. Even though *Melba's Gift Book* was entirely Australian in terms of its contributions, in its set-up it was very similar to the British gift books and had several ties with the situation facing the Belgian refugees (Declercq 2015: 280).

11   In a similar vein, Hodder and Stoughton went on to publish another gift book. *The Queen's Gift Book* (1915) was published in aid of Queen Mary's Convalescent Auxiliary Hospitals for Soldiers and Sailors Who Have Lost Their limbs in the War. Although it cannot be but for Belgian wounded soldiers also to have been accommodated by the scheme, this gift book for charity was not included in the overview as books whose proceeds went in support of Belgians in Britain.

12   Markland was also known as the poet R M Ingersley.

13   The second part included poems by Lord Byron, Walter Scott, William Wordsworth, Robert Browning and Dante Gabriel Rossetti.

14   The poem had also been used in *Poems of the Great War*.

References

Primary sources – books

(BBG) *A Book of Belgium's Gratitude* (1915/1916?), London: John Lane.

(COB) Comité Officiel Belge pour l'Angleterre (1917), *Rapport Addressé à Monsieur le Ministre de l'Intérieur*, Brussels and London: Adhémar Dumoulin.

(ESBRN) *Everyman Special Belgian Relief Number* (1914), Edinburgh: Everyman.

(GOB) *The Glory of Belgium* (1915), London: Erskine MacDonald.

(KAB) *King Albert's Book* (1914), London: The Daily Telegraph / The Daily Sketch / The Glasgow Herald / Hodder and Stoughton.

(PGW) *Poems of the Great War* (1914), London: Chatto and Windus.

(PMGB) *Princess Mary's Gift Book* (1914), London: Hodder and Stoughton.

(RWU) *Report on the Work Undertaken by the British Government in the Reception and Care of the Belgian Refugees* (1920), London: HMSO.

(THW) *The Times History of the War*, vol. IV (1915), London, The Times.

Bryce, J. and A. Toynbee (1916), *The Treatment of Armenians in the Ottoman Empire*, London: Hodder and Stoughton.

Melba's Gift Book of Australian Art and Literature (1915), London: Hodder and Stoughton.

Poems of the Great War (1916), New York: Macmillan.
Pro Patria et Rege (1915), London: J. and J. Bennett.
The Lady Galway Belgium Book (1916), Adelaide: Hussey and Gillingham.
The Master of Man, book review (1921), *The North American Review* 214: 716–17.
Told in the Huts: The YMCA Gift Book (1916), London: Jarrold and sons.
Wharton, E. (1916), *The Book of the Homeless*, New York: Charles Scribner's Sons.

Primary sources – newspapers

Globe, 16 December 1915, 3.
Inverness Courrier, 13 November 1896, 6.
The Derby Daily Telegraph, Saturday 8 August 1914, 2.
The Times, 16 December 1914, 9, 12.
Westminster Gazette, 17 December 1915, 8.

Secondary sources

Allen, V. (2011), 'Caine, Sir (Thomas Henry) Hall (1853–1931)', Oxford Dictionary of
    National Biography Online, https://doi.org/10.1093/ref:odnb/32237 (accessed 14 April
    2020).
Altenhöner, F. (2017), 'War Propaganda Bureau', in U. Daniel, P. Gatrell, O. Janz et al.
    (eds), *1914–1918-Online: International Encyclopedia of the First World War*, Berlin:
    Freie Universität Berlin. DOI: 10.15463/ie1418.11200.
Amara, M. (2008), *Des Belges à l'épreuve de l'Exil. Les réfugiés de la Première Guerre
    mondiale: France, Grande-Bretagne, Pays Bas 1914–1918*, Brussels: Editions de
    l'Université de Bruxelles.
Buitenhuis, P. (1989), *The Great War of Words: Literature as Propaganda 1914–18 and
    After*, London: B.T. Batsford.
Cahalan, P. (1977), *The Treatment of Belgian Refugees in England during the Great*,
    Unpublished PhD diss., McMaster University.
Cunliffe, M. (1974), *The Age of Expansion, 1848–1917*, London: Weidenfeld and Nicolson.
Declercq, C. (2015), *Belgian Refugees in Britain 1914–1919: A Cross-Cultural Study of
    Belgian Identity in Exile*, Unpublished doctoral diss., University of London (Imperial
    College).
Declercq, C. (2019), 'The Odd Case of the Welcome Refugee in Wartime Britain: Uneasy
    Numbers, Disappearing Acts and Forgetfulness Regarding Belgian Refugees in the
    First World War', *Close Encounters in War* 2: 5–26.
Doyle, P. and J. Walker (2012), *Trench Talk: Words of the First World War*, Stroud: The
    History Press.
Freeman, M. (2003), 'Victorian Philanthropy and the Rowntrees: The Joseph Rowntree
    Charitable Trust', *Quaker Studies*, 7 (2): 193–213.
Grant, P. (2012), *Mobilizing Charity: Non Uniformed Voluntary Action during the First
    World War*, Unpublished doctoral diss., University of London.
Harris, K. D. (2012), 'Rudolph Ackermann', in F. Burwick (ed.), *The Encyclopedia of
    Romantic Literature*, Vol. I, 18, Chichester: John Wiley and Sons.
Hayman, E. (2014), *Inimical Languages: Conflicts of Multilingualism in British Modernist
    Literature*, Unpublished doctoral diss., Columbia University.

Horne, J. and A. Kramer (2001), *German Atrocities, 1914: A History of Denial*, New Haven: Yale University Press.

Hughes, L. (2016), 'Finding Belgian Refugees in Cymru1914.org: Using Digital Resources for Uncovering the Hidden Histories of the First World War in Wales', *Immigrants & Minorities; Historical Studies in Ethnicity, Migration and Diaspora*, 34 (2): 210–31.

Jefcoate, G. (2020), *An Ocean of Literature: John Henry Bohte and the Anglo-German Book Trade in the Early Nineteenth Century*, Hildesheim: Georg Olms Verlag.

Laybourn, K. (2015), 'The New Philanthropy of the Edwardian Age: The Guild of Help and the Halifax Citizens' Guild, 1905–1918', *The Transactions of the Halifax Antiquarian Society*, 23: 73–94.

Lehuu, I. (2000), *Carnival on the Page: Popular Print Media in Antebellum America*, Chapel Hill: University of North Carolina.

Messinger, G. S. (1992), *British Propaganda and the State in the First World War*, Manchester: Manchester University Press.

Potter, J. (2007), 'For Country, Conscience and Commerce: Publishers and Publishing, 1914–1918', in M. Hammond and S. Towheed (eds), *Publishing in the Great War: Essays in Book History*, 16, 49, London: Palgrave-Macmillan.

Prieto, S. (2018), *Reporting the First World War in the Liminal Zone: British and American Eyewitness Accounts from the Western Front*, London: Palgrave-Macmillan.

Rankin, N. (2008), *Churchill's Wizards: The British Genius for Deception 1914–1945*, London: Faber and Faber.

Roddy, S., J.-M. Strange and B. Taithe (2019), *The Charity Market and Humanitarianism in Britain 1870–1912*, London: Bloomsbury Academic.

Sanders, M. L. (1975), 'Wellington House and British Propaganda during the First World War', *The Historical Journal*, 13 (1): 119–46.

Siemens, L. (2011), 'Annuals and Gift Books', in S. Mitchell (ed.), *Victorian Britain: An Encyclopedia*, 27, London: Routledge.

Towheed, S. and E. King (2015), 'Introduction', in S. Towheed and E. King (eds), *Reading and the First World War: Readers, Texts, Archives*, 1–25, London: Palgrave-Macmillan.

Tusan, M. (2012), *Smyrna's Ashes: Humanitarianism, Genocide, and the Birth of the Middle East*, Berkeley, Los Angeles and London: University of California Press.

Waller, P. J. (2006), *Writers, Readers, and Reputations: Literary Life in Britain, 1870–1918*, Oxford: Oxford University Press.

Wollaeger, M. (2008), *Modernism, Media, and Propaganda: British Narrative from 1900 to 1945*, Princeton: Princeton University Press.

Part IV

Post-war

Introduction to Part IV

Marguerite Helmers

The chapters in this final section of the volume draw attention to the contributions of the First World War to global rhetorical practices, tracing a time period from roughly 1910 to 1955. By the fiftieth anniversary of the conflict in 1964, against the backdrop of the Vietnam War, a public rhetoric that amplified the pity of war became dominant. But in the intervening decades until that time, the legacy of the war was still in flux. In these chapters, the authors are primarily concerned with larger post-war institutional rhetorics; their work ranges from discussions of single words to broader considerations of philosophical idealism.

Speech act theory points out that language use is deployed across different registers, ranging from descriptions of reality to utterances designed to persuade (Austin 2009; Searle 2012). Within this latter register, speech acts shape beliefs and actions; rhetorical theory and social epistemics intersect, providing a rich ground for textual and cultural studies of intention, power and reception. Such insights into the relationship between language, belief and social behaviour are particularly relevant when considering a range of publications dating from after the First World War, a time when traditional regimes and hegemonies splintered, rivalled by competing efforts to make the social fabric cohere around shared constructions of sacrifice and remembrance. Conservative efforts to preserve memory through physical and textual war memorials shared ideological space with the radical artistic experimentations of modernism (Winter 2014: 93). Revolutions, riots, strikes, anarchy and fascism emerged in the decades after the war, and new social groups shaped the 'lost generation' into pacifists and radicals.

And certainly, the conflict of discourses that emerged in the 1920s and after – what could be talked about in America, Australia and Europe after the war and what societies would bear – included everything from frank descriptions of sex to exterminating ethnic groups. Post-war rhetoric not only brought a kaleidoscope of languages together that spawned neologisms such as napoo and Anzac and plonk, but introduced new identities for individuals: the tourist, the pilgrim, the veteran and the hero.

None of the texts studied by the contributors to this section are descriptive of the 1914–18 crisis. These are not chapters that interrogate memory, but ones that examine texts that actively sought to shape public opinion against the backdrop of war. To borrow again from J L Austin and John Searle, none of the utterances studied are purely locutionary. Rather, the collection of texts under scrutiny are powerful illocutionary acts, performative texts designed to persuade—to warn, to guide, to unite, to divide. The contributors turn to the publications that emerged after the troops returned home and the philosophical reflections on the causes of war began (although Van Samang and

Witt also are curious about the continuities between pre-war and post-war discourse). Amanda Laugesen and Véronique Duché catalogue the new words that emerged from Australian veteran's organizations; Mark Connelly looks at the structure and aims of battlefield travel books; Jonathon Green examines the bawdy autobiographical text by T E Lawrence titled *The Mint*; Fabian Van Samang investigates genocidal rhetoric; and Steve Witt offers an overview of the optimistic language of internationalism.

Certainly, as Julian Walker points out in *Words and the First World War*, the conflict gave rise to hundreds of new words and expressions, many of which remain with us today, their now invisible origins offering a silent testament to the cataclysmic changes that the conflict wrought on global societies (Walker 2017). In this volume, Laugesen and Duché present a list of seven words that became prevalent among Australian forces during the war and remained in use for decades after, marking 'the distinctive community and voice of the returned soldier'. Importantly, these neologisms were intended to shape public perception, drawing attention to the achievements of Australian soldiers at Gallipoli and on the Western Front and sacralizing their experience.

Like Laugesen and Duché, Connelly points out that there was discursive power in the primacy of battlefield experience. Guides to the battlefields of the Western Front took on the task of not only providing condensed histories of significant battles, but instructing tourists on how to behave in these spaces. The guides codified a moral attitude towards the war, exemplified by the frequent use of the term 'sacrifice' to reference the deaths of the combatants and they positioned the tourist 'as a pilgrim on a spiritual journey with significant implications for expected behaviour'.

If veterans and battlegrounds could be sanctified through language use, as Laugesen, Duché and Connelly stress, the military might also be exposed as obscene. Green provides an overview of T E Lawrence's memoir, *The Mint*, which chronicles his service with the Royal Air Force between 1922 and 1926. The book tears away the idealized image of Lawrence. Slang, brutal sexual language and crude swearing mark him as a literary anarchist prefiguring the iconic counterculture frankness of Allen Ginsburg and William S Burroughs.

Marking the section's turn to broader political concerns, Van Samang queries whether Adolf Hitler and the rhetoric of National Socialism copied speech acts of Ottoman officials responsible for the Armenian genocide. His particular concern is with semantic entropy, a degree of ambiguousness in official publications that could both mask genocide with other terms, offering plausible deniability to officials and members of the public who encountered those documents.

Concluding this group of chapters is Witt's examination of the aspirational rhetoric of the 'international mind', an educational and political network sponsored by the Carnegie Endowment for International Peace (CEIP) that attempted to achieve international understanding through mass literacy initiatives. Founded in 1910, the CEIP continues to have a presence on the world scene, with think tanks located across the world.

The editors note in the introduction to this volume that before and after crisis points in history, conservative and radical discourses compete for dominance, transmitting values that are codified, worked over, forgotten and resurrected for generations after. The vast cultural changes that took place following the Armistice were fertile ground for experimentation and iconoclasm. As these five chapters demonstrate, the languages and rhetorics of the First World War created a transnational and transhistorical legacy. The foundation laid by these chapters and the considerable scholarship of the war's centenary has opened new areas of research that push the boundaries of war rhetoric far beyond 11 November 1918.

References

Austin, J. L. (2009), *How To Do Things With Words*, Oxford: Oxford University Press.

Searle, J. (2012), *Speech Acts: An Essay in the Philosophy of Language*, Cambridge: Cambridge University Press.

Winter, J. (2014), *Sites of Memory, Sites of Mourning*, Cambridge: Cambridge University Press.

Walker, J. (2017), *Words and the First World War*, London: Bloomsbury.

14

Tracing the afterlife of war words in Australia, 1919–29

Amanda Laugesen and Véronique Duché

In 1939, an article was published in *The Daily News* (Perth) that observed that the 'dinkum Aussie' vocabulary of the 1914–18 war was about to be revived and used by a new generation of Australian soldiers (MacLean 1939: 7). The author described how that language had not been forgotten by those who had fought the earlier war, but it was now a mystery to those who had not experienced that war. Where had these words gone? Were they going to come back into use?

The story of the revival (or not) of war words in the Second World War remains a subject to be taken up elsewhere, but in this chapter, we trace something of what happens to war words once war has ended. How does the story of the afterlife of war words illuminate the aftermath of the First World War, the evolving identity of the returned soldier, and the way the war was remembered and understood?

Many war words are ephemeral for a reason – there is not much place in civilian life for words that describe the horrors of the trenches, the distinctive weaponry of trench warfare or the burdens of military routine. It can also be a challenge to trace them – we do not have the same rich body of wartime writing such as letters, diaries and soldier publications for the period that follows war. On the whole, memoirs and post-war fiction tend to not include many 'war words', even when they recount events of the war. Julian Walker argues in his *Words and the First World War* (2017) that much war slang quickly became 'quaint'; first, it appears with inverted commas (and sometimes with explanations or definitions), and then it starts to drop out of usage altogether (Walker 2017: 270).

But is it quite as simple as this? We suggest that investigating the question of where war words go merits closer inspection. What can these words' disappearance from usage tell us? And which words, if any, continued to be used and why? This chapter proposes a preliminary foray into answering some of these questions, restricting our chronological and geographical focus to Australia and to the decade immediately following the war (1919–29).

Beyond focusing on Australia in the first post-war decade, in this chapter we also restrict our investigations to selected words. They are all words in use during the First World War, and for which there is substantial wartime evidence of use by Australians. They illuminate different elements of the wartime experience and the identity of the Australian soldier. The words selected for study are: *Anzac, Billjim, buckshee, digger, gutzer, hop-over* and *napoo*. This list includes Australianisms, words used by all the Anglophone forces and borrowings from both Arabic and French.

Where do we find war words after the war?

War words can be traced in a variety of sources in the post–First World War period. For example, slang dictionaries sought to record such words before they were lost: Australia produced two significant collections, W H Downing's published *Digger Dialects* (1919) and an unpublished glossary compiled by the Australian War Museum (later Memorial) over the years 1921–4 (Arthur and Ramson 1990). Novels and non-fiction accounts of the war might also capture some of these words. Literary accounts are worthy of a separate study, however, and so are not included in our discussion.

One of the most useful sources for tracing the path of war words in popular usage are contemporary newspapers. A good number of Australian newspapers are available for searching through the Australian database *Trove*, hosted by the National Library of Australia.[1] Returned soldier periodicals produced by the Returned Sailors and Soldiers League of Australia (RSSILA) provide us with another very useful and relatively consistent source. These publications remain vastly underutilized sources for studying veteran culture in Australia more generally. To these two sets of sources, we add one additional periodical from the 1920s, *Aussie: The Cheerful Monthly*. This publication was a continuation of one of the most well-known soldier magazines produced during the war, *Aussie: The Australian Soldiers' Magazine*. However, it became a much more 'general' type of publication in the decade following the war, as it sought to find a wider audience in post–First World War Australia.

Our analysis employs both quantitative and qualitative methodologies for examining the afterlives of war words. We use a corpus of *Aussie* that incorporates both wartime and post-war issues,[2] as well as a corpus of selected RSSILA periodicals, *The Diggers Gazette* (South Australian branch), *The Listening Post* (West Australian branch) and the *Queensland Digger*.[3] We also make use of the Trove digitized newspaper database, which, aside from throwing up examples of how war words, were used in the period 1919 to 1929, also helps us to estimate frequency and trends in usage over time.

Quantitative methods provide us with, as J M Winter suggests in his statistical analysis of the word *glory* through using Google n-Grams, 'questions rather than answers' (Winter 2017: 12). However, corpus analysis offers a range of useful approaches to analysing language historically. For example, we can examine changes across time and space, but we can also identify features such as the most frequently found collocations (words found side by side or in close proximity). We hope to demonstrate something of the value of combining qualitative analysis with corpus methodologies for historians.

Australian soldiers return

Australia sent about 300,000 troops overseas. 60,000 were killed or missing in action, and 150,000 wounded, maimed or psychologically impaired (Garton 2014:

129). The First World War had a significant impact on Australian society. The war divided opinion in Australia, especially as a result of two controversial and highly emotional conscription referendums. In addition, some returned Australian soldiers were significantly traumatized by war. There were many psychiatric casualties, as well as physical injuries: alcoholism and suicide occurred, and incidents of violence were reported. As one historian writes, 'return' was a process that involved years, and sometimes decades, of support for some soldiers. War left physical and mental scars (Straw 2017: 7, 73).

Return was perhaps made even more complex because Australia was divided politically and socially during the war and in the years immediately after. In 1919 and 1920, there were around twenty significant returned soldier riots in Australia in all the major capital cities. Some of these were fuelled by industrial unrest, some were driven by demands for improved entitlements for the returned soldier (Garton 2014: 136). Unrest settled down as the 1920s went on, but divisions lingered and were reflected in the politics of the period.

A complex system of pensions and support was introduced to assist returning soldiers, beginning during the war and continuing with a number of Repatriation acts in the post-war period. Pensions were provided for returned soldiers and dependents, and there was some assistance for helping soldiers gain employment. In 1920, a War Gratuity was also introduced. These efforts were specifically framed not as charity but rather as support to help the returned soldier re-establish himself in civilian life.[4]

The RSSILA took an active role in supporting ex-servicemen and became an important force in Australian politics, but its membership fluctuated dramatically through the first years of its life. The League was however widely considered to be the official representative body for returned soldiers, and it had a dominant voice in interwar culture and politics with respect to the returned soldier. It also aimed to perpetuate the idea of a community for returned soldiers.

The RSSILA took a fundamentally conservative stance with respect to politics, notably opposing industrial action, labour organizing and socialism. They took up a rhetoric of 'loyalty', presenting 'disloyalty' as something associated with trade unions, Bolshevism, the Industrial Workers of the World and other forces considered to be suspect. This rhetoric of loyalism drew on the flowering 'Anzac legend' (the idea of the sacred and heroic Australian soldier) for legitimacy (Garton 2014: 137). Alistair Thomson argues that after the war, digger culture was primarily sustained within the RSSILA, but was more tightly contained within, and influenced by, an official culture of Anzac (Thomson 2013: 128).

Returned soldier publications served to further the agenda of the RSSILA and to amplify its political and cultural rhetoric, while also conveying a variety of messages to its members and the broader community. But as Stephen Garton argues, we should recognize that returned soldier publications could contain within them contradictions and tensions (Garton 1996: 56). And as Frank Bongiorno also argues, the politics of the RSSILA was perhaps more complex than has been traditionally been portrayed (Bongiorno 2019: 102).

It is important to note the distinctive culture that Australian veterans created for themselves in the years following the end of the war. This culture justified the value of their experiences but also underpinned the claims that they made on pensions, benefits and the right to speak about the war experience and the role of veterans in the Australian public sphere. Returned soldier periodicals provide us with some insight into this culture that is not fully captured in, for example, contemporary newspapers.

Returned soldier culture centred on the powerful mythology of Anzac – the loss at Gallipoli that became foundational to Australian nationalism. There was also a strong element of imperial nationalism to the rhetoric of returned soldiers in this period (perhaps even more so than during the war itself), but the language of returned soldiers focused on asserting the achievements and distinctive qualities of the Australian ex-soldier.

There was never the same sense of disenchantment that can be seen as marking British cultural output of this period. Carolyn Holbrook writes that interwar Australian literary culture largely eschewed irony and the message of futility – it was closer to a form of middlebrow culture (Holbrook 2014: 88). To an extent, returned soldiers' magazines continued and amplified the tradition of 'big-noting' that Robin Gerster identified in Australian war writing, although there are complexities to this.[5] The magazines certainly worked to continue to cultivate the idea of the quality and superiority of the Australian fighting soldier.

Returned soldier magazines thus produced a distinctive language and vocabulary that marked the distinctive community and voice of the returned soldier. They helped in the process of creating a myth of the digger and of the war that gave returned soldiers a sense of belonging not just to a community of veterans but also to the national polity. In this, they formed an essential part of the process and culture of repatriation itself.

Returned soldier periodicals and language

During the war, trench publications became a key site of generating a common digger culture, marked by a distinctive language (slang), a particular attitude (for the Australians, the anti-authority larrikin was a key figure), the development of a particular style of humour, the cultivation of an idea of home through sentimental pieces, and the elevation of the Australian 'digger' as a superior figure (notably as an effective fighter, and physically superior to others, especially the British).

Returned soldier periodicals served both different and similar functions to trench periodicals. They helped to cultivate an 'imagined community' of returned soldiers, but were also devoted to communicating a great deal of practical information that would enable the transition of the ex-soldier from military to civilian life, and integrate effectively into society. They were often perhaps more an expression of an 'official culture' than an organic soldier (or ex-soldier) culture than trench periodicals, but there were still important ways in which returned soldier periodicals could express a common culture for these men.

Returned soldier publications typically contained a variety of material including articles about war pensions and soldier settlement; recorded accounts of activities undertaken to commemorate Anzac, Armistice Day and other occasions of importance to returned soldiers; and often described and promoted the meetings and celebrations of various RSSILA sub-branches. Magazines also reported on sub-branches and other associations of allied nations, including Canadian and South African returned servicemen organizations. They often reprinted stories and pieces from elsewhere, often including humorous anecdotes from publications such as *Aussie: The Cheerful Monthly* and *Smith's Weekly*. Popular topics for humour included women and marriage, as well as stories that made fun of figures of authority, as well as wartime anecdotes.

These returned soldier publications became an important place in which war words continued to have currency and to circulate, forming an important part of the returned soldiers' imaginative world. Wartime language was most often revisited in a self-conscious way in humorous stories, and/or stories about the war. The *Queensland Digger*, for example, included several articles written by E A (Emil Augustus) Tardent, who wrote articles such as 'Plain Bill on Army Rations' and 'Plain Bill and Aristocracy'.[6] These stories featured an average soldier, 'Plain Bill', talking about army life, his speech rendered with a Cockney-style accent (a technique that was commonly used at the time to represent the Australian accent). Plain Bill made use of war slang such as *whizz-bang*, *Froggy*, *vin blanc*, *possie*, *Jacko the Turk* and *gutzer*.

Other stories about the war also occasionally made use of the slang of the war years, keeping alive war words such as *Woodbine* 'an English soldier', *stoush* 'a fight; to fight', *brass hat* 'a high-ranking officer' and *babbler* (from *babbling brook*) 'cook'. While these words might have dropped out of returned soldiers' active vocabulary, they may well have appealed to a nostalgic revisiting of the war. For some soldiers, the RSSILA represented an important means to connect to their wartime identity and community, and language was one way in which to do this. While we cannot know what returned soldiers said to each other at their reunions, it is likely that there was at least some use of wartime language, especially slang, to facilitate their revisiting and reviving of wartime comradeship.

The language of war could also be mobilized in other ways during the post-war period. Words that had particular wartime uses and meanings could be transferred to other uses, or be used for particular purposes. One example of this can be found in an obituary for Lieutenant Colonel D G Marks, who died in 1920 saving a woman in the surf at Palm Beach. He was described as having gone 'over the top – for the last time'.[7] Here *over the top* was used to invoke a connection between death in battle and the heroic death of a returned soldier. *Over the top* was mobilized for other purposes also: in 1922, returned soldiers in Western Australia were asked to support an MP in an upcoming election; he asked 'all Diggers to get over the top and support him on polling day'.[8]

Aussie: The cheerful monthly

Aussie: The Australian Soldiers' Magazine was a trench periodical produced during 1918 in France by Philip Harris, a journalist (who came from a publishing family) serving with the Australian Imperial Force (AIF). He decided to continue publication of *Aussie* at home after the war, continuing to edit the magazine until 1923, after which it was taken over by Walter Jago.[9] *Aussie* continued to be published until 1931.

The periodical aimed to carry 'the diggers' esprit de corps into a peace-time esprit de nation', and declared that it promoted a 'cheerful nationalism' in opposition to the disunity and discord that Australia was experiencing at the time.

Aussie maintained some aspects of the digger culture established in trench periodicals but became a significantly different publication. David Carter has observed that the post-war *Aussie* was 'at the centre of processes by which the community of the nation was re-imagined after the First World War through a certain form of populist nationalism' (Carter 2013: 67). The new *Aussie* was never only a periodical for returned soldiers; it aspired to cater to a much broader urban readership of both sexes. But it retained something of the digger culture, primarily through its column 'Aussiosities' (also in the 1918 wartime editions) which contained 'diggerisms'.

To this end, *Aussie* provides us with a publication that bridged the print culture that circulated with and for soldiers and ex-soldiers, and the print culture that was aimed at a younger urban and increasingly cosmopolitan and modern readership. It also shows how print culture and the language employed therein helped to mediate a new identity for Australians in the interwar period.

What we find is that words that appear in returned soldier periodicals and even newspapers at the time do not appear in any great frequency in post-war *Aussie*. We might even speculate that the publication was deliberately moving away from the use of wartime slang as part of its attempt to reshape Australian culture through this critical interwar period. Here, the *absence* of words, rather than the *presence*, provides us with important insights into the complexities of Australian culture in the interwar period.

The words

What, then, are some of the words of war that continued to have currency in the post-war period? The words whose stories we trace here continued to be used, sometimes with inverted commas, sometimes not – suggesting that the currency (or self-conscious use) of these words varied.

Digger, Anzac, Billjim

During the war, several names evolved to describe Australian soldiers. They included *Billjim, Anzac* and *digger*.[10]

Billjim, an Australianism in use from 1898 meaning 'the typical man in the street', and often used in the popular Australian periodical *The Bulletin* before the war, was transferred to refer to the soldiers during the war. This use was popularized in the press more so than by soldiers themselves. Wartime *Aussie* in 1918 rejected *Billjim* as a word that was actually used by soldiers: 'The word is certainly not a Digger's word. It doesn't fit' (quoted in Laugesen 2015: 23).

Anzac was an initialism derived from Australian and New Zealand Army Corps. It first came into use at the Gallipoli landings in April 1915, and was initially only used to refer to the soldiers who had seen action at Gallipoli. 'Digger' became a widespread term for the Australian soldier by 1918. Its origins are disputed. *Aussie* claimed it was transferred from the diggers of the Western Australian gold fields, while the New Zealanders claimed it as transferred from the New Zealand gumdigger. Others claimed that it derived from the soldiers 'digging in' while at Gallipoli.

All of these terms associated the Australian soldier with particular qualities of character. *Billjim* invoked the 'ordinary bloke', and this came to adhere to the *digger*, who also became championed for his knockabout, larrikin and stoic attitude to the war. His superior fighting qualities were often invoked in particular through the use of *Anzac*, a term that associated all Australian soldiers with the heroism of Gallipoli. *Digger* came to signify both the larrikin qualities of *Billjim* and the heroic qualities of the *Anzac*.

Returned soldier periodicals worked to shape a language for talking about returned soldiers, perpetuating a language of mateship (by this point a core Australian 'value') on the one hand and reinforcing the ongoing special and privileged status of the digger in Australian society on the other. So which of the three terms were preferred by the returned soldiers themselves?

'Digger' was the dominant term by which ex-soldiers referred to themselves in their own periodicals. It is used as much as or even more so than any other term, with twice as many occurrences of *digger* than *returned soldier* and *returned men* combined, in the returned soldier periodical corpus. In the contemporary press, *digger* enjoyed considerable popularity, but *returned soldier* and *returned men* were more commonly used. This supports some continuation of wartime practice, where 'digger' was often a term soldiers used of themselves, and also functioned as a term of address to each other.

Common words that collocate with *digger* in the returned soldier periodical corpus include 'comrade', 'unfortunate', 'fellow' ('fellow digger') and 'pals'. These collocations attest to the general sentiments of mateship and comradeship associated with the use of *digger*. 'Dinkum digger' is another term that appears, attaching the Australianism *dinkum*, popular during the war years, much used by soldiers (including of other soldiers – for example, *he's a real dinkum*), and meaning 'genuine, true', to the *digger*.

The occasional rarely used term is also revealing of the connotations that were accreting to *digger*. The *Diggers Gazette* used the term 'superdigger', and a few other occurrences of the word can be found in the contemporary press. The word suggests a singling-out of a *digger* (usually a prominent military or RSSILA figure) but its rarity may suggest how the distinguishing of individual diggers was antithetical to the more egalitarian ethos promoted by post-war digger culture.

'Digger' was also a word that could suit multiple purposes in returned soldier discourse. Soldier settlers were sometimes called *Land Diggers*. Women who had served as nurses were sometimes referred to as 'diggeress' during the war, and this term continues to be around through the 1920s although quickly dropping off in usage after about 1922–3. The term *feminine Digger* can also be found. General Birdwood was referred to as the *Boss Digger* – he was very popular with the soldiers, and there were numerous articles written about him in returned soldier periodicals.

'Billjim' is a term of interest in relation to the returned soldier identity, especially given that it had been a word used *of* soldiers, rather than *by* them. In the corpus of returned soldier periodicals, there is some use in 1919 and 1920, but the word subsequently does not appear more than three times. The occurrences identified suggest very much its use in the context of talking about wartime exploits (and often in contrast to soldiers of other nationalities, for example, Billjim and Tommy), and never in reference to returned soldiers. So, it had little currency in returned soldier discourse, perhaps because it was a word never truly owned by the soldiers and not seen as applicable to the returned soldier.

'Anzac' is a term found many times over in returned soldier periodicals. *Anzac* could refer to the place, Anzac cove at Gallipoli, as well as to those men who fought there. It also had general adjectival use, to refer to things associated with commemoration such as *Anzac (Day) services*, *Anzac (day) celebrations* and *Anzac (day) commemorations*, as well as those related to the Anzac landing including *Anzac landing, Anzac cove, Anzac division* and *Anzac beach*.

The word had special meaning from almost the beginning. In Australia, parliament passed legislation in 1916 that stated that no one could 'assume or use in connexion with any trade, business, calling, or profession that word "Anzac"'. As Jo Hawkins observes, this legislation was 'an indication of the growing awareness by the federal government that the word Anzac embodied a potent social currency that needed to be protected and controlled' (Hawkins 2018: 16). *Anzac* started to be truly sacralized through the 1920s, as 'Anzac' started to take on mythic form.

In terms of a returned soldier, the term 'Anzac' as a noun and referring to a person was rare in the 1920s in singular use, but had some currency in plural form. The individual returned soldier was very rarely referred to as 'an Anzac' but he was very commonly referred to as 'a digger'. Both terms continued to evolved after the 1920s, but in the 1920s they speak to the rapid development of particular mythologies around the terms, albeit still closely linked to the Gallipoli campaign.

By contrast, the post-war *Aussie* corpus indicates a steady drop-off of use of all of these terms through the 1920s. This supports David Carter's argument that the periodical was reorienting its content to gain a much broader readership that moved beyond wartime discourse to remake a particular vision of the Australian imagined community (Carter 2013: 67, 71). As it sought to find new readers who had no experience of war and were looking towards a modern future, wartime language had little relevance.

Buckshee and napoo

Australian soldiers borrowed a number of words from languages and people they encountered while overseas. These words were shared with the other Anglophone armies, and, in most cases, the borrowing may well have come from contact with the British army as much as speakers of Arabic or French. Nevertheless, such borrowings were a feature of the wartime vocabulary. What was their currency after the war?

The term 'buckshee' was already in the British soldiers' vocabulary and was adopted and frequently used during the war by the Australians. Borrowed from the Arabic, it was quickly adopted for a range of situations (e.g. *buckshee stew, buckshee shovel*). In the corpus of returned soldiers' periodicals, its frequency of use is not particularly high, but there are occasional and regular uses across the 1920s. *Buckshee* was used in reference, for example, to free meals provided for returned soldiers ('The result was a buckshee meal for 150 diggers'[11]).

Interestingly, *buckshee* came to be used adjectivally meaning 'free' as in the example just cited, while post-war examples of the variant *backsheesh* were more commonly as a noun meaning 'something given for free' ('just as we were beginning to think we had cast good backsheesh before a perfect swine'[12]). Both terms are found in contemporary newspapers in the 1920s, used in similar ways and with numerous hits for both forms. They fall out of use soon after the Second World War.

When the new post-war *Aussie* was first launched, it included in its advertising: 'AUSSIE wants his Digger cobbers to sustain him with literary pabulum in the same spirit as they did at the Front: but it will not now be a buckshee stunt. Everything used will be paid for' (Aussie 1920: n.p.). But, as in the returned soldier periodicals, *buckshee* disappeared from usage as time went on. For post-war *Aussie*, the magazine's initial intent to continue its wartime imagined community was changed to gain a different, and more commercially viable, broad readership.

Julian Walker comments in his *Words and the First World War* that *napoo* is a candidate as the iconic word of the war (Walker 2017: 269). John Brophy and Eric Partridge in their *Songs and Slang of the British Soldier 1914*-1918 memorably glossed it with the comment: 'the word came to be used for all the destructions, obliterations and disappointments of war' (Brophy and Partridge 1930: 141). *Napoo* was a corruption of the French *il n'y en a plus* 'there's no more'.

While *napoo* only brings up a few hits in the returned soldiers' periodicals corpus, it is used in a general sense rather than in a way that invoked a wartime connection. For example, in a discussion of a British ex-soldier business venture involving trade with Germany, *The Listening Post* commented: 'When Fritz was permitted to trade with England, one of his first acts was to swamp the market with toys considerably cheaper than the British articles. Result – napoo the ex-soldier ventures.'[13] In contemporary newspapers, we also find much general use of *napoo*, suggesting it had some possibility to find its way into general Australian English, establish itself, and lose its wartime connotations; however, by the end of the 1930s, it largely fades away, only being attached to a popular dog race known as the 'Napoo Stakes'.

Gutzer and hop-over

A number of war words were intimately connected to fighting, death and injury. Many of these words had limited, if any, currency beyond the war years and dropped out of usage very quickly (e.g. slang words for weapons like *coal box* and *pineapple*). But a few did gain some currency, as we'll see. These ongoing usages reveal that a few wartime slang words could be remade or find some relevance in civilian life.

Gutzer (also *gutser*) had its origins in a wartime context in 1917, in both the sense of a 'heavy fall' and in the phrase *to come a gutzer* 'to fail as a result of miscalculation'. Wartime usage varied from *coming a gutzer* because your pay-book was overdrawn, to failing at an attack on the battlefield. *Gutzer* came to have some post–First World War currency. While never widely in use, it has maintained a steady presence in Australian

English through to the 2000s, and might well constitute what Ross Wilson calls the 'ethereal' lexical legacy of war (Wilson 2013: 54).

'Gutzer' is in the *Australian National Dictionary* in the noun sense 'a heavy fall, a collision'; in the phrase *to come a gutzer*; and in the verb sense 'to fail miserably'. Just why this word was able to transition so effectively from wartime/soldier use to general Australian English is unclear but perhaps a clue lies in its use by notable interwar authors including Leonard Mann and Norman Lindsay; these writers may well have helped it to make a transition to more general usage.

Soldiers also sought to remake words that were intimately associated with the nature of the war. *Hop-over* (also *hop over*) was widely used during the war to the action of 'going over the top' in an attack. It continued to have currency in Australian English in the interwar period, but the sense shifted. W H Downing in *Digger Dialects* defined *hop-over* as '(1) A battle. (2) An assault on an enemy position. (3) A riotous convivial celebration'. But the final sense was much less used during the war (perhaps for obvious reasons) than the former two.

However, in the post-war period and in the context of returned soldier culture, *hop-over* came to be used primarily in reference to a kind of social event for returned soldiers (and sometimes also more generally to refer to a fight or ruckus of some sort). It is possible to find a great many references to the 'social event' sense in both returned soldier periodicals and contemporary newspapers. The following is an example: 'The "hopover" which took place on the "supper-room front" on June 17, at "zero," was highly successful from every viewpoint'.[14] This example clearly used language to revive memories of wartime life.

'Gutzer' and 'hop-over' are just two of a number of wartime words that continued to have currency; some of these retained currency because of their evocation of wartime life, but others began to lose their wartime origins and connections as they moved into general currency. More work remains to be done on these kinds of words.

Conclusion

'Is the Digger language which has developed over here during the last four years, going to establish itself in Aussie after the boys return?', asked soldier 'A.X.' in *Aussie* in January 1919.[15] The answer was largely 'no'. Most words had no real relevance for a civilian life. Yet there was a place for such language within the returned soldier community, and through the public interaction with the legacy of the war and with the returned soldiers themselves.

Language has a key role to play in articulating and shaping identity and community. During the war, language, especially slang, helped to carve out a distinct Australian identity while also tying soldiers into a broader Anglophone identity. We have seen that while much of the language mobilized to make sense of the experience of war disappeared quickly, some of it was retained, if only for a period of time and only in specific contexts. Some words continued to be retained within the returned soldiers' vocabulary, tying these men to each other and asserting their status as veterans and their special place within Australian culture and society.

Some words lived on to become part of the broader Australian vocabulary, existing, as Ross Wilson's work has suggested in the British context, as a form of intangible heritage. Notably, the deep significance accorded to the words 'digger' and 'Anzac' have been central to the ongoing evolution of Australian national identity, even as they mutated in new and different ways in the decades that followed. Much more work remains to be done in examining the afterlife of war words.

Notes

1 *Trove*, National Library of Australia, https://trove.nla.gov.au/.
2 Compiled by Véronique Duché and Daniel Russo-Batterham. Python, Django and Dash were used to create a searchable database of First World War magazines as part of a project funded by the Digital Studio at the University of Melbourne.
3 Compiled by Amanda Laugesen using LancsBox.
4 For details, see Crotty (2019).
5 See Gerster (1987).
6 *Queensland Digger* 1, no. 2 (May 1925): 9; 1, no. 1 (15 April 1925): 13.
7 *Diggers Gazette*, 1, no. 8 (March 1920): 21.
8 *Listening Post*, 1, no. 5 (25 April 1922): 18.
9 Walter Jago (1885–1943), second president of the Fellowship of Australian Writers, was also the last editor of *The Lone Hand* (1919–28), a monthly magazine of literature and poetry.
10 All definitions and etymological information is hereafter drawn from Amanda Laugesen 2015 and Moore 2016.
11 *Diggers Gazette*, 1, no. 12 (May 1920): 11.
12 *Queensland Digger*, 2, no. 4 (1 September 1926): 48.
13 *Listening Post*, 1, no. 1 (20 December 1921): 5.
14 *Eastern Districts Chronicle*, 25 June 1926, 2.
15 *Aussie* 10 (January 1919), 1.

References

Arthur, J. M. and W. S. Ramson (1990), *W.H. Downing's Digger Dialects*, Melbourne: Oxford University Press.
Bongiorno, F. (2019), 'Australian Politics in the Wake of the First World War', in Carolyn Holbrook and Keir Reeves (eds), *The Great War: Aftermath and Commemoration*, 101, Sydney: UNSW Press.
Brophy, J. and E. Partridge (1930), *Songs and Slang of the British Soldier 1914–1918*, London: Scholartis Press.
Carter, D. (2013), *Always Almost Modern: Australian Print Culture and Modernity*, Melbourne: Australian Scholarly Publishing.
Crotty, M. (2019), 'The Veteran Challenge: Repatriation Benefits for Australian Soldiers', in Carolyn Holbrook and Keir Reeves (eds), *The Great War: Aftermath and Commemoration*, 58–68, Sydney: UNSW Press.
Garton, S. (1996), *The Cost of War: Australians Return*, Melbourne: Oxford University Press.

Garton, S. (2014), 'Demobilization and Empire: Empire Nationalism and Soldier Citizenship in Australia after the First World War, *Dominion Context*', *Journal of Contemporary History*, 50 (1): 124–43.

Gerster, R. (1987), *Big-noting: The Heroic Theme in Australian War Writing*, Carlton: Melbourne University Press.

Hawkins, J. (2018), *Consuming Anzac: The History of Australia's Most Powerful Brand*, Crawley: UWA Publishing.

Holbrook, C. (2014), *Anzac: The Unauthorised Biography*, Sydney: New South.

Laugesen, A. (2015), *Furphies and Whizz-bangs: Anzac Slang from the Great War*, Melbourne: Oxford University Press.

Maclean, R. O. (1939), 'How they Said It Last Time', *Daily News (Perth)*, 6 December 1939, 7.

Moore, B. (ed. with Amanda Laugesen, Mark Gwynn and Julia Robinson) (2016), *The Australian National Dictionary: Australian Words and Their Origins*, Melbourne: Oxford University Press.

Pretty, A. G. (2003), 'Glossary of Slang and Peculiar Terms in Use in the AIF (1921–24)', original in the Australian War Memorial, AWM 93 [18/1/1] and online edition (with annotated version edited by Amanda Laugesen). Available at: https://slll.cass.anu.edu.au/centres/andc/glossary-slang-and-peculiar-terms-use-aif-1921-1924

Straw, L. (2017), *After the War: Returned Soldiers and the Mental and Physical Scars of World War I*, Crawley: University of Western Australia Publishing.

Thomson, A. (2013), *Anzac Memories: Living with the Legend*, Melbourne: Oxford University Press.

Walker, J. (2017), *Words and the First World War: Language, Memory, Vocabulary*, London: Bloomsbury.

Wilson, R. J. (2013), *Cultural Heritage of the Great War in Britain*, Farnham: Ashgate.

Winter, J. M. (2017), *War beyond Words: Languages of Remembrance from the Great War to the Present*, Cambridge: Cambridge University Press.

15

The language of battlefield guidebooks, 1919–25

Mark Connelly

The battlefields of the Western Front gripped the imaginations of the British people throughout the conflict. Gaining an understanding of the nature of the trenches and no man's land was something that drove millions of Britons to see war films such as *The Battle of the Somme* (1916) and attend exhibitions of photographs and art and of displays of war equipment and trophies.[1] The interest whetted the appetite to see the battlefields themselves, and during the course of the conflict certain VIPs and other key groups the government wished to influence were taken on carefully constructed battlefield tours.[2] At the end of the conflict, the desire to visit was expressed widely with many frustrated by the government's official ban on travel to France and Belgium through the maintenance of wartime restrictions. However, the cessation of hostilities led to an immediate influx, as people found ways around the regulations. In turn, this stimulated a specialist travel industry in which guidebooks played a crucial role shaping expectations, rhetorical and moral constructions of the battlefield and establishing a lens through which they could be seen and interpreted. In Britain, guidebooks began to be published in 1919, and they rapidly formed into two slightly different styles and natures. The first might be deemed a slight variant on the classic tourist guidebook, as already well established in European culture by 1914. The second was much more focused on the emotions and moral of the war and treated the visitor not as a tourist, but as a pilgrim on a spiritual journey with significant implications for expected behaviour and demeanour.

The first guides to the battlefields appeared during the conflict itself with Michelin pioneering the way in 1917 with its works on the Marne.[3] Having set the precedent, Michelin, already famous for encouraging motoring through its careful creation of tourist circuits and grading of hotels and restaurants, followed up with a series of guides to all the major battlefields of the Western Front.[4] These guides were published in English, often with subtle variants on the original French to make them more interesting and relevant to British readers and visitors. As such early entries into the market, Michelin could not provide much detail on areas in which it usually excelled, namely places of accommodation and refreshment. The devastated battlefield zone lacked any infrastructure at the moment they went to print, so what they provided instead was an authoritative overview of each major battlefield. Using what Foucault deemed the 'magisterial' gaze of the nineteenth-century museum, which translated into the language of the tourist guidebook, Michelin's texts explained the context of each battle with great clarity and insight.[5] The tone of the official historian was evident in the careful classification of different chronological and geographical zones of each battlefield. Its definitions of the Somme battle spaces exemplify this approach:

> *North of the Somme* – The battle zone, bounded by the rivers Ancre, Somme and Tortille – the latter doubled by the Northern Canal – forms a strongly undulating plateau (altitude 400-520 feet), which descends in a series of hillocks, separated by deep depressions, to the valleys of the rivers (altitude 160 feet). The Albert-Comblés-Péronne railway runs along the bottom of these depressions. (The Somme 1919: 11)

Maps lent further weight to the instructive tone, as did the lavish use of photographs, carefully annotated to allow the visitor to orient herself/himself in the landscape. Through this combination, the Michelin guides managed to include a world of battlefield wonders well worth gawping at, but covered in a language of cool detachment and information. They were perfect for the visitor who wished to appear engaged and wanting to understand what had happened, and not someone intent on a joyride seeking thrills and sensations by traversing sites of trauma.

The famous *Blue Guide* series took a similar approach to Michelin. In 1920, it produced *Belgium and the Western Front* and in 1922 *North-Eastern France*. Both contained extensive introductory essays covering the history of the war written by the distinguished British General Sir Fredrick Maurice. Maurice's style was spare, matter-of-fact and peppered with military language, particularly in its obsession with topography. His detached, clipped approach gave the impression of factual accuracy and impartiality which was doubtless meant to inspire confidence in the text.[6] An excerpt from his analysis of the Battle of Mons provides a perfect example of his approach:

> Sir Horace Smith-Dorrien's 2nd Corps held the Bois la Haut, which dominates the town of Mons to the S.E., the loop of the Canal de Condé at Nimy, N.E. of the town, and a forward position along the canal just N. of the town, extending W. in the direction of Condé, with Allenby's cavalry on his left flank. The canal line was intended to be little more than out outpost position, and Smith-Dorrien had selected a main position S. of the town on the more open ground near Ciply. (Maurice in Muirhead 1920: xxxv–xxxvi)

As with the Michelin guides, the assumption of the Muirhead guides was that the visitor had the means to travel independently. Of course, Michelin's guides were designed for those who could afford to own, run and drive their own car, or had the wealth to hire a chauffeur. Other guidebooks were also designed to meet the wealthy traveller market, and imitated the style established long before the war by the tourist industry. A particular variant was provided in the guides aimed at American tourists. A M Sommerville Story, a British writer long domiciled in Paris with a string of articles and books about the city already published, produced a series with great rapidity for this market. Here, the emphasis was on practical travel details to ensure the easiest way of touring the great sites of the battlefields. The tourist gaze was fully reflected in the title of his 1920 work, *Present Day Paris and the Battlefields: The Visitor's Handbook with the Chief Excursions to the Battlefields*. The guide gives the distinct impression of seizing an opportunity to exploit a market, but without having to put in an exhaustive amount of research. Given his knowledge of France and Paris, it appears to have been a relatively easy task to put together a text based on existing knowledge and work and complete it with a brief chapter on the battlefields. He very definitely decided to keep within his comfort zone for much of the book starting with the introductory chapter, 'Paris of to-day', which makes only one reference to the war, and then it is in the chapter's final sentence. Thirteen further chapters on various aspects of Paris, its history and culture, follow before the battlefields are finally addressed in a whistle-stop tour through the main battle sites.

Like much of the literature aimed at the American market, the foregrounding of Paris was probably made on the assumption that after making such a long journey, American visitors would naturally gravitate towards the capital for both logistical and touristic reasons. Having arrived by ship, the rail links would take them through to Paris first, and there was then little point in not exploring the city at either the start or the end of a trip to France. The French capital was therefore at the centre of the whole text and the nodal point for all exploration and experiences. When Sommerville Story finally focused on the battlefields, he made the point that they could easily be reached from Paris, and much could actually be seen in a day trip. He told readers that the trains were generally reliable, but accommodation in the devastated regions 'is still not very high-class', which was offset by the easy availability of good food. That there was already a set of established itineraries is revealed in his comment, 'the tourist agencies have mapped out the devastated regions to correspond with the different battlefields and to enable tourists to see the utmost in the minimum of time and with the least inconvenience' (Sommerville Story 1920a: 142).

Orientation was also made dependent on sites of interested to American visitors. Verdun thus became the gateway to the American cemetery of Romagne, rather than as a site of significance purely because of the immense Franco-German struggle fought around it. American feats of arms were celebrated and underlined by quotations implying authoritative judgement: 'St Mihiel, which 'has been called the "twenty-seven hour, clean-cut American victory"'. There was also the neat coincidence of Paris being so close to Château Thierry and Belleau Wood, two sites where American troops were heavily engaged. Both 'can easily be visited in one day' meaning a return to Paris in time for dinner and lunch in Château Thierry itself (Sommerville Story 1920a: 143).

Writing of the Ypres battlefields, he noted that the battlefields could be visited in numerous ways – by car, by train and thence on foot, by bicycle 'or on foot entirely'. But the latter two were deemed to require 'a good deal of time and patience and will be found highly fatiguing under the circumstances'. He then deployed a didactic language of instruction: 'Still another method is the personally conducted tour, and there is much to recommend this in the case of visits to the battlefields. In the first place one's route of travelling will be followed in accordance with expert guidance and after careful study, and in the circumstances of the battlefields this is a great advantage' (Sommerville Story 1920b: 3).

Listing and ranking facilities by standards and costs was another important element of guidebooks prior to the war, and it remained equally significant to the battlefield guide. The *Pilgrim's Guide to the Ypres Salient* commented on five hotels using direct, spare and economical language, perfect for the visitor wishing to make a rapid decision. The Splendide was declared 'rather expensive'; the Ypriana 'Cheerful, clean, cooking good'; the Metropole 'excellent cooking of a French type' rooms nice, but a bit small (The Pilgrim's Guide 1920: 50).

The literature aimed at the tourist market, rather than that trying to straddle the divide with those designed to have a deeper level of reflection on the war, also made a point of emphasizing the sites of wonder on the former battlefields. Having become stars in their own right during the course of the conflict, tanks continued to have an almost mesmeric effect, and places where they could still be seen in their ruined and abandoned condition were very deliberately highlighted. The Ypres battlefields had two locations labelled as either 'Cemetery of the Tanks' or 'Tank Cemetery'. One was near the village of Poelcappelle. But the more famous of the two was on a bend in the Menin road near Hooge labelled 'Clapham Junction' by the troops. *Muirhead's Belgium and the Western Front* of 1920 flagged it up, as did Ward, Lock and Company's 1921 *Handbook to Belgium and the Battlefields*.[7] They even attracted comment from those works produced for the more committed visitor. Another early guide, J O Coop's 1920, *Short Guide to the Battlefields*, referred to the 'dismantled tanks' that could be seen along the Menin Road (Coop 1920: 32). Similarly, *The Pilgrim's Guide to the Ypres Salient* of 1920, called attention to the 'Tank Cemetery' where the country was 'strewn with the wreckage of over a dozen tanks' (*The Pilgrim's Guide* 1920: 61).

The nature of the guides aimed at the visitor wishing a deeper interaction with the battlefields was made explicit in their high diction titles such as *The Pilgrim's Guide to Ypres and the Salient* (1919), *Ypres: Holy Ground of British Arms* (1919), *The Immortal Salient* (1925) and *Ypres: outpost of the Channel Ports* (1929). In these works, the moral emphasis on the visitor to act reverently and commit themselves to not just understanding what happened factually on the battlefields, but also immersing themselves in the challenge of coming to terms with the scale of sacrifice made on their behalf was obvious. Indeed, the regular use of the term 'sacrifice', rather than 'killed' or 'died', added to the emotional power and degree of instruction. Rather than mirroring the official army language of 'killed, dead and missing', or the essential facts of guidebooks, 'sacrificed' turned every soldier into an imitator of Christ, freely giving his life that others might live. It is also noticeable how many of the guides built around a high diction related specifically to the Ypres Salient. Ypres was regarded as the most important of the war's battlefields throughout the period, as it was the site on which every British and imperial unit that served on the Western Front fought at some point. The mythologizing of Ypres also commenced from the earliest stages of the war during the first great battle fought in its environs in the autumn of 1914. As such, these guidebooks maintained continuity with wartime representations and language.

A significant element of the earliest guidebooks was the provision of a welter of detailed advice. This was extremely important in the immediate post-war years, as the Western Front was a devastated zone lacking many basic amenities and infrastructure. As some of the earliest guides were written by former soldiers or other members of the armed forces, the style of the military instruction manual can be detected in the mix of advice bordering on direct order. Lieutenant Colonel T A Lowe was extremely prescriptive in his approach, and in the process revealed the status and culture of the officer class. He told his readers to take an old golfing suit combined with stout boots and leggings so as to avoid snagging on the copious amounts of barbed wire still scattered across the battlefields. The exposed nature of the battlefields also demanded a waterproof coat, which was deemed a crucial necessity 'except when there is no doubt about the weather', and as any soldier knew, when carefully rolled a mackintosh would give 'little trouble . . . on the back and shoulders' (Lowe 1920: 3). The Reverend J O Coop, former chaplain to the 55 (West Lancashire) Division, was equally direct in his guidebook. 'Above all things the traveller must be weather-proof', he warned, adding that the visitor needed to be 'well prepared against mud and rain'. Just in case the prospective visitor could not understand the nature of the Western Front, he spelt it out graphically: 'it is perfectly astonishing what a change a shower of rain will bring about – especially in Belgium.' He went on: 'A good portion of the battle area, even in good weather, is difficult to negotiate; in or after wet weather it is indescribable' (Coop 1920: 13). A walking stick was therefore necessary, as were thick-soled, stout boots (Coop 1920: 13).

When advising on suitable clothing and useful kit, the ex-service guidebook writer also revealed the paternalistic language and style of the officer class determined to ensure the well-being of those under their command. As might be expected, ensuring rations was also a focus for the experienced ex-serviceman-writer. Referring to the needs of the 'inner man', Lowe said it was possible to survive on sandwiches and something to drink, but also advised making provision for a good meal at lunchtime (Lowe 1920: 3). Coop was a little more sybaritic, but started by hinting at possible dangers, noting 'accidents and contingencies may arise when a supply of food is most welcome, and an emergency ration, therefore, should invariably be carried' (Coop 1920: 13). In addition, he believed it wise to carry a Thermos flask, tin opener and a corkscrew to 'prevent subsequent exasperation. . . . Little details like these are apt to make the difference to the comfort of a day's journey in the battle area', he added (Coop 1920: 14).

The veterans also brought the soldier's eye for country and topography into their guidebooks. As such, only by walking the battlefields could they be truly understood. Lowe referred to the motor tour, but recommended against it. Instead, he advocated the advantage of the poor man (and he conceived it in masculine terms) unable to afford such a luxury. By exploring on foot, the visitor would achieve a far deeper understanding of the battlefields than the chauffeur-driven person. In addition, the walker would gain insight into the wartime lot of the soldier: 'he will feel that he is tramping as they were obliged to, minus the burden of a rifle, equipment and heavy pack – details which are well calculated to minimize the delights of a walking tour' (Lowe 1920: 2). In this respect, Lowe implied that the visitor should shift from being the engaged, but detached, tourist, to the emotional and intellectual empathizer.

The battlefield guidebooks produced in the immediate aftermath of the Great War therefore revealed a number of linguistic and stylistic traits. Many of them adopted the format and style of the pre-war tourist guide, and simply inserted the new addition into an existing matrix. This ensured that the battlefields were primarily understood as sites of touristic interest. Any moral qualms about the propriety of visiting sites of misery and trauma were overcome by the deployment of a detached language of historical investigation or museum annotation overlaying the visitor with the veneer of the interested observer wishing to understand the ebb and flow of battle. Other guides adopted a more emotional tone perceiving the visitor as a pilgrim who was obliged to tread reverently and engage spiritually with the landscape. Both had to include many practicalities, as navigating a devastated zone was a difficult proposition, and here ex-service writers often adopted a tone bordering on military language in its directness. Battlefield guidebooks were thus a fascinating hybrid in which different language codes and styles were blended together as they attempted to deal with a landscape that was both spectacular and sacred.

Notes

1   See Wellington (2017).
2   For an example, see Masefield (1917).
3   *The Marne Battlefields (1914)* (1917).
4   For a study of tourist literature, see Buzzard (1993).
5   For a discussion of Foucault's influence on tourism studies, see Hollinshead, Ivanova and Caton (2015: 17–35).
6   Muirhead (1920); Muirhead (1922).
7   *Muirhead's Guide to Belgium and the Western Front* (1920: 49); Ward, Lock and Co. (1921: 55).

References

(The Somme) *The Somme. Volume I. The First Battle of the Somme* ([1916–1917] 1919), Albert-Bapaume-Péronne, Clermont-Ferrand: Michelin.

Buzzard, J. (1993), *The Beaten Track. European Tourism, Literature and the Ways to 'Culture', 1800–1918*, Oxford: Oxford University Press.

Coop, J. O. (1920), *A Short Guide to the Battlefields*, Liverpool: Daily Post.

Handbook to Belgium and the Battlefields (1921), London: Ward, Lock and Co.

Hollinshead, K., M. Ivanova and K. Caton (2015), 'Destination and Discipline: Foucault and the Transformation of Place Makers', in Y. Reisinger (ed.), *Transformational Tourism: Host Perspectives*, 17–35, Wallingford and Oxon: CABI.

Lowe, Lieutenant-Colonel T. A. (1920), *The Western Battlefields: A Guide to the British Line. Short Account of the Fighting, the Trenches and Positions*, London: Gale and Polden.

Masefield, J. (1917), *The Old Front Line*, London: William Heinemann.

Muirhead, F., ed. (1920), *The Blue Guides: Belgium and the Western Front British and American*, London: Macmillan.

Muirhead, F., ed. (1922), *The Blue Guides: North-Eastern France*, London: Macmillan.

Muirhead's Guide to Belgium and the Western Front (1920), London: Macmillan.

Sommerville Story, A. M. (1920a), *Present Day Paris and the Battlefields: The Visitor's Handbook with the Chief Excursions to the Battlefields*, New York: D. Appleton and Co.

Sommerville Story, A. M. (1920b), *The Battlefields of France and Belgium V. Ypres and the Struggle for Calais*, Paris: La Renaissance du Livre.

The Marne Battlefields (1914) (1917), Clermont-Ferrand: Michelin.

The Pilgrim's Guide to the Ypres Salient (1920), London: Herbert Reiach.

Wellington, J. (2017), *Exhibiting War: The Great War, Museums, and Memory in Britain, Canada and Australia*, Cambridge: Cambridge University Press.

16

The Mint by 352087 A/C Ross[1]

Jonathon Green

In the introduction to his dictionary, published in 1859, the slang lexicographer John Camden Hotten posits the sources of slang as 'the congregating together of people . . . the result of crowding, and excitement, and artificial life' (Hotten [1859] 1860: 45). He was thinking of cities, but nowhere could qualify any better for his description as does military life. And if the use of cant, criminal slang, in studies and novels of crime confers unarguable authenticity to the texts, so too does slang to those of the armed forces.

It is not simply proximity that produces fertile soil for slang's generation. The battlefield was, and largely remains, a male territory. Whether in the training depot, in the barracks or in combat, the soldier's, sailor's and airman's basic existence was alongside other men. Slang, while widely and for many centuries regularly used by women, remains largely a 'man-made' language and projects a male point of view. Extend that combination, as in the First World War, for four years, and the opportunity for extending this innately male language seems almost limitless. Those books which come out of the era's military life reflect this. T E Lawrence's *The Mint*, written post-war but a primary repository of slang, is undoubtedly one of them. But *The Mint*, I suggest, was not wholly like its peers.

T E – Thomas Edward – Lawrence was born in 1888, the second of five illegitimate sons of Thomas Chapman, an Anglo-Irish baronet who had abandoned his aristocratic life – a wife, four daughters and a country estate – to elope with the girls' governess. After a peripatetic boyhood, he went up to Oxford, and in 1909, as part of his degree work, visited Syria where he went on an 1,100-mile tour of crusader castles. Two years later, he was part of an archaeological team, excavating Carchemish, a Hittite mound on the border with Turkey.

By December 1914, he had joined up and was serving with British intelligence in Cairo; in 1916, he became liaison officer with Prince Feisal of Mecca, leader of a revolt against the Turks. He worked with the prince as a guerrilla, wrecking railways, looting trains and distributing British cash to the rebels. In October 1918, by now a lieutenant colonel, he was among the Arab forces who took Damascus.

Back in London he was a popular, if wholly unwilling, hero. He rejected all honours but could not stop a romanticized and adulatory lecture-cum-film show devoted to 'the uncrowned King of Arabia'. He worked as an adviser to the then Colonial Secretary

Winston Churchill and helped establish Feisal and his brother as rulers of Iraq and Trans-Jordan. In 1922, tossing aside all connections and changing his name to John Hume Ross, he enlisted in the still nascent RAF. (This had not been simple, his first application was turned down by one W E Johns, later the creator of the fictional flying ace Biggles). A year on, his true identity was uncovered and 'Ross' was ejected from the air force. He joined the Royal Tank Corps (with yet another name: Shaw), and in 1925 was allowed back into the RAF. Here he stayed until two months prior to his death, in a motorbike crash in 1935. He was just forty-six.

Lawrence is known for two books: *Seven Pillars of Wisdom*,[2] an autobiographical account of his experiences during the Arab Revolt (and the basis of the 1962 hit movie, David Lean's *Lawrence of Arabia*), and *The Mint*, an account of his post-war experiences as an RAF recruit, complete with the barrack-room language that such an experience entailed; it was signed 'by 352087 A/c Ross'. While the former text, abridged as *Revolt in the Desert*, added literary stardom to his role, albeit reluctant, as popular hero, *The Mint*, written up from notes, as he put it in a letter to his friend the Bloomsbury writer David Garnett, 'about 15000 words…scribbled at night, between last post and lights out, in bed' had a different role. These notes, he suggested, would create, 'an iron, rectangular, abhorrent book, one which no man would willingly read'. At his own request it was embargoed until after his death or at least until 1950.

In the event, other than a tiny print run in 1936, so as to secure US copyright (just ten copies, priced at half a million dollars each), it appeared in 1955 in two editions: one expurgated of all supposed obscenity, the other, in a luxury format reminiscent of what booksellers termed 'curiosa' and others 'porn', being Lawrence's text in full. Contemporary reviews seem to have sidestepped the language; as was the way in 1955, bowdlerization was perfectly acceptable: one would not have one's wife or servants, let alone one's children, given access to such filth. The purchasers of pricey, unexpurgated 'curiosa' were considered immune.

Slang of course was not mandatorily obscene. But in the context of the First World War and its aftermath, the suggestion that soldiers might use slang, but avoid its grosser instances, was probably born of wishful thinking and propagandizing. The playwright and novelist Ian Hay (1876–1952) wrote three wartime books – starting with the best-selling *First Hundred Thousand* in 1915: they offered a humorous-but-never-negative take on a conscripts' army. Their motto reflected the stiff upper lip as required: 'War is hell, and all that, but it has a good deal to recommend it. It wipes out all the small nuisances of peace-time' (Hay 1915: 120) The army and the navy both had popular chroniclers. (Like Lawrence, they opted for pseudonymity, but presumably to mask their active military rank rather than to express a serious trauma.) 'Sapper' (Herman Cyril McNeile, 1888–1937) would go on to worldwide fame as the creator of Bulldog Drummond, but as a serving officer during the war (he quit the army in 1919 as a lieutenant colonel) offered a steady output of often quite sombre stories from the trenches. His equivalent in the senior service was 'Bartimeus' (Capt Lewis Anselm Da Costa Ricci, 1886–1967). Again, drawing on personal experience, he poured out short stories of navy life, generally among the midshipmen and junior ranks, in titles that included *Naval Occasions* (1914), *The Navy Eternal* (1918) and the tellingly titled *An Awfully Big Adventure* (1919). 'Taffrail' (H Taprell Dorling, 1883–1968), another pseudonymous naval officer, produced similar works such as *Stand By!* (1916), *Sea, Spray and Spindrift* (1917) and *The Watch Below* (1918). Both sailors were still writing in the Second World War. In all instances, while there was plenty of slang to establish the necessary authenticity, it remained wholly 'clean'.

The truth was less soothing. We know that the average serviceman spoke with neither Rupert Brooke's mawkish sentimentality nor Wilfred Owen's acerbic disdain. Brutal experiences produced brutal language. Kipling, without using it, made it clear that the Indian Army's favourite adjective was 'fucking'.[3] (Some claimed it as 'bloody' but that all-purpose favourite had been taken off Down Under and proudly characterized as 'The Great Australian Adjective'.[4]) Conscripts may have outnumbered old sweats as the conflict went on, but Kipling's 'adjective' remained paramount. For those who had doubts, there was Frederick Manning's punningly titled First World War memoir, *The Middle Parts of Fortune* (1929). Like *The Mint*, though involuntarily, this too was held back. Aside from a limited edition, authored by 'Private 19022' in 1929, it was unavailable to the mass market until 1977, although an expurgated edition, now entitled *Her Privates We* (both titles punning on an exchange between Hamlet and the courtiers Rosencrantz and Guildenstern) was published in 1930 and in 1943 Manning was posthumously credited with the authorship.

With peace declared, the collection of slang was given over to the glossarists, the memoirists and the writers of fiction. In October 1921, the *London Times* announced that the Imperial War Museum, using the scholarly journal *Notes and Queries* as a collection point, was canvassing for contributions to a collection of war slang.

> The Secretary of the Imperial War Museum will be glad to receive any notes on the subject, giving the slang, terms used in the British Army, together with the meaning of the term, and, if possible, the derivation. It is quite understood that many of these terms are not entirely fit for polite conversation, but at the same time it is considered that they will be valuable for record purposes. (*The Times*, 6 October 1921, 6)

On 1 November, the paper devoted a leader on the first list to appear in *Notes and Queries (N&Q)*. Further lists of reader-submitted material were added on 12 November 10 December 1921, and 7 January, 4 February, 18 March 1922, and 29 July (on the Mesopotamian campaign):

> Buckshee, lash-up, all cut, lead-worker, hard skin, wangle, lit, talking wet, napoo, san-fairyann, the duration, soaked, stiff, touch-out, blighty, windy, click, cushy, win, jam on it, swinging the lead, oojar, scrounge, stunt, umteen, wash-out, go west, cold feet, strafe, work your ticket, where are you working, soft job, some lad, issue, muck in, sweating, and the gear. (*The Times*, 18 November 1921, 5)

Around two-thirds would survive into modern use. These are relatively anodyne, but in 1921 a correspondent to *N&Q*[5] noted that

> the soldier's[6] actual speech . . . was absolutely impregnated with one word which (to use it as a basis for alliteration) the fastidious frown at as 'filthy'. . . . Words were

split up to admit it : 'absolutely' became 'abso------lutely', and *Armentieres* became 'Armen------teers'. 'Bloody', so popular and helpful a word in civil life, quite lapsed as being too polite and inexpressive. (N&Q 12 Ser. IX, 1921: 415)

Why? *N&Q* had no doubts: 'The explanation is of course simple: conditions and regulations of active service were so exasperating that only frequent use of the foulest word in the language could afford any adequate relief.' The use of 'exasperating', more usually applied to incompetent servants or tradespeople than to a worldwide cataclysm, is a fine example of British understatement, but the essential finding was not denied. The selection of citations is always serendipitous, but it is surely not so surprising that the next citation I have for the infix form is from Lawrence's text: The sergeant stared: then whispered to himself, 'Jesus fucking Christ.[7]

America, for the time, seemed less censorious. In 1922, as 'Ross' joined up, the American writer E E Cummings published *The Enormous Room*, the story of his four months incarceration in a French prison camp for alleged 'anti-war sentiments'. Slang plays its role, as might be expected, but the appearance, at that time, of so many examples of *fuck* or *fucking*, and a good representation of the remainder of the obscene canon, must have shocked many.

So Ross' fellow *erks*, as aircraftsmen termed themselves, were hardly unique. Yet *The Mint* feels different, and reads as such, not merely through its post-war backdrop. Slang comes in many guises, coarse, naturally, but often playful and far from devoid of wit. *The Mint*, I believe to a greater extent than almost all of the thousands of texts I have researched, is wholly lacking in this 'positive' side of slang. The world that Lawrence depicts, the denizens thereof and the slang that he uses quite deliberately to underline the fact are sordid, foul and hellish, in every sense. Manning's uses convey emotion and sometimes humour; Lawrence's slang is a grim litany, an inescapable punctuation. It takes us nowhere. This, it has been suggested, is an offshoot of Lawrence's sexuality: not just homosexual, he was also a masochist. He may not be beaten physically at the depot, as he notoriously claimed to have been in the *Seven Pillars*, but everything about the place serves to beat him and his fellows down. *The Mint* makes it clear that this, for him at least, was wholly sought after: a terrible, deliberate self-purging and the destruction, as far as possible, of what he found an inadequate self.[8] I am neither Lawrence expert nor psycho-analyst: those who wish to pursue his inner demons can do so via a number of biographies. So let us return to slang.

'Mint' means brand new and a mint strikes out new coins. Thus the text, which deals in the coining of new airmen, who are not just new, but like coins are identical in their various value groups. But the shininess and newness stops there. The keynote is rather a beating into shape. Slang exists here as an agent of dirt, both literal and figurative. Slang can be ludic, but this is not. There is no wit. Just brutality. Slang as its negative stereotype, what feminists would term a 'man-made language' in its worst aspects. Its latrinal obsessions are reminiscent of a supposedly amusing scene in an Irvine Welsh novel where when his apprentices arrive back at their factory on a Monday morning, each defecates onto a newspaper, the winner being he who excretes the lengthiest turd.

Lawrence himself did not swear. This may have been true of many young officers when they arrived at the war, although those on the Western Front may have absorbed at least some of language of their men. Perhaps Lawrence, fighting among Arabs, would have been insulated at least from the United Kingdom's four-letter vocabulary. But he was, one might say, a good reporter. The four-letter words and their many peers were undoubtedly included as part of his creation of *The Mint's* grim atmosphere, but they were also what he heard and scrupulously took down.

Whether it reflected innocence/ignorance or self-censorship, like the *N&Q* lists, officers' memoirs were similarly restrained. They had, presumably, picked up some slang at their public schools, but no glossary of such speech even hints at anything coarse. Some terms may have filtered through from the men. One such junior officer was Robert Graves whose *Goodbye to All That* (1929, contemporary with Manning's novel) offers relatively few slang terms, although in reporting speech from 'the men' the text offers a harder edge. Presiding over a defaulter's parade and recounting a soldier's obscene accusation, Graves recalls that 'The Bandmaster, who was squeamish, reported it as: "Sir, he called me a double-effing c—"' (Graves [1929] 1995: 79), (wherein, one might note, the NCO was himself protecting his officer's supposedly tender ears). As for Graves himself, the strongest term seems to have been 'balls-up', a mess.

One can differentiate the specific instances of slang in *The Mint* – swearing, exclamations, terms of address, descriptions of individuals and objects – but in the end the slang is all of a piece. Just as it is in the slang lexis, the obscenities, whether taken from the short canonical list thereof or plucked from slang's vast synonymy, dominate the vocabulary, are not alone. So let us consider everything that Lawrence found to make his case. I shall not quote: if the slang is generally short and brutal, so are its appearances. It is the slang vocabulary in its entirety, as a micro-lexis, that I suggest underpins Lawrence's desired effect.

Let us start with general terms, used in print for the first time in *The Mint*. Such 'first uses' are fluid; research constantly pushes dating further back, and the first rule in dictionary making is simple: it's always older than you think. As things stand, Lawrence may still be credited with the introduction, at least in print, of a number of such terms. They include

'aerated' (angry), 'axe' (to close down, to dismiss), 'bind' (to bore) and 'binder' (a bore; thus the name of a later RAF-related radio show, *Much Binding in the Marsh*), 'bit of skin' (girlfriend), 'blanket drill' (masturbation), 'bob on' (anticipate), 'bolshie' (in the non-political but still derogatory use of a complainer), 'brama' (enjoyable, good), 'eff and blind', 'erk' (any of the lowest ranks of the RAF), 'with knobs on', 'oppo' (a friend), 'pack up' (to stop doing something), 'have a pot on' (to be drunk), 'pound-note' (pompous) and 'toffee-nosed'.

Other slang, already in use, covered the counter-linguistic waterfront. There is drink or rather drunk: *fuddled, roaring*, to *have a pot on* or a *smell of the barman's apron*. There is food, or *scran*: *Zepps in a cloud*: sausage and mash, *adam and eve on a raft*: (a phrase he describes as 'Hoxtonian' for fried eggs on toast but was long since known in the United States); *cow juice*: milk and *slop*: bad tea.

There are, naturally, some purely military references: *rookie*: a neophyte, *harry freemans*: for free, *old man*: the commandant, *Pompey*: Portsmouth, *she*: an airplane, *swaddy*: soldier, *old sweat*: a veteran and *biscuit*: an army mattress. The rest are a non-differentiated mishmash:

> *crease*: to exhaust, *jannock*: OK, *scatty*: emotional, *chaffer*: to bargain, *easy meat*: a pushover, *jammy*: easy, *beastly*: the current euphemism for gay, *swing it*: to get away with, *half a dollar*: 2/6, *lofty*: a nickname for tall man and *shorty* for a small one, *oppo*: partner, *put a sock in it*: shut up, *click*: to come up with, *half-inch*: steal or 'pinch', the dismissive *put it where the monkey puts his nuts, mum*: silent. The suffix –*ology*, here as *toffology*: overly 'clever' talk, *sweat*: to make an effort, *do*: to serve (of an enlistment), *block*: the head, *gob*: a lump of phlegm, *half* as in *can't half. jazz*: energetic time-wasting (the musical use was barely ten years old), *tool someone along*: to accompany, *lightweight*: a weakling, *doo-dah*: an adornment (on a skirt), *the Smoke*: London, *have a weed on*: angry (from SE *weed*, a mourning garment), *run(in)*: arrest, *yaffle*: talk.

Some of these were very well established: *gob* went back to 1555; *mum* to 1575; *block* to 1608. The mid-nineteenth century gave some: *half-a-dollar* in 1843 and *run in* in 1859, while others were recent: *doodah* in 1900, *jazz* in 1912 and *swing it* in 1914. All represent slang's regular tropes: insult, physicality, money, speech and so on. But there is an absentee: whether or not Lawrence deliberately excluded them, keen to intensify his depiction of a claustrophobic all-male camaraderie, there are no words for 'woman', even dismissive.

Then are the obscenities, disproportionately represented as they were. Of the 150-odd slang terms 'Ross' used, 60 were obscene (for comparison, Manning also used 150 examples of slang, but only 20 qualified as 'filth'). Unsurprisingly, there is *fuck* and its creations:

> fuck the —, go fuck —, will I fuck!*, fuck about, fucking (as adj. and infix), fucker (as an abusive term); meanwhile F* (euphemising fuck), for fuck's sake!*, fuckpig*, fucked* (unhappy, exhausted), fucking well*, fuck it!*, fuck you Jack, I'm fireproof*all make their printed debut here. None of which, it will be noticed, refer to actual sex; that is reduced to the sourly reductive cunt* (which as 'vagina' was much older but never recorded as 'copulation' before this).

There are others that like *fuck* are positioned in slang's front rank[9]:

> *arsehole, ballock* and *drop a ballock** (as yet unknown), *balls-up, buggered* and *like buggery** (again a novelty), *cheese* (smegma), *clinker* (a piece of excrement), *doggy* (sex-obsessed), *knob* (the penis) and *doings* (testicles), *flash* (to reveal the genitals), *frig* and *shag* (to have sex), *pissed* (drunk), *pull someone's pisser* (to tease or deceive), *gnat's piss* (weak drink and a first-timer here), *piss off* (to leave), *all prick and no pence, short-arsed, sodding, split-arse* (daring), *swing the dolphin* (masturbate), *turd* (of a person), *twat* (a fool) and *up you!*

In the realm of the obscene, the book offers more coinages than established terms. Lawrence heard, and then wrote out, *not know if one's arsehole is bored, punched, drilled or countersunk**, *arseways** (head-over-heels), the emphatic *bastard-well**, *bicycle pump and tool-bag** (the genitals and cognate with *musket and bandoliers* (of 1663) and *watch chain and seals* (of 1781)). We find *bullshit** (an object or task that is seen as annoying, irritating or nonsensical), *bullshitter**, *chew someone's balls off**, *cunting** and *like a cunt** (used as an intensifier), a *map of Ireland** (a semen stain on a sheet which in Australia became a *mapatassie*, that is, Tasmania, like Ireland, a conveniently shaped piece of land), *piece of piss** (something easily accomplished), *pull one's plonk**, *prick** (as meaning a fool), *spunking** (as a negative intensifier) and *chew up for arse-paper** (to reprimand aggressively). Finally, a group devoted to shit: *shit-bag**, *knock seven kinds of shit out of**, *shit in it!** (i.e. one's hat), *shit oneself** (to be terrified); *little shit* (an obnoxious person), *shit cart* (a refuse wagon and used here to name a chapter), *shitty* (unpleasant) and *shit the bed* were all long established.

Slang has always been used to confer authenticity. A pillar of crime writing – both fact and fiction – ever since the form existed, but elsewhere too. Lawrence may add new perspectives, but he follows a well-trodden path. Yet *The Mint* seems to add another take on authenticity: not that of the station house, the brothel or anywhere else along the traditional mean streets of noir fiction, but as the evocation of a man's unhappy mind. The authors of noir may be seen as enjoying the language they use. Lawrence, it seems, used it consciously as something quite repellent, the perfect evocation of an experience both emotional and actual that he irredeemably despised yet in which he had chosen to immerse himself.

Listing words without context makes proof hard but rarely, perhaps never have I encountered a text that uses slang so brutally and nihilistically, a literary writer's co-opting of the scrawlings on a lavatory wall. This is not, however, to judge and I certainly have no problems with any of slang's words, however gross. After all, this is the effect that the author of *The Mint* sought. The text, with its insistent drumbeat of nihilist slang, would suggest that this is also what he achieved.

Notes

1   All examples of slang (and if cited, their dating) comes from greensdictofslang.com.
2   Manuscript was completed in 1922, and privately published in 1926; the unabridged text did not appear until 1997.
3   Edgar Wallace praised him as 'the poet of the cuss-word and the swear', but there were limits. In 'In the Matter of a Private' (1899), he suggests that 'Thomas [i.e. the generic Tommy Atkins] really ought to be supplied with a new Adjective [*sic*] to help him express his opinions' but we never read it and see only blanks.
4   Coined by W.T. Goodge in his eponymous poem, published in the Sydney *Bulletin* on 11 December 1897.
5   N&Q 12 Ser. IX (1921: 415).
6   One should probably stress 'soldiers', that is, 'other ranks'. In the generally praised film *1917* (2020), a colonel tells a messenger to 'Fuck off!'; this was generally considered unlikely, although officers' private conversations may have been more obscene than was admitted in memoirs, and so on.

7 Lawrence (1955): 121.
8 It is perhaps arguable that 'Ross', in his unflinching promotion of the obscene, was consciously using such language to distance himself even further from Lawrence.
9 'first uses' as currently recorded are marked with a *

References

Cummings, E. E. (1922), *The Enormous Room*, New York: Boni and Liveright.
Graves, R. ([1929] 1995), *Goodbye to All That*, London: Penguin.
Hay, J. B. (1915), *The First Hundred Thousand*, Edinburgh and London: Blackwood.
Hotten, J. C. ([1859] 1860), *A Dictionary of Modern Slang, Cant and Vulgar Words*, London: John Camden Hotten.
Lawrence, T. E. (1926), *Seven Pillars of Wisdom*, London: Subscribers.
Lawrence, T. E. (1955), *The Mint*, London: Jonathan Cape.
Notes & Queries, 12 Ser. IX (1921), 415.

17

When words kill

Armenians, Jews and the nature of genocidal discourse

Fabian Van Samang

Introduction

In recent years, there has been a tendency in holocaust scholarship to historicize and universalize genocide. Whereas the first generation of holocaust historians considered genocide as a pre-eminently modern and Western phenomenon (Hilberg 1961; Poliakov 1986; Bauer 2001) – thus excluding instances of mass violence prior to the second half of the nineteenth century in Africa, Asia or Latin America – recent scholarship has stressed its universality and its roots in prehistorical and ancient history (Kiernan 2007; Carmichael 2009; Bloxham 2010b).

Despite this extended conceptual range, the extermination of the European Jews (1941–45) – in which an estimated six million people perished – remains the most important benchmark when trying to define genocide (Gerlach 2016: 3). While arguing why a specific outbreak of mass violence should be regarded as genocide, scholars rarely refer to the persecution of heretics, the destruction of seventeenth-century French villages or anti-Bab pogroms in late nineteenth-century Iran. On the contrary, while assessing the genocidal character of mass violence, historians (and politicians) typically refer to the Holocaust as their most important yardstick (Fein 2007; Rosenbaum 2009; Hayden 2010; Power 2008: 279–368).

The fact that the Holocaust is often used as a touchstone against which other genocides are measured also applies to the massacre of possibly over a million Armenians by the Ottoman regime during the First World War (Kaiser 2013). If Nazi rulers were inspired by the Armenian bloodbath to wipe out European Jews, the argument goes, then the slaughter of the Armenians definitively must have been genocidal (Peterson 2004: 160; Desbois 2008: 63). Yet, the historical evidence linking the genocidal policy of the Third Reich to the Armenian question is very scant. There is Eduard Scharrer's note (30 December 1922), indicating Hitler's self-professed concern to find a solution for the Jewish Question: 'Failing that, there will be only two alternatives: either the German people will come to resemble a people like the Armenians or the Levantines;

or there will be a bloody conflict' (Hitler 1980: 775; translation from Weber 2017: 276–7). Hitler's remark of 5 July 1941 contended that Russians had to be driven out of the Crimea, where until half a century ago Germans were still a majority. But gradually, Hitler claimed, the region had been colonized by 'Tartars, Armenians and Jews – and finally Russians. We have to reconquer all of this' (Hitler 1982: 101–2). In July 1942, Alfred Rosenberg, the head of the Reich Ministry for the Occupied Eastern Territories, had a lengthy change of mind with Hitler, concerning the designation of the Caucasian (Georgian, Armenian) territories (Rosenberg 2016: 462–3, entry 14 July 1942). Hitler's infamous, much debated and highly controversial speech of 22 August 1939, in front of his senior officers, referred to the killing of millions of people by the Mongol tribesman Genghis Khan, demanding a similar ruthlessness of the German troops towards the Polish civilian population. German generals shouldn't worry about history's judgement, Hitler is reported as having said, for 'who, after all, speaks of the annihilation of the Armenians nowadays?' (Baumgart 1968: 120–69).

Our research focus is on genocide and discourse performativity. More specifically, we try to assess when, how and why discourses turn genocidal, in other words how genocidal discourses can be distinguished from non-genocidal speech acts, and how these genocidal discourses trigger genocidal policies. In this chapter, we will elaborate on two points. First, what were the main characteristics of Hitler's written and verbal speech acts and, by extension, of National Socialist (NS) discourse as a whole? In addition, how did this discourse relate to the extermination of about six million Jews (Dawidowicz 1990: 480; Benz 1996: 1–20) during the Second World War? And second, to what extent did the speech acts of Ottoman officials resemble this NS discourse?

Semantic entropy, National Socialism and the destruction of the European Jews: An analysis

In order to address the question of Hitler's discourse, the main characteristics of his speech acts had to be made first. These are a selection of his letters, notes and speeches, as far as the Jews and the so-called Jewish Question (*Judenfrage*) is concerned. Since his war years, discourse possibly diverged from his earlier speech acts, we distinguished between four carefully demarcated periods: 1919 (his first political writings) to 1925 (the publication of *Mein Kampf*), 1925 to 1933 (from Hitler's re-entry in the political realm until his seizure of power), 1933 to 1939 (his years as chancellor, until the outbreak of the Second World War) and 1939 to 1945 (the war years and the implementation of the Holocaust). An analysis of his public and private discourses in those four periods was made on a lexical-semantic, pragmatic-discursive and intertextual level.

With respect to the lexical-semantic level, twenty-five German and non-German bibliographic reference books, dating from 1808 to 1989, were analysed for references to 'Jews', 'Jewish' and 'Judaism' for the purpose of possibly relating these to Hitler's speech acts. Although real, imagined or stereotyped characteristics of Jews are mentioned in some articles which are absent in others, there seems to exist a broad consensus in those reference works as far as the core (prototype) meaning of the concepts 'Jew' and 'Judaism' is concerned. Typically, Jews are described as a 'people' of 'mosaic' 'belief' or 'religion', a 'Semitic' 'tribe' 'driven' from their 'land', the 'kingdom of Judaea', being 'dispersed' all over the world (e.g. 'Jude', *Das deutsche Wörterbuch. Ein umfassendes Nachslagwerk des deutsche und eingedeutschten Sprachschatzes*, I (1959): 349; 'Jude', *Brockhaus Wahrig deutsches Wörterbuch*, III (1981): 826). Only in the second place, some authors (e.g. 'Jude', *Deutsches Wörterbuch von Jacob und Wilhelm Grimm*, IV (1877): 2352–3; 'Jude', *Sanders Wörterbuch der deutschen Sprache*, I (1969): 842–3; 'Jude', *Weigand deutsches Wörterbuch*, I (1909): 953–4) also refer to a 'beard' and accusations of 'usury', or Jews being 'profit-driven', 'imposters', 'suffering' and sometimes living in 'ghettos' (Van Samang 2010: 95–112).

Next, an analysis was made of references to 'Jude', 'Judentum', 'jüdisch' in Hitler's discourse (1919–45) – 891 references were found, coupled to 833 different adjectives and nouns. Two features clearly stand out. First, Hitler's concept of 'the Jew' diverged to a very large extent from the prototypical semantic meaning of the Jew as described in bibliographic reference books. To him, Jews were an internationally (forty-four references) oriented race (twenty-nine), linked to a Bolshevik (twenty-eight) and Marxist (twenty-six) world view, dominating the press (twenty-six); they were war- and battle-prone (twenty-four and eleven references), dangerous (eighteen), aiming to conquer world dominance, while exterminating (eleven) and destroying (four) others in the process. Second, Hitler's description of 'the Jew' became increasingly contradictory over time – Jews were referred to as capitalists and Bolsheviks, as pacifists and warmongers, as democrats and tyrants, as nationalists and internationalists at the same time (Van Samang 2010: 113–15). In our opinion, this increasing attribution of contradictory peripheral meanings is the main characteristic of Hitler's (anti-Jewish) discourse on the lexical-semantic level.

On a second, pragmatic-discursive level, it should be considered whether Hitler's discourse can be considered a coherent, explanatory model. A model can be defined as an explanation for a strictly delineated phenomenon, demonstrating the meaningful relationship between this phenomenon and a limited number of other phenomena. A model is not a mere description of an event, an opinion or an attitude, but tries to explain its raison d'être, its genesis and its possible future, in order to better understand or to explain related phenomena. As such, Samuel Huntington's 'Clash of civilizations' is an explanatory model, as is the work of his major opponent, Francis Fukuyama ('The end of history and the last man'). To determine as accurately and as objectively as possible whether a speech, a treatise or a private conversation can be regarded as a model, an analysis of eleven criteria was made, going from the historical explanation of a specific problem, addressed in a speech or a note, over existing and alternative theories and solutions, to the empirical underpinning of statements, predictability and logical consistency. Judged against these criteria, one can safely state that, to a large extent, *Mein Kampf* (1925) offered a firm explanatory discursive model to its readers (see Table 17.1).

An analysis of Hitler's public discourse shows that in the period 1919 to 1925 the speaker/author (i.e. Hitler) often explicitly referred to a certain theme, problem or phenomenon that, in his opinion, needed to be addressed (e.g. his 1920 speech 'Why are we antisemites'; see Phelps 1968: 390–420 and Nolte 1961: 584–606). In general,

Table 17.1 *Mein Kampf* as an explanatory model (° = meets criterion, - = doesn't meet criterion)

	Factor	*Mein Kampf*
1	Well-defined problem/theme	°
2	Historical framework	°
3	Standard explanation	°
4	Alternative explanation	°
5	Alternative solution	°
6	Supported by empirical data	-
7	Potential to explain	°
8	Further evolution	°
9	Textual consistency	°
10	Intertextual consistency	°
11	Refined conceptual framework	°

he tried to put this theme in a broader historical framework (in his aforementioned 1920 speech he went back to an alleged long-lost ancient Germanic and Roman culture and to 'inferior', 'primitive' Abrahamic times) and went through great lengths to give an alternative explanation or solution for the problem he dealt with (in his 1920 speech he claimed that Jews aimed at the destruction of the social meaning of labour; they wanted to pollute the so-called Arian blood and tried to destroy the culture that hosted them – that's why, according to Hitler, they had to be removed ['Entfernung der Juden aus unserem Volke, nicht weil wir ihnen ihre Existenz nicht vergönnten . . . aber weil uns die Existenz der eigenen Volkes noch tausendmal höher steht als die einer fremden Rasse'; Phelps 1968: 415–17]). His speech acts in those early years (1919–25) were formulated in an unequivocal and consistent manner and, as a whole, can be considered an explanatory discursive model (his speech acts in the years 1919–25 met 68.48 per cent of the selected criteria shown in Table 17.1). But as years went by, the consistency, the logic, the coherence – in other words, the explanatory model – little by little disappeared from his public discourse. Whereas 4.48 per cent of the criteria were met in the earlier speeches (1919–5), those standards were met increasingly less in the next two decades, namely 38.64 per cent in the period 1925–33, 34.27 per cent in the years 1933–9 and 4.04 per cent in the period that covers the Second World War. The dissolution of the explanatory model is also clear from Hitler's private discourse – whereas *Mein Kampf* (1925) met ten out of eleven selected criteria (see Table 17.1), Hitler's unpublished *Second Book* (1928) met no more than seven, his *Tischgespräche* (1941–2) on average three and his political will (April 1945) merely two. Moreover, whereas the 'Jewish Question' initially seemed to be firmly interwoven into his discourse – he referred to Jews in 120 of the 401 paragraphs of his speeches dealing with the Jewish Question (29.93 per cent, 1919–25) – this was no longer the case after he seized power in 1933. Jews were referred to in no more than 55 out of 448 paragraphs (12.28 per cent) of his war years speeches (1939–45). Since words and sentences partly derive meaning from the surrounding text, the dissolution of the explanatory model in Hitler's discourse substantially increased potential diverging interpretations. We will call this phenomenon 'discursive dissolution', and we consider it to be the main characteristic of Hitler's discourse on the pragmatic-discursive level.

As far as the third, intertextual level is concerned, Hitler's image of the Jew and his anti-Jewish policy were established in interrelated textual units (e.g. his speeches on the Jewish Question dating from 1941, juxtaposed to his contemporary table talks). Our analysis shows that the radicalization of National Socialist (NS) anti-Jewish policy (to outlaw, confiscate, harass, expel, ghettoize and exterminate) clearly wasn't coupled with a radicalization of Hitler's discourse. On the contrary, whereas anti-Semitic praxis gradually intensified, became harder and more murderous over time, Hitler interchangeably made statements with an undeniable genocidal potential, while toning them down in interrelated speech acts. For example, while in his famous letter to Adolf Gemlich of 16 September 1919, Hitler affirmed that partial liquidation (pogroms) to deal with the Jewish Question would not suffice, he favoured a so-called rational anti-Semitism, which – according to Hitler – would lead to a harsher policy. However, the measures he proposed were limited to the withdrawal of German-Jewish privileges and 'zur planmässigen und gesetzlichen Bekämpfung' (Deuerlein 1959: 177–227). In any case, Hitler argued, the final goal of the anti-Semitism of reason must be the 'irrevocable removal of the Jews in general' ('unverrückbar die Entfernung der Juden überhaupt', Deuerlein 204), without specifying what that 'removal' exactly meant. On 13 August 1920, he again spoke of the removal of the Jews ('Entfernung der Juden aus unserem Volke'; Phelps 1968: 417), while – almost simultaneously – he spoke of the extermination of this 'blood angel' ('muss ausgerottet werden – der Jude als Blutengel', undated note; Maser 1973: 238–9), calling them a 'mortal enemy' in 1922 ('dass das Judentum als Volk für sich uns als Todfeind gegenübersteht'; Hitler 1934: 25), at the same time (in April 1922 and 1923) referring to the 'arian-Jewish' struggle that would end in de destruction of one of both ('Entweder Sieg der arischen Seite oder ihre Vernichtung und Sieg des Juden'; Hitler 1934: 15, 17 and 55). Remarkably enough, while he asked for 'the destruction of the Jews', on 18 September 1922, he demanded no more than the 'immediate expulsion of the Jews who immigrated since 1914' ('Sofortige Ausweisung der seit 1914 eingewanderten Juden'; Hitler 1934: 39). Obviously, as 'Entfernung', 'Beseitigung', 'Auswanderung' and even 'Ausrottung' or 'Vernichtung' constantly referred to different social and political realities, it was extremely hard, if not impossible, to unravel its one and only true meaning. In fact, it could mean practically anything. This 'intertextual obscenity' might be the key trait of Hitler's discourse on the third, intertextual level.

The convergence of discursive dissolution, the increasing attribution of contradictory and peripheral meanings and intertextual obscenity above all else typify Hitler's discourse. Rather than the fundamental poverty of NS speech acts ('And here a more profound explanation for the impoverishment of the LTI opens up from beneath the obvious one. It was poor not only because everyone was forced to conform to the same pattern, but rather – and indeed more significantly – because in a measure of self-imposed constraint, it only ever gave expression to one side of human expression'), as the German linguist and philosopher Victor Klemperer argued (Klemperer 2010: 20), it is this configuration of features that characterized Hitler's discourse, a dynamic while incessantly changing discursive phenomenon we would term 'semantic entropy'.

Semantic entropy is not limited to Hitler's discourse, but characterizes the linguistic acts of almost all NS echelons involved in the preparation and execution of the Holocaust, as is shown from the analysis of twenty-nine terms, possibly related to genocide. These terms include (*ab-, aus-, ein-, rück-, übersee-, weiter-* and *zu-*)*wandern*, (*an-, aus* and *um-*)*siedeln, abschieben, ausmerzen, ausrotten, ausschalten, austreiben, beseitigen, emigrieren, Endziel, entfernen, erledigen, ermorden, erschiessen, evakuieren, exekutieren,* but also combinations of (*End-*)*Lösung* and *Judenfrage*, and *liquidieren, vernichten, verschieben and zerstören.* The terms appear 1,294 times in 403 different documents (including 228 internal notes, 166 speeches, 4 essays, 3 diaries and 1 service calendar). The source material originated from eleven different NS institutions such as security services, ministries, the Plenipotentiary for the Four-Year Plan, the *Einsatzgruppen* and the *Wehrmacht.* The analysis of these terms reveals the erosion of the concepts used, the loss of the explanatory model and the ongoing intertextual inconsistency (Van Samang 2010: 219–340).

How then does semantic entropy relate to genocide? How does it affect the relationship between the perpetrator, the bystander and the victim on the one hand, and the step-by-step development of policies of mass violence on the other? To address this question, it may be useful to appeal to Leon Festinger's theory of cognitive dissonance (Festinger 1957; Festinger, Riecken and Schachter 1958: 156–63; Aronson 1969: 1–34). Festinger asserted that by modifying an opinion, view or belief (a cognition), reflected in a change of behaviour, human beings seek to reduce mental stress (they minimize dissonance), triggered by two or more antithetical cognitions. Little children, given the opportunity to pick one out of two (identical) objects, tend to overrate the features of the chosen object, thus reducing the mental stress caused by the knowledge that one object had not been chosen while having identical features (the free-choice model) (Brehm and Cohen 1959: 373–8). When exposed to information that substantially contradicts firmly held beliefs, people tend to reduce dissonance by either changing their positions, or – more generally – by avoiding, ignoring or simply reinterpreting the information in a non-confronting way (exposure-to-information model) (Festinger 1957: 162–76; Bramel 1962: 121–9). Within a forced-compliance model, test persons who receive a single dollar to perform a boring, repetitive task, afterwards tend to think of it as more enjoyable and more important to scientific research, and are more willing to participate in a similar test than test persons who were given $20 (Festinger and Carlsmith 1959: 203–10; Scott 1957: 72–5; Aronson and Mills 1959: 177–81). With regard to the history of the Third Reich, unambiguous expressions of eliminatory anti-Semitism may have given rise to cognitive dissonance within the liberal segment of the German population, whereas an unequivocal plea for anti-Jewish legislation might have provoked quite some dissonance with NS hardliners (who thought of these measures as being too soft). Senior bureaucrats – who in the early years of National Socialism still had vivid memories of the democratic principles of the now defunct Weimar republic, but who had to cooperate in drafting new anti-Jewish legislation after Hitler's seizure of power – probably experienced considerable cognitive dissonance, as did the railway clerk who signed the documents required for the deportation of a large group of Jews from ghetto A to extermination centre B. But by broadening or blurring the semantic field of certain concepts ('the Jew'), by deconstructing the explanatory model, apparently justifying a certain policy ('the solution of the Jewish Question') and by incessantly switching meanings – in other words, by creating semantic entropy – individuals could safely participate in a murderous regime, not experiencing cognitive dissonance and leaving their most profound beliefs as good as unaltered.

Semantic entropy, the Ottoman Empire and the Armenian question

When the First World War broke out in August 1914, little was left of the powerful and magnificent Ottoman Empire that for centuries had dominated the Eastern part of Europe, Northern Africa and considerable parts of Asia and the Middle East. Successive sultans had been driven out of Algeria (1830), Romania, Serbia and Bulgaria (1878), Tunisia (1881, Egypt (1882) and Libya (1912), while most of their European possessions were lost in the wake of the Balkan Wars (Rogan 2009). The instability of the Ottoman regime created opportunities for Turkish nationalists, united in the Committee of Union and Progress (CUP), who forced Sultan Abdulhamid II to reintroduce the constitution, and who eventually took power in 1913 (Akçam 2006; Kévorkian 2011). Given the close relations between Germany and the Ottoman Empire in the years preceding the First World War, the latter decided to take part in the war on the German side (McMeekin 2011). As a result, the Ottomans very soon had to deal with the military threat of Russian troops in the northeast, Allied troops in the southwest and British-Indian troops in the southeast. On top of this, in the last months of 1914 and the first trimester of 1915, the Ottoman army was decimated by disease – about 60,000 soldiers died of typhoid fever and dysentery (Rogan 2015: 159–84). It was in these perilous circumstances that the decision was made to deal with the Armenians, whom the Turkish nationalists saw as an unreliable fifth column in the Ottoman Empire. Estimates vary widely, but historians consider it likely that between 600,000 and 1.2 million Armenians perished as a result of forced deportations to the Syrian deserts, hunger, deprivation, suicide and massacres on a massive scale (the Turkish government refers to a flawed study of the 'Center for Strategic Studies'; 2007, 40: 'It can be concluded that the number of the Armenian losses was around 300.000'; Kiernan, 2007: 415; Bloxham and Göçek 2010a: 345; 1.1 million according to Kaiser 2013: 382–3).

If Nazi discourse can be regarded as a genocidal discourse, and semantic entropy is the main feature of speech acts by Adolf Hitler and by extension also the NS regime, then the question arises whether or not this type of discourse can be found in the writings of Ottoman officials before and during the First World War. To answer this question, we made an analysis of 385 historical sources, which were collected, translated (into French) and published by the leading French-Armenian historian Raymond Kévorkian and his colleague Yves Ternon (Kévorkian and Ternon 2014). We made a distinction between Ottoman and Armenian sources, and sources that came from bystanders or third parties. Only contemporary sources were retained, as far as they specifically refer to the Armenians.

At the lexical-semantic level, we made an analysis of the keyword 'Armenian' in twenty-three bibliographic reference books in six different languages, covering the

Table 17.2 The term 'Armenia(n)' in bibliographic reference books (1854–2005)

Lemma	Bibliographic reference book	Volume	Year
Armenier/armenisch	*Brockhaus Wahrig*	I (A-Bt)	1980
Armenië	*De Katholieke Encyclopaedie*	III	1949
Armeno	*De Mauro – Il Dizionario della Lingua Italiana*	I	2000
Armenier	*Der Grosse Herder*	I (A-Battenberg)	1931/1939
Armenien	*Deutsches Wörterbuch*	I (A-Biermolke)	1854
Armenio	*Diccionario de la Lengua Española*	I (A-G)	1992
Armenia/Armenio	*Diccionario Enciclopédico Abreviado*	I	1957
Arménien (/-ienne)	*Dictionnaire de l'Académie française*	I (A-ENZ)	1992
Arménien (/-ienne)	*Dictionnaire Quillet*	I	1956
Armenien	*Duden-Lexikon*	I (A-F)	1965
Arménien (/-ienne)	*Grand Dictionnaire Universel du XIXe siècle*	I	1866
Armenio	*Gran Diccionario de Uso del Español Actual*	I	2001
Arméniens	*Grand Larousse Encylcopédie*	I	1960
Armeniërs	*Grote Spectrum Encyclopedie*	II	1990
Armeniërs	*Grote Winkler Prins*	II	1990
Arménien (-/ienne)	*Le Grand Robert de la Langue Française*	I	2001
Arménien (/-ienne)	*Le Nouveau Petit Robert*	I	2004
Arménien (/-enne)	*Nouveau Larousse illustré*	I	s.d.
Armeni/Armeno	*Nuovissimo Vocabolario Illustrato della Lingua Italiana*	I	1997
Armenia (catholic church in)	*The New Catholic Encyclopedia*	I	1967
Armenia(n)	*The New Encyclopaedia Britannica*	I	2005
Armeniër/Armenisch	*Van Dale's Groot Woordenboek der Nederlandsche Taal*	I	1914

period from 1854 to 2005 (see Table 17.2). Please note that we do not try to establish one fixed meaning of the concept 'Armenia' or 'Armenians'. Rather it is our intention to establish a prototypical definition of these key words, that is as objective and temporarily and geographically as broad as possible. In the reference books we selected, Armenians were described as an 'ancient' (eight references) 'Christian' (six) 'people' (ten) of 'Indo-European' (eight) descent, speaking an 'Indo-Germanic' (four) or 'Armenian' (seven) 'language' (fifteen), inhabiting a region ('country' or 'land', seven references) that covers parts of 'Asia' (nine), 'Russia' (three) and present-day 'Turkey' (four). Subsequently, as with Hitler's discourse earlier, all references were listed when related to *Armenian* (adjective – 486 references) and *Armenians* (noun – 1,259 references); then the sources from Turkish origin in Kévorkian's collection were added (there were 360 references to Armenian(s) in 129 sources) as well as adjectives and nouns surrounding both lemmas (there were 209 references to 142 different keywords). Among those are references to a 'Christian' (two) 'people' (seven), 'population' (four) or 'community' (two), led by a 'patriarchate' (two), inhabiting certain 'provinces' (eight), 'villages' (six), 'regions' (five) and 'cities' (five) in the 'Ottoman' (two) empire or in 'Anatolia' (two). Contrary to Hitler's discourse, there seems to be a considerable convergence, rather than a divergence, of the Ottoman discourse with the prototypical lexical-semantic meaning of the word *Armenian* compared to the reference books. Neither is there an increasing attribution of contradictory meanings, as was the case in Hitler's discourse. On the contrary – we found references to Armenian attacks (one), but not to defense, to migrants or 'expatriates' (two) but not to immigrants, to dangerous (three), but not to harmless or inoffensive. On a lexical-semantic level, there seems to be a considerable difference between Hitler's discourse prior to and during the Second World War, and that of Armenian officials prior to and during the First.

On a second, pragmatic-discursive level, we argued that Hitler's private and public discourse (in the period 1919–45) was characterized by the gradual loss of textual coherence (see earlier text). To find out whether this was also the case in the discourse of Ottoman officials with reference to the Armenian question, we selected sixty-seven Ottoman sources from Kévorkian's collection (Kévorkian and Ternon 2014), of which twelve came from the pre-war years (1902–14) and fifty-five from the years 1914, 1915 and 1916. To these sources we applied the same criteria that we used to determine whether Hitler's discourse can be considered an explanatory 'model' (see Table 17.1). Our research results show that, in the rare cases that a well-defined problem/specific theme is present in the Ottoman sources we analysed (criterion 1), this problem is only on very few occasions put in a broader historical context (criterion 2). If ever, commonplace or alternative ideological explanations are very rarely given for the problems the speaker or writer refers to (criteria 3 and 4); and when these explanations do occur, the claims are not supported by empirical data (criterion 6). Historical laws ('things are bound to turn out this way') (criteria 7 and 8) hardly ever occur in the speech acts of the Ottoman officials; and a refined, sophisticated conceptual apparatus is virtually non-existent in most textual units (criterion 11). Our analysis indicates that, as far as the first period of the discourse of Ottoman functionaries (1902–14) is concerned, only about one-fifth of the speech acts (speeches, letters, notes) meets the criteria necessary to define them as a coherent and explanatory model (in the formative years of National-Socialism this was about 70 per cent). This large discrepancy may be explained by the small number of speeches made by Ottoman officials on the Armenian question at the time. Indeed, in the first decade and a half of the twentieth century, the Armenian question does not seem to have been an essential part of Ottoman ideology. In fact, when the First World War broke out, this type of discourse hardly changed. In 1915 and 1916 (the second period), while hundreds of thousands of Armenians were deported and killed, our data do not show the disintegration of a model-based discourse, since in no more than 18 per cent of the cases the criteria for a systematic discourse were met (as to one-fifth in the years 1902–14). Even if we distinguish between the years 1915 and 1916, this does not substantially alter the research results: from 1902 to 1914, 22 per cent of the criteria were met for the entire period, as to 17 per cent in 1915, and 20 per cent on average in the year 1916. On a pragmatic-discursive level, the structure of NS and Ottoman discourse prior to and during the First (in the case of the Armenians) and the Second World War (as far as the Jewish Question is concerned) could hardly be more dissimilar.

This brings us to the third level of our discourse analysis, the intertextual level. Let's keep in mind that Hitler's discourse, and that of other NS leaders, did not reflect the gradual implementation of a certain policy, but that NS functionaries – in their public as well as in their private discourse – interchangeably referred to killing, deporting or exterminating, to force into migration, to partially eradicate or to outlaw the Jews, thus leaving it to imagination of the audience to figure out what 'Ausrottung', 'Vernichtung', 'Auswanderung', 'Liquidierung' or 'Ausweisung' really meant. But that is not what we see when we study the language acts of Ottoman officials. In a telegram by Mehmet Talât – also known as Talaat Pasha, one of the three de facto rulers of the Ottoman Empire – to the prefecture of Erzerum, East Turkey, on 10 May 1915 the intentions are much less clear: 'Taking into account the local circumstances, Armenians from the towns and villages of your province *will be deported and settled* in places designated by the government. . . . When the Armenians reach the places to be designated, *they will be installed* according to the circumstances' (Kévorkian and Ternon 2014: 136–7 – italics by the author). This is entirely in accordance with his order of 20 May 1915 to the Secretary-General and commander of the 5th Army: 'Generally, in many cases, Armenian notables have been *arrested and deported* to other regions not too far away and under similar conditions. . . . The Ministry of the Interior has ordered . . . that measures be taken against those Armenians who, because of their personality and relations, may be involved in criminal acts' (Kévorkian and Ternon 2014: 137). About one month later, Colonel Sehabeddin sent a request to the commander-in-chief of the Third Army: 'Please provide me with the necessary instructions on the individuals, whose names are included in the attached list, whose *deportation is considered indispensable* by both the court martial and the local authorities. . . .These are the regions where Armenians should be *dispersed and settled* in a [maximum] proportion of ten percent of the Muslim population' (Kévorkian and Ternon 2014: 137–8). On 24 July 1915, General Faik Pasha – also known as Süleyman Faik – informed the vali (governor) of Mamuret-ul-Aziz that some Committee of Union and Progress officials used 'the *deportations* of the Armenians' (Kévorkian and Ternon 2014: 276–7) as a pretext to enrich themselves – a suspicion that was confirmed by the research section of the court martial of the Ninth Army corps in October 1916 ('during *the deportations*, they took or stole personally or [had] accomplices [steal] the precious objects and money of Armenians on the way') (Kévorkian and Ternon 2014: 152–3). In July 1915, governor Sabit Bey reported to the Interior ministry: 'Apart from the town of Malatya, *where the deportations will start* in a few days, the province and its surroundings are completely cleared of Armenians' (Kévorkian and Ternon 2014: 277). Even in the autumn of 1916, Ottoman officials still described the fate of the Armenians in more or less the same words: 'In the course of the deportations, they seized or personally stole . . . valuables and money from the Armenians'; 'they participated in the events which took place last year, during the expulsion of the Armenians' (Kévorkian and Ternon 2014: 153–4).

There are some notable exceptions to this unambiguous, consistent use of language. In March 1915, during a meeting of CUP leaders, some attendants reportedly said that 'a heavy blow on the heads of the Armenians would immediately shut up our adversaries, and the policy against the Armenians would be a nightmare for Greece'; another participant, Dr Nâzim, went even further, arguing that they [the CUP] had to 'eradicate the Armenian question at its root, by totally exterminating this [Armenian] nation'. But this text is a compilation of speeches and documents, handed over to the Armenian patriarchate in 1921 by an Armenian survivor. It was published for the first time in 1929, and its authenticity is dubious, as the editor himself acknowledges: 'So it is with some reserve that we hereby enclose the translation of the minutes of this meeting' (Kévorkian and Ternon 2014: 104–6). Other references to killings or liquidations are questions from local officials who inquire what happened to the deported Armenians, or refer to penal procedures against Armenian individuals or groups of Armenians. Apart from those exceptions, the speech acts of Ottoman officials seem to be very consistent on the intertextual level, and does not resemble in any way the intertextual obscenity that characterized NS discourse.

Conclusion

Our analysis shows that the discourse of representatives of the Turkish-Ottoman state at the lexical-semantic, pragmatic-discursive and intertextual level does not exhibit the characteristics we observed among NS officials. Therefore, the mechanisms of mass violence that we believe are generated by semantic entropy do not seem to apply as far as the period 1915–16 is concerned. There may be various explanations for this discursive divergence: maybe the research material used was insufficient or not representative; maybe there are several types of genocidal discourses; maybe the mechanisms of violence we saw in the Ottoman Empire and the Third Reich were of a different nature. A heated debate has been raging for quite some time about the status of the killings of the vast majority of the Armenian population by officials of the Turkish state and their collaborators. Whereas numerous sovereign states (including most European, half a dozen of Latin-American countries and Russia) have officially recognized that the massacres amount to genocide in the legal sense of the word, a number of major actors in the international arena are wary of such recognition (including the White House [in spite of two resolutions having been passed by the US House of Representatives and the US Senate], Australia, Israel and – for obvious reasons – Turkey). Although defining genocide and taking the Armenian case to the test is not the subject of this chapter and therefore should not be addressed here, the current analysis calls for further research, new analytical instruments and a strong academic debate on the relationship between discourse and the outbreak of mass violence and/or genocide.

References

Akçam, T. (2006), *A Shameful Act: The Armenian Genocide and the Question of Turkish Responsibility*, New York: Metropolitan Books.

Anonymous (2007), *Armenian Claims and Historical Facts: Questions and Answers*, Ankara: Center for Strategic Studies.

Aronson, E. (1969), 'The Theory of Cognitive Dissonance: A Current Perspective', in L. Berkowitz (ed.), *Advances in Experimental Social Psychology*, vol. IV, 1–34, New York: Academic Press.

Aronson, S. and J. Mills (1959), 'The Effect of Severity of Initiation on Liking for a Group', *The Journal of Abnormal and Social Psychology*, 59: 177–81.

Bauer, Y. (2001), *Rethinking the Holocaust*, New Haven and London: Yale University Press.

Baumgart, W. (1968), 'Zur Ansprache Hitlers vor den Führern der Wehrmacht am 22. August 1939. Eine Quellenkritische Untersuchung', *Vierteljahrshefte für Zeitgeschichte*, 16 (2): 120–49.

Benz, W. (1996), 'Die Dimension des Völkermords', in W. Benz (ed.), *Dimension des Völkermords. Die Zahl der jüdische Opfer des Nationalsozialismus*, 1–20, München: Deutscher Taschenbuch Verlag.

Bloxham, D. and F. Göçek (2010a), 'The Armenian Genocide', in D. Stone (ed.), *The Historiography of Genocide*, 344–72, Houndsmills: Palgrave Macmillan.

Bloxham, D. ([2009] 2010b), *The Final Solution: A Genocide*, Oxford and New York: Oxford University Press.

Bramel, D. (1962), 'A Dissonance Theory Approach to Defensive Projection', *The Journal of Abnormal and Social Psychology*, 64 (2): 121–9.

Brehm, J. and A. Cohen (1959), 'Re-evaluation of Choice Alternatives as a Function of their Number and Qualitative Similarity', *The Journal of Abnormal and Social Psychology*, 63 (3): 373–8.

Carmichael, C. (2009), *Genocide Before the Holocaust*, New Haven and London: Yale University Press.

Dawidowicz, L. (1990), *The War against the Jews, 1933–1945*, Harmondsworth: Penguin Books.

Desbois, P. (2008), *The Holocaust by Bullets: A Priest's Journey to Uncover the Truth behind the Murder of 1.5 Million Jews*, New York: Palgrave MacMillan.

Deuerlein, E. (1959), 'Hitler's Eintritt in die NSDAP und die Reichswehr', *Vierteljahrshefte für Zeitgeschichte*, 7 (2): 177–227.

Fein, H. (2007), 'A Formula for Genocide: Comparison of the Turkish Genocide (1915) and the German Holocaust (1939–1945)', in M. Lattimer (ed.), *Genocide and Human Rights*, 271–94, New York: Routledge.

Festinger, L. (1957), *A Theory of Cognitive Dissonance*, Evanston: Row, Peterson.

Festinger, L., H. Riecken and S. Schachter (1958), 'When Prophecy Fails', in E. Maccoby, M. Newcomb and E. Hartley (eds), *Readings in Social Psychology*, 156–63, New York: Holt.

Festinger, L. and J. Carlsmith (1959), 'Cognitive Consequences of Forced Compliance', *The Journal of Abnormal and Social Psychology*, 58 (2): 203–10.

Hayden, R. ([2008] 2010), 'Mass Killings and Images of Genocide in Bosnia, 1941–5 and 1992–5', in D. Stone (ed.), *The Historiography of Genocide*, 487–516, Houndsmills: Palgrave Macmillan.

Hitler, A. (1934), *Adolf Hitlers Reden*, edited by E. Boepple, München: Deutscher Volksverlag.

Hitler, A. (1982), *Monologe im Führerhauptquartier 1941-1944*, edited by W. Jochmann, München: W. Heyne.

Kaiser, H. (2013), 'Genocide at the Twilight of the Ottoman Empire', in D. Bloxham and A. Dirk Moses (eds), *The Oxford Handbook of Genocide Studies*, 365–85, Oxford and New York: Oxford University Press.

Kévorkian, R. ([2006] 2011), *The Armenian Genocide: A Complete History*, London and New York: I.B. Tauris.

Kévorian, R. and Y. Ternon, eds (2014), *Mémorial du genocide des Arméniens*, Paris: Editions du Seuil.

Kiernan, B. (2007), *Blood and Soil: A World History of Genocide and Extermination from Sparta to Darfur*, New Haven and London: Yale University Press.

Klemperer, V. ([1947] 2010), *LTI. Lingua Tertii Imperii. The language of the Third Reich: A Philologist's Notebook*, translated by M. Brady, London and New York: Athlone Press.

Maser, W. (1973), *Hitlers Briefe und Notizen. Sein Weltbild in handschriftlichen Dokumenten*, Düsseldorf and Vienna: Econ Verlag.

McMeekin, S. (2011), *The Berlin-Baghdad Express. The Ottoman Empire and Germany's bid for world power 1898-1918*, London: Penguin Books.

Nolte, E. (1961), 'Eine frühe Quelle zu Hitlers Antisemitismus', *Historische Zeitschrift*, 192 (3): 584–606.

Peterson, M. (2004), 'Starving Armenians.' *America and the Armenian Genocide, 1915–1930 and after*, Charlottesville and London: University of Virginia Press.

Phelps, R. (1968), 'Hitler's "grundlegende" Rede über den Antisemitismus', *Vierteljahrshefte für Zeitgeschichte*, 16 (4): 390–420.

Poliakov, L. ([1951] 1986), *Bréviaire de la haine. Le IIIe Reich et les Juifs*, Brussels: Editions Complexe.

Power, S. ([2003] 2008), *'Een problem uit de hel.' Amerika, het Westen en het tijdperk van de genocide* ['A problem from hell.' America and the Age of Genocide], Amsterdam: Uitgeverij Olympus.

Rogan, E. (2009), *The Arabs: A History*, New York: Basic Books.

Rogan, E. (2015), *The Fall of the Ottomans: The Great War in the Middle East, 1914–1920*, London: Allen Lane.

Rosenbaum, A., ed. ([1995] 2009), *Is the Holocaust Unique? Perspectives on Comparative Genocide*, Boulder: Westview Press.

Rosenberg, A. (2016), *Journal 1934-1944*, edited by J. Matthäus and Frank Bajohr, Paris: Editions Flammarion.

Scott, W. (1957), 'Attitude Change through Reward of Verbal Behavior', *The Journal of Abnormal and Social Psychology*, 55: 72–5.

Van Samang, F. (2010), *Doodgewone Woorden: NS-taal en de Shoah*. Leuven: Universitaire Pers Leuven.

Weber, T. (2017), *Becoming Hitler: The Making of a Nazi*, Oxford and New York: Oxford University Press.

18

Creating the international mind

The language of internationalism and the battle for global public opinion (1912–38)

Steve Witt

Introduction

This chapter explores the proliferation of the phrase 'international mind' as a trope used to both promote internationalism around the world and create a new globalized mindset that could employ public opinion to support institutions of global governance for a peaceful world order. As Marco Duranti pointed out, 'the language of internationalism served as a mechanism for demarcating the boundaries of transnational communities of peoples, excluding those who did not respect civilized norms' (Duranti 2016: 442). Beginning in the build-up to the war and engaged on a global scale during the interwar period, the Carnegie Endowment for International Peace (CEIP) promoted the international mind through academic networks, political circles and a transnationally conceived community to change global public opinion. Led by Columbia University's Nicholas Murray Butler, the international mind campaign was a direct response to the conditions that led to the First World War and the worldwide human and material impacts of the conflict. Creating the international mind became the answer to replacing the nationalism that begat war with an internationalism that bound personal and national self-interest to global civil and economic interests.

International history of the twentieth century is often seen as a series of catastrophes caused by a nationalism that fuelled two world wars, and the history of interwar internationalism is often viewed as insignificant given its apparent failure (Pugh 2012; Winter 2008). The role of internationalism as an effort to develop a means to sustain peace within the international system, however, is an increasingly important facet of the historical narrative of the twentieth century (Iriye 2002; Gorman 2017). Glenda Sluga describes interwar internationalism as having distinctive roots in the same political realism that generated nationalism. This form of internationalism was a product of the social and political modernity of the times, 'including new international institutions, new international forms of sociability, and [an increased regard for the power of public opinion]' (2013: 2). Predating and responding to the pressures that led to the

First World War, internationalism was enabled and informed by increased economic integration and the 'transnational spread of ideas and power of public opinion that accompanied mass literacy' (Sluga 2013: 2). Michael Pugh describes internationalists in this era as embracing transnationalism as a mode of organizing and asserting the importance of public opinion based on the assumption that knowledge and education would create within the population the capacity to make rational choices about war and peace (Pugh 2012). This was an internationalism that was 'liberal, nation-embracing, and anticommunist', which included 'leaders of powerful Western states, middle-class women and feminists, anti-colonists, social scientists, and moral reformers' organized around the idea of being internationally minded (Sluga 2013: 5).

In both the foreground and background of these internationalist activities were large philanthropic foundations. Among them, the Carnegie Endowment for International Peace (CEIP) stands out for its uniquely extensive efforts to impact public opinion globally. The CEIP integrated the development of what it referred to as the 'international mind' with the organization and dissemination of knowledge through library collections, the media and academic networks aimed at reaching a broad and globally conceived public (Witt 2015). Through these efforts, the CEIP helped to create the language of internationalism while developing a corpus of knowledge aimed to move public opinion and the social psychology of the nation state system towards support for global institutions built to maintain peace and economic development.

The international mind in the pre-war era

Prior to the outbreak of the First World War, peace activists and internationalists established the framework from which the international mind developed conceptually. Specifically, the normative ideal of the international mind seems to have derived from the French, '*l'esprit international*', a term that emerged from within the transatlantic peace movement that revolved around the work of Henri La Fontaine and Paul Otlet. In 1907, this term was used when describing the *Société Belge de Sociologie's* publication, *Le Mouvement Sociologique International* (1907). Published in collaboration with the Belgian peace activist, bibliographer and League of Nations architect Paul Otlet's Institut International de Bibliographie, *Le Mouvement Sociologique International* was centred within a vast network that bound the work of sociologists, peace advocates and international academic associations (Van Acker 2014). By 1912, Henri La Fontaine's Union of International Associations' journal, *Le Vie International,* was using *L'esprit international* as a normative ideal, which figuratively and literally crossed the Atlantic to join the ideas shared within the Lake Mohonk, New York, conference on International Arbitration.

During the eighteenth Mohonk Conference in May of 1912, Nicholas Murray Butler, who was simultaneously the president of Columbia University and director of the CEIP's Division of Intercourse and Education,[1] coined the English version of *l'esprit international*, the international mind, to expound the phenomena used by his acquaintances Otlet and La Fontaine. As Butler explained to the American audience, the international mind was nothing else than that habit of thinking of foreign relations and business, and that habit of dealing with them, with regard the several nations of the civilized world as friendly and co-operating equals in aiding the progress of civilization . . . in spreading enlightenment and culture throughout the world. (1912: 102)

To gain an 'international mind', Butler informed the conference one must 'learn to measure other peoples and other civilizations than ours from their own point of view and by their own standards' and to hasten the time when 'races and nationalities are able to cease preying upon and oppressing one another, and to live together as fellow-sharers in a world's civilization' (Butler 1912: 16–17). With the goal of securing peace, Butler universalized ideas of global order while excluding individuals, nations and societies that operated outside the internationalist's civilized world (Clinton 2017). The idea of the international mind attempted to counter problems of nationalism with an internationalist perspective that balanced nationalism and globalism. Almost immediately, *l'esprit international* crossed back over the Atlantic as the translation of Butler's speech was published by La Fontaine's organization, *Du Bureau International de la Paix a Berne*. The *Bureau* was funded by the CEIP. The French term '*l'esprit international*' soon became associated with Butler and the CEIP's efforts to create the international mind. Butler's Mohonk speeches were published as *The International Mind: An Argument for the Judicial Settlement of International Disputes* immediately after the conference with the preface published in July of 1912 and the book in 1913.

Although reflecting Western notions of civilization, culture and the role of enlightenment thinking in bringing about common perspectives and outcomes regarding international relations (Curti 1963; Rietzler 2011; Weber 2015), the CEIP aimed the campaign for the international mind at the American public, Western Europe and peoples around the world. Internationalism and the international mind included an element of a civilizational mission from the Western nations when exported and of a pacifying mission when implemented within the borders of the Western world (Weber 2015). Butler dedicated his collection of essays on the *International Mind* to

that large and growing company of men and women who, in Europe, Asia, Africa, and the two Americas, are working to hasten the coming of the day when justice shall take the place of force in the settlement of difference between nations. (1913: i)

In 1913, the staff of the CEIP disseminated Butler's book. By mid-year, the book had been translated to French and Spanish, and 2,200 books shipped to American professors of international law, cabinet members, congressional delegates, governors and all members of the American Political Science Association, American Economic Association and American Society of International Law (Mailing list 1913). In the early fall of 1913, the Pan American Union provided the names of ministers and academics within the twenty-one American Republics represented within the Union for distribution throughout Latin America (Hale 1913). The global campaign to promote peace through the international mind was in full gear despite or perhaps because of the threat of war in Europe. Aimed at influencing a political and intellectual elite, the mass dissemination of this book exemplified attempts to influence and network academics and representatives of the public through the distribution of knowledge of internationalism (Laqua 2011; Rietzler 2011).

In addition to exploiting academic networks, the national and international press aided in promoting the idea of the international mind. Immediately after the Mohonk talk, newspapers published articles recounting Butler's speech. (International Mind Urged by Mr. Butler 1912; Peace Advocates Meet 1912). The English international press distributed the term. On 9 May 1913, *The Daily Post* of Hobart, Australia, published a compilation from both Butler and German philosopher and Nobel laureate Rudolph Eucken on the 'International Mind' in a clear attempt to introduce the international mind and promote peaceful relations between Germany and England (1913). On 20 May of the same year, the front page of Japan's English newspaper, the *Japan Times*, introduced Butler's concept 'in order to call the attention of Japanese statesmen, public men and press, to the fact that the international mind is becoming the attitude of thinkers of the leading nations' (International Mind 1913: 1). The article introduced the international mind to Japan and used the term as a normative standard to criticize politicians in the United States for their anti-Japanese policies. By 1916, the term was translated into Japanese and introduced as *kokusaishin* (国際心) by the prominent Japanese scholar Inazo Nitobe (Nitobe 1916), who would become the League of Nations Under-Secretaries General in 1920. In only three years, the international mind entered the global imagination, representing the ideals of internationalism while exemplifying enlightened political behaviour.

As war erupted across Europe, Butler and the CEIP moved from prevention to advocacy, viewing the actions of Germany and the Central Powers as antithetical to civilized internationalism. The war contrasted the ideal of the international mind, which persisted as a vision for the future. Looking beyond the war, British economist John A Hobson paraphrased Butler's description of the inevitable evolution towards 'international mindedness' that Hobson also characterized as driven by the 'web of international relations, economic, social, scientific, philanthropic, which everywhere testifies to a liberal-mindedness and a community of interests and purposes transcending the limits of country and nation' (1914: 191). Like Butler, Otlet and La Fontaine, Hobson posited that the integration of 'the railroad, shipping, postal, telegraphic, financial, journalistic apparatus, by which these communications are carried on, constitutes an immense structure of social-economic government' that would bring together the races, languages and cultures, requiring new approaches to diplomacy and international relations (Hobson 1914: 192). Not taking the spread of the international mind for granted, in July of 1916, as troops were fighting in the Somme, Henri La Fontaine called on civil society groups 'imbued with the spirit of brotherhood and the international mind' to build a post-war vision for action and 'propaganda' across nations and languages to promote supranational institutions to maintain peace (La Fontaine 1916: 199–20). Operating in the ambiguous space of an anti-nationalist movement that serves national interests, the international mind operated as an inevitable condition driven by globalizing technological progress and an ideal to promote around the world.

The psychological basis for the international mind

The international mind campaign relied on the belief that reading the right books would lead to altered perceptions and changes in behaviour – in essence it was cognitive therapy enacted on a massive scale. In Europe, Henri La Fontaine and Paul Otlet were motivated by the idea of organizing the world's knowledge in ways that would promote internationalism and peace (Rayward, 2003). In March of 1911, when La Fontaine sought funding for the Central Office for International Institutions, he requested funding from the CEIP, sharing a short essay titled *Salus Mundi Suprima Lex* (the Welfare of the World is Supreme Law) (1911) and proposed to change the anarchical international system towards peace through what he described as the use of 'facts' and 'institutions'. The 'facts' that La Fontaine sought to share were

> Those which tend to bring men in contact and induce them to enter in relation the ones with the others, notwithstanding the difference of their languages, opinions and races. The facts are the improvements realized by the conscious and unconscious contributions of men of sciences and technics [sic] pertaining to the most various peoples. (p. 1)

Many of the underlying concepts for making the international mind conscious corresponded with George Mead's psychological theories of social construction of the self as applied to the internationalization and civilization of states (Fischer 2008). Mead considered nationalism 'largely a psychological problem, for it has to do with the change of attitude, the willingness to accept the whole international fabric of society' (Mead 1914: 605). The notion of both a social psychology of the nation and the ability to affect cognitive change on a global scale drove the campaign to develop international minds.

It is no surprise that the First World War inspired scientists to focus on the social psychology of nationalism and ways to overcome its negative consequences. Walter Pillsbury's *Psychology of Nationality and Internationalism*, which was published almost immediately after the War, tried to provide solutions to the perceived incompatibility between national perspectives and internationalism. Pillsbury, like others in the internationalist movement, rationalized that the combined forces of information technologies and literacy will work towards creating a global consciousness that will limit, if not eliminate, the problems of nationalism. Noting the ability of modern communications to shrink the world, Pillsbury observed:

> For the purpose of obtaining news and the diffusion of ideas all parts of the world are mechanically one through the agency of the press and the telegraph. The general spread of literacy has increased the possibility of a common understanding, and furthered the development of common ideals and the resulting common control. (1919: 293)

The intense reaction to the war's ability to upend civilization combined with progressive social theories about the power and malleability of public opinion inspired interwar efforts to change both the ability of the state and the desire of citizens to engage in war.

Promoting the international mind in the interwar era

After the war, the cultivation of the 'international mind' became a key means to promote a Western liberal democratic economic system animated by populations of globally conscious citizens. In 1926, Dr J C Maxwell Garnett, secretary of the League of Nations Associations, addressed the Geneva Institute of International Relations in a talk titled *The Psychology of Patriotism and the Aims of the League of Nations Associations*. Garnett informed the group of scholars, administrators and politicians that 'the aim of League of Nations Associations is. . . . to create the international mind. . . . with the organization of public opinion' (1927: 326). By the late 1920s, the international mind had become a common trope and normative description for the manner by which internationalists thought and reacted to cultural, racial and linguistic differences within society and the world. It had become symbolic of a perspective that could bind the world together and unify an interconnected humanity with the same zeal that animated patriotism and nationalism. Within the League of Nations, cultivating the international mind had become an aspirational force that required the strategic organization and engagement of international organizations (Wöbse 2006). To impact the thinking of a broad public, the promotion of the international mind required educational campaigns that could influence public opinion on a transnational scale. In the early twentieth century, this meant the mass dissemination of books and the use of libraries to drive access.

International Mind Alcoves

By the war's end, the CEIP was prepared to promote internationalism by working extensively with the library community to disseminate books (Witt 2015). In 1917, the CEIP partnered with J W Hamilton, a librarian and internationalist from St Paul, Minnesota, and Mary Chase, a leader in peace advocacy and the women's suffrage movement from Andover, New Hampshire, to develop collections on foreign countries in small public libraries. Called International Mind Alcoves (IMA), these collections transformed what had quickly developed as the psychological embodiment of internationalism into a selection of books aimed to introduce people to concepts of global governance and sensitize them to the world's cultures. As reported by Chase, the CEIP promised 'to send books, free, to any part of the world, as long as the supply lasted' (Chase 1919: 361). In a year, the CEIP established 'about one hundred so-called international mind alcoves' (CEIP 1919: 67). A curated collection of books was designed to create the psychological ideal of the international mind through the language of internationalism.

Within the United States, the CEIP strove to promote membership in the League of Nations and convince an isolationist public that Americans should engage the world. Their efforts focused on rural America. IMAs were only awarded in the United States to state libraries and public libraries in cities with populations under 10,000. From the beginning, however, the collections were simultaneously domestic and global in distribution, incorporating domestic efforts to internationalize the perspectives of US citizens and international aims to export the CEIP's vision of internationalism abroad. These internationalizing activities followed the pattern of a civilizing activity outside of Western nations and a pacifying activity within the West. The Tokyo Commerce College, an elite Imperial institute focused on trade (now Hitotsubashi University), received its first IMA shipment in August of 1918 which included Butler's *The Basis for a Durable Peace*, a book soon to be translated into Japanese by faculty from Waseda University. By 1919, Mary Elizabeth Wood,[2] founder of China's Boone University Library (now University of Wuhan), had requested to join the IMA programme (Haskell 1919). IMAs were also sent to libraries in England, Scotland, Wales, Canada, Australia, South Africa, India and New Zealand. By 1924, Butler described the programme as 'one of the surest agencies at the disposal of the Division for developing an instructed public opinion on all that pertains to international understanding and international relations, and for providing a background of intelligent comprehension when new events and new policies are discussed' (CEIP 1924: 21). The programme had grown to eighty-one collections in the United States and twenty-two in other countries.

Distributed for nearly fifty years from 1918, the IMAs included roughly 350 adult and 250 children's titles published between 1909 and 1946. These books introduced people to both the League of Nations and the United Nations whilst attempting to promote a better understanding of cultures, economics and international relations. The books profiled nearly fifty nations, taking a regional approach to introducing the global public to the world's nations, cultures and politics. Famous works of fiction by authors such as Pearl S Buck (*The Good Earth*) and E M Forster (*A Passage to India*) provided readers with cultural escapes across India and China among other locations. Books also included those from established academics such as John Maynard Keynes' *Economic Consequences of Peace*. Also included were journalists like Sir Norman Angell, who won the 1933 Nobel Peace Prize and was active in organizations such as the World Committee against War and fascism. Angell's work the *Unseen Assassins: Peace with Dictators?* (1932) focused on the battle for public opinion that raged within the struggle for internationalist solutions versus militarism. Although dominated by American and European authors often writing in a manner later to be criticized in Edward Said's *Orientalism*, these collections also reflected the rise of Japan as an international power, including books by eleven Japanese scholars on topics that ranged from Japanese immigration to Kakuzo Okakura's early pan-Asianist title *Awakening of Japan*.

Within the United States, these collections became fodder for the ongoing debate about the role of America in the world. The IMAs were criticized as 'arguing for internationalism as against Americanism . . . [and] these activities should all come under the classification of foreign propaganda' (Scope of Propaganda 1927: 2). A 1930 *Chicago Daily Tribune* article titled 'Virtue for Tiny Tots' complained that the children's collections were a part of a trend to water down history and children's stories with 'substitutes for the heroism of two-gun patriots' (1930: 14).

The CEIP countered negative press by promoting information collected from librarians about the growth of the IMAs domestically and abroad:

> Librarians all over . . . report that the man in the street, formerly interested in fiction, detective stories and in the stock market . . . has, in the last few years, been awakened to a consciousness of other countries, with their different customs, finances, and morals. (Many Study World Topics 1930: 54)

The collections symbolized a connection between the seemingly isolated communities in rural America and the rest of the world. An early article in the *Charlotte Observer* described an IMA as 'a collection of books which shall be a definite contribution toward the formation of public opinion along international lines' (Library receives fine collection of books 1922: 7).

In 1925, the CEIP's European bureau in Paris, the *Dotation Carnegie Pour La Paix Internationale*, began to develop a European version of the IMA. The US office of the CEIP asked their colleagues to 'initiate work along the lines of the 'International Mind Alcoves'' and encourage their establishment in European public libraries and smaller colleges and universities. The American office described how the CEIP inspired librarians' personal interest in the programme to ensure that the books were promoted to 'entice' the public to read them (CEIP 1925a).

To create what would be called the 'Collection de la Pensée Internationale', the Paris office consulted scholars and political leaders in England, France, Germany and Czechoslovakia. The CEIP wrote for advice regarding the best contemporary periodicals and recent books on international questions and peace for students and their teachers. Specifically, the letters requested books published in their home country that would be suitable for readers in another country. The CEIP noted, 'we do not call a "good" book, a work of mere propaganda for peace, neither a pamphlet representing the ideas of a "party", but any publication (including novels) the spirit [*sic*] of which might develop better international understanding' (CEIP 1925b: 2). The letters implored: 'As you know, the great evil which we have to overcome is ignorance. France knows hardly anything of Germany, neither does England, I presume, know much about France, etc.' (CEIP 1925b: 2). By early spring, lists of books and periodicals began to arrive at the St Germain offices of the CEIP.

From Germany came suggestions noting works on the sociology of religion, political philosophy and the contemporary states with recommendations for books such as Alfred Weber's reaction to the First World War and fascism in Italy, *Die Krise des Modernen Staatsgedankens in Europa* (the Crisis of the Modern State in Europe) and Thomas Mann's most recent novel, *Der Zauberberg* (Magic Mountain). From England, scholars and politicians suggested periodicals like the *Round Table: The Commonwealth Journal of International Affairs*, *Headway* from the League of Nations Union, *Goodwill* from the World Alliance of Churches and the *Arbitrator* from the Arbitration League, and books like the Norman Angell's *International Affairs*, *Geneva Protocol* by Phillip Baker and *The Revival of Europe* by Horace Alexander. In total, recommended titles represented works on the study of religion, economics, sociology and political science that examined problems revealed by the First World War (CEIP 1925c).

The means of compiling and selecting for the IMA collection suggests a methodological approach to ensuring the presence of highly relevant and contemporary scholarship on international affairs that was also representative of the countries that were the focus of the European collections. In addition to the IMA collections for Europe, the CEIP continued to promote dialogue about the international mind through the journal *L'Esprit International*, which was published from 1927 to 1940. The European office, however, also had its sights on influencing the Near East.

In 1927, the CEIP sent Florence Wilson to engage in a survey of educational institutions in Greece, Turkey, Syria, Palestine and Egypt. Wilson in many ways exemplified the transnational network that bound the international mind campaign. As the former League of Nations Librarian, Wilson was supervised by Japan's Inazo Nitobe, who promoted the international mind in Japan. (Dale 1972). Wilson went from a librarian under Butler's supervision at Columbia University in 1917 to serving as the American Library Association's liaison to the Paris Peace Process and the only female member of the American Peace Commission. Just prior to her departure to the Near East, Butler sent her a personal letter outlining her charge and his ambitions for the journey to help establish IMA collections and give 'men and women of open mind new knowledge and new sympathy with all of that that relates to foreign relations' (Butler 1927: n.p.).

Wilson consulted with institutions that ranged from the American University of Cairo to small missionary schools on the administration of libraries and assessed their potential for IMAs. Wilson reported general enthusiasm. Like the rural American public libraries, Near East institutions expressed interest in international relations among their readers and a need for books on political science, history, and international events. Wilson informed the CEIP that IMAs could contribute to the development of the peoples of the Near East, who, 'held in restraint by despotic rulers and the domination of foreign governments, and without education facilities, need, as a preparation for their new democracies and to combat rather violent nationalism, a knowledge of international affairs' (Wilson 1928: 15). Through the growth and expansion of the IMA programme, it was clear that the CEIP's solution to the development needs around the world were similar to needs in the rural United States: an exchange of knowledge on cultural affairs and international practices through the distribution of books would change the minds of people and transform societies. Although the collections abroad were clearly aimed at an elite class of people with knowledge of English and access to private educational systems, the IMAs presented opportunities to develop an intellectual foundation leading to international mindedness. As Butler reported on adult education activities in 1927:

> Public libraries and reading rooms, International Mind Alcoves and International Relations Clubs are to be strengthened or brought into being not in one land, but in many lands, that the public mind, which in the modern democracies is in the last resort the source of authority, may be opened and broadened and deepened and instructed in all that relates to international understanding and international cooperation. (CEIP 1927: 27)

The IMA project continued through the Second World War, turning its focus on supporting what the CEIP considered a just war against forces antithetical to internationalism (Witt 2015). Butler passed away in 1947. By 1948, the CEIP had established over 1,500 adult and juvenile international mind collections across the United States and throughout Africa, Asia, Europe, Latin America and the Near East.

Conclusion: From international mind to global competency

By 1948, the CEIP moved its attention to the establishment of the United Nations, working to develop new international institutions and integrating the language of the international mind into UNESCO programmes such as those for public libraries (Intrator 2016). In many ways, this ended the common usage of the international mind as a trope to promote internationalism, whilst its rhetoric continued to proliferate.

The political power of the language of the international mind campaign, however, continued to linger during the Cold War. By the early 1950s, the international mind was once again in the news as the target of US congressional investigations amidst the communist scare and fears that foundations and foreign influence were undermining US national interests (Globalistic and Red Propaganda 1951; Foundation Inquiry 1952). The US Congress analysed the IMA collections, concluding that books such as Harold J. Laski's *Studies in the Problem of Sovereignty* were 'opposed to the "national interest" and inclines toward extreme left' (US Congress, House, Special Committee to Investigate Tax-Exempt Foundations 1954: 926). Pearl Buck's *The Good Earth* was labelled 'slightly leftist' and other titles were categorized as 'globalist' and 'Marxist' with some IMA authors linked to reports from the McCarran committee on Un-American Activities. Overall, the congressional committee concluded that the IMA books presented a perspective that did not promote the national interest.

The term 'international mind' and its globalizing rhetoric is still seen behind mass educational movements to create 'global citizens' and 'cultural competence' in schools and universities around the world. One-hundred years after the First World War ended and the IMA collections launched, the OECD's Programme for International Student Assessment (PISA) developed the 'Global Competence Framework' and testing instrument with language that parallels Butler's Lake Mohonk speech:

> Global competence is the capacity to examine local, global and intercultural issues, to understand and appreciate the perspectives and world views of others, to engage in open, appropriate and effective interactions with people from different cultures, and to act for the collective well-being. (PISA 2018)

The battle for the international mind continues with new vectors of public opinion shaping world views. The globalized media and publishing environment continue as a vehicle to influence the public and legitimacy of global institutions designed to arbitrate differences among states with social media and memes disseminating many of the same symbols of nationalism and internationalism that were shared in print during the early twentieth century. The language and aspirations of these movements remain whilst modes of dissemination have evolved.

Notes

1   Despite the peace building rhetoric of the international mind, Nicholas Murray Butler was a controversial figure in US and international academic, political and cultural life during the early twentieth century. As the president of Columbia University, Butler was both lauded and criticized for his heavy-handed leadership, including the dismissal of faculty that opposed the First World War. It is also important to note that Butler shared much of the anti-Semitism that flourished in the United States during the time, marring his legacy as a leader of Columbia University (Rosenthal 2006: 333). In addition, Butler maintained a close relationship with Benito Mussolini and was initially enthusiastic about the manner by which fascism transformed Italy politically and economically. It was not until Mussolini invaded Ethiopia in 1936 that Butler's relationship with Mussolini ended. Butler, however, never harboured fondness for Hitler and German fascism (Rosenthal 2006). At the same time, Butler shared the 1931 Nobel Prize for Peace with Jane Addams. Like other facets of the internationalist movement, Butler's actions, disposition and achievements create troubling and conflicting views when assessed by contemporary ideas of nationalism, social justice, human rights and racial equity.

2   Mary Elizabeth Wood is often credited with bringing Western library practices to China through the Boone University Library and the library school she founded there. This library school is now part of Wuhan University and considered one of the top Library Science programmes in China (Zhang 2014).

References

Butler, N. (1912), *The International Mind: The Eighteenth Annual Lak Mohonk Conference on International Arbitration, May 15, 1912*, Mohonk Lake: Lake Mohonk Conference on International Arbitration.

Butler, N. (1913), *The International Mind: An Argument for the Judicial Settlement of International Disputes*, New York: Charles Scribner's Sons.

Butler, N. (1927), March 3. Letter from N. Butler to F. Wilson, 3 March 1927. CEIP European Center Records, 1911–1940. *Box 47.4*, CEIP Archives, Columbia University.

CEIP (1919), *Annual Report*, New York: CEIP.

CEIP (1924), *Annual Report*, New York: CEIP.

CEIP (1925a), 'Project de Creation en Europe de Petites Bibliothèque'. CEIP European Center Records, 1911–1940. *Box 37.4*, International Mind Alcoves, 1925–27. CEIP Archives, Columbia University.

CEIP (1925b), [Untitled Letter Template, 30 March 1925]. CEIP European Center Records, 1911–1940. *Box 37.4*, International Mind Alcoves, 1925–27. CEIP Archives, Columbia University.

CEIP (1925c), CEIP European Center Records, 1911–1940. *Box 37.4*, International Mind Alcoves, 1925–27. CEIP Archives, Columbia University.

CEIP (1927), *Annual Report*, New York: Carnegie Endowment for International Peace.

Chase, M. (1919), 'The New Hampshire Peace Society: February, 1918-1919', *The Advocate of Peace*, 81 (12): 361–3.

Clinton, D. (2017), 'Nicholas Murray Butler and 'The International Mind" as the Pathway to Peace', in M. Cochran and C. Navari (eds), *Progressivism and US Foreign Policy Between the World Wars*, New York: Palgrave.

Curti, M. (1963), *American Philanthropy Abroad*, New York: Transaction Publishers.

Dale, D. (1972), 'An American in Geneva: Florence Wilson and the League of Nations Library', *Journal of Library History*, 7 (2): 109–29.

Duranti, M. (2016), 'European Integration, Human Rights, and Romantic Internationalism', in N. Doumanis (ed.), *The Oxford Handbook of European History, 1914–1945*, Oxford: Oxford University Press.

Fischer, M. (2008), 'Mead and the International Mind', *Transactions of the Charles S. Peirce Society: A Quarterly Journal in American Philosophy*, 44 (3): 508–31.

Foundation Inquiry (1952), *New York Times*, 11 December 1952.

Garnett, J. C. M. (1927), 'The Psychology of Patriotism and the Aims of the League of Nations Associations', in H. Milford (ed.), *Problems of Peace: Lectures Delivered at the Geneva Institute of International Relations*, 326–51, Geneva: League of Nations.

Globalistic and Red Propaganda (1951), *Chicago Daily Tribune*, 15 October 1951, 1.

Gorman, D. (2017), *International Cooperation in the Early Twentieth Century*, London: Bloomsbury Academic Press.

Hale, A. (26 September 1913), Letter to Dr. S. N. D. North. CEIP. New York and Washington Offices Records, 1910–54, *Vol. 38* (4078585). CEIP Archives, Columbia University.

Haskell, H. (15 July 1919), Letter from Haskell to Boone University Library, 15 July 1919. CEIP European Center Records, 1911–1940, *Box 35.5*, International Mind Alcoves, 1923–27. CEIP Archives, Columbia University.

Hobson, J. (1914), *Towards International Government*, New York: Macmillan.

Institut International de Bibliographie (1907), *Le Mouvement Sociologique International*. Bruxelles.

International Mind (1913, May 9), *Daily Post*.

International Mind (1913, May 20), *The Japan Times*.

International Mind urged by Mr. Butler (1912, May 15), *The Christian Science Monitor*.

Intrator, M. (2016), 'UNESCO, Reconstruction, and Pursuing Peace through a "Library-Minded" World, 1945–1950', in Poul Duedahl (ed.), *A History of UNESCO*, 131–50, London: Palgrave.

Iriye, A. (2002), *Global Community: The Role of International Organizations in the Making of the Contemporary World*, Berkeley: University of California Press.

La Fontaine, H. (1911), *Salus Mundi Suprima Lex*, CEIP, New York and Washington Offices Records, 1910–1954., *Volume 35*(4078585). CEIP Archives, Columbia University.

La Fontaine, H. (1916), 'An Appeal for a United Pacifism', *The Advocate of Peace*, 78 (7): 199–200.

Laqua, D. (2011), 'Transnational Intellectual Cooperation, the League of Nations, and the Problem of Order', *Journal of Global History*, 6: 223–47.

Library receives fine collection of books (1922), *Charlotte Observer*, 12 November, 7.

Mailing list for 2200 copies (1913), CEIP, New York and Washington Offices Records, 1910–1954, *Vol 38* (4078585), CEIP Archives, Columbia University.

Many Study World Topics (1930), *New York Times*, 7 December, 54.

Mead, G. (1914), 'The Psychological Basis of Internationalism', *Survey*, 23: 604–7.

Nitobe, I. (1916), 'Kokusaishin no yōsei', *Kaitakusha*, 11 (1): 6–10.

OECD (2018), *PISA 2018 Global Competence*, https://www.oecd.org/pisa/pisa-2018-global-competence.htm

Pillsbury, W. (1919), *Psychology of Nationality and Internationalism*, New York: D. Appleton.

Peace Advocates Meet (1912). *New York Times*, 16 May, 9.

Pugh, M. (2012), *Liberal Internationalism: The Interwar Movement for Peace in Britaini*, New York: Palgrave.

Rayward, B. (2003), 'Knowledge Organisation and a New World Polity: The Rise and Fall and Rise of the Ideas of Paul Otlet', *Transnational Associations*, 55: 4–15.

Rietzler, K. (2011), 'Experts for Peace: Structures and Motivations of Philanthropic Internationalism in the Interwar Years', in D. Laqua (ed.), *Internationalism Reconfigured: Transnational Ideas and Movements between the World Wars*, London: I.B. Tauris.

Rosenthal, M. and P. O'Toole (2006), *Nicholas Miraculous: The Amazing Career of the Redoubtable Dr. Nicholas Murray Butler*, New York: Columbia University Press.

Said, E. (1978), *Orientalism*, New York: Pantheon.

Scope of Propaganda (1927), 10 September, *Berkeley Daily Gazette*.

Sluga, G. (2013), *Internationalism in the Age of Nationalism*, Philadelphia: University of Pennsylvania Press.

US Congress. Special Committee to Investigate Tax-Exempt Foundations (1954), *Tax-exempt Foundation: Report of the Special Committee to Investigate Tax-Exempt Foundations and Comparable Organizations House of Representatives Eighty-third Congress second session on H. Res. 217. 83rd Congress*, US Government Printing Office.

Van Acker, W. (2014), 'Sociology in Brussels, Organicism and the Idea of a World Society in the Period before the First World War', in W. B. Rayward (ed.), *Information beyond Borders: International Cultural and Intellectual Exchange in the Belle Époque*, Surrey: Ashgate.

Virtue for Tiny Tots (4 February 1930), *Chicago Daily Tribune*, 14.

Weber, P. (2015), 'The Pacifism of Andrew Carnegie and Edwin Ginn: the Emergence of a Philanthropic Internationalism', *Global Society*, 29 (4): 530–50.

Wilson, F. (1928), *Near East Educational Survey; Report of a Survey Made During the Months of April, May, and June 1927*, London: Hogarth.

Winter, J. (2008), *Dreams of Peace and Freedom: Utopian Moments in the Twentieth Century*, New Haven: Yale University Press.

Witt, S. (2015), 'International Mind Alcoves: The Carnegie Endowment for International Peace, Libraries, and the Struggle for Global Public Opinion, 1917–54', *Library & Information History*, 30 (4): 273–90.

Wöbse, A. (2006), 'To Cultivate the International Mind', *Zeitschrift fur Geschichtswissenschaft*, 54 (10): 852–63.

Zhang, Y, (2014), 'The Development of Library and Information Science in China (1840–2009)', *IFLA Journal*, 40 (4): 296–306. DOI: 10.1177/0340035214541033.

Conclusion

Up the line with the best of luck

Julian Walker and Christophe Declercq

Modern studies of the First World War through the lens of language mostly stem from Odile Roynette's *Les Mots des tranchées. L'Invention d'une langue de guerre, 1914-1919* (Paris, éditions Armand Colin, 2010), Doyle and Walker's *Trench Talk* (History Press, 2012) and Amanda Laugesen's *Furphies and Whizz-bangs: Anzac Slang from the Great War* (OUP, 2014). However, Hilary Footitt's still valid proposal that 'on the whole, the historiography of war continues to develop its key research questions within contexts which are foreign language free' (2012: 4) shows that this approach to conflict carries huge potential for future research. Focusing on slang terms used by Australians during wartime, Laugesen had been working on *Diggerspeak: The Language of Australians at War* (2005).

The First World War clearly played an important role in the development of an Australian identity, and Laugesen extended its linguistic foundations to a period from the Boer Wars to the Vietnam War. Footitt, along with Mike Kelly, founded the Languages at War series at Palgrave in 2012, which up to time of writing has fifteen titles in its portfolio, including work by Baker and Kelly (2013), Footitt and Tobia (2013), Walker and Declercq (2016), Declercq and Walker (2016), and Laugesen and Gehrmann (2020). Walker published *Words and the First World War* (Bloomsbury 2017), an in-depth examination of the effect of the war on the English language. Given that the major impetus to commemorating the conflict came from Anglophone countries (particularly Britain, Australia, New Zealand and Canada), France and Belgium, for whom the history of the war has been portrayed over the past century as a contributor to the creation myths of the modern history of these countries,[1] it was perhaps inevitable that the studies should be initiated in English and French.[2]

Thus, the discipline of the critical study of influences between languages and developments within languages during, and as a result of, the conflict has developed the language of its representation and the delimiting of single-language platforms of memory within the lead up to the period of and the aftermath of the centenary, and cannot be divorced from that extended experience of commemoration.

With greater ease of access to a wider range of material, the centenary period has given researchers both the opportunity and the incentive to look beyond the Western Front and Gallipoli and soldier slang. Forms of non-academic research, personal interest and family history have revealed as much, if not more than, academic processes. The centenary period has allowed the extension of the reach of evergrowing available material to broaden the locatedness of examining language through history and history through language, and to look to future areas of research for Languages and the First World War (LFWW) – effectively an episode in the sociolinguistic impression of languages in times of conflict.

From a small number of sites, focusing largely on the Western Front, the British Home Front and the relationship between English and other languages, the project has spread out to other European fronts, and other European languages, to non-European languages seen in terms of their relationship to European languages, and from there to non-European languages outside these parameters. It has been important to note the various patterns of emerging centrism, and for them to be seen as the perhaps necessary conditions for engaging with a subject which has been historically centred on Europe, America, Canada, Australia, New Zealand and, to a lesser extent, India and South Africa. One benefit of building up a strong subject area based on the potential strength of the European linguistic experience is that it provides a context for seeing other linguistic encounters as part of a global historical story, rather than as isolated encounters and anecdotes. A large amount of work therefore remains to be done on the stories of Chinese, Japanese, Thai, South American Spanish, Portuguese, the languages of Russia and indigenous languages of North America, and we hope that the project retains its purpose as a framework for this as well as to break down what Hilary Footitt described as: 'traditional historical scholarship on war [which] has been markedly ethnocentric' (2012: 1).

If using foreign languages and code switching was initially exclusive to those soldiers who had left the native sphere and joined their national forces at a front in a foreign field, then the locatedness of the linguistic enrichment was first physical. The foreign code as a sense of native solidarity among troops then translocated as a linguistic element into the native tongue as slang. Despite possible imperfections and assumptions, such as the anticipation that everyone in Belgium spoke French (see *Introduction*), language use and location became/were interdependent spheres of linguistic contact and inclusion. This translocation of language use and otherlingual spheres was the ultimate translation of scenario projection as exemplified by phrasebooks (see *Introduction* and chapters by Kuldkepp and Walker). Translocation at times of conflict therefore provides a common denominator to the world of crisis and otherlingual responses moving across fragmented (geo-)localized spheres.

Focused research, carried on via online forums, has been a major feature of recent military history studies, much of it done by non-academics, and dependent on contributions from individual family histories or personal collections. As a model, the online forum and blog of the Languages and the First World project – managed and edited by Julian Walker – has proved appropriate for the study of individual phrases and incidences, alongside Lynda Mugglestone's blog analysing the Rev Andrew Clark's diary, which provided an impetus for wider studies of journalistic usage during the war. Since early 2014, the LFWW project's blog has focused equally on individual postcards or letters, as well as usages in the popular press, government telegrams, ships' signals and song lyrics. What the subject provides is an extended series of often overlapping case studies, in which influences may go back and forth. But equally, parallel development may occur where cross influencing might be expected: the expression 'Send it down David/Davy' was noted in Fraser and Gibbons as 'A soldier's greeting to a shower of rain likely to postpone a parade' (1925: 72), and was claimed to be Welsh in origin, with the Australian/New Zealand variant being 'Send it down Hughie'. In *A Dictionary of Slang and Unconventional English* (1923), Eric Partridge noted that 'New Zealanders and Australians say *Send her down, Hughie!*', this being extended in his later *A Dictionary of Catch Phrases American and British* as the following:

> 'send it down, David (with var. "Davy lad")!'. The *var.* belongs to the Regular Army; and the basic 'send it down, David' is often intensified by the addition of a repetitive 'send it down': late C19-20. In the army, esp. during WW1, it was used to implore David, the Welsh patron saint, to send a preferably very heavy shower, notably when it might cause a parade to be postponed or cancelled. Parts of Wales have a notoriously wet climate: and, what is more, Wales is 'the Land of Leeks' (leaks). (1977: 265)

The *Macquarie Dictionary* also gives instances of 'Steve' and 'Jimmy', alongside possible pre-war origins for the use of 'Hughie', with the citation of *Digger Dialects* for 'Steve', also noting the use of 'her' for 'it', following a common Australian model of pronoun substitution (2014).

But slight differences of language may carry strong nuances. This was seen in the language consultation for the BBC's radio production running throughout the centenary period, during which the appropriateness of the expression 'man down' arose. Whilst there was evidence of the expression 'another man down' dating from 1915 and *My Year of the Great War*, a book by Frederick Palmer, no evidence of the more peremptory 'man down' was found.[3] The danger in the use of this expression was that it would feel too American and too modern, thus shifting the linguistic script from the past to the present. Yet this left the potential problem of the script being too identifiably historic in immediate comparison with a well-known more modern phrase, when the exercise, as proposed by the social diary format, was intending to emphasize the lived experience of the war. Whilst, in this case, language operates both to distance and to highlight the universality of how we, then and now, comprehend experience, language can also provide an interference, one 'past' – perceived or not – getting in the way of another. Here too translocation appears, with existing – typically older occurrences of – language use being relocated retrospectively, away from the anticipated newer usage.

The locatedness of language use also takes place between two different spheres. Despite the influence of seminal works like Paul Fussell's *The Great War in Modern Memory* (1975), the concentration on the written rather than the spoken word could scarcely be avoided given its physical survival. However, this approach has inevitably ignored popular phraseology from the war period and environments. Considering the often-fugitive nature of material such as silent film captions, serialized fiction, music hall patter and advertising slogans, the cross-movement of terms between popular usage and popular culture is a huge area of research. Cinema has had a huge influence on how the experience of the war was shaped in later minds, more so probably than literature.

The question of authenticity in representing the language of the period raises the issue of different registers in different environments. Historians of language would note 'why don't we go over?' and 'pushing up daisies' in Maxwell Anderson's dialogue script for the 1930 film of *All Quiet on the Western Front*, and applaud the accurate representation of language, but this is in a register specific to time and cultural context – much of the audience would recognize these expressions as authentic Anglophone soldier terms from the Western Front. However, the application of various forms of censorship in cinema and society at the time would not have allowed the use of 'fuck', the repetitive application of which was so clearly noted by John Brophy in 1930 and Claude Sisley in 1919. Sisley recognized both the value of the word and its limitations:

> the one word that won the war was the well-known obscenity containing four letters. From generals downwards everyone used it, and everyone was comforted by saying it. No dialogue pretending to represent military conversation ever rings quite true because this essential word is omitted. Of course, in public writings it can't be very well referred to, but only those who have soldiered out here realized what a companion in adversity that little word has been. (Sisley, C, *Athenaeum*, 1 August 1919)

Brophy and Partridge noted that 'it became so common that an effective way to express emotion was to omit this word' (Brophy and Partridge 1930: 17). For T E Lawrence, as shown here by Jonathon Green, the constant stream of obscenities was 'repellent', but as Green points out, it 'confers authenticity'. 'Fuck' itself Brophy and Partridge found 'meaningless', a noise, and as the form 'fucking' doing nothing much more than signalling the approach of a noun. The sparing use of 'fuck' and 'fucking' in the 2019 film *1917*, directed by Sam Mendes, matched the codes of acceptability of the twenty-first century rather than the year it aimed to convey. Pragmatically, any authentic – that is, true to the original situation – usage would be, as Brophy and Partridge, and Sisley suggest, dull to the point of meaninglessness, and of course not authentic to the film context. We have then a situation where authenticity becomes fugitive and an object of censorship, in a situation where the linguistic act of censorship is both authentic to its own context and an act of suppressing authenticity.

The overlapping of different nuances in different registers and contexts may be difficult to unravel, especially when the end results overlap. For example, Remarque's script uses the sentence 'Come on! Grab your rifles!'; whilst this might overlap with John Brophy's observation that for greater urgency a sergeant would say 'get your rifles' rather than 'get your fucking rifles' (Brophy and Partridge 1930: 17), the linguistic evidence for urgency is in effect an absence of an expected word. Thus, the omission of an utterance can function simultaneously as authenticating agent and its opposite. Whilst this is merely part of a truism that every generation rewrites history, it is less observed that both the retention and the alteration of the time- and context-accurate language is an influential agent in the rewriting process.

Any overview of this project would then show that it has moved from the expected subjects of the central areas of physical conflict to the civilian areas, the theatres of war that feature less often in the history books, and that it affords an opportunity for less-known subjects of research to be brought into, and related to, a wider whole. This then gives a direction to future research, which may both enrich the subject and broaden perspectives of what is meant by global war in the modern era.

The more the areas of research that have emerged during this journey through extended sociolinguistic case studies, the more the details have revealed the potential for more work, chance comments and anecdotes opening up whole fields. Furthermore, revelatory accounts increasingly create cross-disciplinary approaches on the one hand, but also the aspect of linguistic translocation within a shared locatedness on the other, as is the case with cross-no-man's-land communication.

> 'While our guns were giving the Prussians opposite us hell, the Saxons opposite the Middlesex applauded the hits. Later they shouted across, "We are being relieved by Bavarians tonight. Give us time to get out and then shoot the ---s"', though one attempt to get a German soldier to speak accent in order that he should reveal a regional accent failed because the German soldier was determined to speak English. (Dunn [1938] 2004:113)

Whilst there was no reason to assume that accent should have revealed more than the soldier's shoulder tag, the reputation of differing degrees of belligerence or recklessness identifiable through place of origin remained widespread; Australians, Prussians and Canadians were credited with outstanding ferocity and were identifiable through accent as much as uniform. It is not yet known to what extent attempts to gain advantage through the manipulation of accent were myths of war or actual tactics; and whilst anecdotal evidence has emerged from the Western Front, the policy of getting the enemy to reveal himself by any means would have been relevant in all theatres.

Linguistic tensions within countries were strongly noticeable for Germany, and indeed for France, where the army and the pursuance of costly tactics were a catalyst for the rekindling of tensions between people of different regions, exemplified by their linguistic differences, notably speakers of Breton, Languedoc and standard French; these distinctions were quite apart from those between other French speakers, Alpine *chasseurs*, 'Turcos' from North Africa, Senegalese and Annamites from present-day Vietnam. Trench magazines were used to bind together a wide range of dialect speakers in the Italian army (Du Pont 2016: 149–58), and the potential for chaos lay as a shadow over the Austro-Hungarian armies (Scheer 2016: 62–78). Anne Samson, in this volume, reveals the complexities of communication across languages within forces serving in Africa. A vast field of comparative research remains to be done carrying this question into other armies, particularly the Russian and Ottoman armies. This new research also allows for cross-communication, interactions beyond the entity of the own army, with troops aligned with the own cause or with citizens from the local area, and in the case of population movement such as the mass migration of the Arameans in 1915.

The spreading of research from the conflict zones to the home fronts and internment and prisoner-of-war camps, as exemplified here by Calladine, Connelly and Golubinov, points to the work remaining to be done on the linguistic engagement of East Asian countries, particularly the Chinese Labour Corps, for whom an extensive phrasebook was published (*A Chinese phrase book for Chinese labour*, n.d.). Xu (2011) explores the problems facing Chinese labourers, and Achiel van Walleghem mentions in passing that Flemish traders learned a few words of Mandarin (Walleghem 2017).

Chinese labourers during the war also played a role upon return. If triumphant sentiments over China's contribution to the Allied victory were to start immediately after Armistice, the May Fourth Movement certainly turned around the celebratory mood. On 4 May 1919, a crowd of 3,000 students stormed Tiananmen Square in protest at the Paris Peace Conference. The wartime commitment and emotional attachment to the European allies had been replaced by critical reflections on the war for intellectuals and labourers alike. In 1919, Fu Xingsan, a labourer, published a record-detailing critical reflections on war. He also depicted the lack of equality on the home front as well as limited membership in terms of partaking in camaraderie with the Allied soldiers they set out to support (Zhong 2017: 135–51). Also, Chinese labourers arrived at the Western Front through the British use of Canada as a pathway for transporting those labourers to France, a 'process that was later reversed' for the same labourers to be returned home (Rowe 2012: 243). This patronizing attitude towards subject races (Anderson 2017: 150) not only poses questions about space, race and place, but the work done by Chinese labourers is also a prime example of how the First World War needs to be analysed as a global conflict.

The linguistic management of campaigning by East Asian and south-east Asian forces is wide ranging. For example, Anglo-Japanese operations overcame a huge linguistic divide and typically involved other languages. The Siege of Tsingtao (now Qingdoa) – a port for which the Germans had held a ninety-nine-year lease since 1898 – by Anglo-Japanese forces at end of August 1914, involved several hundred Sikh soldiers joining the British contingent. Early in 1915, Japanese military support helped quash a mutiny against the British government by Indian troops in Singapore, and Japanese naval support extended to the eastern Mediterranean in 1917 (Dickinson 1999, 2013; Melzer 2017). Meanwhile on the British Home Front, and building on previous orientalist themes in British art and literature (De Gruchy 2003: 16–33), the Japanese theatre exerted a cultural influence throughout the war, particularly on W B Yeats and Ezra Pound.

Confirming the global aspect of the world war and its countless intersections renders essential the inclusion of the linguistic engagement by those nations who were involved in the last years of the conflict, though this itself throws open the question of when exactly the war finished. In the Spanish and Portuguese-speaking countries that entered the war following the United States' declaration in April 1917, from Peru to Nicaragua, established German-speaking communities came under attack, and German-speaking institutions were closed, mirroring the Austrian ban on the use of Italian in public notices, street signs and newspapers in Trent, Trieste and Zara (*Yorkshire Evening Post*, 6 September 1916). Even though Siam was the only country in south-east Asia to remain independent from the great empires during the colonial era and, as such, entered the First World War relatively unconnected, it did declare war on Germany and Austria-Hungary in July 1917: 'Twelve German vessels docked in Siamese ports were immediately seized. The crews and other Central Power nationals were detained and sent to India to join their fellow citizens in British India's existing civilian internment camps' (Stricklin 2020: 268). But it was Siam's decision to send troops to fight on European soil that marks the Siamese involvement as a deeper confirmation of the disruption of traditional expectations and balances (Hell 2015). Siamese troops, medics and pilots joined the Entente forces' operations in October 1918, but the peremptory attitudes of French interpreters, possibly in the stress of pursuing the endgame of the conflict, caused huge operational and diplomatic problems. To relieve these tensions, Siamese troops were directed to serve in the post-war occupation of Germany, specifically in Neustadt an der Weinstraße, located in the French area of control.

Many intriguing areas of research remain: the linguistic preparations for the failed Stockholm Conference of 1916; the creation of the fake signals luring German ships towards British battlecruisers in the Battle of the Falkland Islands (December 1914); the language dispositions for the engagement of Portuguese troops on the Western Front, and the 1,200 Icelanders who enlisted in Canadian forces and served in France and Flanders. Given that David Lloyd George's 19 September 1914 speech laid great store on the offence against the 'little countries' of Europe, it is important to bring to the forefront the lesser-known environments, histories and engagements, and particularly those that continued after November 1918; the phrase *on ne se tue pas* (the killing has stopped) manifests a relief that has lasted for a century, but as a marker tends to throw a shadow over post-war conflicts, occupations, mutinies and lost opportunities.

In the study of conflict, and more particularly the First World War, focus has been on the war's impact on localities (location of armies, front lines, battle zones). Assuming that the very locatedness of events is one field of research, language brings in a second field, a dimension that ties the locations together and yet remains local, tied to location on the one hand, but cross-cutting that geographical dimension with a linguistic one on the other. The stereotypical group of soldiers fighting the enemy can always be found taking in local experiences, but they not only move from one location to the next – in the case of the stalemate Western Front, this was not far – they also transpose their language onto a new local one, and the translocation carries familiar elements of belonging as well as allowing for new linguistic contact zones.

How does this relate to current conflict, which is without clear geophysical boundaries, but in which information and data are among the most potent weapons? Does language act as a marker, inflaming suspicions of xenophobia? Certainly in stressed urban environments, the growth in the use of languages recognized only as 'foreign' and unlocatable due to an absence of associations of skin colour was an influence on xenophobia during the UK Brexit debate in 2016. Over the past two centuries, language has increasingly governed the concept of identity, within frameworks of nation, religion, social class and other tribes. How the war acted as a catalyst to the management of language as creating or reinforcing boundaries of what is meant by 'we' is the subject of chapters in this volume by Kempshall, Ribeiro, Ilea, Laugesen and Hutečka. Many of the writers in this volume are the grandchildren of people directly involved in the war, and thus embraced in the same grouping involving what we choose to describe as 'us'. In many cases, this concept of 'we' sits within a cultural context currently interpreted as overwhelmingly positive, for whilst it is subject to re-examination, rebalancing and revision, it is still the history of winners. But, for millions of those engaged in the conflict, the concept of 'we' changed as nation states emerged or dissolved: the former Irish soldier in the BEF, rendered almost persona non grata after Irish independence; the former Ottoman soldier with a nationality invented by the Sykes-Picot Agreement; the Hungarian orphan shunted to Belgium and back again. Any 'we' link has largely dissolved, any surviving relationship between 'we' in 1914, 'we' in 1918 and 'we' in 2018 is far more complex when examined globally than the comfortable grandparent–grandchild link between BEF soldier and modern academic would suppose, rendering that relationship a privilege of simplicity. The study of the linguistic effects of the war lies at the heart of the study of the changes of identity provoked by the conflict, which set up many of the challenges of the modern world.

A further question stands in the shadows: What do we hope to gain from the study of war, and specifically war and communication? How do we retain an academic voice whilst knowing that war is something we have sought through the past 100 years to avoid? And this is especially important in a world of surrogate, forgotten and deliberately ignored wars whose effects we fail to ignore at our peril in terms of migration, energy supply and geopolitical balances affect the West. The popular confusion of 'celebration' with 'commemoration' in the centenary period highlighted the dangers of triumphalism and behind them the relationship between accepting that history is history, and past, and the ongoing effects of past conflict. Acts of genocide matter; they stand as self-condemnatory, no matter when they happened. The First World War saw weapons of mass destruction employed by entities we still choose to address as 'our' culture: huge numbers of civilians were displaced, starved and killed, and fake news demonized entire nationalities and cultures, including their languages; whilst there is tragedy in the symbolic loss of a generation of young men, more than one generation was brutalized and culturally distressed. Whilst the subject is its own condemnation, the search for meaning is itself always a moral stance.

Notes

1   One such myth in Belgium was that 80 per cent of the Belgian army did not understand French and that only 20 per cent who did commanded the others. For more on the issue, see De Vos and Keymeulen 1989. Following on from that a further myth emerged on the back of the First World War, during the 1920s, on how Flemish counter-nationalism created myths around their martyrs. For more on the issue, see De Schaepdrijver 2018.

2   Relating to the previous footnote, a seminal and early myth busting study – one about German atrocities and Belgian civilians, rife with mythification – was published in English by Horne and Kramer (2001).

3   A profound search in the British Library Newspaper Archive for 'man down' in the second half of 1914 did not land any results relating to the debate. Instances concerned headings or collocations such as 'to knock a man down'.

References

Primary literature

Anderson, M. (1930), *All Quiet on the Western Front*, dialogue script.
Brophy, J. and E. Partridge (1930), *Songs and Slang of the British Soldier: 1914–1918*, London: Eric Partridge Ltd.
Dunn, J. ([1938] 2004), *The War the Infantry Knew*, London: Abacus.
Fraser, E. and J. Gibbons (1925), *Soldier and Sailor Words and Phrases*, London: Routledge.
Palmer, F. (1915), *My Year of the Great War*, Toronto: McClelland, Goodchild & Stewart.
Partridge, E. (1923), *A Dictionary of Slang and Unconventional English*, London: Routledge.
Partridge, E. (1977), *A Dictionary of Catch Phrases American and British*, London: Routledge.
Sisley, C. (1919), *Athenaeum*, 1 August 1919.
Yorkshire Evening Post, 6 September 1916

Secondary literature

1917 (2019), feature film (S. Mendes dir.).
Anderson, K. J. (2017), *Egyptian Labor Corps: Logistical Laborers in World War I and the 1919 Egyptian Revolution*, PhD diss., Cornell University.
Baker, C. and M. Kelly, eds (2013), *Interpreting the Peace*, London: Palgrave-Macmillan.
De Schaepdrijver, S. (2018), 'Belgium', in Ute Daniel et al. (eds), *1914–1918-Online: International Encyclopedia of the First World War*, issued by Freie Universität Berlin. DOI: 10.15463/ie1418.11285.
De Vos, L. and H. Keymeulen (1989), 'Een definitieve afrekening met de 80%-mythe?' [A final conclusion for the 80%-myth?], *Belgisch Tijdschrift voor Militaire Geschiedenis* [Belgian Journal for Military History], 28 (2): 81–104.
Declercq, C. and J. Walker, eds (2016), *Languages and the First World War: Representation and Memory*, London: Palgrave-Macmillan.
Dickinson, F. R. (1999), *War and National Re-invention Japan and the Great War, 1914–1919*, Cambridge, MA: Harvard University Press.
Dickinson, F. R. (2013), *World War I and Triumph of the New Japan, 1919–1930*, Cambridge: Cambridge University Press.
Doyle, P. and J. Walker (2012), *Trench Talk*, Stroud: The History Press.
Du Pont, K. (2016), 'Sociolinguistic Aspects of Italian War Propaganda: Literacy, Dialects and Popular Speech in the Italian Trench Journal L'Astico', in J. Walker and C. Declercq (eds), *Languages and the First World War: Communicating in a Transnational War*, 142–58, London: Palgrave-Macmillan.
Footitt, H. (2012), 'Introduction', in H. Footitt and M. Kelly (eds), *Languages at War*, 1–15, London: Palgrave-Macmillan.
Footitt, H. and S. Tobia, eds (2013), *War Talk*, London: Palgrave-Macmillan.
Fussell, P. (1975), *The Great War in Modern Memory*, Oxford: Oxford University Press.
Hell, S. (2015), 'Siam', in U. Daniel, P. Gatrell, O. Janz, H. Jones, J. Keene, A. Kramer, and B. Nasson (eds), *1914–1918-Online: International Encyclopedia of the First World War*, issued by Freie Universität Berlin. DOI: 10.15463/ie1418.11285.

Horne, J. N. and A. Kramer (2001), *German Atrocities, 1914: A History of Denial*, New Haven: Yale University Press.

Laugesen, A. (2005), *Diggerspeak: The Language of Australians at War*, Oxford: Oxford University Press.

Laugesen, A. (2014), *Furphies and Whizz-bangs: Anzac Slang from the Great War*, Oxford: Oxford University Press.

Laugesen, A. and R. Gehrmann, eds (2020), *Communication, Interpreting and Language in Wartime*, London: Palgrave-Macmillan.

Melzer, J. (2017), 'Warfare 1914–1918 (Japan)', in U. Daniel, P. Gatrell, O. Janz, H. Jones, J. Keene, A. Kramer, and B. Nasson (eds), *1914–1918-Online: International Encyclopedia of the First World War*, issued by Freie Universität Berlin. DOI: 10.15463/ie1418.11285.

Rowe, S. E. (2012), 'Strangers on the Western Front: Chinese Laborers in the Great War', *First World War Studies*, 3 (2): 243–4.

Roynette, O. (2010), *Les Mots des tranchées. L'Invention d'une langue de guerre, 1914–1919*, Paris: éditions Armand Colin.

Scheer, T. (2016), 'Habsburg Languages at War: The linguistic Confusion at the Tower of Babel Couldn't have been Much Worse', in J. Walker and C. Declercq (eds), *Languages and the First World War: Communicating in a Transnational War*, 62–78, London: Palgrave-Macmillan.

Stricklin, W. A. (2020), *The Prince and I - Miss Olive*, Pittsburgh: Dorrance Publishing.

Walker, J. (2017), *Words and the First World War*, London: Bloomsbury.

Walker, J. and C. Declercq, eds (2016), *Languages and the First World War: Communicating in a Transnational War*, London: Palgrave-Macmillan.

Walleghem, A. ([1917] 2017), *The Year of Passchendaele: The British Army in Flanders: The Diary of Achiel Van Walleghem*, Brighton: E.R. Root.

Xu, G. (2011), *Strangers on the Western Front*, Cambridge, MA: Harvard University Press.

Zhong, Y. (2017), 'Sacred, the Laborers: Writing Chinese in the First World War', *Cross-Currents: East Asian History and Culture Review*, 1 (22): 135–59.

Online sources

Send It Down Hughie! (2014), Macquarie Dictionary Blog, online: https://www.macquariedictionary.com.au/blog/article/89/ (accessed 01 September 2020).

Index

Lightning Source UK Ltd.
Milton Keynes UK
UKHW022136250521
384369UK00002B/208